Espionage and Counterintelligence in Occupied
Persia (Iran)

Also by Adrian O'Sullivan

Nazi Secret Warfare in Occupied Persia (Iran): The Failure of the German Intelligence Services, 1939–1945

Espionage and Counterintelligence in Occupied Persia (Iran)

The Success of the Allied Secret Services, 1941–45

Adrian O'Sullivan

To Phil
with best wishes

Adrian
O'Sullivan

palgrave
macmillan

First published 2015 by
PALGRAVE MACMILLAN

Palgrave Macmillan in the UK is an imprint of Macmillan Publishers Limited, registered in England, company number 785998, of Houndmills, Basingstoke, Hampshire RG21 6XS.

Palgrave Macmillan in the US is a division of St Martin's Press LLC, 175 Fifth Avenue, New York, NY 10010.

Palgrave Macmillan is the global academic imprint of the above companies and has companies and representatives throughout the world.

Palgrave® and Macmillan® are registered trademarks in the United States, the United Kingdom, Europe and other countries.

ISBN 978–1–137–55556–4

This book is printed on paper suitable for recycling and made from fully managed and sustained forest sources. Logging, pulping and manufacturing processes are expected to conform to the environmental regulations of the country of origin.

A catalogue record for this book is available from the British Library.

A catalog record for this book is available from the Library of Congress.

Typeset by MPS Limited, Chennai, India.

For my daughter, Claire

Contents

List of Figures

Preface

When I began drafting my first book on occupied Persia, *Nazi Secret Warfare*,[1] I intended to write only one on the subject. However, the sheer mass of neglected material on Persia that I discovered in the British, American, and German archives soon made it apparent that my *oeuvre* would have to be split asunder. So here is the second half of my narrative, in which I concentrate not on the Nazis but on the activities of the Allied secret services — mainly the British — in their fight against various kinds of Axis threat which menaced the Persian polity, the Lend-Lease supply route, the oil infrastructure, and the communications links between Britain, the Indian subcontinent, Australasia, and the Far East. This story begins properly after the settling of the desert dust, stirred briefly in the late summer of 1941 by Operation COUNTENANCE, which saw several divisions of British, Indian, and Soviet soldiers crashing across the western and northern frontiers of Persia and fanning out to occupy the provinces along the Caspian coast, the major urban centres, the oilfields and refineries of Khuzistan, the Trans-Iranian Railway (TIR), and the ports on the Persian Gulf.[2] From the moment that the Anglo-Soviet invasion and occupation began, these infrastructural assets instantly became potential sabotage targets of strategic significance which had to be secured and protected against Nazi-inspired attack: in the northern zone of occupation by Soviet counterintelligence and security-intelligence forces (NKVD), and in the rest of the vast hinterland by various British services, most notably MI5 (known regionally as Security Intelligence Middle East [SIME]), the Special Operations Executive (SOE), and the Field Security Sections of the Intelligence Corps (FSS).

After what Germans call *die Wende* (the turning point) — in other words, after they had fought and lost the fierce, crucial battles of El Alamein, Stalingrad, and Kursk — there occurred in the twilit world of political intelligence and counterintelligence what we would today term a 'paradigm shift'. From 1943 onwards, British and American intelligence priorities veered from the covert activities of the Nazis, whose ultimate military defeat was now assured, towards the political manoeuvres and manipulations of the Stalinist Russians in the Transcaucasian and Black Sea region, as they repositioned themselves in such a way as to maximize their postwar power and influence over the lands bordering the soft southern underbelly of the Soviet Union, to extend their hegemony to the shores of the Persian Gulf, and to exercise maximum control over the world supply of oil.

On the face of things, the convenient Stalinist proxy in Persia was the Tudeh Party, whose existence absolved the Soviets of the need to construct and remotely control a large propaganda apparatus to influence Persian political opinion. However, such a transparent entity could be monitored equally conveniently by the diplomats of the British and American legations, largely relieving the security forces of any need to surveil communist activities in Persia at the party and *Majlis* level. Nevertheless, as I discovered during my archival research, the British Secret Intelligence Service (MI6) and the US Office of Strategic Services (OSS), independently of each other, saw fit to insert active-intelligence operatives into the region, mainly to monitor Soviet activities within the sealed northern occupation zone, despite the fact that a moratorium existed, mutually agreed by the occupying powers, which expressly prohibited active-intelligence activities anywhere in Persia for the duration of the war.

However, the focus of this book is not on active intelligence but on security intelligence. Here the emphasis remained firmly on the Nazi menace and the task of identifying, surveilling, pursuing, and neutralizing German or pro-German elements within the Persia and Iraq Force (PAIFORCE) theatre, including saboteurs and political subversives. This was the extensive remit of the British security forces: SIME's Combined Intelligence Centre Iraq and Persia (CICI) and its Tehran branch, the Defence Security Office Persia (DSO Persia). For their part, the US security forces – the Counter Intelligence Corps (CIC) – bore responsibility only for the behaviour of their personnel operating the Lend-Lease supply route and for railway operations, not for the security of the route itself, though they routinely dealt with cases of small sabotage against railway equipment and infrastructure, as well as the frequent pilfering of materiel by the local population.

As this book reveals, Joe Spencer and the officers of DSO Persia faced a daunting task. With a staff of 20–25 people, supported by eight area liaison officers in the outposts, they policed a country 6.71 times the size of the United Kingdom. Here they maintained such routine security controls as postal and press censorship, travel and visa control, and positive vetting. At the same time they were responsible for active surveillance, prisoner interrogations, the Sultanabad (Arak) internment camp, interservice and external liaison, regular security summaries, and the establishment and maintenance of a large central registry. One disputed remit was responsibility for political counterespionage, which overlapped with the conventional jurisdiction of MI6, thinly disguised as the Inter-Services Liaison Department (ISLD). As the war progressed, however, a comfortable informal compromise evolved without the need for intervention from London: ISLD watched the Russians, whilst DSO Persia watched the Persians and fugitive Germans.[3] Fortunately, DSO Persia were able to delegate some routine operational responsibilities to the Intelligence Corps FSS and even to the Free Polish, whose soldiers they came to regard highly as dependable prisoner escorts and guards. In fact, the DSO employed no fewer than eight Poles on their permanent staff as bodyguards, doorkeepers, and general 'strongarm men'.[4] From the Persians, however, the DSO could expect nothing, for the Persian police and gendarmerie were utterly corrupt, demoralized, disorganized, and unreliable, despite zealous American attempts to advise and reform them, all of which failed.

Like my first book, this one is about Persia the operational theatre, not Persia the nation, and my narratives tell not of grand Persian endeavours, but merely of a few unsuccessful attempts by certain misguided Persian individuals, mostly exiles, to ally themselves with the odious Nazi cause, until such time as it suited them to switch sides or disappear into postoccupational obscurity. Of course, a few of these personalities — like the malignant Fazlollah Zahedi, for instance — would succeed in projecting their political survival into the postwar era. However, resurrected and anointed arbitrarily with Machiavellian intent by the British and American secret services, Zahedi is an atypical exception to the general rule that supporting fascism ultimately benefited no one in Persia and cost some dearly. Tribal leaders like Nasir and Khosrow Khan Qashgai, for instance, changed sides late in the war and prolonged their struggle with the central regime, ultimately with that of the Islamic Republic, but they paid heavily for their 'nomadic romanticism', and few beyond their tribe remember them today.[5] The Second World War is hardly a proud period of Persian political and diplomatic history, but it is a caesura that nevertheless merits closer study and analysis by Western political and diplomatic historians.

The rest of the story belongs to the intelligence historian, as most of the events of the period transpired in the secret world and were documented in records that have remained secret until quite recently. Unlike my first effort on German clandestine warfare in Persia, a field supported by limited documentation and therefore fairly easily comprehended, this book on Allied secret operations in the PAIFORCE theatre is about a significantly more fertile, more richly documented field. Therefore I hope that this book – based on a deeper and wider tranche of British and American records than *Nazi Secret Warfare* – will not only expose yet another hitherto opaque, neglected narrative of the Second World War, but will also provide ample scope and stimulus for a younger generation of intelligence historians to raid the archives more adventurously and thoroughly than I have been able to do. Like a pathfinder, I have therefore dropped some flares in Chapter 12 and in the Epilogue to mark the target for them by surveying the current state of the archives, warning of certain traps to avoid, and offering some unapologetically subjective advice about 'good' and 'bad' historiography. I wish them good hunting among the records, and I look forward to witnessing their attempts to eradicate the still gaping lacunae in the history of the region and of the time.

They will of course quickly learn that lacunae come in various shapes and sizes. In writing this book I encountered many minor ones that irritated rather than gaped, calling in places for a minimally speculative approach to the source material in order to ensure some measure of narrative unity. But there is a fundamental difference between informed speculation and conspiracy theory. Unlike other historical disciplines, the historiography of secret intelligence in all its manifestations (espionage, counterintelligence, subversion, etc.) is rendered especially challenging because it often depends upon primary sources that have been weeded, redacted, or restricted to a degree that makes the construction of a wholly verified and corroborated narrative impossible. The younger intelligence historian will then be faced with a radical dilemma: to write or not to write? Whether 'tis nobler in the mind to suffer passively the consequences of the weeder's black felt pen or take arms against a sea of deletions and blank pages by proactively supplying a moderately speculative narrative based on a combination of fragmentary evidence, educated guesswork, and commonsensical analysis.[6] The latter, I would suggest, is a perfectly acceptable methodological solution, provided it is applied proportionally, judiciously, and as a conjunctive rather than substantive process. It is all about using connective tissue to assemble a body of historical events, not fabricating it from scratch, which is what revisionists and conspiracy theorists do. It is often the only way in which to glue together and publish in a coherent form those scattered bits of truth about the secret world that need to see the light of day, but for which the archival evidence is incomplete. We must simply trust the individual historian, young or old, to go about such delicate surgery in a skilled, enlightened manner. In fact, to ensure that this process is handled ethically, the requisite skills have more to do with language than with history. It is essentially about marking one's speculative state-ments with clear transitional expressions that say to the reader, loudly: the next bit is not based entirely on verified, corroborated archival sources, but it shows what likely happened (or did not).

Therefore, words and phrases like 'probably', 'possibly', 'perhaps', and 'it can be safely assumed that' or 'it is highly unlikely that' can and should be included in the historian's legitimate thesaurus. Fail to use them, boldly and consistently, and one's historiography will be timid, tentative, and very dull. Worse yet, one might even find oneself with no stories to tell and no books to publish. But obviously, intelligence history needs to be written and published; it cannot be hobbled by purists who see a conspiracy behind every imaginative stroke of the historian's pen as he or she seeks to complete a jigsaw puzzle that often has many missing pieces. In this book I have therefore tried hard to label my occasional speculative moments clearly, either in the text itself or in the endnotes, in the hope that readers will always know when a modicum of cohesive force has had to be applied to a fragmentary narrative that would oth-erwise have flown apart.

Adrian O'Sullivan
West Vancouver, British Columbia
July 2015

Notes

1. Adrian O'Sullivan, *Nazi Secret Warfare in Occupied Persia (Iran): The Failure of the German Intelligence Services, 1939–45* (Basingstoke: Palgrave Macmillan, 2014), abbreviated throughout to *NSW*.
2. *NSW*, 25–31.
3. See Philip H.J. Davies, *MI6 and the Machinery of Spying* (London: Frank Cass, 2004), 128–9.
4. Cooperation with Russian Security, Supplementary Report No. 3, 30 August 1945, KV 4/225, The National Archives, Kew, Surrey (TNA).
5. Not long after returning as *ilkhan* (supreme leader) from exile in the United States and Germany, Khosrow was executed publicly by the new revolution-ary regime in Shiraz in 1982, after he had 'confessed' to being a CIA agent. His older brother Nasir died in exile in 1993. For more about the lives of Nasir and Khosrow Khan Qashgai, see Abbas Milani, *Eminent Persians: The Men and Women Who Made Modern Iran, 1941–1979*, vol. 1 (Syracuse, NY: Syracuse University Press, 2008), 261–6.
6. Cf. *Hamlet*, 3.1 (with apologies to the bard).

Acknowledgements

Hundreds of hours spent on research in museums, archives, and libraries both great and small have been made more congenial and productive for me than they might have been by the knowledgeable and supportive professional staff I have encountered during the past few years in Britain, Germany, Canada, and the United States. To them all, too numerous to mention, go my sincere thanks. I also appreciate the ongoing support and encouragement I have received from various colleagues and friends at home and abroad, among them most notably Julian Brooks (Simon Fraser), Bernd Lemke (ZMSBw Potsdam), Katrin Paehler (Illinois State), and André Gerolymatos (Simon Fraser), who originally suggested that I turn my attention to Persia. A permanent expression of gratitude is owed to my former doctoral supervisors in South Africa, Tilman Dedering (UNISA) and Ian van der Waag (Stellenbosch), without whose benign patronage and constructive advice neither of my two books would have seen the light of day. When one writes in retirement, without even emeritus or adjunct status at any academic institution to bolster one's confidence, historiography can become a lonely endeavour, unless one has recourse to such a rich vein of scholarly wisdom.

As a non-affiliated historian with limited personal funds, I also greatly appreciate the kindness of those representatives of for-profit entities and other institutions who have supplied photographic materials and miscellaneous documents without charge or for a negligible sum. Thanks therefore go to Ralph Gibson (RIA Novosti) for permission to publish a rare image of two obscure KGB operatives; to Tom Neiman (Stock Montage) for permission to use an image of the US minister to Persia, Louis G. Dreyfus; to Douglas J. Wilson (USACE Office of History) for the clearance of images from the Donald Connolly Collection; to Samar Mikati Kaissi (AUB) for locating and clearing a fine image of Stephen Penrose, when those found in the CIA records proved to be of unacceptably poor quality; and to Timothy Engels (Brown) for facilitating the reproduction of a rare award certificate signed by Adolf Hitler. For ransacking resources on my behalf in my relentless but often fruitless quest to reconstruct the lives of personalities expunged from the historical record, who deserve a better fate, I also wish to thank Geoffrey P. Megargee (USHMM) and Jürgen Förster (Freiburg). For interesting insights into the current state of the Russian military archives, I thank Alex Statiev (Waterloo). For tracing the history of the Field Security Sections and providing obscure details about the special duties performed in Persia by certain serving personnel, sincere thanks go to a fellow member of the Special Operations Executive Group, Alan F. Judge (Military Intelligence Museum and Archives, Defence Intelligence and Security Centre [DISC], Chicksands). For kindly providing me with certain valuable but overlooked Middle East records, I must also thank another member of the SOE Group, Steven Kippax, whose tireless work at Kew over the years has disclosed many an elusive archival treasure. For clarifying questions of copyright and for tracking down elusive rightsholders, many thanks go to Debbie Usher (St Antony's College, Oxford). Last but on no account least, I wish to thank Gerhard L. Weinberg for personally granting me permission to quote from his definitive book on Nazi foreign policy. The snippets I have used cannot truly measure the profound influence that Professor Weinberg's illuminating, magisterial works have had on my understanding of Allied and Axis strategy.

I wish to thank the Trustees of the Imperial War Museum for allowing access to the collections held in the IWM Sound and Documents Section. I also wish to thank Malcolm Bell Macdonald and Jeffrey Maunsell for kindly granting me permission to quote from their fathers' memoirs held at the IWM. Unfortunately, however, despite every effort, it was not possible to trace the copyright holders of the unpublished private papers of D.W.A. Mure and E.N. Sheppard. Both the IWM and I would be grateful for any information which might help to trace those whose identities or addresses are not currently known. The same goes for the published works of George Lenczowski, Paul Leverkuehn, David Mure, Sir Reader Bullard, and Lord Wilson of Libya. Of course, every effort has been made to trace and acknowledge all copyright holders, but if any have been inadvertently overlooked, the publisher will be pleased to make the necessary arrangements at the first opportunity.

It was thrilling to interview Dr Francis Shelton, one of few remaining SOE veterans, now over 100 and in splendid intellectual form, about his Middle East adventures and the many colourful personalities he encountered there. In late-1930s Budapest, with war and persecution looming, Shelton abandoned a promising career in law, and ventured forth to Turkey and Persia with some young friends and his trusty cello as an itinerant night-club musician. Before being posted to SOE in Cairo and working for PWE in Bari, Shelton wrote propaganda for Ann Lambton at the Tehran legation and knew, among others, Herbert Underwood (the military attaché) and David Turkhud (who recruited him after he had begged Jumbo Wilson to let him join up). He was invited by Reza Shah and Queen Esmat on several occasions to play his cello at the imperial palace, not at grand gatherings but intimately, with the fearsome shah-in-shah and his consort mere inches from him. Shelton's fascinating stories of life in occupied Persia are legion, and he tells them with great eloquence, charm, and wit, bringing to life the tumultuous era of war and intrigue that this book depicts. Meeting this fine man was a pleasure and a privilege, and I thank him and his son Anthony for making our long conversation possible.[1]

Finally, as in my previous book on Persia, I must acknowledge Winston Churchill's characteristic common sense when he insisted, on the eve of the Anglo-Soviet invasion in 1941, on official use of the term *Persia* instead of *Iran*, to avoid 'dangerous mistakes [that] may easily occur through the similarity of Iran and Iraq'.[2] Most contemporary British spoke of the country as *Persia*, and this usage is reflected in most of the documents that are the basis of this book.

Notes

1. While available in English at the Imperial War Museum (IWM), Dr Shelton's memoirs have only been published in Magyar: Francis Shelton, *Különleges küldetésem: Ügynök cselloval a II. vilaghaborüban* (Budapest: Scolar, 2010).
2. Minute M785/1, 2 August 1941, Prime Minister's printed personal minutes, CHAR 20/36/8, Churchill Archives Centre, Churchill College, Cambridge (CAC); *NSW*, xiv. Churchill showed similar concern about the possible confusion of Iceland with Ireland, directing that Iceland always be followed by a parenthetical upper-case 'C'. See Winston S. Churchill, *The Grand Alliance*, vol. 3 of *The Second World War* (London: The Reprint Society, 1952), 356.

Abbreviations

AA	Auswärtiges Amt (Auslandsamt) (Berlin)
Abw	Abwehr
Abw I L	Abwehr I Luft [= German air force intelligence]
Abw I M	Abwehr I Marine [= German naval intelligence]
Abw II SO	Abwehr II Südost
ADSO	Assistant Defence Security Officer
'A' Force	= Cairo-based unit responsible for Middle East strategic deception
AFHQ	Allied Force Headquarters
AGEA	Arbeitsgemeinschaft ehemaliger Abwehrangehöriger (Association of Former Members of the Abwehr) [Abwehr veterans' organization]
AIOC	Anglo-Iranian Oil Company
ALO	Area Liaison Officer
Amt VI	= RSHA Foreign Intelligence Department
Amt VI C 3	= Kurt Schuback's desk at Amt VI
Amt VI C 14	= Roman Gamotha's desk at Amt VI
AOC	Air Officer Commanding
AUB	American University of Beirut
B	= counterespionage [as in MI5 B Branch]
B1A, B1a	= MI5 counterespionage subsection administering double agents
B1B, B1b	= MI5 counterespionage analysis subsection
BArch	Bundesarchiv [Berlin-Lichterfelde]
BArch-MArch	Bundesarchiv-Militärarchiv [Freiburg]
BAOR	British Army of the Rhine
BBC	British Broadcasting Corporation
BDC	Berlin Document Centre
BL	British Library

BND	Bundesnachrichtendienst [Federal Intelligence Service]
BOAC	British Overseas Airways Corporation
BSC	British Security Coordination
BSM	Bronze Star Medal
BTE	British Troops in Egypt
C, 'C'	= Head of SIS (MI6)
CAC	Churchill Archives Centre [Churchill College, Cambridge]
C&CS	*see* GC&CS
CBE	Commander of the Order of the British Empire
CC	Creative Commons
CCS	Combined Chiefs of Staff
CE	counterespionage
CEV	Centre d'Examination des Voyageurs [Aleppo, Syria]
CI	counterintelligence [OSS]
CIA	Central Intelligence Agency [USA]
CIC	Counter Intelligence Corps [USA]
CICI	Combined Intelligence Centre Iraq and Persia
CID	Criminal Investigation Department [India]
CinC, C-in-C	Commander-in-Chief
CMG	Commander of the Order of St Michael and St George
CO	Colonial Office; commanding officer
CREST	CIA Research Tool
CS	countersubversion [OSS]
CSDIC	Combined Services Detailed Interrogation Centre [Maadi, Egypt]
CUCTU	Central United Council of Trade Unions [Persia]
DCOS	Deputy Chief of Staff
DDMI	Deputy Director of Military Intelligence
DDSP	Deputy Director of Special Planning [SOE]
DIB	Director of the Intelligence Bureau [India]

DSO	Defence Security Office(r); Distinguished Service Order
DSP	Director of Special Planning [SOE]
Exko	Executive Committee [Hizb-i-Melliun]
FBI	Federal Bureau of Investigation [USA]
FDR	Franklin Deleanor Roosevelt
FHW	Fremde Heere West (Foreign Armies West)
FKI	Freikorps Iran
FO	Foreign Office
FSB	Federal'naya sluzhba bezopasnosti Rossiyskoy Federatsii (Russian Federal Security Service)
FSO	Field Security Officer
FSS	Field Security Section(s) [Intelligence Corps]
FUSAG	First US Army Group [notional formation under General Patton]
G2, G-2	Divisional Intelligence Staff Officer
GC&CS, GCCS	Government Code and Cipher School
GENMISH	United States Government Mission to the Persian Gendarmerie
Gestapo	Geheime Staatspolizei (Secret State Police) [RSHA Amt IV]
GHQ	General Headquarters
GHQ (ME)	General Headquarters Middle East
GI	US serviceman [colloquialism]
GMDS	German Military Document Section [Camp Ritchie, MD]
GOC	General Officer Commanding
GOI	Government of India
GRU	Glavnoye Razvedyvatel'noye Upravleniye (Russian Armed Forces Main Intelligence Directorate)
GSI, GS(I)	General Staff Intelligence
GSI(c)	= original designation for SIME
HM	His (Her) Majesty('s)

HMG	His (Her) Majesty's Government
HMI	Hizb Mille Iran (Persian National Party)
HMSO	His (Her) Majesty's Stationery Office
HQ	headquarters
HUMINT	human intelligence
IA	Indian Army
IARO	Indian Army Reserve of Officers
IB	Intelligence Bureau [India]
i/c	in command of
IDB	illegal diamond buying
INA	Indian National Army
IO	intelligence officer; interrogating officer
IP	Iran Parastan [political party]
IPI	Indian Political Intelligence
ISLD	Inter-Services Liaison Department [= MI6 Middle and Far East]
ISOS	Intelligence Service Oliver Strachey [= Abwehr manual ciphers]
IWG	International Working Group
IWM	Documents Collection, Imperial War Museum
JCS	Joint Chiefs of Staff
KGB	Komitet Gosudarstvennoi Bezopasnosti (Committee of State Security) [USSR]
KONO	Kriegsorganisation Nahost [= Abwehr outstation in Istanbul]
LO	Liaison Officer
LOM	Legion of Merit
MA	Military Attaché
MBE	Member of the Order of the British Empire
ME	Middle East
MEC	Middle East Command
MECA	Middle East Centre Archive [St Antony's College, Oxford]

MEF	Middle East Forces
MEIC	Middle East Intelligence Centre
MEW	Ministry of Economic Warfare
MHQ	Mohammed Huseyin Qashgai
MI5	Military Intelligence Dept 5 [colloquial designation for the Security Service]
MI6	Military Intelligence Dept 6 [colloquial designation for the Secret Intelligence Service]
MI9	Military Intelligence Dept 9 [escape and evasion]
MI14	Military Intelligence Dept 14 [surveillance of Germany]
MilAmt	Militärisches Amt (RSHA Military Department)
Mil C	Militärisches Amt C [= post-merger RSHA equivalent of Abwehr I Ost]
Mil D	Militärisches Amt D [= post-merger RSHA equivalent of Abwehr II]
MilKo	Military Subcommittee [Hizb-i-Melliun]
MMQ	Malek Mansour Qashgai
MTS	Motor Transport Service [US Army]
NARA	National Archives and Records Administration [USA]
NCO	non-commissioned officer
NKVD	Narodnyi Kommissariat Vnutrennikh Del (People's Commissariat for Internal Affairs) [USSR]
NOIC	Naval Officer in Charge
NSW	*Nazi Secret Warfare in Occupied Persia (Iran)*
NUS	National Union of Students
OBE	Officer of the Order of the British Empire
OC	Officer Commanding
OIC	Officer in Charge
OKH	Oberkommando des Heeres (High Command of the German Army)
OKW	Oberkommando der Wehrmacht (High Command of the German Armed Forces)

OPD	Operations Division [US War Department]
OR	other ranks
OSS	Office of Strategic Services [USA]
OTI	Office of Technical Information [USA]
PAIC	Persian and Iraq Command
PAIFORCE	Persia and Iraq Force
PD	public domain
PGC	Persian Gulf Command (December 1943 onwards) [USA]
PGSC	Persian Gulf Service Command (up to December 1943) [USA]
PIAW	Preventive Intelligence Arab World
PICME	Political Intelligence Centre Middle East
PoKo	Political Subcommittee [Hizb-i-Melliun]
POLINT	Political intelligence
POW	prisoner(s) of war
PWE	Political Warfare Executive [created in 1941 from the SOE propaganda department (SO1)]
RAF	Royal Air Force
RAMC	Royal Army Medical Corps
RfA	Reichsstelle für (den) Aussenhandel (Reich Office of Foreign Trade)
RGVA	Russian State Military Archive
RIA	Russian Information Agency
RNOH	Royal National Orthopaedic Hospital
RNVR	Royal Naval Volunteer Reserve
RSHA	Reichssicherheitshauptamt (Reich Security Administration)
SAS	Special Air Service
SBS	Special Boat Service
SD	Sicherheitsdienst (SS Security Service)
SHAEF	Supreme Headquarters Allied Expeditionary Force
SI	secret intelligence [OSS]

SIFE	Security Intelligence Far East
SIGINT	signals intelligence
SIME	Security Intelligence Middle East [= MI5, Cairo]
SIS	Secret Intelligence Service (MI6)
SK	Sonderkommando (special squad) [in the SS this was a euphemism for extermination squad, but not of course in the German army (for example, SK Bajadere)]
SKL	Seekriegsleitung (Maritime Warfare Command) [German supreme naval HQ]
SMERSH	Smert' Shpionam (Death to Spies) [Red Army counter-intelligence] [USSR]
SNOPG	Senior Naval Officer Persian Gulf
SO1	= SOE propaganda department which became PWE in 1941
SOAS	School of Oriental and African Studies [University of London]
SOE	Special Operations Executive
SS	Schutzstaffel [Nazi Party security forces]
SSE	special source exploitation
SVR	Sluzhba vneshney razvedki (Russian Foreign Intelligence Service)
TAP	Truck Assembly Plant [US Army]
TASS	Telegrafnoye Agentstvo Sovetskogo Soyuza (Telegraph Agency of the Soviet Union)
TIR	Trans-Iranian Railway
TJFF	Transjordan Frontier Force
TNA	The National Archives [UK]
UCL	University College London (University of London)
UK	United Kingdom
UKCC	United Kingdom Control Commission
UNISA	University of South Africa
USACE	United States Army Corps of Engineers
USAFIME	United States Army Forces in the Middle East

USGPO	United States Government Printing Office
USHMM	United States Holocaust Memorial Museum
USS	United States Ship
WCNA	Whitman College and Northwest Archives
WD	War Department
WDGS	War Department General Staff
WDSS	War Department Special Staff
WE	war establishment
WO	warrant officer
WO2	Warrant Officer Class 2 (Company Sergeant-Major or equivalent)
W/T	wireless telegrapher/telegraphy [= radio operator/radio]
X-2	counterespionage [OSS]

Chronology

8 Nov 1940	Mayr and Gamotha arrive in Pahlavi under commercial cover.
19 May 1941	Schulze-Holthus arrives in Tabriz under diplomatic cover.
30 May 1941	Rashid Ali Gailani flees to Persia from Iraq.
Jun-Jul 1941	SIME establishes CICI in Baghdad.
25 Aug 1941	Operation COUNTENANCE: British and Soviet troops occupy Persia.
Jan 1942	CICI remit extended to include Persia; Spencer posted to Tehran as DSO.
29 Jan 1942	Anglo-Soviet-Persian Treaty of Alliance signed.
23 April 1942	Japanese legation in Tehran closed; Japanese diplomats expelled.
22 Jun 1942	Schulze-Holthus joins Nasir Khan in Qashgai territory
Jul 1942	Mayr and Vaziri organize *Hizb-i-Melliun*.
August 1942	PGSC established; CIC deployed.
3 August 1942	Harris-Griffiths murder in Lorestan.
2 Nov 1942	Mayr's house in Isfahan raided and key documents seized.
Nov 1942	Wilson, Bullard, Maunsell, and Wood plan operations against *Melliun*.
9 Nov 1942	Schulze-Holthus's Farrashband landing ground discovered.
8 Dec 1942	Operation PONGO: Zahedi arrested and interned.
14 Jan 1943	Force Kalpak expedition sent to southern Persia.
22 Mar 1943	FRANZ expedition dropped at Siah Kuh.
May 1943	Persian troops occupy parts of Qashgai territory.
15 May 1943	Penrose posted to Cairo as head of OSS SI.
28 Jun 1943	DORA group sent by Mayr to Bakhtiari territory.

17 July 1943	ANTON expedition dropped near Shiraz.
2 Aug 1943	Schulze-Holthus joins the ANTON group.
11 Aug 1943	Spencer releases his fifth-column master plan.
15 Aug 1943	Spencer arrests Mayr at gunpoint.
29 Aug 1943	The entire FRANZ group is now in custody.
9 Sep 1943	Persia ends its neutrality and declares war on Germany.
23 Sep 1943	Schulze-Holthus and the ANTON group transferred to Boir Ahmedi custody.
28 Nov 1943	Churchill, Roosevelt, and Stalin meet in Tehran.
Jan 1944	Crawford succeeds Penrose as head of OSS SI.
1 Mar 1944	Schulze-Holthus and the ANTON group returned to the Qashgai by the Boir Ahmedi.
21 Mar 1944	Dreyfus transferred to Iceland.
22 Mar 1944	KISS establishes contact with MARQUIS.
23 Mar 1944	Schulze-Holthus and the ANTON group surrendered by the Qashgai.
31 Mar 1944	Qashgai Brothers return to Persia from 12-year exile.
Apr 1944	Kellar first visits DSO Persia.
Aug 1944	OSS inserts two active-intelligence agents into the Soviet zone.
17 Jan 1945	Schulze-Holthus repatriated to Germany in exchange for British agent.
2 Apr 1945	Last German agent (Jakob) captured on Persian soil.
3 May 1945	MARQUIS transmits final farewell message to KISS.
Dec 1945	Last US forces leave Persia.
Feb 1946	Last British forces (73 FSS) leave Persia.
Apr 1946	Last Soviet forces leave Persia.

'Things Look Black for the Persians: The "American Century" Begins!'

Anti-American racist cartoon in the official SS newspaper, Das Schwarze Korps *(12 November 1942)*

Under overall Sicherheitsdienst (SS Security Service [SD]) editorial control, with the rabidly antisemitic Günther d'Alquen of the Waffen-SS as editor-in-chief, this weekly propaganda broadsheet featured articles laden with race hatred, some of which proudly proclaimed the splendid work of SS Death's Head units in the Nazi concentration camps. The paper's wide popularity, with a circulation in the hundreds of thousands, makes a nonsense of claims by ordinary Germans that they knew nothing of the camps.

When this cartoon appeared, a couple of months before their staggering rout at Stalingrad, the Germans still planned to occupy Persia themselves. Despite the lip-service paid cynically by Nazi ideologues like d'Alquen to pure Persian 'Aryanism', which explains the smug condescension displayed here towards the blackface American occupiers, things would no doubt have looked far 'blacker' for the racially tolerant Persians, had they been forced to host a permanent army of arrogant, bigoted, 'Aryan' SS-men for a millenium, instead of about 4000 African-American GIs – mostly egalitarian, easy-going, hard-working truck drivers, train drivers, and clerks – for a mere couple of years.

Prologue: MI5 in the Middle East

> The importance of retaining the use of Abadan refin-
> ery cannot be overestimated. If this refinery were
> destroyed, we have not sufficient tanker tonnage to
> supply the wants of the Middle East and India, and
> our position in the Middle East would dry up for lack
> of oil. (War Cabinet Joint Planning Staff)[1]

To many it may seem curious that the Royal Air Force (Air Staff
Intelligence Iraq) should have been responsible throughout the Second
World War for the administration of the predominantly British and
Indian army ground formation, Combined Intelligence Centre Iraq
and Persia (CICI), that answered for the security of occupied Iraq and
Persia, including the great Anglo-Iranian Oil Company (AIOC) refinery at Abadan and the oil infrastructure of Khuzistan. Traditionally,
however, ever since the First World War, responsibility for Middle East
and Central Asian intelligence had rested solely with the RAF, mainly
because the vast distances involved in maintaining an intelligence presence in those remote regions could only be covered by aircraft. The
strongest advocate for this system of aerial control and policing was
Winston Churchill, who was compelled as Secretary of State for War
and Air during the 1920s to find an operational alternative to land-
based forces in Mesopotamia, mainly because of their iniquitous cost.[2]
Interestingly, one of those most closely associated with the elaboration
and implementation of Churchill's air-substitution policy at the Middle
East Department of the Colonial Office was none other than Reader
Bullard, who as British minister (and later ambassador) in Tehran figures
prominently in this book.[3] Clearly, because of this high-level experience, from the very onset of his posting to the Persian legation in 1939

Bullard must have possessed far greater regional security expertise than would normally be attributed to a diplomat, even one so senior. It may partially explain why he, as we shall see, so resolutely supported and facilitated the work of the secret services and security forces operating within his Persian bailiwick throughout the war.

And so – a full decade after British and Indian land forces had ceded overall command of Iraq to the air force[4] – RAF Habbaniya, a large strategic air and seaplane base, was constructed at enormous but relatively acceptable expense in the mid-1930s about 89 km west of Baghdad. It became the logical choice as the administrative nerve-centre for all intelligence, counterintelligence, and security operations east of Suez, once the Hashemite Kingdom had been established (in 1932), and the RAF had abandoned its operational centre at Rowanduz in Iraqi Kurdistan.[5] Lest it be thought that the RAF's mandate in the region as originally conceived by Churchill was provisional rather than permanent and merely perpetuated by expediency at the outbreak of war in 1939, the following description of Habbaniya by the well-connected, highly observant, and hugely popular British star of stage and screen Joyce Grenfell has set the record indelibly straight. In her 1944 diary, on her way to entertain the troops in Persia, Grenfell described an enormous 'impersonal' camp of incomparable luxury in the middle of the Iraqi desert near the Euphrates which had cost many millions to build in the 1930s. Grenfell believed that her aunt, Nancy Astor, had asked a lot of 'silly and awkward questions' about spending public money on it at the time. Anyway, it was spent, lavishly, and the result was very splendid and rather unreal. 'It's got everything,' Grenfell wrote, 'pools, polo, football, tennis, a huge movie house, clubs galore, a first-class hospital ... , bungalow quarters for everyone with bathrooms to every room, trees, gardens – everything. And in 1935 it was just twelve square miles of dust.'[6]

In fact, RAF Habbaniya was a very large base indeed. At its height (1941–42) it was staffed by no fewer than 7500 personnel (446 officers, 5603 other ranks [ORs], and 1571 civilians); how many of these people were involved in intelligence and security operations is unclear. Two years later, however, after the strategic turning points in the war at El Alamein and Stalingrad and the subsequent transfer of Allied land and air forces to other theatres, the base had swiftly shrunk to nothing more than a token operational presence, useful mainly as a refuelling station for RAF and BOAC long-range aircraft heading for India, the Far East, and Australasia, including flying boats, which could berth on the 140 km² lake.[7] Whereas in 1942 two entire Habbaniya-based Hurricane squadrons had been exclusively dedicated to flying regular sorties to the east over the Abadan oil refinery in southwest Persia, by June 1943 only four aircraft were left at Habbaniya to perform that and other tasks, two of which were venerable Gladiators. They were even outnumbered by the 8–10 dummy aircraft deployed on the tarmac to bamboozle the enemy into believing that Habbaniya was still an operational threat. On 19 June, the Air Officer Commanding (AOC) minuted that there was no fighter squadron left in the entire Iraq Command; that the defence of the two most vital enemy targets in the region (the Abadan and Kirkuk oil refineries) devolved entirely on the anti-aircraft artillery stationed in those places; and that there remained no air reporting system anywhere in the Command to warn of approaching enemy aircraft.[8] By this time, however, the RAF had fortunately been relieved of all but its administrative responsibility for intelligence and security operations. Its successor was Security Intelligence Middle East (SIME): the improbable anomaly of an MI5-controlled, interservice counterintelligence and security-intelligence organization, administered by the 'Brylcreem Boys', but staffed predominantly by British and Indian army personnel, whose backgrounds and training reflected an extensive legacy of expertise in colonial policing and management. Even less probable is the fact that this peculiar structural combination not only worked, but it proved from the start to be immensely successful, mainly because of the vision and rigorous consistency of its leaders.

Originally, it was Sir Archibald Wavell who, during the first month of the war, had conceived of the need for security intelligence to be organized on a Middle East basis.[9] At Wavell's insistence, Raymond Maunsell, a former tanks officer who had served with the Transjordan Frontier Force (TJFF) between 1930 and 1931,[10] and who had been based in Cairo as Defence Security Officer since 1937, was seconded to the army from MI5 in October 1939 and submitted a series of proposals for an 'MI5 of the Middle East', all of which were rejected for budgetary and administrative reasons by two successive Deputy Directors of Military Intelligence (DDMI).[11] Nevertheless, the extraordinarily efficient and successful organization called SIME was eventually developed from Maunsell's original concept owing to the persistent feeling both in London and in Cairo that, notwithstanding administrative objections, the central coordination of counterintelligence was necessary and that the problem was 'an indivisible whole' in the Middle East.[12] It was originally intended that SIME should be called Preventive Intelligence Arab World (PIAW); however, since the area to be covered included Persia, Turkey, and parts of Abyssinia, the more suitable title of Security Intelligence Middle East was adopted.

SIME was therefore 'to coordinate information of all anti-British agents whether or not of German nationality working in [the] area covered by MEIC [Middle East Intelligence Centre]'.[13] The object was to locate them, keep track of their movements, and deal with them, 'should opportunity offer'.[14] In fact, this defensive nexus of coordinated security-intelligence measures, in concert with the deception operations run by Dudley Clarke's 'A' Force, proved so effective that the manifestly uncoordinated German, Italian, and Japanese espionage services were unable to obtain any useful information from the Middle East, despite the existence of disaffected, pro-Axis elements among the indigenous populations. According to David Mure, one of Clarke's staff officers, 'in the whole of the Middle East there literally was no genuine Axis espionage network',[15] and Guy Liddell of MI5 wrote conclusively in his diary: 'It is probably true to say that the Abwehr have failed to obtain any reliable information of strategic importance.'[16] Meanwhile, the skilful doubling, tripling, and playback by the Allied services of enemy agents also ensured that a great deal of disinformation reached the Axis spymasters. By far the most interesting source on these Middle East deception operations is David Mure, who was directly involved in them at an executive level and who wrote: 'we were able to control the German military espionage service in all areas occupied by the Western Allies and supply all their information'.[17]

The Allied view of the German intelligence services operating in the Middle East was never complimentary, yet neither was it complacent. Shortly after the Anglo-Soviet invasion of Persia, the head of SIME noted that the enemy espionage organization in the Middle East had never been efficient; that, being newcomers in the area, the Germans were in the process of making all the mistakes that the British had long forgotten; and that recent events in Persia had disorganized whatever organization existed. But he went on: 'I am not suggesting that we have any cause for complacency and we have no intentions of "sitting back," as we know that the enemy is directing every effort to reconstituting his espionage organization.'[18]

Raymond Maunsell's boldly innovative leadership of SIME was characterized both by his unique leadership style and by the operational principles he instilled in his officers, ORs, and civilians. While SIME was technically part of Middle East Forces (MEF), Maunsell simply could not see the point of applying a rigid military hierarchy and a unified code of behaviour to a heterogeneous interservice/civilian staff. He felt there was nothing to be gained by having a military-type discipline in a body consisting of regular army, RAF, and RNVR officers, and civilians with honorary or temporary commissions, to say nothing of the extremely efficient and hard-working 'lady civilians' – all were 'part of the show'. Maunsell encouraged the use of first names. 'I particularly strove to encourage the SIME [organization] to be a friendly and quick-working one, and I didn't give a damn how they wore their uniforms or, indeed, what they wore', he wrote.[19]

Maunsell thoroughly believed that his was the best paradigm for '"working" a mixed bag of people engaged in operations of complexity, nicely seasoned with embarrassments, successes, and occasional absurdities'.[20] Yet, when it came to operations, there was nothing lax or inefficient about SIME. Indeed, Maunsell insisted on the strict observance of certain 'general working principles' throughout the organization: careful and exact administration; unending patience, accessibility, and an 'inexpungable' sense of humour; the importance of 'dedramatization', which Maunsell defined as the stressing of the 'ordinariness' of human activities ('the necessity of trying to interpret dramatic police or other reports, e.g. the apparently suspicious behaviour of individuals may often be due to the secret pursuit of homo- or heterosexual relationships');[21] the necessity for constant, if not daily, contact with local commanders, other British intelligence organizations, and the local special police; the importance of consultation with each other; the importance of vetting; and, finally, the importance of cutting across channels. In this connection, Maunsell wrote: 'It was a principle of operation that different SIME areas (Defence Security Offices) and, indeed, individual officers in different areas, should communicate directly with each other and only refer to SIME Head Office if help was required or if it was vital for the Head of SIME to know about the matter in question at once ...'.[22] So, the absence of formality in Maunsell's organization was clearly not associated with any absence of rigour or professionalism in operational procedures. Indeed, as David Mure has pointed out, in the Middle East all the security and clandestine organizations – SIME, ISLD, and 'A' Force – were service-staffed and functioned admirably in far more difficult circumstances than those obtaining in the UK. Being service organizations, they were free of 'the plague of the civilian MI5 in 1944 ... indiscipline'. A man under service conditions was forced to maintain a high standard of conduct as he was liable, rightly, to be sternly disciplined for the slightest misdemeanour. 'One immediately thinks of homosexuality, then a criminal offence,' wrote Mure, 'perpetual drunkenness, drug taking, black market operations. People like Burgess [and] Blunt ... would not have survived six weeks in the Middle East intelligence services.'[23] One wonders what Mure made of the flamboyantly camp Alex Kellar of B Branch, whom he probably encountered during the war, and who served MI5 in exemplary fashion well into the Cold War era.

Certainly, none of the Cambridge Five would have felt at home amidst the regulation and discipline of SIME's security-intelligence HQ in occupied Tehran – the Defence Security Office Persia (DSO Persia), also known as CICI Tehran or just DSO – where things under Joe Spencer's able command were managed strictly, efficiently, and anything but casually. From his arrival early in 1942, Spencer established comprehensive security systems and procedures, and he expected them to be applied and managed with rigour, precision, and consistency, which they were. Rank mattered, and army traditions prevailed, notwithstanding the organization's close liaison with the predominantly civilian Security Service in London. It is these few 'Ratcatchers of Tehran' – no more than 25 officers, ORs, and civilians – who are at the centre of this book (see Appendix A.1). When they first gathered in Tehran, few had any background in security intelligence, yet by the end of the war – a mere 28 months later – all had become highly professional operatives. Their astonishing success in protecting the security of an immense region in the face of German military threat and clandestine warfare, Persian fifth columnists and saboteurs, Soviet manoeuvres and postures, American disingenuousness and anglophobia, and the volatility of the pro-Nazi tribes undoubtedly merits this attempt to identify their achievements, construct their neglected narrative, and describe the historical context within which they functioned so effectively.

Notes

1. Eastward extension of the war in the Middle East, Report by the Joint Planning Staff, War Cabinet, 9 July 1941, CAB 79/12/41, The National Archives, Kew, Surrey (TNA).
2. The development of air control in Iraq, October 1922, AIR 19/109, TNA. See also David E. Omissi, *Air Power and Colonial Control: The Royal Air Force, 1919–1939* (New York: Manchester University Press, 1990), 20–1; Jafna Cox, 'A Splendid Training Ground: The Importance to the Royal Air Force of Its Role in Iraq, 1919–32', *Journal of Imperial and Commonwealth History* 13 (1985): 157–84. For a jaundiced view of the genesis of RAF aerial policing, interesting in that it examines the socio-cultural and intellectual rather than intelligence roots of air control in Iraq, see Priya Satia, 'The Defense of Inhumanity: Air Control and the British Idea of Arabia', *American Historical Review* 111, no. 1 (February 2006): 16–51; Satia's bibliographical footnotes are detailed and useful.
3. Satia, 'Defense of Inhumanity', 28.

4. In October 1922. Ibid., 32.
5. *NSW*, 191.
6. Joyce Grenfell, *The Time of My Life: Entertaining the Troops, 1944–1945* (London: Hodder & Stoughton, 1989), 165.
7. Location and estimated strength of units in Iraq Command, AIR 23/5858, TNA.
8. Edwards to HQ RAF Middle East, Air Defence Iraq, 19 June 1943, AIR 23/5860, TNA.
9. An excellent recent biography of Wavell is Victoria Schofield, *Wavell: Soldier and Statesman* (London: John Murray, 2006). He was of course a general who later became a field marshal (and an earl); however, except for the occasional mention, especially when the first name is unknown, I have deliberately avoided the use of military ranks in this book, not out of disregard for such titles but because they changed like shifting sands during the war, and their use would become very muddled and confusing for the reader.
10. 'Brigadier Raymond John Maunsell', *The Peerage*, http://www.thepeerage.com/p45209.htm#i452081.
11. Maunsell to Head of MEIC, 6 June 1942, KV 4/306, TNA.
12. Memorandum on counter-intelligence in the Middle East area with special reference to Iraq and Persia, KV 4/223, TNA. The official narrative of SIME's establishment is to be found in F.H. Hinsley and C.A.G. Simkins, *British Intelligence in the Second World War*, vol. 4, *Security and Counter-Intelligence* (New York: Cambridge University Press, 1984), 149–53.
13. Ibid., quoting MEIC telegram no. 5069, 4 October 1939. The brief history (1939–43) of the Middle East Intelligence Centre (MEIC), effectively superseded in mid-1943 by the Political Intelligence Centre Middle East (PICME), is described in H.O. Dovey, 'The Middle East Intelligence Centre', *Intelligence and National Security* 4, no. 4 (1989): 800–812. The security summaries provided by both organizations tended to concentrate on the Arab Middle East, to the exclusion of Persia, which was adequately covered by a separate series of summaries released by DSO Persia, now to be found in WO 208/1567–1569 and WO 208/3088-3089, TNA. Unfortunately, the first 15 summaries in the series, located in WO 208/3087, are listed as 'wanting' (i.e. although catalogued by TNA, they were never actually transferred to Kew from the War Office).
14. Memorandum on counter-intelligence in the Middle East area with special reference to Iraq and Persia, KV 4/223, TNA.
15. David Mure, *Practise to Deceive* (London: William Kimber, 1977), 49.
16. Diary of Guy Liddell, 22 October 1943, KV 4/192, TNA.
17. Mure, *Practise to Deceive*, 12. See also David Mure, *Master of Deception: Tangled Webs in London and the Middle East* (London: William Kimber, 1980), 15–16 passim.
18. Maunsell to Petrie, 18 September 1941, KV 4/306, TNA.
19. Memoir of work in the intelligence service in the Middle East, 1934–1943, Private papers of Brigadier R.J. Maunsell, 4829:80/30/1, Documents Collection, Imperial War Museum (IWM). I wish to thank the Trustees of the Imperial War Museum for allowing access to this collection held in the IWM Sound and Documents Section.
20. Ibid.

21. Ibid.
22. Ibid.
23. The role and control of secret intelligence in support of both operations and security, Private papers of D.W.A. Mure, 2194:67/321/3, IWM. I wish to thank the Trustees of the Imperial War Museum for allowing access to this collection held in the IWM Sound and Documents Section.

1
Ratcatchers

Mopping up the well-concealed Germans was not a task for conventional military forces. It was a rat-catching operation, and our little group were the rat catchers … . (Bill Magan [MI5])[1]

Early in the war, Persia was an independent neutral state in which no British intelligence organizations were operating, with the exception of individual travelling agents working for the Royal Air Force (Air Staff Intelligence, Iraq), which held responsibility for Persia as well as Iraq. Initially therefore, Security Intelligence Middle East (SIME) permitted this arrangement to continue, providing the RAF with direction on counterintelligence matters concerning Persia and providing them with funds for this and other purposes. Then, a few months after the Allies had invaded the country, SIME appointed a security officer (Edward Leslie 'Joe' Spencer, Royal Artillery) and a small staff to Tehran to open a Combined Intelligence Centre Iraq and Persia (CICI) office there, answerable to CICI HQ in Baghdad, which was under the command of a highly capable Indian Army colonel, Edwin (or Edward) Kyme 'Chokra' Wood of The Corps of Guides (Cavalry), IA.

Chokra Wood was a professional soldier, born in York in 1900. His distinguished father, Colonel Cecil E. Wood, CMG, had been mentioned in despatches during service as an officer of the York Volunteers in the Boer War and had commanded 5th Battalion, West Yorkshire Regiment during the First World War, becoming an honorary colonel in 1922. Chokra Wood first went out to Wellington Cadet College in the Nilgiri Hills as an officer cadet in 1919. He was commissioned as a second lieutenant six months later as part of the first intake of 80 cadets at Quetta and Wellington destined to become the new postwar generation of regular IA officers.[2] After passing out, Wood was attached as a squadron officer to the Queen Victoria's Own Corps of Guides (Frontier Force) (Lumsden's) Cavalry in January 1920, serving in this élite Punjabi regiment for 15 years before retiring with the rank of captain to the UK and becoming a senior hospital administrator in 1937.[3] Returning to military life and promoted to major in 1940, Chokra Wood moved at some point from India to the Middle East, possibly with his regiment. The Guides Cavalry, who were now the 10th Queen Victoria's Own Frontier Force, became mechanized in September 1940, were sent to Iraq as a light reconnaissance unit, and took part in Operation COUNTENANCE, during which one of the Guides' squadrons captured the city of Khorramshahr as part of 18th Indian Infantry Brigade.[4] Whether Wood was then detached for staff duties or had been transferred earlier remains unclear, as does the matter of how he originally came to the attention of Raymond Maunsell and was recruited for intelligence duties. Traditionally, the Corps of Guides had always performed a reconnaissance and intelligence role on the North-West Frontier; perhaps a background in tactical intelligence led to Wood's secondment to SIME. Given his pedigree, not least his years of civilian senior-management experience, it is understandable that those – mostly much younger men, some of them American – who encountered Wood as a Baghdad spymaster readily deferred to him as a rather eccentric, 'old-style' British Indian colonel: a formidable character worthy of considerable respect.[5]

When Wood despatched him to Tehran, Joe Spencer immediately took over the counterintelligence functions hitherto being performed – with considerable difficulty – by the military attaché (Herbert John Underwood of the 15th Punjabis, IA) at the Tehran legation. However, by November 1942 – over a year after the Anglo-Soviet invasion and two years after the arrival in Persia of the German spies MAX and MORITZ (Franz Mayr and Roman Gamotha)[6] – it was felt that counterintelligence was not being adequately covered under the existing arrangement, because of severe underresourcing, not because of any incompetence on the part of the CICI Tehran staff. Therefore, properly organized Area Liaison Officers (ALOs) were posted to Persian regional centres in December 1942, answerable to Spencer, whose official title was now (and would remain until late-1944) Defence Security Officer (DSO) Persia. This decision, shortly after the establishment of Persia and Iraq Command (PAIC) under Sir Henry Maitland 'Jumbo' Wilson, was largely a response to strong pressure from Sir Reader Bullard, the British minister (later ambassador) in Tehran, for a beefing up of the

CICI organization in Persia, in the light of heightened Axis covert activities. In October 1942, Bullard wired the British minister of state in Cairo as follows:

> At present [the] staff of CICI Tehran is quite inadequate for the duties it has to carry out, and they are overworked to a point at which efficiency is bound to suffer. Of the total Tehran strength of five officers and seven other ranks, one officer has had to be detached for interrogation duties at Sultanabad [Arak]. The military authorities also want an ALO at Qum. Meanwhile the control of suspects suffers.[7]

On October 20, there had been no fewer than 40 investigations pending against Germans supposed to be hiding. The careful control of entry and exit visas arranged the previous summer had had to be abandoned, as it was physically impossible to check all the applications with the staff available, without intolerable delays.[8] Bullard also made it abundantly clear to London that there was no alternative but to reinforce CICI, as they alone had to bear the full burden of responsibility for internal security within the British zone of occupation:

> It has been suggested that [the] Persian police should help more. As you will realize, this shows total incomprehension of the situation here. Members of [the] Persian police are themselves suspected of complicity in fifth-column activities, and at the best they tend to use any evidence we bring forward as a means of extracting bribes from the accused. No more help can possibly be expected from [them] than is now being given.[9]

After full consideration of this undesirable state of affairs, Bullard recommended most strongly that six more officers and six ORs be sent out, and provided with additional transport. This would enable the vast and important problem of security to be tackled more effectively.[10]

In the same cable, Bullard was also unstinting in his praise of Joe Spencer and the staff of DSO: 'Nothing in this telegram should be read as a criticism of Major Spencer and his staff. They are most capable, but they cannot be expected to shoulder their greatly increased responsibility until they are strongly reinforced at [the] earliest possible moment.'[11] Pressure also came from the military leadership. Like Archie Wavell, who was renowned for his insatiable appetite for intelligence product, Jumbo Wilson, who assumed command of Persia and Iraq on 21 August 1942 – almost one year after the Anglo-Soviet occupation began – was

Figure 1.1   PAIFORCE commander (21 August 1942 to 17 February 1943): Sir Henry Maitland 'Jumbo' Wilson, the extremely popular general who encouraged and oversaw the establishment of an adequately resourced CICI security-intelligence organization throughout his command.
Source: Wikipedia Commons/PD.

an extremely security-conscious commander, who strongly supported and relied heavily upon CICI. Of course, Wilson's main concern was that the internal security of Persia should remain sound at a time when he was assembling his military forces to defend Persia against an anticipated German attack through the Caucasus, in the event of a Russian collapse, possibly as early as mid-November 1942.[12] Even later PAIC commanders, like Sir Henry Pownall, whose appointment lasted from 23 March 1943 until 12 October 1943, after the invasion crisis (in other words, after El Alamein and Stalingrad), were concerned that the internal security situation should not deteriorate to the detriment of the general prosecution of the war.[13]

Meanwhile, at CICI headquarters in Baghdad, Chokra Wood compiled his own general prescription for success in Persia, which he saw as dependent upon making the right policy decisions. After defining the main causes of disaffection and unrest in the country as being (1) an oppressive, corrupt, and inefficient administration, (2) economics, (3) government inability to enforce its authority outside the urban areas, and (4) enemy agents, the outspoken Wood concluded that enemy agents were widespread throughout the country, and in this category he included many Persian officials of high and low degree, as well as foreign nationals. For reasons of policy, the Persians, in most cases, were being temporarily left at large but under observation. The foreign nationals were receiving Persian and tribal protection and, although every effort was being made to round them up, the difficulty of this task was considerable. Wood went on:

> When considering a remedy for the situation in Persia our policy towards that country has to be considered. Our policy at present consists of support for the central government and noninterference in Persia's internal affairs. The support is given to a very shaky structure and the noninterference, which is belied in practice, has been construed as an evasion of responsibility. Whatever the result of the policy, it rules out any suggestion of Allied administration of the country and any possibility that the root causes of Persia's ills might be speedily and effectively removed.[14]

According to Wood, there remained the problem of ensuring security in British military areas and on the lines of communication. 'Since time is a consideration, it appears that finer political feelings should be disregarded and the issue decided by Allied force or by British or Allied negotiation with those elements which are the causes of insecurity.'[15] In fact, the concerns of Bullard, Wilson, and Wood were effectively dealt with in 1943 by various measures taken at the policy level and by the deployment of greater numbers of security personnel and advisers, including American field security units, in the region.

Whilst CICI was essentially a combined-services organization, the original supremacy of the RAF in matters concerning the administration of Allied security intelligence in the region inevitably led to all

manner of difficulties, especially as the War Office saw fit to perpetu-
ate the RAF's responsibility for administrative arrangements connected
with CICI. The main problem seems to have been that, although the
operational work of CICI prospered and multiplied from 1942 onwards,
the administrative resources of the RAF did not. The administration of
officers' pay, for instance, seems to have been fraught with difficulties.
The officers' war-establishment strength from December 1942 to June
1944 included a Royal Navy officer, British Army officers on British rates
of pay, British officers on IA rates of pay, regular IA officers, emergency-
commissioned IA officers, and RAF officers. All officers drew their own
service pay and allowances; travelling claims had to be submitted to
their own service. This meant that, as the RAF adjutant and orderly-
room staff could not possibly deal with the many and varied queries
which were continually arising regarding army pay questions, a separate
army officer had to be appointed to deal with those and other army
questions.[16] By August 1943, two years after the Anglo-Soviet invasion,
the total war establishment of CICI Baghdad and Tehran numbered
75 officers and 20 ORs.[17]

Another area in which an underresourced RAF ran into difficulties
was transport. When CICI was formed, the RAF were responsible for
issue and maintenance, but as they could not deal with the problem,
they asked the army to accept responsibility, which they did. This was
the first break in the administration, and CICI from then on found itself
responsible to the army for transport and having to comply with army
rules, forms, etc., which the RAF orderly-room staff were not able to deal
with.[18] There were also apparently 'endless difficulties' with hirings,
equipment, and staff replacements, for which neither the army nor the
RAF would accept responsibility. In other words, what had originally
seemed to be a feasible arrangement when CICI was being formed ultimately became a cumbersome burden for all service branches to bear,
especially since the RAF administrative staff was 'constantly changing'.[19]

A unique symbiotic relationship developed between SIME, headquartered in Cairo, and its offspring CICI, headquartered in Baghdad. In turn,
an equally special, mutually beneficial working arrangement evolved
during the years of the Allied occupation of Persia between the latter
organization and its virtually autonomous 'branch office' in Tehran,[20]
which, under the extraordinarily able command of Joe Spencer and his
deputy Alan Roger, is the leading protagonist in the operational history
this book portrays. Edward Leslie 'Joe' Spencer was originally commissioned during the 1930s as a Territorial Army infantry officer but was
transferred to the Royal Artillery in 1938 when 21st London Regiment

was disbanded. Spencer was from a patrician London family (his father was a Kensington 'society' doctor) and had a petroleum-engineering background, probably first in Chile and later at Abadan with AIOC, which gave him some knowledge of Persia; however, he had no experience at all with security-intelligence operations. He was personally recruited by Raymond Maunsell as DSO Persia early in 1942; how he originally came to Maunsell's attention remains unclear, though Spencer (D/H79)[21] was at the time already working in the secret world of the Special Operations Executive (SOE), which Maunsell probably saw as a talent pool.[22] One artillery officer visiting Tehran in 1943 depicted Spencer as 'an ex-Gunner colonel who looks as though he did all the rough stuff with blackjacks and automatics'.[23] After the war, Sir Reader Bullard described Spencer as 'an able man of good and calm judgement'.[24]

Spencer was competently assisted and ultimately succeeded as DSO Persia by his Assistant Defence Security Officer (ADSO), Alan Stuart Roger of the 6th Rajputana Rifles, IA. Roger, heir to a substantial family fortune and educated at Loretto School and Trinity College, Oxford, where he read history, came to Persia like Spencer from a position of social privilege. Before his arrival in Tehran, the sum total of Roger's war experience had been with the British Red Cross in northern France prior to Dunkirk and a spell at the Ministry of Supply in Delhi.[25] However, these two officers proved to be no lightweights: their personal intelligence, adaptability, versatility, and executive ability were extraordinary inasmuch as neither they nor the officers and NCOs on their staff were trained security-intelligence professionals. The sole exception, Bill Magan of Hodson's Horse, IA, who served with CICI as Indian Intelligence Bureau (IB) Liaison Officer,[26] and who was a career intelligence officer, praised them highly, saying that they appeared to have been hand-picked, as they were 'a very gifted lot of people' and included some Persian speakers. 'The officers consisted of a petroleum engineer [Spencer], a stockbroker [Roger], a schoolmaster [Carstairs], an Englishman who had formerly been a [White] Russian army officer [Caird], and a university don [Wickens]'. The two NCOs consisted of a university don who was fluent in Persian and an Englishman who had been brought up in Persia and was also fluent in the language.[27] To support the Tehran staff, security officers (ALOs), with the rank of major or squadron leader, were also posted to eight regional centres: Hamadan, Kermanshah, Sennandaj, Qum, Isfahan (with vice-consular cover), Shiraz (with vice-consular cover), Ahwaz, and Abadan.[28]

Strong personalities ruled these roosts, yet it is testimony to the professionalism of these leaders that their relations remained generally amicable and, as the narrative shows, particularly in the case of Persia, highly productive. Raymond Maunsell's deputy at SIME was Kenyon W. Jones of the Welch Regiment, a former Welsh rugby international and managing director of Ronson's, while the somewhat eccentric Chokra Wood presided over CICI Baghdad, ably assisted by H.K. Dawson-Shepherd of the RAF, a highly competent Arabic speaker. Also on Maunsell's staff, at least for a while, was Jumbo Wilson's son, Patrick Maitland Wilson of the Rifle Brigade.[29] In fact, Joe Spencer's service record in Tehran was so spectacularly successful, it brought him substantive promotion to lieutenant colonel and a 'gong'. Recommended for the Distinguished Service Order (DSO) by both Bullard and Pownall, Spencer was lauded not only for his achievement in capturing Franz Mayr, his documents, and the FRANZ/DORA parachutists,[30] but also for his physical courage. 'In the course of his investigations and particularly in making the arrest,' wrote Pownall, 'Lt Col Spencer has knowingly and continuously risked his life, and I consider that his action is one which ... fully justifies a gallantry award'.[31] Spencer was earmarked in 1944 as the most worthy successor to Raymond Maunsell as head of SIME, a promotion which ultimately, however, never came his way. In fact, Maunsell was immediately succeeded by Douglas Roberts (who later became head of counterintelligence at MI6) and ultimately by Alex Kellar of MI5, as first civilian head of SIME.[32] In 1947, the Americans made Spencer an Officer of the Legion of Merit; in 1953,[33] on leaving MI5, he also received the OBE.[34]

It is true that there was some irritation between Raymond Maunsell, head of SIME, and Chokra Wood, head of CICI Baghdad, over the former's strong views that he must control all Defence Security Officers (DSOs) throughout the Middle East and PAIFORCE, even though PAIFORCE was an independent command under the War Office. However, Maunsell subsequently agreed that he was quite content with his charter and that of CICI,[35] so he and Wood buried the hatchet. According to paragraph 4 of the CICI Charter, CICI Persia was in fact directly responsible to CICI Baghdad, with SIME retaining responsibility solely for methods and policy. Maunsell subsequently noted that it was important that SIME's overall coordination of security-intelligence matters should extend to CICI and that this was 'amiably achieved'.[36] Far from resenting advice and requests for assistance from SIME, Wood actually welcomed them, along with visits by SIME officers, though few took place. What Maunsell ended up with was simply the general coordination of security throughout the Middle East and PAIFORCE, which was his chief, entirely justifiable priority. Far less amicable, however, was the external relationship between CICI and the Persian branch of the Inter-Services Liaison Department (ISLD), which was the name adopted by the Secret Intelligence Service (MI6) for its Middle and Far East operations. Their ongoing vendetta, which came to a head in April 1944, is examined in a later chapter.[37]

One visitor to Baghdad came away with the following positive impression of the effectiveness of the CICI organization that Wood had established:

> Wood was not a Middle East expert, but he was an excellent and experienced administrator and had plenty of expertise on his staff. His organization had an air of purpose and discipline about it which was noticeably lacking in most of the other mushrooming intelligence and propaganda organizations which I encountered in the Middle East and India.[38]

In August 1943, for his outstanding leadership of CICI, Chokra Wood was awarded the OBE.[39]

By the beginning of January 1942, when CICI's remit was extended to cover Persia as well as Iraq, and the Tehran office began to investigate subversive activities, only a few security controls had been introduced.[40] While most German nationals in Persia had been rounded up and interned by the British and Soviet occupying forces, and joint Anglo-Soviet-Persian censorship measures had been introduced, only rudimentary records of enemy aliens had been established. Those that existed were fragmentary, inaccurate, and often even highly speculative. Most remaining Germans had gone to ground, the Japanese legation was still operating with impunity, Persian laws for dealing with fifth columnists were inadequate, and there was no travel or visa control at all. The CICI office in Tehran – which later became known as DSO Persia (or simply DSO) – and the ALOs were not wholly responsible for the evolution of the various security controls, normally subject to diplomatic negotiation with the Persian authorities. However, the investigation and pursuit of the fifth column so often brought to notice the many flaws in the existing arrangements that CICI Tehran seized the initiative. As a precursor of what was to become their routinely pragmatic, inventive, yet thoroughly consistent *modus operandi*, they proposed a series of bold remedies and unilaterally created the expedient security arrangements that remained in effect until the end of the war.[41]

The routine controls established by DSO Persia included postal and press censorship. The former occupied a unique place among them, not least because Spencer's team could not rely upon the Persian police, whom they quickly came to regard as enemies rather than allies. Furthermore, the ALOs who supplied regional intelligence to the Tehran office were only stationed in southern Persia; consequently, they were unable to report on events in the north, in the east, and on the borders. DSO therefore had to rely upon censorship to acquire intelligence on the intended and actual movements of suspects throughout the entire country. Visa control too came to depend as much upon censorship intercepts as upon actual visa applications to the police. In view of the venality of the Persian police and the laxity of the Soviet authorities in the north, it was found advisable to use censorship to reduce to a minimum all travel between Persia and Turkey, the route used by most enemy agents and couriers. The main problem was that the Persian police and gendarmerie were grossly underpaid, not least because the officers would routinely steal their men's wages; consequently, both forces were utterly corrupt and considered by many to be beyond redemption.[42] Even when their American adviser, H. Norman Schwarzkopf (whose son would become celebrated as 'Stormin' Norman', the commanding general of US and Coalition forces in the First Gulf War [1990–91]), attempted to introduce gendarmerie reform measures in 1944, he had his budget arbitrarily slashed from 600 million to 290 million rials by Dr Arthur Millspaugh, the US economic adviser, who stated at the time that the security forces in Persia were 'not worth the money expended on them'.[43]

Ultimately, the joint Anglo-Soviet-Persian censorship administration, established formally by the tripartite treaty of January 1942, in which DSO was evidently compelled by circumstances to invest far greater effort than its Russian partners – with the Persians contributing virtually nothing – assumed far more importance in Persia than censorship measures in other theatres. The Anglo-Soviet-Persian Treaty of Alliance was signed on 29 January 1942, after what the British minister described as 'endless attempts at procrastination and amendment by the [*Majlis*] deputies and the Persian government'.[44] Under the terms of the treaty, the Persian government formally agreed to cooperate with the Allies in maintaining internal security on Persian territory and to cooperate in the censorship measures required. Despite the delays, a complete censorship scheme was sanctioned as early as November 1941, and – with the help of volunteers – telegrams and outgoing press messages were quickly placed under control. Significantly, the Persians were also persuaded by the British censors to abandon all wireless communication with Axis countries. Censorship was not only used by DSO as a substitute for general security controls, but also as a counterespionage weapon. By examining a large number of censorship extracts, it proved possible to establish the identity of the principal couriers between the pro-Axis fifth column in Persia and the German intelligence services in Turkey. Censorship also revealed plain-language communications between agents using other people's names.

The routine work was painstaking. For example, on a daily basis, the censorship liaison officer at DSO would examine the list of all correspondence between Turkey and Persia. Then he would decide which letters to report in full and which to paraphrase. The translations were always attached to the originals, so that handwriting could be examined and a decision on disposal quickly made. This arduous process meant that fewer letters could be reported; however, it guaranteed more accurate investigations into particular cases. As the correspondence subject to examination was multilingual, many nationalities were represented on the staff of the Anglo-Soviet-Persian censorship administration. Despite positive vetting by DSO, some individuals could have been recruited by various intelligence organizations, either before or after joining the censorship staff. It was therefore necessary to keep a general watch on the censorship officials themselves, which complicated matters considerably. Even cases of possible connections between Jewish censors and the Zionist movement proved to be a cause of anxiety and extra work.[45] The possibility of sabotage by Zionist agents was of very real concern. For instance, the British embassy reported to DSO early in 1944 that 130 Palestinian Jewish technicians employed in the Abadan refineries were members of a Jewish sabotage organization.[46] As early as March 1943, it had been reported that Haganah had established an intelligence post in Tehran as a preliminary to organizing a complete network in Persia. Also, during a recent visit to Tehran a senior Jewish Agency official had made contact with the Soviet secret services.[47]

After the expulsion of the Nazi diaspora in 1941, approximately 600 aliens who technically belonged to Axis countries but who were politically aligned with the Allied cause remained in Persia. They generally posed no security threat and were of little concern to DSO; however, they were all carded in the DSO registry. There were 160 Germans and Austrians, more than half of whom were Jews. They were fairly prosperous and engaged in such professions as engineering and medicine. A number were employed in posts by British and American civil authorities. There was even a small, unofficial Free Austrian movement with some 25 members. There were approximately 200 Hungarians, fewer than half of whom were Jews. They were on the whole a wealthy community, engaged chiefly in engineering, with a number of cabaret artistes and musicians among them. The great majority were members of the Free Hungarian movement led by Forenc Bodansky, a Jewish Palestinian of Hungarian origin, and a Hungarian named Bela Kertesz, though many seem to have been indifferent towards the Allied cause. A few members were self-declared communists. The Italians, generally lacking cohesion and organization, numbered about 100, of whom only two were of Jewish origin. Except for a few engineers, most were builders or labourers. Giovanni Polesello was titular head of an unofficial, effete Free Italian movement, even though his wife and children were living in Germany. Fewer than 100 Bulgarians were legitimately at large; they were said to be a rude and undisciplined community without any 'free' organization but with a fair proportion of criminals. Of the 25-odd Romanians, most were artistes and musicians, while a few had industrial jobs.[48]

The second set of routine security controls developed by DSO concerned travel and visas. The arrangements established formed part of a general Middle East movement-control scheme; however, there were certain peculiarities about conditions in Persia which made any attempt at control very difficult, even when the Persian government had agreed to the arrangement. For instance, after the abdication of Reza Shah in September 1941, Persians felt that for the first time they were free to travel abroad, visas having been extremely difficult to obtain under the old regime. The result was that, instead of the war's leading to a restriction of travel, it merely stimulated the demand for visas, and the DSO's office was continually faced with the problem of hundreds of Persians blandly trying to go abroad in wartime for trade or simply for the novelty of the thing. Ever since the last war, Germany had exercised an extraordinary fascination on the wealthier Persian, and one could therefore never be sure that a Persian who applied for a visa to go to Turkey would not go on to Germany afterwards, or at least get in touch with the Germans in Istanbul. Neither the breaking off of diplomatic relations nor the declaration of war had any effect on this, and the only remedy was to try to cut down all traffic with Turkey to a minimum.[49]

However, this policy raised a second difficulty: the northern frontier was not controlled by the British, but by the notoriously lax Russians. Only from censorship intercepts could DSO determine whether their decisions about exit visas were being respected or not. Thus, although it was possible to have one of the fifth column's couriers arrested in Aleppo because his journey was through British-controlled territory, much more important couriers were able to travel to and fro across the northern frontier without hindrance. As the northern route was much cheaper than that via Syria and Iraq, DSO's inability to control it adequately was a serious weakness in the general control of movement throughout the Middle East. The only restriction on the use of the northern route was imposed by winter conditions, and even these did not prevent the determined from making the journey, among them enemy agents.[50]

Ultimately, it took formal diplomatic negotiations to resolve the question; somewhat unexpectedly, the impetus came from the Russians, not the British, and not until late in 1943. At that time, the Soviet ambassador in London requested that all precautions be taken to prevent Axis agents from entering Persia via Turkey. As a consequence, it was decided that, 'as there were full facilities for interrogation at Aleppo', the Persian government would be asked to close the northern frontier with effect from 21 November 1943.[51] This was done, although the border proved to be as leaky as a sieve until the end of the war, since most Russian border guards were illiterate and incapable of recognizing suspect identity papers and other bogus travel documents.[52] Furthermore, the Soviets were highly selective in their choice of whom to detain and whom to allow passage. Ultimately, however, DSO turned this situation to their own advantage by shrewdly using the Russians' choices (as revealed in censorship intercepts) to identify possible Soviet agents (or double agents).[53]

Besides these general difficulties with the effective implementation of routine visa controls, there were also specific technical issues associated mostly with passport control, including the question of the validity of pre-existing visas (i.e. those issued before the visa-control arrangements were introduced), the automatic issuing of exit visas in renewed passports, the automatic right of every Persian to re-enter the country, the inaccurate transcription of Persian names, and the systemic corruption among Persian officials. DSO accepted these challenges with vigour and largely resolved them. They persuaded the Persian police to limit the validity of exit visas and to withdraw passports from Persians re-entering the country. They also redesigned the application form to be submitted by Persians seeking exit visas for trips to Turkey, requiring full details of the applicant and ensuring that the information was distributed to DSOs throughout the Middle East.

The third area of routine security control was that of positive vetting, which was originally carried out by DSO Persia for various Allied services and organizations more or less as a courtesy on an unofficial basis. Later, however, this evolved into a formal cooperative role, although CICI records were never directly accessible to other agencies. Among other responsibilities, it was necessary to maintain close liaison with a large international community in Persia, which included many nationalities other than those of the three major Allies. For instance, many Poles evacuated from the Soviet Union after the launching of Operation BARBAROSSA in 1942 remained in Persia for a lengthy period before moving elsewhere in the Middle East; some even settled in Persia permanently. Additionally, there were over 500 Czechs, as well as Greeks, Yugoslavs, French, and Danes, all of whom were liable to be conscripted by the Free Forces of their respective countries, especially as the establishment of a second front in Europe became imminent. To deal separately with Poles and Russians when neither were on speaking terms with the other and to fathom the intrigues inherent in all exiles' communities taxed the diplomacy of British security to the full. The only workable criterion which could be adopted was to make the authorities of each community responsible for their own nationals. If there was a special security authority, as with the Poles, then the word of that authority was taken rather than that of their legation, but in most other cases the diplomatic representative was looked upon as responsible for the security of his own compatriots.[54]

It is some measure of the high esteem in which British security held the Polish forces in general that they chose Polish soldiers to guard CICI premises in Tehran and even CICI prisoners and suspects, whenever British soldiers were unavailable. Although there was sometimes internal dissension between the Polish security authorities and the diplomats at the Polish legation, and although Polish security occasionally adopted an unacceptably anti-Soviet – or even antisemitic – line of enquiry, Anglo-Polish cooperation was always cordial. Polish security also rendered technical assistance to DSO in the form of much needed photographic and reprographic services for less sensitive documents. But it was clearly disappointing to Spencer's staff that the Poles could not be more useful as providers of pure intelligence; however, constant Polish intrigues rendered any collaboration 'almost fruitless'.[55]

Unlike the Poles, most other Allied nationalities in Persia lacked any specific security organizations of their own. CICI therefore had to maintain contact with Allied diplomatic missions on questions of security. DSO not only helped in the disposal of suspect Allied nationals and in the general control of visas and employment of all Allied nationals, but even went so far in the case of the Greeks as to help them conscript all Greek men of military age. With most of the exiled nationalities, however, the most significant problem for CICI was the fact that the policies pursued by their legation diplomats did not always sit well with the majority of the exiles themselves. Consequently, Spencer's officers were frequently obliged to monitor both sides in any resulting disputes in order to respond objectively to any requests that were submitted to them, either by diplomats or private individuals. Naturally this compounded CICI's workload.

All three occupiers evolved different strategies for coping with the incompetence of the Persian security authorities. Buoyed by a seemingly ingenuous faith in their own particular brand of democracy, the Americans tried to reform the Persians with something akin to missionary zeal ... and failed. The American police adviser died after accomplishing nothing, and was not replaced. The advisers of the United States Mission to the Persian Gendarmerie (GENMISH), led by the capable and resourceful Norman Schwarzkopf, though able and invested with wide powers, battled against incredible corruption without any appreciable sign of headway.[56] The force was in a deplorable state. As Sir Reader Bullard noted, its administration had been neglected, and in its operations it had not often had that support from the army which had been the essence of its effectiveness in the time of Reza Shah. It was grossly underpaid; its detachments were badly housed and almost unfed, except for what they could beg or steal. Consequently, its numbers and its morale were low. The miserable conditions offered attracted few volunteer recruits: its numbers could only be maintained by drafting to it unwilling conscripts from the army. Owing to its almost complete lack of transport and means of communication, its effectiveness in protecting communications was very limited. The arrival of three American officers as advisers had done little to improve the state of affairs. 'They have blinded themselves to the needs of the immediate present', wrote Bullard, 'by fixing their eyes on a beautiful but quite impractical, ideal organization, which would only be justified if the army were to be abolished.'[57]

In the face of such dysfunction, the British were generally content to regard the Persians as sleeping partners, consulting them as little as possible and usually ignoring and circumventing them at the operational level. It was clearly felt by MI5 in London that the Persian police would remain of negligible value to DSO unless or until reformed by the Americans ... which never happened. In the view of the Security Service, no doubt informed by Alex Kellar and Joe Spencer, the inefficiency, corruption, and anti-British attitude of the Persian police had made effective liaison with them impossible. Information from them was small in quantity and valueless. From the executive point of view they were untrustworthy, so it had been found necessary to make most arrests direct.[58] Joe Spencer could not recall a single case in which the Persian police had detected a pro-Axis agent or agitator on their own initiative. If information of a proposed raid on a suspected hiding place was given to the police in advance, the target was almost always warned and given time to escape.[59] After arrests, Persian police interrogators and interpreters had even been caught grooming German prisoners: showing them answers given during previous interrogations of other subjects.[60]

The security of the TIR was gravely affected by the incompetence of the Persian gendarmerie. In the summer of 1942, with German armies advancing rapidly from the north, the key points on a railway line over 1000 km in length were guarded by only 200 ragged, underpaid, poorly officered gendarmes. Though the Persian prime minister had pledged that their number would be increased to 1000 (approximately one gendarme per kilometre of track), there appeared no hope that his promise would ever be fulfilled. Volunteers were called for, but without response, since no increase in pay was offered, and there was little prospect of unofficial 'perquisites'. The British security authorities reached the conclusion that they could rely only on their own troops. If there were enemy pressure in the north, the Persian technical and administrative staff would probably quit, and the railway would be brought to a standstill.[61]

In the absence of any effective local police or gendarmes, DSO came to rely upon the availability of the Field Security Sections of the Intelligence Corps as their police force – their eyes, ears, and 'boots on the ground' throughout Persia. These highly effective British and combined British/Indian units were under PAIFORCE (10th Army) command and were generally at Joe Spencer's disposal whenever he needed 'backup' in the form of armed men with intelligence and policing skills. Sometimes FSS NCOs were actually seconded full-time to DSO; one sergeant (George Wickens) even remained permanently, becoming a commissioned officer on Spencer's staff. Seven sections served at various times in Persia: 72 FSS (Tehran, 1942–43), 73 FSS (Ahwaz, TIR, Gulf ports, 1943–46), 296 FSS (TIR, 1943), 402 FSS (TIR and throughout Persia, 1943–45), and 408 FSS (Bisitun, October 1942), with 266 FSS and 401 FSS manning the Iraqi-Persian border, and 403 FSS doing that, as well as providing security for the Tehran Conference. An FSS could vary between platoon and company strength; it usually comprised at least one commissioned officer (the Field Security Officer [FSO]), at least one warrant officer (usually with the rank of WO2), and an indefinite number of NCOs. Some units, such as 72 FSS and 73 FSS grew much larger than this, whilst others remained relatively compact. As in the military police, some kind of rank (at least lance corporal) was considered necessary for the effective exercise of authority. Like the legendary mounties who pioneered the vast forests, prairies, and mountains of Canada, it was not uncommon for an FSS corporal in Persia to be given responsibility for patrolling a huge rural area whose inhabitants would turn to him in all kinds of situations, bringing him into contact with senior civil and military leaders. These amazingly versatile, highly mobile units were capable of a wide range of military-intelligence and security functions, including prison-camp administration and security, border control, searches and arrests, field reconnaissance and surveillance, rail-supply protection, port security, and general crime prevention.[62]

Compared with the unenviable lot of the infantry soldier or the relatively monotonous routine of the military policeman, FSS duties were interesting and varied; they often involved travelling immense distances in the execution of regular duties, though the men generally described their working conditions as varying between 'uncomfortable' and 'unbearable'; the only reasonably comfortable detachment was apparently considered to be Tehran itself. Those who were assigned military-intelligence duties could have an especially interesting war. One sergeant of 72 FSS, for instance, frequently rode in deep disguise on a donkey into remote areas to gather intelligence from tribal leaders; two others from the same unit helped Joe Spencer arrest the SD representative Franz Mayr at gunpoint in Tehran. In April 1942, with German armies at the gates of Transcaucasia, 73 FSS found itself responsible – alone – for protection of the entire 1100 km-long line of communication between the Persian Gulf and the Caspian Sea. FSS border guards often found themselves at the uniquely sharp end of Anglo-Soviet liaison, as they were in close daily contact with soldiers of the NKVD.[63]

By 1943, at the zenith of German covert activity in the region, MI5 and SIME seem to have become increasingly aware that US interest in Persia was transient and Soviet interest intransigent. The truth is that there was never any concerted Allied effort in Persia during the four years of joint occupation. The occupying powers operated strictly within their assumed or allotted competencies, which is why effective liaison, as Joe Spencer rightly surmised, became of paramount importance. A policy of self-reliance – combined with sound tradecraft and consistent methodology – therefore appeared the best approach to solving the knotty counterintelligence problems presented by covert Axis subversion and sabotage initiatives. At the same time, DSO maintained close liaison with the Russians throughout the occupation, meeting two or three times a week with the Russian security officers in a generally cordial atmosphere and, as far as possible, deciding upon a uniform policy towards the Persians.[64]

While the Americans attempted reforms, the Russians in the northern zone preferred simply to control the Persian authorities (or at least to influence them ideologically). First, they disarmed the Persian gendarmerie and police, and then they refused to help them maintain law and order on the ground that this would constitute interference in the civil administration. Eventually an agreement was concluded for the rearming of a limited number of gendarmes and police in the Russian zone. According to Bullard, 'the Russians arrested most of the police and gendarmes in their area, and ... they haggled long and tenaciously about the number ... to be kept at each post, and whether they should be armed or not'.[65] The process left Persians with the accurate impression that an attempt was being made by the Soviet occupiers to weaken the authority of the Persian government in preparation for a campaign of ideological propaganda.

The propaganda campaign indeed followed, and was sustained throughout the years of joint occupation. No doubt partly to alleviate pressure on the Persian polity and to ensure internal security and political stability, the British security authorities tried to intervene by using the Tripartite Censorship Commission to intercept printed propaganda from Moscow, which usually came by post. A game of tit-for-tat ensued in which the Soviet censorship section tried to suppress all British propaganda, while the British section – without disputing the Soviets' right to act as they had – attempted to obtain reasoned explanations of their actions. In a despatch to London, Sir Reader Bullard described the outcome as follows:

> No explanations in the least satisfactory or detailed were ever forthcoming. The truth is probably that the Russian section, true to Soviet political principles, considered wholesale suppression as laudable and natural action, from the performance of which it had only refrained in the past owing to the necessity for accommodating valuable allies. Some of the suppressed British material was indeed critical of Soviet affairs in varying degrees; but for the most part the criticism was not only fair, but also extremely mild – far more so than the habitual tone of the Soviet press in regard to the Western Allies.[66]

Cooperation was also necessary with the Americans, whose main interest in Persia appears to have been in political rather than security intelligence, as well as in targeting their Russian ally rather than their Axis enemy. However, the initial focus of the US mission to Persia was the coordination and supervision of the Lend-Lease supply route to Russia – an engineering project of enormous scale (see Appendix A.4). Consequently, matters of intelligence – whether to do with espionage, counterespionage, security intelligence, sabotage, propaganda, or subversion – were given scant consideration. Later, after the establishment of Persian Gulf Service Command (PGSC) in August 1942,[67] when the Americans decided to deploy the field-security forces of the Counter Intelligence Corps (CIC) in Persia, their decision was logically prompted by the need to secure their strategic project by safeguarding the vital lines of communication and supply between the Persian Gulf and the Soviet Union.[68] Less logical, however, would seem their decision to send to Persia active espionage and counterintelligence agents of the Office of Strategic Services (OSS), particularly in a theatre where a moratorium on positive intelligence operations existed – mutually agreed between the British and the Soviets.[69] The British were not informed of this move, and Joe Spencer was left to discover independently the presence of American secret agents operating on his turf in Tehran. The existence of an inter-Allied agreement on operational intelligence in Persia seems clear; however, despite exhaustive searches, no such document could be found in the British or American records. The clearest statement on record is by OSS head of Near East Secret Intelligence (SI), Stephen B. L. Penrose Jr, who said that the PGSC commanding general had been 'prevailed upon by the Russians to withdraw all military intelligence' and that the British too had been instructed 'to do no intelligence work in Russian-occupied areas'.[70] Nevertheless, by the end of the war, OSS Near East Section controlled eleven positive-intelligence officers under various kinds of cover in Persia and Iraq: three senior representatives – Joe Upton (TIGER or 'Richard Lowe') and Donald Wilber (TAPIR or 'Eliot Grant') in Tehran, and 'Walter Donor' (BUFFALO) in Baghdad – together with the writer Harold Lamb (TIMUR), the Viennese psychiatrist Hans Hoff (BUNNY or 'Henry Ibsen'), 'Robert Craig' (IBEX), 'Gordon Scott', 'Herdic' (probably Ed Wright of PGSC/PGC [TIMBER WOLF]), 'Fennel' (probably Art Dubois of PGSC/PGC [TEDDY BEAR]), 'Leland', and 'Loy'.[71] The OSS Near East Section records are muddled and (deliberately?) challenging. Upper-case animal cryptonyms (e.g. TIGER) – so-called 'menagerie report names' (plants were reserved for Greece and birds for Turkey) – were used interchangeably with code names (e.g. 'Richard Lowe') and sometimes even real names (e.g. Harold Lamb). Senior field men also used alternative code names, and the distinction between sources and subsources was often unclear, easily leading to false estimates of how many operatives were deployed in any given region at any one time. Some 70 years on, certain senior field men remain unidentifiable even by this trained archival sleuth, which is of course greatly to the credit of those originally charged with preserving OSS cover.[72]

The American CIC in Persia kept only meagre security records, preferring to rely upon the resources of CICI when it came to security matters common to the three main Allies. The sheer volume of the records created and maintained by the DSO registry are a testimony to the diligence and organizational ability of Spencer and his staff – by late 1944, 50,000 index cards and 1700 case files; a year later, 61,000 cards.[73] So much of intelligence work involves identity and personality. It is this which makes the writing of intelligence history very different to the writing of military history, where behaviour of the formation is of far greater significance than character, personality, and individual behaviour. Like the artist or the writer, what the security officer in Persia feared most was the blank canvas, the blank page: the unknown enemy. The most dangerous agent was the one about whose personality nothing was known, displaying no perceptible patterns of operational behaviour, nor even any behavioural possibilities or probabilities. Without them, even the agent's unpredictability could not be rendered predictable, nor his or her inconsistency consistent. No operational profile could emerge: there was no *modus operandi*. Thus, most counterintelligence and security-intelligence investigations consisted essentially in a dynamic inductive process whereby fragmentary knowledge drawn from disparate sources was painstakingly assembled and crossreferenced to form a unique construct or identity which could itself be registered and indexed, so that it might contribute to the compilation and construction of other constructs or identities.

In those days, security-intelligence registries were accessed by requesting any number of personality traces (known in the trade as 'lookups'), from which numerically crossreferenced and often minute facts could, if deemed significant and relevant, be laboriously extracted and transposed into a new profile. In this way the blank canvas was painted, the blank page was slowly filled, and the enemy was revealed and identified. Such was the routine task of the 'ratcatcher' in Tehran during the Second World War, and to do it he had no modern technology. Just a pile of blank index cards; a typewriter; some clerical help (perhaps); the ability to send signals or letters up the line to Baghdad, Cairo, or London; and probably a huge backlog of human intelligence (HUMINT), signals intelligence (SIGINT), and case files to be processed, all flagged 'most secret' and 'immediate'.

By September 1944, Alan Roger was complaining that it was impossible – during the period of the arrests of Mayr and the FRANZ/ DORA group and of Schulze-Holthus and the ANTON group – to keep the records up-to-date, and that a serious bottleneck had developed in the carding process. However, when one realizes that 7,000 names were carded during the month of August 1944 alone, it seems astonishing that such a small staff could have generated so many records in such a brief period. In connection with the arrests, it should be remembered that the voluminous documents captured from the Germans, as well as most of the interrogation dialogues, were of course in German and had to be translated. Since many of the original translations were produced under extreme time pressure and proved to be of inferior quality, they frequently had to be re-translated, placing an additional burden on those responsible for creating and maintaining the relevant case files.[74] Another problem was the fact that everything had to be written out in longhand, as no suitable candidate with shorthand qualifications could be found locally. Steps were eventually taken to send Spencer and Roger a trained secretary from MI5 in London, but not until May 1944.[75]

In addition to the case files on captured German agents in Persia, one group of records was accorded significant priority: the files that CICI had compiled on the principal Persian suspects in enemy territory. They included not only full details of the careers and contacts of Persians who had been or could have been recruited as agents, but also a fairly comprehensive survey of German connections which would be of use in counteracting any long-term German plans for the resurrection of German influence in Persia at some future date.

In view of the inefficiency of the Persian police, whose records were 'in a chaotic state', DSO's records were in fact probably the only comprehensive ones in the entire country; without them the Persian police would frequently have been unable to arrest their own citizens. In other words, by default, CICI had to constitute itself its own police force in the matter of records as in everything else. The way in which DSO's activities had been extended showed that the organization filled a definite need in Persia, where it had become, along with its ALOs and the FSS, a sort of independent police force. It operated general security controls and had probably the only up-to-date records in the country. It had carried out investigations into the fifth column, effected its own arrests, made its own interrogations, and done its own interning. Although first and foremost a security and counterintelligence organization, it had inevitably been drawn into other branches of intelligence, working a double-agent case, interrogating about conditions in enemy territory, investigating oil intrigues, and providing the embassy with 'hot' news of political events. At the same time, DSO had had to warn the local military commander of impending trouble in Persia and keep him *au courant* with the political situation. As the German threat receded, these subsidiary activities grew in importance, though constant vigilance was still necessary in view of the surprisingly sustained German interest in Persia.[76]

What remains to be mentioned in this chapter is the positive and productive relationship which grew and matured during the war years between the staff at DSO in Tehran and the B Branch staff at MI5 HQ in London.[77] In no small measure it is the effectiveness of this liaison that enabled a mere handful of albeit very enthusiastic young British security officers in Tehran to succeed in protecting an enormous territory like Persia from enemy threat and incursion. They were attached umbilically to the immense resources of the Security Service, and access was guaranteed them by one particularly gifted and able desk officer: Alexander James 'Alex' Kellar, who had in turn established liaison with various other government departments, thereby significantly widening his own subsection's resource base. Alex Kellar was known to have useful contacts at the Foreign Office, the Colonial Office, and MI6 (see Appendix A.2).[78]

John Le Carré's early but exquisitely crafted novella of counterespionage, *Call for the Dead*, juxtaposes two character foils of note: the professional field officer George Smiley, who was to become in subsequent novels Le Carré's most celebrated protagonist, and a highly politicized desk jockey named Maston, 'the man with cream cuffs'.[79] It is said that David Cornwell (Le Carré) based the latter character on an officer he had known during his years at MI5: Alex Kellar.[80] However, though occasionally described as 'eccentric', the real Kellar who emerges from the archival records bears little resemblance to his 'flamboyant' fictitious counterpart.[81] While Maston expends his energy on currying favour with his political masters, much to George Smiley's distaste, the factual Kellar ran the Middle East desk in London thoroughly professionally throughout the occupation, and in that capacity liaised directly and very effectively with Joe Spencer and Alan Roger at DSO Persia. Kellar was a former barrister from the Middle Temple who had specialized in international law, and who, as a law student at Edinburgh

University during the 1930s, had been president of the National Union of Students (NUS), which had no doubt not escaped the notice of the Security Service, always on the lookout for talent and leadership ability, and had led to his ultimate recruitment.[82]

Director General Sir Dick White took a great interest in Persian security during the war and visited SIME in 1943. During this visit, at the SIME Annual Conference held in Beirut early in 1943, White outlined the genesis of Kellar's Middle East desk, created about a year previously, which was to prove so supportive during the critical period in which DSO Persia succeeded in arresting all but one of the known Nazi agents in the region. According to White, consideration would be given on his return to London to the question of adapting this subsection as far as possible to meet the interests of SIME and ensuring that SIME received from London all available and relevant intelligence. White went on to enumerate the 22 sources from which such intelligence could be acquired by MI5 (see Appendix A.2).[83]

Kellar's special responsibility for Middle East security intelligence and counterespionage came about almost accidentally. Prior to 1941, B Branch's interest in the Middle East had been restricted to monitoring communist activity, and Kellar worked in B4B, one of the communist subsections. Once it had been recognized that MI5's principal interest in the Middle East had nothing to do with communism but was connected with the region as an important centre of military operations, and that the Abwehr was very interested in those operations, Kellar's specialized subsection was transferred out of B Branch and moved successively to F Branch and E Branch (which had no access to ISOS W/T intercepts), finally ending in March 1943 as part of B Branch again (B1B). Such muddle meant that Raymond Maunsell was urgently needed in London to organize and solidify the liaison between MI5 and SIME; however, because no visit could be arranged, there was no alternative but to send T.A.R. 'Tar' Robertson and Dick White out to the Middle East to sort things out. This they did, separately, in the spring of 1942 and in early 1943. Both MI5 officers made similar recommendations for improvement. While it proved impossible to implement their main shared recommendation – that SIME should be amalgamated with MI5 – significant structural and procedural changes were made to SIME, including the establishment of the Centre d'Examination des Voyageurs (CEV) at Aleppo. From this point on, especially during the crucial year 1943, Kellar's close special liaison with DSO Persia seems to have grown and flourished.[84]

The immense scale of MI5's global intelligence acquisition, analysis, and distribution operation is impressive: one realizes how much

Spencer's comparatively tiny counterintelligence organization in Persia must have benefited from its liaison with Kellar's desk in London. In fact, it was the active liaison between Joe Spencer and Alex Kellar that was to become the key ingredient in the ultimate overwhelming success of British security intelligence in Persia. This liaison, maintained largely by wired (cabled) correspondence and reports – and to a far lesser extent by personal visits – effectively fortified and compounded the strength of DSO, enabling Joe Spencer's small local staff of no more than 13 officers, eight ORs, and three civilians (see Appendix A.1) – responsible for surveilling an immense region – to draw upon the limitless global resources of MI5, which were in turn extended by Alex Kellar's 'old boy network', which offered many personal contacts within other organizations, such as MI6, the Foreign Office, and the Colonial Office (see Appendix A.2).[85] Over drinks and dinner at White's, the Athenaeum, or the 'In & Out' Club, secret affairs of state were discussed, and the great driving-wheels of a huge Empire-wide intelligence machine were kept well lubricated (often literally) and constantly turning. It was all handled with poise, discretion, and civility, in a uniquely British, 'public-school' way.

The cordial correspondence between Kellar and Tehran (Spencer and Roger) testifies to this; many of the letters have been preserved in the records of the Home Office. To a considerable degree, this liaison with Kellar undoubtedly compensated for the dysfunction of DSO's local liaison with the MI6 representative in Tehran. During wartime at least, however uneasy their relationships at various regional and local levels, MI5 and MI6 appear to have shared intelligence on the Middle East with relative ease at the headquarters level in London.[86] According to David Mure, former 'A' Force officer, the two services cooperated well even in Cairo: 'SIME was a marvellously successful amalgam of all security intelligence affecting the Middle East, and officers of MI5 and MI6 worked together in it irrespective of their original allegiance.'[87]

Ultimately, however, German covert operations in Persia would likely have failed, whatever the circumstances and regardless of the solidarity of the security forces deployed against them. As Raymond Maunsell, the architect and founder of SIME, has pointed out, it is in the very nature of covert warfare that it always favours the defender:

> Counter-intelligence in war, properly organized, will always have the upper hand, since its defences and resources are based on the whole nation, with its different security and secret services, police, frontier controls, etc and a watchful wartime public. The enemy, i.e. the spy

or saboteur, has to break through a 'defensive ring' and starts off with the disadvantage of being frightened, i.e. doesn't know whether, if caught, he will be tortured before being executed.[88]

Maunsell's analysis of course echoes Clausewitz's insistence on the primacy of defence over offence; in fact, Clausewitz's axiomatic theory is analogous to what occurred in the case of Germany's clandestine intentions towards Transcaucasia and Persia as its military campaign in southern Russia evolved, its resources became progressively overextended, and its field agents ever more isolated, especially when he writes:

> By initiating the campaign, the attacking army cuts itself off from its own theatre of operations, and suffers by having to leave its fortresses and depots behind. The larger the area of operations that it must traverse, the more it is weakened – by the effect of marches and by the detachment of garrisons. The defending army, on the other hand, remains intact. It benefits from its fortresses, nothing depletes its strength, and it is closer to its sources of supply.[89]

Thus, in Persia there was little of the 'cat-and-mouse' play popularly associated with counterintelligence operations, for that is not at all how things happened. It was rather a case in which a robust defensive security-intelligence system, soundly conceived and efficiently run, succeeded in sustaining preventive measures which covered all aspects of potential offensive enemy movements and activities. Into this solid wall of British determination, the Germans of the FRANZ and ANTON initiatives blundered – ill-prepared, isolated, and fugitive from the start – with little realistic hope of survival. In operational terms, apart from sending a few radio messages to Berlin, they achieved nothing. The stories told after the war by Paul Leverkuehn and Berthold Schulze-Holthus of German agents tying up thousands of British troops are a nonsense. The truth is that by the latter half of 1943 the British only had a few battalions of fighting forces in Persia, having transferred most PAIFORCE units to the Italian campaign or returned them to India. Clearly, the strategic deception perpetrated by Dudley Clarke's 'A' Force, which greatly inflated the number of British and Indian troops deployed as part of 10th Army in Persia, had its effect and continued to be believed by the Germans even after the war. The PAIFORCE 10th Army deception operation was part of Clarke's highly successful Middle East order-of-battle deception codenamed CASCADE, which was initiated in March 1942, fully implemented by July 1942, and terminated in February 1944.[90] Thus Paul Leverkuehn hyperbolized Schulze-Holthus's achievements in his 1954 memoir as follows:

> Far away and cut off from his superiors he showed both courage and imagination of a high order, and he made the utmost of the possibilities inherent in his position. Nor did his efforts go unrewarded; he tied down a number of British troops, the forces and material which the enemy had to bring into action were considerable, and around this solitary man a complete little theatre of war was developed.[91]

Sir Reader Bullard was highly critical of Schulze-Holthus's claims in this regard and accused him of megalomania no less for 'supposing, quite wrongly, that he was keeping large numbers of British troops occupied'.[92]

Dick Thistlethwaite, future senior MI5 officer, who served under Joe Spencer and Alan Roger in Tehran as an operations officer responsible for many of the counterintelligence reports and summaries on which this book relies, took a slightly different, much more accurate view after the war of British successes against German covert operations in Persia. Thistlethwaite sensed not only that Spencer was an extraordinarily able leader, but also that – given the same degree of integrated and consistent support by the SD in Berlin that Spencer could rely on from MI5 in London – Franz Mayr might have been a far more formidable opponent than he ultimately proved to be:

> If Berlin had done as Mayr asked and only sent a trained Persian W/T operator with lots of gold and sporting rifles, things could have been quite sticky with us. He was however let down by his own side, who thought they knew better and hampered him with a lot of useless Germans. By the time the [Big-Three] Conference met, there wasn't a single German agent at liberty in Tehran. It was really due to a splendidly led, but extremely small team, which it now seems to me had a remarkable esprit.[93]

Notes

1. William T. Magan, *Middle Eastern Approaches: Experiences and Travels of an Intelligence Officer, 1939–1948* (Wilby, Norfolk: Michael Russell, 2001), 24.
2. See inter alia *London Gazette*, 28 May 1920, 5964; *London Gazette*, 5 October 1920, 9697; *The Quarterly Indian Army List, April 1921* (Calcutta: Superintendent Government Printing, 1921), 964; T.A. Heathcote, *The Military in British India: The Development of British Land Forces in South Asia, 1600–1947* (Manchester: Manchester University Press, 1995), 204–5.

3. The Cripples Training College was officially opened at the Royal National Orthopaedic Hospital (RNOH) on 20 July 1937; 'Capt. E.K. Wood, late of the Indian Army, was appointed as Superintendent, with his living quarters in Lymes Farm House.' *Lost Hospitals*, http://ezitis.myzen.co.uk/rnohstanmore. html; Paul Wood, email message to author, 14 March 2015.

4. 'Queen's Own Corps of Guides (Punjab Frontier Force)', *The British Empire*, http://www.britishempire.co.uk/forces/armyunits/corpsofguides/corpsofguides.htm; Hans Houterman, email message to author, 15 March 2015.

5. See, for example, Preliminary report of trip of S.B.L. Penrose, Jr, Aug–Sept 1943, 21 September 1943, RG 226, Entry 215, Box 3, National Archives and Records Administration, College Park, MD (NARA); Warne to Art [Arthur Dubois?], 25 February 1944, RG 226, Entry 217, Box 1, NARA.

6. See *NSW*, 108–43.

7. HM Minister to Minstate, 23 October 1942, 138/25/42, WO 201/1400A, TNA.

8. Ibid.

9. Ibid.

10. Ibid.

11. Ibid.

12. Later revised to end-December 1942. See various despatches in PREM 3/237/9 and PREM 3/401/13, TNA.

13. Despatches, Persia and Iraq Command, 12 October 1943, CGS/1740/2, WO 32/10540, TNA.

14. Wood to Quilliam, 12 December 1942, WO 201/1401, TNA.

15. Ibid.

16. History of Combined Intelligence Centre, Iraq and Persia, June 1941–December 1944, 15 December 1944, KV 4/223, TNA.

17. War Office Organization Table: Persia and Iraq Command, 27 August 1943, WO 33/2122, TNA.

18. Ibid.

19. Ibid.

20. See Appendix A.1 for a comprehensive chart of the DSO Persia organization.

21. SOE symbols 6, HS 8/971, TNA. If traceable in the SOE records, I have appended the symbols to the first mentions of known SOE operatives in Persia, most of whom retained their original symbols even when they changed their jobs and/or locations. D/H was the section symbol for the Balkans and the Middle East (Cairo Group); D/N, for Persia. Cf. Neville Wylie, ed., *The Politics and Strategy of Clandestine War: Special Operations Executive, 1940–1946* (Abingdon: Routledge, 2007), 25n8.

22. See 'London Gazette of Tuesday, January 14' published in *The Times*, 15 January 1936; Private papers of Brigadier R.J. Maunsell, 4829:80/30/1, IWM.

23. Diary entry for 16 October 1943, Private papers of Captain A.M. Bell Macdonald, 10786:PP/MCR/C49, IWM. I wish to thank the Trustees of the Imperial War Museum for allowing access to this collection held in the IWM Sound and Documents Section.

24. Bullard to Farago, 3 November 1966, GB-165-0042-3/11, Middle East Centre Archive, St Antony's College, Oxford (MECA).

25. 'Alan Stuart Roger (Obituary)', *The Herald*, 9 August 1997.

26. See Chapter 9.

27. Magan, *Middle Eastern Approaches*, 23. My identifications in brackets, deduced from references and cross-references scattered among the British archival records. See inter alia Captain Archibald Mitchell Carstairs, RASC in WO 339/77659, TNA.
28. Appendix IX, Security: Persia, 16 February 1943, KV 4/240, TNA.
29. See Patrick Maitland Wilson, *Where the Nazis Came* (Lancaster: Carnegie, 2002), 86–7 passim.
30. For the full story of Mayr's diary and documents, and the Nazi parachute operations, see *NSW*, passim.
31. Pownall to Under Secretary of State, Immediate awards, August 1943, WO 373/62, TNA.
32. Note on certain points of interest concerning security matters in the Middle East, 22 January 1944, WO 373/62, TNA.
33. Legion of Merit (Officer) recommendation, WO 373/148, TNA.
34. See Private papers of Brigadier R.J. Maunsell, 4829:80/30/1, IWM; WO 373/62, TNA; WO 373/148, TNA; Spencer to Bullard, 5 October 1959, GB 165-0042-3/7, MECA.
35. See Adrian O'Sullivan, 'German Covert Initiatives and British Intelligence in Persia (Iran), 1939–1945' (DLitt et Phil diss., UNISA, 2012), Appendix A2.
36. Private papers of Brigadier R.J. Maunsell, 4829:80/30/1, IWM.
37. See Chapter 7.
38. Geoffrey Wheeler Collection, GB165-0298, MECA.
39. *Supplement to the London Gazette*, 5 August 1943, 3523.
40. Extract from report from CICI Tehran on the plan for breaking the German 5th column in Persia, 11 August 1943, KV 2/1492, TNA.
41. History of Combined Intelligence Centre, Iraq and Persia, June 1941–December 1944, 15 December 1944, KV 4/223, TNA.
42. Bullard to Eden, 26 May 1942, E 3655/3655/34, IOR/L/PS/12/3472A, India Office Records, British Library, St Pancras (BL).
43. Bullard to Eden, 9 March 1945, E 2050/31/34, IOR/L/PS/12/3472A, BL.
44. Bullard to Eden, 17 June 1942, E 3655/3655/4, and 26 March 1943, E 2450/239/34, IOR/L/PS/12/3472A, BL.
45. Ibid.
46. Minutes of the SIME Annual Conference, held in Beirut 2–4 April 44, KV 4/234, TNA.
47. Security Summary Middle East No. 130, 1 May 1943, WO 208/1562, TNA.
48. Ibid.
49. History of Combined Intelligence Centre, Iraq and Persia, June 1941–December 1944, 15 December 1944, KV 4/223, TNA.
50. Ibid. The detailed rules to be followed when controlling Allied and neutral couriers at the CEV are specified in General Directive No. 41, Examination of Arrivals at Aleppo, RG 319, Entry 134A, B17, NARA. Overriding them was the clause: 'These rules are a general guide and are not intended to prevent full examination whenever there are grounds for suspicion.'
51. Extract from SIME Quarterly Summary for the months Sept–Dec inclusive, SIME GHQ MEF, 17 January 1944, KV 2/1480, TNA.
52. Security Summary No. 158, 30 November 1943, WO 208/1562, TNA.
53. Extract from SIME Quarterly Summary for the months Sept–Dec inclusive, SIME GHQ MEF, 17 January 1944, KV 2/1480, TNA.
54. Ibid.

55. Ibid. For more about the Polish experience in Persia, see Wladyslaw Anders, *An Army in Exile: The Story of the Second Polish Corps* (London: Macmillan, 1949).
56. Bullard to Eden, 9 March 1945, E 2050/31/34, IOR/L/PS/12/3472A, BL.
57. Bullard to Eden, 26 March 1943, E 2450/239/34, IOR/L/PS/12/3472A, BL.
58. Appendix IX, Security: Persia, 16 February 1943, KV 4/240, TNA.
59. Security Summary Middle East No. 66, 30 July 1942, WO 208/1561, TNA.
60. Security Summary Middle East No. 67, 3 August 1942, WO 208/1561, TNA.
61. Security Summary Middle East No. 58, 30 June 1942, WO 208/1561, TNA.
62. A.F. Judge, 'The Field Security Sections of the Intelligence Corps, 1939 to 1960', unpublished MS, Military Intelligence Museum and Archives, Chicksands, Bedfordshire.
63. Ibid.
64. Appendix IX, Security: Persia, 16 February 1943, KV 4/240, TNA.
65. Reader Bullard, 'Persia in the Two World Wars', *Journal of the Royal Central Asian Society* 50, no. 1 (1963): 14.
66. Bullard to Eden, 9 March 1945, E 2050/31/34, IOR/L/PS/12/3472A, BL.
67. Persian Gulf Service Command (PGSC) was recast as Persian Gulf Command (PGC) in December 1943.
68. Beware of a grandiosely entitled but thoroughly unreliable and poorly sourced history of CIC, according to which — among other glaring errors — Franz Mayr was tried and executed (!): Ian Sayer and Douglas Botting, *America's Secret Army: The Untold Story of the Counter Intelligence Corps* (New York: Franklin Watts, 1989). See Chapter 13 for more about the role of CIC and CICI–CIC cooperation.
69. On the finely nuanced sociocultural differences between CIC and OSS, see Michael John, 'Anglo-amerikanische Österreichpolitik, 1938–1955', *Historicum* (Winter 1999/2000, http://www.wsg-hist.jku.at/Historicum/HABIL/Beer.html.
70. Penrose to Warne, 8 July 1943, RG 226, Entry 217, Box 1, US National Archives and Records Administration, College Park, MD (NARA).
71. The latter name may not be code, but may refer in clear to the US minister-resident in Baghdad, Loy Henderson.
72. See inter alia: Notes on representatives in Iran and Iraq based on field trip made by Gordon Loud, November 11–24, 1944, RG 226, Entry 210, Box 261, NARA.
73. Roger to Kellar, 29 August 1945, KV 4/223, TNA.
74. Secret summary by Alan Roger, 4 September 1944, KV 4/223, TNA.
75. Report on visit by Mr A.J. Kellar to SIME and CICI organizations, May 1944, KV 4/384, TNA.
76. History of Combined Intelligence Centre, Iraq and Persia, June 1941–December 1944, 15 December 1944, KV 4/223, TNA.
77. See John Curry, *The Security Service, 1908–1945: The Official History* (Kew: PRO, 1999), 271–4.
78. Ibid., 273.
79. John Le Carré, *Call for the Dead* (London: Victor Gollancz, 1961), 12 passim.
80. Cf. Christopher Andrew, *The Defence of the Realm: The Authorized History of MI5* (Toronto: Penguin Canada, 2010), 350. Andrew suggests that Le Carré may have known Kellar personally.

81. See 'Scots MI5 Spy Was Hero in Terror Plot', *The Herald*, 21April 2014. Both adjectives were frequently used as contemporary ciphers for the modern term 'gay'.
82. Ibid; Mike Hughes, *Spies at Work: The Rise and Fall of the Economic League* (Bradford: 1 in 12 Publications, 1994), 176. http://www.1in12.com/publications/archive/spiesatworkcontents/spieschapter9.html.
83. Minutes and notes on the meeting of SIME representatives held at Beirut 12-13 Feb 43, KV 4/240, TNA.
84. Curry, *Security Service*, 271–4. See Chapter 10 for more about White's visit and about CEV Aleppo.
85. Ibid., 273.
86. The role and control of secret intelligence in support of both operations and security, Private papers of D.W.A. Mure, 2194:67/321/3, IWM.
87. Mure, *Master of Deception*, 66. See also Curry, *Security Service*, 273.
88. Private papers of Brigadier R.J. Maunsell, 4829:80/30/1, IWM.
89. Carl Clausewitz, *On War*, ed. and trans. Michael Howard and Peter Paret (Princeton, NJ: Princeton University Press, 1976), 365. Cf. Michael I. Handel, *War, Strategy, and Intelligence* (London: Frank Cass, 1989), 71–4.
90. See Michael Howard, *Strategic Deception in the Second World War* (New York: Norton, 1995), 41; H.O. Dovey, 'The Eighth Assignment, 1941–1942', *Intelligence and National Security* 11, no. 4 (1996): 672–95.
91. Paul Leverkuehn, *German Military Intelligence* (London: Weidenfeld & Nicolson, 1954), 10. Cf. Julius Berthold Schulze-Holthus, *Daybreak in Iran: A Story of the German Intelligence Service* (London: Mervyn Savill, 1954), 149, 193, 203, 213 passim.
92. *International Affairs* 31, no. 3 (July 1955): 392–3. See also the interesting exchange of opinions between Wolfgang G. Schwanitz and Burkhard Ganzer about Leverkuehn and Schulze-Holthus in *Sehepunkte* 9, no. 6 (June 2009) and *Sehepunkte* 9, no. 10 (October 2009), http://www.sehepunkte.de/archiv/ausgaben/.
93. Thistlethwaite to Bullard, 30 December 1954, GB165-0042-3/7, MECA.

2
Security Threats and Operational Channels

> The difficulties of the security organization in Persia are greater than those in any other Middle East country. (K.W. Jones)[1]

It is clear from Sir Henry Pownall's report on the period of his command in Persia between March and October 1943, which included the major German covert initiatives mounted against Persia and Iraq – Operations FRANZ, DORA, ANTON, and MAMMUT – that German operational priorities in the theatre had become tactical, not strategic, and that their general intent had become disruptive and destructive rather than preparatory (i.e. for military invasion) and constructive. In Pownall's words

> evidence already gained by our intelligence service indicated that there was in being a strong fifth column in Persia, instigated by a group of German agents and supported by a considerable number of ill-disposed Persians. This organization was doubtless created with a view to assisting the German invasion of Persia which, until the spring of 1943 at least, had been confidently expected. The turn of the tide of operations in South Russia must have disappointed these expectations, and a reorientation of the German outlook in Persia was therefore to be expected.[2]

According to Pownall, several valuable objectives offered themselves to aggressive action by the Germans, by which they could impede Allied war efforts and further their own. Any material reduction in the output of oil in South Persia would inflict far-reaching damage on the Allies; a steady and increasing flow of military supplies was reaching Russia by the Persian Gulf, and any interruption of this supply would directly assist the German armies in Russia; finally it would detract from grow-ing Allied offensive power if British troops could be embroiled in tribal operations in Persia, or locked up in increasing numbers in protecting British installations and lines of communication in that country.[3]

General Pownall felt that two forms of Nazi aggression might be expected: first, sabotage of oil installations or vulnerable points on the Persian lines of communication; second, attempts to stir up the tribes against the Persian government. His analytical judgement, based no doubt on that of Joe Spencer and his staff at DSO Persia, was to prove unerringly correct. All subsequent German covert operations had as their primary tactical objectives either sabotage against Persian infrastructure; subversion of the Qashgai, the Bakhtiari, or the Kurds; or both. Pownall was particularly concerned about possible German operations against Abadan and the oilfields and installations of western Persia, against the TIR, against various port installations operated by the Russians and the Americans, and in support of rebellious tribes, especially the Qashgai of southwestern Persia. In this context, the general wrote:

> Tribal attack presented the simplest solution of all, and the most imminent danger was removed by the decision, taken in consulta-tion with the American commanding general, to close Bushire as a port of entry and so avoid the long mountain road by Shiraz and Isfahan through the Qashgai country. ... In general it is fair to say that no widespread or well-conceived campaign of sabotage has yet been undertaken by the enemy in Persia or Iraq.[4]

In late 1940, Amt VI – the Auslandsnachrichtendienst (Foreign Intelligence Service) of the Sicherheitsdienst (SS Security Service)[5] – sent two potentially effective but very young SS intelligence officers – Franz Mayr and Roman Gamotha – out to Persia under commercial (rather than diplomatic) cover with no agent training and only vague instruc-tions to go to Persia, find out what they could, and await further instruc-tions, which never came.[6] Furthermore, Mayr and Gamotha's cover as logistics experts was flimsy at best, since neither knew much about the transport business, and the Tehran office of Schenker & Co was riddled with Persian informers and under constant police surveillance.[7] This is but the first instance of Amt VI's operational dysfunction and commu-nicative disarray; it was to be followed between 1940 and 1945 by many more instances, with little substantial improvement over that five-year period. No serious lessons seem to have been learned from successive fail-ures, which seems inexplicable until one realizes that, unlike the British, neither the Abwehr nor the SD spymasters seem to have acknowledged the importance of operational literacy and communications efficiency when mounting intelligence operations over very long distances. It is perhaps an indication of how far in this respect the Germans lagged behind the British, whose centuries of imperial management experience had led them to appreciate the importance of maintaining lively lines of communication between London and their far-flung outposts. There was a sharp discrepancy between Germany's desiring 'a place in the sun'[8] and its ability to achieve and maintain it in Persia, some 3700 km from Berlin, with regular, reliable communications.

After the Anglo-Soviet invasion and occupation of Persia in August–September 1941, both Mayr and Gamotha decided to avoid internment in Australia and became staybehind agents, improvising their own subversion plans – Gamotha in the Russian zone; Mayr in the British. Left to his own devices and anticipating an imminent German invasion of Persia from the north, Franz Mayr soon became a potent security threat. Astonishingly, he succeeded within one year in establishing a powerful subversive organization called the *Melliun*, which had the potential to cause great difficulty for the security forces of the occupying powers.[9]

Mayr's remarkable covert initiative was identified by British security intelligence as 'The Fifth-column Channel'[10] in accordance with Joe Spencer's security summaries, which attributed all German clandestine operations and Persian sympathy or collaboration to one of three operational channels (see Appendix A.3). To the north, Roman Gamotha was soon captured and turned by the Russians, ultimately returning to Germany in March 1943 as a Soviet mole with access for two years to the very highest level of SS foreign-intelligence operations.[11] Once back in Berlin, Gamotha attempted, with little apparent success, to manage and manipulate a restive group of Persian exiles, whom Joe Spencer identified as part of 'The Persian Quisling Channel',[12] whose activities required surveillance and intervention by British security when attempts were occasionally made, especially by Abwehr naval intelligence (Abw I M), to infiltrate their quisling agents into the region. To the south, among the rebellious Qashgai tribe, a third German intelligence officer from Abwehr air-force intelligence (Abw I L), Berthold Schulze-Holthus, was identified as belonging to 'The Tribal Channel',[13] which also merited constant monitoring, as it involved all three of the principal German agencies (Abwehr I, Abwehr II, and Amt VI of the Reichssicherheitshauptamt [Reich Security Administration (RSHA)]) interested in exploiting the troubled relationship between the Persian tribes and the Tehran government.

DSO Persia were right to predict that attacks on the TIR and oil installations would become the priority for the Germans in 1943, but wrong to suppose, as they did, that Franz Mayr was minded to undertake such sabotage or capable of it.[14] Certainly, Abwehr II and Amt VI embraced such a priority; however, Mayr had neither the will nor the local capacity for a sabotage offensive. As can be seen from Pownall's appreciation, British security also felt that the Qashgai tribe, with Schulze-Holthus's military counsel, would be capable of inflicting significant damage on the TIR, while the fifth column under Mayr fomented unrest and created civil disturbances. But they did not know of course how disorganized the German intelligence services really were, both in Berlin and at the regional level in Persia. Abwehr II–Amt VI liaison and coordination barely existed; when it did sputter into life, it quickly became mired in interservice bickering.[15] Worse still, the same was also true of relations in the field between Amt VI's Mayr and Abw I L's Schulze-Holthus. Interservice rivalry and personality issues were merely compounded by poor, primitive communications between Tehran and the southwest, and the unreliability and duplicitous behaviour of such important cutouts as Habibullah Naubakht and Mohhamad Vaziri. As for the pro-German tribes (Qashgai, Bakhtiari, and Boir Ahmedi) who might be enlisted to execute any destructive plans, they were – like Mayr himself – becoming all too aware that there would be no German military invasion from the north through Transcaucasia. Unless Hitler invaded Turkey – and soon – he would never enter the region and would almost certainly lose the war.

DSO could not know of these things, partly because, though the Abwehr and SD codes had been broken in 1941,[16] the absence of regular W/T communication between Berlin and Tehran, together with Mayr's reliance on couriers to communicate with Germany and with Schulze-Holthus in tribal territory, meant that no signals intelligence on Persia existed to be monitored and decrypted. DSO were shooting in the dark, not because their counterintelligence potential was in any way deficient, but rather because of their enemy's communications dysfunction. Consequently, when the Mayr diary and documents fell into their hands in Isfahan in November 1942, Joe Spencer was able to reconstruct at least an entire year's worth of missing intelligence, enabling him to make some educated guesses as to Berlin's true intentions and those of Franz Mayr. In the absence of hard SIGINT, Spencer can hardly be criticized for making a few false assumptions and flawed deductions.

At last it must have become clear to Spencer that there were two distinct areas of German or pro-German activity to be monitored: fifth-column subversion (centred on Tehran and the major cities) and tribal sabotage (centred on the TIR). He was right to attribute to Mayr a significant measure of control over the former. He was wrong, however, to attribute to Schulze-Holthus a similar degree of influence over Nasir Khan, the *Ilkhan* (supreme leader) of the Qashgai. Spencer initially overestimated the strength of the tribes (especially the Bakhtiari), whose support for the Nazi cause became shaky from the moment the Red Army went onto the offensive in southern Russia.

Thus two of Spencer's three operational channels (see Appendix A.3) were defined, largely as a result of the capture of Franz Mayr's diary and documents. It now remained to identify and isolate the third (quisling) channel, which doubtless originally emerged as an independent enterprise from Abwehr decrypts, and which was subsequently confirmed after the interception and capture of quisling agents sent to Persia by Werner Schüler of Abwehr naval intelligence (Abw I M). The challenge for Spencer lay in disentangling the Berlin quisling scheme of Abwehr I, which appeared to have no obvious link with German naval interests in the Persian Gulf, from the tribal channel operated by Abwehr II, which paradoxically did have a link, for the Qashgai winter pastures adjacent to the Gulf offered a potential hinterland for Japanese U-boats intent on delivering supplies, munitions, and possibly even German personnel to the tribal forces.

Japan's role in Persia, which lay at the extreme western periphery of Japanese naval interest, was neither impressive nor especially menacing. After the expulsion of their fellow Axis nationals, the Germans and the Italians, in the summer of 1941, the Japanese legation in Tehran became the natural rallying point for those Persians who were hostile to the Allies and a disseminating centre for anti-Allied propaganda. It was, however, a passive source of inspiration rather than an active force; it is doubtful whether the Japanese in Persia made any attempt to organize active espionage.[17] Nevertheless, there is no doubt that the Japanese legation poured out a constant stream of propaganda against the Allies,[18] and that at one time they even subsidized some sections of the local press. They appear to have made no plans for postoccupational activities:[19] after their departure on 23 April 1942, returning home overland via Baku and Siberia,[20] Japanese influence dwindled into insignificance as the pro-German fifth columnists extended their activities. However, shortly before the expulsion of the Japanese minister and the military attaché, with whom Franz Mayr had been in contact since early 1941, Mayr inherited from the Japanese legation five old, unserviceable Abwehr W/T sets, and much more significantly the valuable Japanese connection with the pro-Axis *Majlis* deputy Habibullah Naubakht and his circle, which subsequntly became an important constituent of Mayr's *Melliun* organization. From April 1942 onwards, there was little evidence of any attempt by the Japanese to conduct subversive activities in Persia, except for occasional reports of the presence in the Persian Gulf of Japanese submarines. But this did not mean that DSO could ever entirely rule out the possibility of a new Japanese intelligence offensive. After all, Tokyo still had 'legal' representations in Turkey, Afghanistan, and the Soviet Union, which no doubt included intelligence officers among their number. DSO certainly thought that the Japanese were not only interested in Persia itself, but in Persia as a means of obtaining information about India, whose border their troops would briefly succeed in penetrating during the spring of 1944.[21]

The potential Axis threat to the Gulf coast and Khuzistan was considered sufficiently serious in early 1943 to warrant the despatch by Chokra Wood at CICI Baghdad of a special Kurdish task force (Force Kalpak) under the command of a rugby-playing Scottish SOE officer, Captain Terence Bruce Mitford of the Dorset Regiment (D/H45),[22] to Bandar Abbas to investigate the matter.[23] The Kalpaks themselves were Kurds from the Turkish borders who had been raised and trained by Mitford to carry out sabotage on communications in the Taurus mountains; after the Persian operation, they were transferred to 9th Army for use as commandos.[24] Mitford, who then moved on to the Special Air Service (SAS) and later served with distinction in the Special Boat Service (SBS) and the Intelligence Corps, was an extremely able officer who had taught classics and archaeology at St Andrew's University before the war.[25] The purpose of the Force Kalpak expedition, which traversed the entire coastal region between 14 January and 8 May 1943 was twofold: first to capture any Axis nationals who might be trespassing in southern Persia, and second to investigate and counter the activities of possible enemy agents on the Mekran and Hormuz coast who might be in touch with Qashgai territory and enemy submarines operating off those coasts. It was quickly established that there had been no contact between the Qashgai and anyone in the region other than a boyhood friend of Nasir Khan Qashgai, the influential and immensely wealthy Sheikh Abdullah Galadari, who, though originally pro-Nazi and well travelled throughout Germany, now firmly supported the Allies, especially after Pearl Harbor and El Alamein. Although there was clear evidence that Japanese submarines definitely lurked in the Gulf, none of the many rumours of enemy submarine landings could be confirmed; certainly, no German saboteurs or other operatives had been inserted by this route. It was concluded that Japanese submarines were in the

Gulf for only one reason, which had nothing to do with the tribes or infrastructural sabotage: they were there to assess the potentialities of mass-scale attacks on shipping, especially tankers. The Naval Officer in Charge (NOIC) Hormuz informed the visiting Kalpak officers that, in his opinion, the Axis would anyway never waste a submarine on extracting agents or landing agents, stores, wireless, bombs, or cash: 'an unheard-of German SS tradition'.[26] Commodore C.F. Hammill, Senior Naval Officer Persian Gulf (SNOPG), concluded: 'it may be taken as established that the landing of arms in the Gulf by the Axis is a myth'.[27]

Until the area was occupied by Persian troops from May 1943 onwards, the question of whether Berthold Schulze-Holthus of Abwehr air intelligence (Abw I L), together with the fugitive engineer Conny Jakob (probably Abw I M), had succeeded in building and maintaining landing grounds on Qashgai tribal territory of sufficient size to permit the infiltration of significant numbers of German troops and munitions was a persistent concern. A landing strip suitable for light and medium aircraft, marked with Schulze-Holthus's codename SABA as a ground signal, was in fact discovered at Farrashband by an RAF reconaissance flight in November 1942.[28] It was subsequently felt that, although the Farrashband aerodrome had clearly been compromised and its boundary markings removed, Schulze-Holthus might have prepared alternative landing grounds at three or four other locations in the Farrashband area, and even as far to the east as Firuzabad.[29] Even further east, near Laghar on flat country across the Mand river from the Kkonj-Ghir road, the RAF suspected the existence of yet another airfield; however, two Blenheim overflights at about 1800 metres above ground level in January and February 1943 yielded no visual or photographic evidence to support these suspicions.[30] Yet, for as long as Nasir Khan and the Qashgai failed to declare openly their rejection of the Nazi cause, the situation remained uneasy, not least because the Qashgai tribal area directly threatened the Lend-Lease supply route (see Appendix A.4) and local Persian garrisons could not be relied upon to act vigorously against the tribe. Joseph Baillon, the PAIFORCE chief-of-staff, felt that there were only two possible courses of action: (1) contact Nasir Khan with an offer of subsidy to win him over to either the British side or at least to neutrality, while strengthening intelligence resources in southern Persia; (2) take military action against the Qashgai, while establishing a permanent garrison in the south.[31] However, a detailed area topographical study revealed how extremely difficult the tribal terrain was, and how tactically challenging and physically gruelling any ground campaign would be for British and Indian troops in one of the hottest, most humid regions of the world.[32]

Whilst Werner Schüler of Abw I M had initiated German interest in establishing a Persian government-in-exile, this had inevitably brought him into contact in Berlin with Nasir Khan Qashgai's younger brothers, Mohammed Huseyin Khan Qashgai (MHQ) and Malek Mansour Khan Qashgai (MMQ), who not only held key positions in the quisling shadow government sponsored by Schüler, but who were also German army officers associated with Abwehr II's Brandenburger special forces. As such, both brothers, especially MHQ, enjoyed a close personal friendship with Gerhard Putz of Abwehr II, who clearly regarded himself as the brothers' mentor, and who may even have lost his life protecting them from the murderous clutches of the SS.[33] Thus, paradoxically, quisling and tribal interests became juxtaposed within Germany, yet intertwined and doubly difficult for DSO Persia to differentiate and extrapolate. By mid-1943, however, Joe Spencer had acquired sufficient intelligence about the Qashgai Brothers to be able to distinguish between their participation as protagonists (MMQ ([shah-designate] and MHQ [premier-designate]) in the quisling shadow government and their utility as bargaining chips in the high-stakes game being played by British security intelligence with the southwestern tribes. Thus the third operational channel, the 'quisling channel', emerged, independent of the specific German intelligence formations that were originally interested in quisling and tribal affairs, and isolated from the other two channels.

Spencer's skilful method of analysing these three diverse threats consisted not of dividing and classifying them rigidly according to their parent organizations, as the Germans did, but instead of deconstructing them according to their operational functions and targets. In other words, Spencer was interested in the situation as seen from Persia, not in what was happening in Berlin. This enabled DSO to isolate each suspected or potential threat regardless of whether it originated from the Abwehr (about whom the British knew a great deal) or the SS (about whom they knew very little). The criteria Spencer applied concerned the potential impact of covert activities on his region, far less than their genesis or point of origin. This approach became particularly effective from 1943 onwards, as the German intelligence services began undertaking joint operations, rendering identification of the originating service more difficult, but of even less importance. Ascertaining the purpose of an operation – for example, subversion or sabotage – also became less significant. After attributing a German operation to one of the three channels Spencer had differentiated, what really mattered was identifying such aspects as operational feasibility, logistics, method of insertion, target location, operational scale, individual identities of personnel (as well as their number and quality, training, weapons and equipment), Persian collaboration and support, and the expedient counterintelligence or security-intelligence response. This kind of practical, target-oriented, open-ended analytical methodology was exactly what was needed in an extremely fluid security situation. As it was applied pragmatically and flexibly by Spencer and his team, it permitted maximum crossreferencing and corroboration of dynamic, malleable intelligence data, and it ensured a greater likelihood of appropriate response. Instead of tilting at elusive windmills in Berlin, DSO found themselves able to work against clearly defined targets on the ground in Persia with an astonishingly high success rate.

From 1943 onwards, of course, their success was also greatly facilitated and accelerated by the generally poor quality of the enemy combatants and agents whom DSO faced. The vulnerable young Germans who were sent out to Persia by their Berlin spymasters at Abwehr II and Amt VI to carry out sabotage operations against the TIR and other strategic installations were hurled – literally – into the dark void of the moonless Persian night from aircraft in a series of blind drops by insecure pilots who, though generally experienced, were flying over unfamiliar, extremely challenging territory. Few of the parachutists had any parachute training, sabotage training, agent training, or linguistic skills; and they had no perceptible talents whatsoever for clandestine operations – with the exception of one experienced Abwehr interpreter/ guide who died of typhus shortly after insertion. Moreover, German operational practice and radio-communication problems dictated that, once dropped into enemy territory, parachutists effectively passed from Berlin's control and were abandoned – expected to fend for themselves in an alien, difficult country. Their sole protection lay with the Abwehr interpreter/guides assigned to their missions, and when these guides died (Operation FRANZ's Karl Korel) or deserted them (Operation ANTON's Homayoun Farzad), they became helpless fugitives incapable of mounting any operations. Finally, had they been even moderately successful and ready to return to Germany, no thought at all seems to have been given to their extraction. These, then, were the helpless, hapless 'rats' whom Joe Spencer and his team had to catch.

Notes

1. K.W. Jones in Appendix IX, Security: Persia, 16 February 1943, KV 4/240, TNA. This conclusion was reached after a lengthy meeting in Cairo in early 1943 between Dick White of MI5, Raymond Maunsell of SIME, and Joe Spencer of CICI Tehran.

2. Despatches, Persia and Iraq Command, 12 October 1943, CGS/1740/2, WO 32/10540, TNA.
3. Ibid.
4. Ibid.
5. See Situation Report No. 8, Amt VI of the RHSA, Gruppe VI C, SHAEF Counter Intelligence War Room, 28 February 1946, RG 263, Entry ZZ17, Box 3, NARA. This report is one of an important series of seven postwar situation and liquidation reports based largely on prisoner interrogations, which are essentially postmortem autopsies on the organization and war history of the SS, including SD foreign intelligence.
6. Thistlethwaite to Wharry, 3 June 1944, KV 2/1480, TNA; see also *NSW*, 1–7.
7. According to the misgivings of SS Brigadier Ettel at the German legation. See Ettel to Berlin, 21 September 1940, Dept Inland II: Geheim: Mayr and Gamotha, GFM 33/464, TNA.
8. Phrase attributed variously to Kaiser Wilhelm II and Prince Bernhard von Bülow.
9. Preface to commentary on the documents left by Franz Mayr in Isfahan, 27 October 1943, KV 2/1482, TNA; see also *NSW*, 111–18, 122.
10. See Chapter 3.
11. For further information on Roman Gamotha, see KV 2/1492, TNA.
12. See Chapter 5.
13. See Chapter 4.
14. The general security situation in Persia February 1943, Appendix 'A' to Security Summary Middle East No. 123, 19 March 1943, WO 208/1562, TNA; also in WO 208/3094, TNA.
15. See *NSW*, 80–85.
16. Hinsley and Simkins, *British Intelligence in the Second World War*, Vol. 4, *Security and Counter-Intelligence*, 163.
17. Security Summary Middle East No. 165, 18 January 1944, WO 208/1562, TNA.
18. Security Summary Middle East No. 34, 7 April 1942, WO 208/1562, TNA.
19. Security Summary Middle East No. 165, 18 January 1944, WO 208/1562, TNA.
20. Security Summary Middle East No. 41, 30 April 1942, WO 208/1561, TNA.
21. Security Summary Middle East No. 165, 18 January 1944, WO 208/1562, TNA; DSO's report on Japanese activities 1941–44, Security Summary Middle East No. 186, 15 June 1944, WO 208/1562, TNA. For more about Japan's invasion across the Indo-Burmese frontier, see B.H. Liddell Hart, *History of the Second World War* (London: Pan, 1973), 538, 542–4.
22. SOE symbols 6, HS 8/971, TNA.
23. Wood to GHQ PAIC, Intelligence report on southeast Persian coast, 19 June 1943, AIR 23/5951, TNA. This file contains full details of the Mitford-Henry mission. About the Kalpaks, see also Henry Maitland Wilson, *Eight Years Overseas, 1939–1947* (London: Hutchinson, 1951), 145.
24. History of SOE in the Arab World, September 1945, HS 7/86, TNA.
25. 'Prof Terence Mitford: Classical archaeologist and explorer (Obituary)', *The Times*, 25 November 1978.
26. Wood to GHQ PAIC, Intelligence report on southeast Persian coast, 19 June 1943, AIR 23/5951, TNA.

27. SNOPG to C-in-C Eastern Fleet, Reports of landing of arms from U-boats on the Persian coast inside the Straits September–December 1942, 4 March 1943, AIR 23/5951, TNA.

28. OC 1434 Flight to AHQ, 215 Group, Photo recce of suspected enemy landing ground, 9 November 1942, AIR 23/5951, TNA; CICI Security Intelligence Summary No. 44, 15 November 1942, WO 208/3088, TNA; Theakston to CIO AHQ, 11 January 1943, AIR 23/5951, TNA; G2 CICI Baghdad to SIO Advanced AHQ, Landing grounds, 23 January 1943, AIR 23/5951, TNA; see also *NSW*, 149, 182, 188.

29. Alternative Landing Grounds in Farrashband area, AIR 23/5951, TNA.

30. HQ 215 Group to Advanced AHQ, Reconnaissance of suspected enemy landing grounds, 10 February 1943, AIR 23/5951, TNA; HQ 215 Group to Advanced AHQ, Reconnaissance of suspected enemy landing grounds, 14 February 1943, AIR 23/5951, TNA.

31. Baillon to Bullard, undated cipher message (after 11 November 1942), AIR 23/5951, TNA.

32. Topographical study of the area Shiraz-Firuzabad-Farrashband-Bushire-Kazerun, 11 November 1942, AIR 23/5951, TNA.

33. See *NSW*, 54.

3
Fifth Columnists

It is easier to drive a camel through the eye of a needle
than to force Persians to cooperate. (Franz Mayr)[1]

The British security authorities were never able to ascertain how many
Germans were in Persia at the time of the occupation in August 1941,
how many escaped into Turkey and returned to Europe, or how many
were captured by the Soviets.[2] Approximately 500 male individuals,
almost all of little importance, were rounded up shortly after the Anglo-
Soviet occupation and were transported to South Australia, where they
were interned under conditions wholly satisfactory to the International
Red Cross.[3] Their wives and children, together with any German
nationals holding diplomatic status, were evacuated and repatriated to
Germany. Hitler retaliated angrily and disproportionately to these altogether humane measures by deporting 825 men, women, and children
from the occupied Channel Islands to internment camps in southern Germany in late September 1941.[4] A maximum of 100 Germans
remained in Persia unaccounted for and possibly in hiding. During the
year that followed, about 15 Germans were tracked down and arrested
by DSO Persia, who were rarely helped and often obstructed by the
Persian police. Rumours of other German fugitives, possibly as many as
30 hidden enemy agents, were frequently received, but circumstances
made it impossible to take any action against them. In addition, there
were concerns about the potential for conspiracy by Persian army
officers, most of whom were undoubtedly anti-British (and even more
deeply anti-Russian). However, in the absence of hard intelligence
about them, British security could only console themselves with gener-
alizations about the shortcomings of the Persian 'character' – notably
a lack of the courage and determination required for fifth-column

work – which rendered Persian officers unlikely to risk themselves in active operations on their own initiative, though it was agreed that they might do so under the direction of German agents.[5]

By mid-October 1942, this rather vague picture was given a decidedly sharper focus: DSO reported that they suspected that some very senior Persian army officers and others closely connected with the Shah's court were involved in fifth-column plans. It was suspected that three groups were active: Franz Mayr's Isfahan group, with branches in Tehran and Shiraz; the Gulmohammedi group in Kermanshah, Tehran, and the Soviet zone; and a third group in the northwest, near the Turkish frontier. Whilst acknowledging the disparate nature of these groups, Joe Spencer already suspected that they were 'fragmentary manifestations of a widespread fifth-column organization'. One month later, Spencer's supicions were confirmed when his security troops raided Franz Mayr's Isfahan home and discovered Mayr's personal diary and documents, which Mayr had been hoarding, most unprofessionally, for some future purpose. Most of the papers consisted of correspondence between Mayr and his right-hand man, Mohammed Hussein Hissam Vaziri, and revealed the structure and extent of Mayr's fifth-column organization, which was supported by Persian army, gendarmerie, and police officers; cabinet ministers; members of the *Majlis*; and civil servants, 160 of whom were named in the documents. Plans had been maturing since the spring, and July had been set as 'zero day', when a German invasion from the north had been expected.[6]

Franz Mayr's diary confirmed that the German-controlled fifth column was not left behind fully organized by the German authorities when British and Russian forces entered Persia. The Abwehr representative, Berthold Schulze-Holthus, for instance, was apparently supposed to make for Erzerum, where a job awaited him. Force of circumstances, however, had sent him south from Tabriz to Tehran, where he eventually entered Mayr's orbit. Though active in propaganda and trade – and in trying to tie Persia to the Axis chariot – the Germans had been unprepared for the Allied invasion and had no proper plans for post-occupational activity. When the blow fell, certain leading Nazis in Persia were simply ordered to stay behind and improvise to the best of their ability. They had had good contacts, but they had lost precious ground between August 1941 and April 1942, when Mayr had finally decided he could safely emerge from hiding (albeit in heavy disguise) and resume his subversive activities.[7]

Any action by Franz Mayr's fifth-column umbrella organization was contingent upon German military support, either by airborne troops or by a direct invasion of Persia via the Caucasus. Without this support, it was considered by DSO highly improbable in November 1942 that the Persians themselves would undertake any operations, however anti-Allied and pro-German they might be, at a time when the prospects of an ultimate Allied victory seemed better than at any time since the war began. Throughout the year, DSO had uncovered piece by piece what at first appeared to be independent pro-German secret societies and isolated German fugitives. Slowly it was discovered that many of these secret organizations were in fact interconnected. Joe Spencer's suspicions were confirmed that he was on the track of a very widespread organization which embraced anti-Allied societies, enemy propaganda, Japanese espionage, suspected sabotage, and all such fifth-column activities. The discovery in November of Franz Mayr's diary and documents during the raid on his house in Isfahan provided the final link which until then had been lacking. It proved that all the anti-Allied secret organizations were in fact semi-autonomous, hermetic cells belonging to one comprehensive pro-German fifth column, whose actions were to be coordinated according to one comprehensive operational plan.[8]

As originally constituted in July 1942, the *Hezb-i-Melliun* (National [German: *völkisch*] Party) was not a political party at all, but it was aptly described by Franz Mayr himself as a 'centre of resistance'. 'It was neutral as to national parties', he added, 'or better – above parties'.[9] It consisted of various secret societies or groups, identified by DSO as follows: *Hezb-i-Nazi* (Gulmohammedi Group), *Hezb-i-Kabud*, *Siahpushan* (SP Group), *Jamiatt-i-Melli* (Workmen's Aid Society), *Iran-Azad*, *Anjuman-i-Tablighat-Iran*, *Iran-Bidar*, the FN Group, and the so-called Railway Section (see Figure 3.1).[10] The first attempt to bring these groups together was a 'Committee of Five' (Naghibzadeh, Naubakht, Neivandi, Kashani, and Namdar [Zahedi's proxy]) formed in May 1942. It met twice and then broke up because of the intrigues among the various members. Mayr then made a second attempt to form an 'Executive Committee' (*ExKo*) in August 1942; its members were Kashani, Hayat, Neivandi, Aghevli, and Pourzand. The first three formed a political sub-committee (*PoKo*); the latter two, being Persian army generals, served as a military subcommittee (*MilKo*). Ali Hayat, a curious choice because he was openly pro-British, was introduced primarily to offset Habibullah Naubakht's aggressive personality.[11] However, Hayat seems to have been a rather unsavoury character, for Mayr assigned to him the task of preparing postoccupational concentration camps and acting more or less as a 'Persian Himmler'.[12] According to Mayr, because of intrigues, *ExKo* accomplished nothing despite repeated meetings between August 1942 and the Isfahan raid in November.[13] Consequently, to see his operational decisions executed effectively, Mayr seems to have bypassed his secret political bureau, preferring to deal directly with his closest aide, Vaziri, who effectively ran things in Tehran while Mayr was in Isfahan for most of 1942, and other more actively engaged members of the organization. Even so, one member of the *ExKo*, Seyyed Abol-Ghasem Kashani, definitely enjoyed Mayr's confidence; however, he ignored this senior cleric at his peril, for Kashani was enormously wealthy, influential, and skilled in anti-British subversion, having closely supported Rashid Ali Gailani before, during, and after his ill-fated coup in Iraq.[14] Even after his arrest in June 1944, Kashani, who was regarded by British security as 'the most dangerous member of the conspiracy', remained implacably anglophobic, openly vowing that when he was released he would do all the damage he could.[15]

Figure 3.1 Sabotage target: Trans-Iranian Railway (TIR). American, British, and Russian officers inspect a trainload of Lend-Lease US tanks destined for the Soviet Union. The *Melliun* Railway Section, which targeted the TIR, was the best organized of Franz Mayr's fifth-column sabotage networks and considered by DSO Persia to be the element that could have done the greatest damage.
Source: Donald Connolly Collection, Office of History, US Army Corps of Engineers (USACE).

The *Melliun* umbrella sheltered a wide variety of constituent members. Mayr appears to have attached the greatest value to winning over the tribal and religious elements of the fifth column, with whom he achieved considerable success: no fewer than 23 tribes were in contact with the *Melliun*. Most significant were the Qashgai, the Bakhtiari, and the bellicose Boir Ahmedi; there was even a widespread network of contacts among the Jangali of Mazanderan, inside the Soviet zone of occupation.[16] Beyond this, Mayr wished to enlist support for Germany among the Kurds and Armenians, though he faced formidable competition among those minorities from Soviet political agencies and the Soviet propaganda machine. Much time and energy was expended by the difficult personalities of the fifth column on internecine strife. Mayr himself had to struggle constantly to assert his authority. He had no sooner settled his differences with the Abwehr representative Schulze-Holthus than he was at loggerheads with their go-between, the *Majlis* deputy Habibullah Naubakht. Joe Spencer commented wryly: 'This man in fact would almost seem an unwitting help to the Allies while at liberty, as he causes almost as much trouble to his fellow conspirators as he does to his enemies.'[17]

To maintain control over these disparate and often unruly elements, Mayr shrewdly kept them as much in ignorance of each other as possible. For a virtually untrained operative, Mayr's largely intuitive tradecraft was remarkably professional and effective. Similarly, he greatly strengthened his control over the *Melliun* cells by distancing himself from them, employing a number of cutouts (intermediaries), such as his factotum Mohhammad Vaziri and his mistress Lili Sanjari, to liaise with the cells indirectly, thereby enhancing Mayr's almost legendary reputation and stature, not only among the Persians but also, it has to be admitted, in the minds of his pursuers – DSO Persia.[18]

The grand Mayr plan was contingent upon the arrival of airborne troops or an attack across the Caucasus and the Caspian Sea (or both combined). It was originally intended to employ the Persian army in conjunction with some of the tribes to rise against the Allied occupying forces. They would seize such key positions as oilfields, refineries, public buildings, utility installations, and the Allied legations in Tehran. Allied sympathizers and nationals would be rounded up, and a puppet government (prefabricated in Berlin) would be installed. These overt activities were to be accompanied by covert subversive measures to cause the greatest possible confusion amongst the Allied forces and amongst Persian elements that might be prepared to help the Allies. As Spencer was quick to perceive, Mayr's plans were not original, but followed closely the common Nazi design – *Blitzkrieg* and *Gleichschaltung* (forcible assimilation) – a lethal combination so frequently and successfully applied by the Germans in recent years to other countries.[19]

DSO had to engage with a perplexing galaxy of interconnected civilian, military, and police personalities associated with the *Melliun* organization. Each had a personal record, which had become complicated and lengthy by the time the fifth column was finally rolled up after the arrest of Mayr and the FRANZ parachutists in August 1943. At that time, Spencer listed some 140 *Melliun* members whose arrest was considered essential, and whose personality profiles make for interesting reading. They ranged from powerful generals and politicians to the humblest local courier, with many of the latter infinitely more important to Mayr's organization and its survival than the former. When things fell apart, some who escaped arrest by heading north into the Soviet zone were perhaps, if valuable, turned and doubled by the Soviets. But, in the absence of relevant Soviet records, we will never know for sure how many of the smaller fry were disposed of by the NKVD, nor how. There is a scattered abundance of CICI documents in the Kew records, including correspondence between Joe Spencer and Alan Roger concerning Soviet counterintelligence activities, which describes the activities and movements of some of these Persian and Azeri agents and clarifies their complex interrelationships. Their original work in the German cause seems frequently to have been more a matter of place and circumstance than of political conviction. What they had in common was their utility: some functioned as local couriers and cutouts, whilst others were professional smugglers whose ability to cross the Turkish frontier unmolested made them useful as international couriers.

Most of those recruited locally who worked for the fifth column within Persia were eventually betrayed by one or other of their associates, and most, if apprehended in the British zone, ended up in the Sultanabad (Arak) internment camp. A few, like Mohammad Vaziri, who seems to have roamed at will throughout the British and Soviet zones, evaded capture until finally intercepted (or possibly kidnapped) by the Russians, probably some time in the latter half of 1942, while he was still working for Mayr and the *Melliun*.[20] Vaziri's father, Hissam Vaziri, was a senior Persian police officer (head of personnel in Tehran), which undoubtedly facilitated his son's migrations. His uncle, General Sadiq Kupal, was also extremely influential, especially in Persian army circles and throughout Turkey, where he was influential enough to facilitate Mayr's courier arrangements.[21] After turning and presumably training Vaziri, the Russians released him to operate as a double agent, now called Ghulam

Reza Abbassian. After returning to work with Mayr in Tehran until the very end of the *Melliun's* existence – right up to the time of Mayr's arrest in August 1943 – Vaziri (as Abbassian) travelled freely from January 1944 onwards as far afield as Turkey, Bulgaria, Switzerland, and Germany, presenting himself to his German or pro-German contacts as a Nazi agent. It is possible that, whilst in the Russian zone, he may have encountered Roman Gamotha and have planned future pro-Soviet activities with him, for it was Gamotha whom Vaziri contacted in Turkey in early 1944 (and possibly in Vienna and/or Salzburg later that year). Certainly, Joe Spencer felt that Vaziri and Gamotha were destined to work together.[22]

Part of the problem in constructing an accurate narrative of what these men did is the fact that both enjoyed Soviet protection; therefore they were never interrogated after the war by the British or the Americans. By late 1945, Vaziri was reported as quite obviously working for the Russians, since he was in constant contact with the Soviet consul in Istanbul and was even learning Russian. He was, however, also observed in contact with US and British intelligence officers.[23] About this time, Dick Thistlethwaite, now working for Alex Kellar at MI5, informed SIME that Vaziri was indeed a fully fledged Soviet agent. In fact, even as early as September 1943, after Franz Mayr's arrest and the collapse of the *Melliun*, Vaziri had been known by DSO to have already been recruited by the Russians. At that time, the Soviet security officer, Gregori Asaturov, frightened that DSO 'ratcatchers' were getting 'too near the mark' in their investigations into the Vaziri family, had admitted that Vaziri was one of his agents and had asked Alan Roger to cease all 'persecution' of him.[24] Furthermore, Asaturov attested to the fact that Moscow Centre – not the local NKVD – had directly recruited Vaziri to penetrate the German organizations in Persia and Turkey, had issued Vaziri with a false passport (later investigated by the Persian justice ministry, almost blowing Vaziri's cover),[25] had got him over the Turkish frontier, and had directly planned and controlled his case.[26] Asaturov's contention is strengthened by the fact that, despite strenuous attempts to plot all Mohammad Vaziri's predominantly Armenian, Azeri, and Turkish connections in order to ascertain if they might also have changed their allegiance, DSO were never able to get the NKVD to admit that they were employing such Vaziri associates as Hissam Vaziri, Firuz and Nadir Khalilnia, Nazifeh Afruz, and Bahlul Zanouzi as agents. Nor did they confirm that they had been responsible for sending Vaziri to Europe. However, the Russians' defensive reactions to British enquiries strongly suggested to DSO that further investigation into the 'wide Vaziri–Khalilnia network' might well reap dividends in the future, as it had always done in the past.[27] While the Soviets never indicated to DSO precisely when they had recruited Vaziri, Franz Mayr was certainly not aware that, possibly from some time in 1942 onwards, his fifth column had been so deeply penetrated and potentially compromised by Moscow Centre.

From the documents captured in November 1942, it became evident that the *Melliun* had its roots in practically every class of Persian society, including members of the *Majlis*, cabinet ministers, army and police officers, and all manner of government officials and civil servants. It was important for DSO to identify each individual as quickly as possible, but this was complicated by the fact that Mayr had encrypted most of their names. Having narrowly evaded arrest and gone into hiding in December somewhere in Tehran, he could not be interrogated in order to break these simple codes. However, by crossreferencing Mayr's documents with their existing records, DSO managed to decipher a number of the cryptonyms and ciphers that Mayr had used, and to their satisfaction discovered that they had already interned a number of *Melliun* subversives as suspects at Sultanabad (Arak) and could now lay charges against them. These charges could be brought effectively because Spencer now had a clear idea of the activities being undertaken 'busily' by the fifth column in the absence of any call to action by Mayr, notably the gathering of intelligence concerning the general disposition and strength of Allied forces in Persia, and the fortifications and installations constructed or under construction. *Melliun* cells were also engaged in preparing to sabotage the oilfields, railways, roads, and ports. Moreover, they were preparing the Persian army and the tribes for the purpose of creating a diversion behind the Allied forces, including the siting and preparation of landing grounds, and a system of prearranged signals.[28] Yet DSO remained unaware of the fifth column's communication problems. They seemed to be under the impression that the *Melliun* had an extensive, effective communications network, with W/T transmitting stations and an elaborate system of couriers shuttling between Persia and Turkey (and Afghanistan) by normal and secret routes on a significant scale. The messages they carried were assumed to have been relayed to Berlin by the Axis legations in Ankara and Kabul. In reality, Franz Mayr had the greatest difficulty communicating with Berlin, and even when his requests and pleas got through to Heinz Gräfe at Amt VI, they were more often than not ignored or contradicted by the VI C chief, who was obsessively preoccupied with operations in Russia. Even Joe Spencer was struck by the number of times Mayr complained in his diary of the lack of communications with the outside world and the way in which he seemed to have been ignored.[29]

Even more surprising was the constant lack of funds. DSO received many reports, reliable and unreliable, of vast sums of money left behind by the Germans, Italians, and Japanese for subversive activities. However, it seemed that many of the inactive Persians to whom the money had been entrusted were quite prepared to embrace German ideals but were not prepared to disgorge the gold deposited with them to support active German agents like Mayr and Schulze-Holthus. Furthermore, as his couriers Mayr preferred to use smugglers of carpets and opium, expert at crossing the difficult and dangerous mountainous frontier between Persia and Turkey: Anvar Hussein, Firuz Khalilnia, Ghulam Kashefi, and Bahlul Zanouzi were among his trusty messengers.[30] Clearly, their loyalty to Mayr was not political but mercenary, and they must have cost him dearly.

Early in November 1942, immediately after the seizure of the Mayr documents, Jumbo Wilson (C-in-C PAIFORCE), Sir Reader Bullard (British minister), Raymond Maunsell (head of SIME), and Chokra Wood (head of CICI) met to formulate plans to deal with the *Melliun* conspiracy. The initial revelation of its size and ramifications had undoubtedly come as something of a shock to all concerned. Wisely, however, rather than advocating widespread arrests, the quartet decided that efforts should be made to penetrate the *Melliun* organization and keep it under close observation. They felt that, since German military intervention in Persia had become highly unlikely, it was equally unlikely that the Persian officer corps or the tribal leaders would be persuaded by their German mentors to undertake any large-scale hostile action. The perceptiveness of the British military, diplomatic, and security-intelligence leadership in recognizing that the Allied victory in the Western Desert and the onset of the Russian winter had a direct bearing on Persian internal security is self-evident. It prevented an overreaction by the Allies to what had in reality become, temporarily at least, a relatively impotent threat.[31]

One month later, DSO considered the security situation in Tehran, Isfahan, and Shiraz to have improved considerably. It was not just that the German drive towards Persia had evidently failed. Nor was it solely because a blow to the *Melliun* had been struck by the capture of the Mayr diary and documents – about which the news seems to have spread rapidly – and by the consequent acquisition of significance amounts of intelligence regarding the identities and activities of Mayr's fifth columnists. Equally important was the simultaneous realization by Mayr's Persian accomplices that his seized documents incriminated them, and that they therefore needed to reconsider their loyalties.

Joe Spencer felt there was reason to hope that some of the conspirators might consequently come forward to make amends for their former subversive activities. During November and December 1942, surveillance certainly revealed a flurry of increased activity involving travel between the major urban centres and Tehran by certain individuals implicated in the fifth column. This may have been a positive sign (of panic); however, Spencer felt that there was still plenty of cause for anxiety, and there was certainly no reason to scale down security-intelligence operations.[32] On the other hand, it must have been greatly reassuring for DSO to learn from Mayr's diary that there had only ever been, besides Mayr himself, three German agents active in the British zone of occupation – all representatives of the Abwehr, not the SD: Berthold Schulze-Holthus (captured on 23 March 1944), Konstantin 'Conny' Jakob (captured on 2 April 1945), and Friedrich Kümel (captured on 20 July 1942).[33]

A further blow to the fifth column was struck on 8 December 1942, when the pro-German general (and future postwar prime minister), Fazlollah Zahedi, under whose protection Mayr's cause had prospered in Isfahan, was arrested by the British military authorities and removed from office.[34] Joe Spencer considered this move – not initiated by his security forces but by 10th Army HQ – to be 'one of the most important security measures taken in Persia since the Allied occupation'. In Spencer's opinion, it would likely serve as a deterrent to similar undesirable persons, who had hitherto relied on their positions of power to protect them in their subversive activities. There had been no visible reactions to Zahedi's internment, except for the congratulations offered to the British authorities by certain leading Persians. However, Spencer thought it likely that other Persian 'obstructionists' would not fail to take warning from the move, the effect of which 'should assist in maintaining our prestige, and improving our security throughout Persia'.[35]

In the spring of 1943, when Abwehr II and Amt VI turned their attention towards Persia as a sabotage target, Franz Mayr briefly attempted to resurrect the *Melliun* and form a slightly different brand of fifth column, no longer the precursor of a German military invasion. By now, however, the organization was a mere shadow of its former self: its ranks had been depleted by waves of arrests and internments; its former members still at liberty were fugitives or under surveillance; its cells were scattered – incommunicado and leaderless; the 'king-pin' of the *Melliun*, Mohammad Vaziri, had long ago deserted Mayr; and public opinion, after Stalingrad and the German retreat from the Caucasus, had begun to turn against the German cause, robbing Mayr of his political influence and financial support. Most telling though was the fact that Mayr's self-confidence, his political convictions, his personal relationship with Lili Sanjari, his health, his stamina, his moods, and his former unquestioning loyalty to his service and his Führer were beginning to disintegrate. A creeping sense of betrayal began to set in, sapping Mayr's operational energy and robbing him of his usual resourcefulness and resilience. Two long years of living as a fugitive in close confinement had clearly taken their toll; we know from Mayr's diary how difficult he found the isolation, the heat, the lack of communication with Berlin, and the increasing sense of failure.

The phenomenal success of DSO in breaking Mayr's fifth column was not improvised; it was achieved by meticulous operational planning. On 11 August 1943, four days before he captured Franz Mayr, Joe Spencer released to the British, American, and Russian authorities his monolithic (57-page) 'Master plan for breaking the fifth column in Persia'.[36] It was indeed a magisterial document which set forth the evidence of past and present activities of the fifth column and German parachutists in detail, including even reports of unidentified aircraft. It defined and elaborated the action to be taken against the resurgent *Melliun* conspiracy, including wholesale reorganization of the Persian police and gendarmerie. The plan acknowledged the changed role of Mayr's resurrected organization, no longer expectant of German military intervention, but now reoriented towards sabotage, civil unrest, and the diversion of Allied military resources.[37] This meant that the policy of noninterventionist surveillance formulated by Spencer in 1942, when the *Melliun* had been constrained by a lack of German military support, was no longer suitable. Now there were SS saboteurs on Persian soil, with more to come perhaps, which could only spur on the fifth columnists. (Of course, Spencer was not aware of how incompetent and inept the parachutists were, nor that Mayr had no use for them.) So, Joe Spencer's intention was to smash the fifth column immediately, or so to disorganize it that it would be unlikely to recover and reform for a very long time. For this reason, it was imperative that the Persian government be convinced that arrests on a large scale were necessary to prevent serious civil disturbances that would gravely effect the position of the government and the Allies. The Persians needed to recognize their treaty obligations under the tripartite agreement, and that fifth-column activities were directed as much against their constitution and their ruler as against the Allies. Such was the scale of Spencer's plan, which was implemented with total success from August 1943 onwards.

Franz Mayr's ultimate capture in August 1943 was followed by a wave of fifth-column arrests (over 100), facilitated partly by his cooperation under interrogation and by the voluminous records so painstakingly assembled by DSO. This marked the end of the *Melliun*; for the rest of the war there was no more fifth-column threat to the Persian polity, the Lend-Lease supply route, the oil infrastructure, or the PAIFORCE theatre. Between July 1942 and the mass arrests in the last quarter of 1943, which were followed by internments and interrogations on a grand scale, DSO's deconstruction and annihilation of Mayr's fifth-column organization was marked by a blend of strategic planning, inspired opportunism, and brilliant inductive analysis. Spencer and his small team pounced like unleashed tigers, eyes burning bright, on every latent scrap of intelligence that came their way, no matter how fragmentary or seemingly innocuous, feeding these scraps into the maw of their massive security registry. Into the DSO records they went, thousands of items, to be indexed, crossreferenced, corroborated, and compounded by the force of existing evidence. Sometimes DSO were lucky, and a windfall like the Mayr documents or a really big fish like Mayr himself came their way. More often it was a relentless, slogging process of acquisition and evaluation which enabled Joe Spencer's team to assemble the big picture, until the *Melliun* menace emerged for what it was, though never perhaps quite as potent a threat as it once purported to be in Franz Mayr's grandiose vision: 'the unification of all forces and associations of Iran which aim at freeing their homeland and who, in their fight against Bolshevik Russia and the Anglo-Saxon world, see in National Socialist Germany their natural allies'.[38]

Notes

1. DSO Persia, Reference DSP/3857, 27 October 1943, KV 2/1482, TNA.
2. For a detailed discussion of the German diaspora in Persia, see *NSW*, 10–31.
3. Auswärtiges Amt, Kult E/Nf. (Zv.), 26 February 1942, R 27330, Politisches Archiv, Auswärtiges Amt, Berlin (AA).
4. For details of the reprisal, see Charles Cruickshank, *The German Occupation of the Channel Islands: The Official History of the Occupation Years* (Guernsey, CI: The Guernsey Press, 1975), 206–19.
5. Security Summary No. 111A, 13 January 1943, KV 2/1477, TNA.
6. Ibid.
7. Comments on the diary of Franz Mayr, May 1943, KV 2/1482, TNA.
8. Security Intelligence Summary No. 44, 15 November 1942, WO 208/3088, TNA. Part of a series signed by Chokra Wood, head of CICI Baghdad, but clearly authored by Joe Spencer, CICI Tehran.
9. DSO Persia, Reference DSP/3857, 27 October 1943, KV 2/1482, TNA. For a more detailed treatment of the *Melliun*, see *NSW*, 111–18.

10. Plan for breaking the German fifth column in Persia, 11 August 1943, KV 2/1477, TNA.
11. Biographical sketch of persons mentioned in the document summarizing the information gained from Franz Mayr, RG 319, Entry 134B, Box 147, NARA; see also *NSW*, 117.
12. Plan for breaking the German fifth column in Persia, 11 August 1943, KV 2/1477, TNA.
13. DSO Persia, Reference DSP/3857, 27 October 1943, KV 2/1482, TNA.
14. Plan for breaking the German fifth column in Persia, 11 August 1943, KV 2/1477, TNA. For more about Kashani, see Abbas Milani, *Eminent Persians: The Men and Women Who Made Modern Iran, 1941–1979* (Syracuse, NY: Syracuse University Press, 2008), 1:343–9.
15. Bullard to Eden, 27 March 1945, E 2050/31/34, IOR/L/PS/12/3472A, BL.
16. Plan for breaking the German fifth column in Persia, 11 August 1943, KV 2/1477, TNA.
17. Comments on the diary of Franz Mayr, May 1943, KV 2/1482, TNA.
18. For more about Mayr and the *Melliun*, see *NSW*, 111–18.
19. Security Intelligence Summary No. 44, 15 November 1942, WO 208/3088, TNA.
20. Soviet activities and the Vaziri case, Defence Security Office, DO/ASR/15, 6 August 1944, KV 2/1317, TNA.
21. Extracted from plan for breaking the German fifth column in Persia, 11 August 1943, KV 2/1317, TNA.
22. Counterintelligence Summary No. 23, 13 April 1944, KV 2/1317, TNA.
23. Extract from DSO Syria's Interrogation Report No. 1 on Firouz Khalilnia, 8 December 1945, KV 2/1317, TNA.
24. Soviet activities and the Vaziri case, Defence Security Office, DO/ASR/15, 6 August 1944, KV 2/1317, TNA; Thistlethwaite to Brodie, 4 January 1946, KV 2/1317, TNA; see also *NSW*, 114.
25. Russian activities and relations, Defence Security Office, DO/ASR/48, 14 September 1944, KV 2/1317, TNA.
26. Soviet activities and the Vaziri case, Defence Security Office, DO/ASR/15, 6 August 1944, KV 2/1317, TNA.
27. Extract from attachment to Defence Security Office CICI Tehran report re cooperation with Russian security, 31 August 1945, KV 2/1317, TNA.
28. Security Intelligence Summary No. 44, 15 November 1942, WO 208/3088, TNA.
29. Comments on the diary of Franz Mayr, May 1943, KV 2/1482, TNA.
30. Biographical sketch of persons mentioned in the document summarizing the information gained from Franz Mayr, RG 319, Entry 134B, Box 147, NARA.
31. Security Summary No. 111A, 13 January 1943, KV 2/1477, TNA.
32. Security Intelligence Summary No. 46, 1 December 1942, WO 208/3089, TNA.
33. Comments on the diary of Franz Mayr, May 1943, KV 2/1482, TNA.
34. See Chapter 8.

35. Security Intelligence Summary No. 48, 15 December 1942, WO 208/3089, TNA. Regarding the effect of Zahedi's removal on the morale of the Persian officer corps, see Stephanie Cronin, *Soldiers, Shahs and Subalterns in Iran: Opposition, Protest and Revolt, 1921–1941* (Basingstoke: Palgrave Macmillan, 2010), 258.
36. Plan for breaking the German fifth column in Persia, 11 August 1943, KV 2/1477, TNA.
37. Ibid.
38. Ibid. See also *NSW*, 111–12.

4

Fierce Tribes and Princely Playboys

> The curse of the Persian tribal system has been the
> great fragmentation of the tribes ... due mostly to the
> broken nature of the mountain terrain, that lies behind
> the disorder, ... and not to the innate wickedness of
> the inhabitants. (Naval Intelligence Handbook)[1]

During the period of the Allied occupation, apart from the Kurds,
the two largest, most powerful tribes of western Persia were the Luri-
speaking Bakhtiari and the Turki-speaking Qashgai to their south.[2] These
were the two Persian tribes which, together with a small but extremely
fierce Zagros tribe called the Boir Ahmedi, fully and actively supported
the German cause until the strategic *Wende* (turning point) of the Second
World War in late 1942/early 1943. From then on, with a handful of idle
or incompetent SS parachutists and an equally disengaged Abwehr spy
on their territory,[3] their tribal leaders grew increasingly less sanguine
about the performance of the Wehrmacht to the north and ever more
aware that no Axis military force would invade Persia and topple
the shah. Clearly, their admiration for the Nazi Führer was never
ideological, but purely opportunistic and transitory. They had obviously
been promised that they would achieve greater political autonomy if
ever the Germans gained control of the country and the central government, especially since Berlin had prefabricated a quisling government
ready to install, with the younger brothers of the supreme leader of
the Qashgai at its head. Essentially, these tribes needed gold and guns,
and as long as the Nazis promised both, they were beholden to Nazism.
However, they would just as readily have accepted such support from
any patron, provided he delivered the goods, and this Hitler failed to do.
So, by the early spring of 1944, both the Bakhtiari and the Qashgai made

their peace with the British and the central government, surrendering their former German 'guests' who had by then become virtual prisoners.

Both the Bakhtiari and the Qashgai lived within virtually autonomous tribal confederations under the authority of their paramount tribal chiefs called *ilkhans*. The tribes existed essentially to protect their interests, members, and property in areas where law and order were not ensured by the Persian gendarmerie or army, from whom they frequently even had to protect themselves. Another major leadership responsibility of the *ilkhans* was the seasonal migration of their flocks, a complicated process which required considerable organization and discipline. The disadvantage of the Persian tribal system was that the tribes were completely fragmented and lacked any central tribal or intertribal authorities to maintain order and to deal with the central govenment, either cooperatively or on an adversarial basis. Historically, the power of the *ilkhans* had generally sufficed to prevent all-out internecine warfare, but local feuds and cattle-raiding remained a persistent problem.[4]

Feuding among the restive Bakhtiari greatly weakened their potential effectiveness and reliability as a subversive force. The Germans must have realized this; it is likely one of the reasons they preferred to work with the Qashgai, who were by contrast a monolithic tribal entity. They were also more autonomous than the Bakhtiari, whose *ilkhans* were generally subject to the approval, and even the appointment, of the shah. Rivalry was inherent in the structure of Bakhtiari society, which pitted common tribesmen (*rayats*) against the ruling *khans*, who formed a separate clan, and the *khans* themselves against each other, especially when an *ilkhan* died. Among the *rayats* analogous rivalries caused fragmentation when a *kalantar* (clan leader) died: traditionally, his sons would set up as rivals and quarrels would ensue. In addition, blood feuds were caused in the migration season by conflicts over loot, which stirred up deadly enmity among the tribes and clans. Also, the tactical mobility of Bakhtiari tribesmen was limited because they would not enter the territory of those with whom they had a feud.[5] Apart from Operation DORA, the scheme extemporized by Franz Mayr in June 1943 to divert two of the idle FRANZ parachutists from Tehran to an area near where the TIR Lend-Lease route ran through tribal territory, neither Mayr, Berthold Schulze-Holthus, Abwehr II, nor Amt VI made any direct attempt during the war to enlist the services of the Bakhtiari, preferring instead to work with the more dependable Nasir Khan and his Qashgai confederacy. The wisdom of this choice is borne out by the fact that, from the moment the leader of Operation DORA, Günther Blume, reached tribal territory, he immediately found himself involved in a typical Bakhtiari feud between two *khans*, one of whom, Abdul Kasim Khan Bakhtiari, sought to exploit Blume's operation as a means of extorting weapons from the Germans to use against his uncle with a simple ultimatum: no arms; no support.[6]

By April 1944, after Berthold Schulze-Holthus had been captured and interrogated, Joe Spencer was in a position to write the definitive document that identified post-factum the three operational channels that he had finally differentiated. His masterly Counter-Intelligence Summary No. 23 of 13 April 1944[7] was a 26-page compendium of operational intelligence and counterintelligence that included a lengthy excerpt from Schulze-Holthus's diary, describing the Abwehr major's experiences as a 'guest' of the bellicose, brigandish Boir Ahmedi.[8] Once Spencer had managed, with the aid of Schulze-Holthus's evidence, coupled with a reassessment of that of Franz Mayr, to disentangle the overlapping elements of the fifth-column, quisling, and tribal channels, as well as the overlapping competencies of Abw I M, Abw I L, Abwehr II, and Amt VI, he could confidently assert that Persia had undoubtedly become a target for joint Abwehr–SD operations. Initially, according to Spencer, it had been a haphazard growth, but the 'admirable' initiative shown by Mayr (SD) and Schulze-Holthus (Abwehr) in dividing their interests into two separate channels – Mayr's fifth column based in Tehran and Isfahan, and Schulze's tribal liaison based in southwestern Qashgai territory – had ultimately shown Berlin the path to interservice cooperation, however fraught with contentious rivalry. Therefore two separate Abwehr–SD missions were sent to Persia: one to support Mayr and the fifth column (FRANZ) and another to support Schulze-Holthus and the Qashgai tribe (ANTON). Later, Mayr sent two of the FRANZ personnel south to join the Bakhtiari (DORA) as a sabotage initiative. What struck Spencer as absurd, however, was the fact that the original purpose of both the FRANZ and ANTON missions somehow became corrupted and transformed before they left Germany into sabotage rather than support operations. He interpreted this – accurately – as evidence of the declining influence of Gerhard Putz and Abwehr II, and the likelihood that Persia had become 'almost entirely an SD commitment'.[9]

For two reasons the head of Abwehr II Orient, Gerhard Putz, was not interested as much in the FRANZ mission as in ANTON: first, because the latter joint operation, though led by an SD officer (Martin Kurmis), was intended to support an Abwehr officer (Berthold Schulze-Holthus); second, because Putz had heavily invested in the interests of his two young Persian protegés, the Qashgai Brothers,[10] because of Abwehr II's desire to foment tribal unrest and to use Qashgai tribesmen to sabotage

Figure 4.1   Baradaran Qashgai: Nasir Khan and his younger brothers. From (l) to (r):
Nasir, Khosrow, Huseyin, and Mansour.
Source: unknown.

the TIR. Consequently, notwithstanding the fact that, once in Turkey, Mohammad Vaziri provided the only link between the brothers in Turkey and Mayr in Persia, this mattered little to Putz, as he was more concerned about tribal affairs than an urban fifth column led by an SD officer. This was of course fortunate for Putz, since he probably had no inkling that Vaziri was completely compromised and had become a Soviet penetration agent. Putz's Abwehr II branch also had no connection with the quislings being run by Werner Schüler of Abwehr I naval intelligence nor with those controlled by Roman Gamotha of Amt VI. Unlike those (inactive) Persian quislings of the 'quisling channel', who were isolated from Tehran politics and consequently of no use (other than perhaps for progaganda purposes) as proxies until some time in the future when they might be activated and transferred to Persia, the two young 'crown princes' of the Qashgai tribe, Mohamed Huseyin Solat Qashgai (MHQ) and Melek Mansour Solat Qashgai (MMQ), known commonly as *Baradaran Qashgai* (the Qashgai Brothers), were 'live' at the epicentre of the 'tribal channel'.[11] They were actively connected via Turkey with their brothers Nasir Khan Qashgai and Khosrow Khan Qashgai in Fars, and quasi-umbilically with their mother, the formidable Khadijeh Bibi Khanum Qashgai. This is not to say that the brothers had not been nominated as members of Schüler's proposed quisling government; however, Joe Spencer rightly chose to focus on their function in the tribal, not the quisling channel, for that was where their true potential lay as influencers of Nasir Khan and as bargaining chips. The trick was to maintain a balance between the official line of British support for the shah and the central government on the one hand, and on the other an innovative, supportive approach to relations with an *ilkhan* who had suffered terribly at the hands of Reza Shah and had supported Hitler and the Nazi cause since the beginning of the war, and with a mother who ardently wished to have her beloved sons return home after a 12-year absence abroad, which only the British could facilitate.

One of the catalysts for Spencer's interest was the fact that, unlike other Persian emigrés from less privileged backgrounds, the Qashgai Brothers had been educated at the American College in Tehran,[12] had once been anglophiles, and had British connections, making them potentially more susceptible than any other quislings to British influence, doubling, and playback. In 1931, after their father had been imprisoned and executed by Reza Shah, the brothers had been sent by their mother to a private school in Bournemouth for 18 months to improve their English. Remaining in England, they then read agriculture at Reading University, transferring two years later to Magdalen College, Oxford. Because MHQ suffered in England from severe asthma, he had moved to Geneva in August 1935, with the intention of later emigrating to California where the climate would be more suitable. After moving to Montreux and Glion a few months later, MHQ was joined by MMQ and some friends. At the end of December 1935, they all drove to Munich and Berlin, where MMQ left MHQ, who wished to undergo further medical treatment in the German capital, and returned to Oxford.[13] For the next four years, the brothers lived apart. MMQ continued his studies at Magdalen until he ran out of money. MHQ studied commerce at Berlin University, had ample funds, and enjoyed a dizzying round of cabarets, cafés, cinemas, and dances, the cost of which ultimately led him to abandon his studies and turn to importing

Qashgai carpets from his brother Khosrow instead, from which he made about 60,000 Reichsmarks. In July 1939, MMQ joined MHQ for a German summer holiday, only to be cut off from England by the outbreak of war in September.[14]

MMQ was first approached directly and unsuccessfully by the Abwehr (probably by Abw I L; possibly even by Bechtle or Schulze-Holthus) in early May 1940. As a neutral, MMQ was asked to accept an assignment to proceed to France and obtain information about French airfields, with the assistance of certain Persians already in France. He was also asked to conceal the approach from his brother. MMQ declined, even when another equally blunt approach was made five days later. It was not until October 1941 that the brothers were contacted in a much more sophisticated manner by a very differently managed Abwehr branch, Abwehr II, in the person of Hans-Otto Wagner (aka Dr Wendel), who was Gerhard Putz's right-hand man responsible for Persian operations. This highly intelligent man disappeared without trace after his transfer from Militärisches Amt C (Mil C) to Militärisches Amt D (Mil D) W (Leitstelle West) in late 1944. However, a recent publication has revealed that Hans-Otto Wagner survived the war: he was captured in France by the Americans and transferred (as one of the so-called 'hillbillies') to the secret German Military Document Section (GMDS) at Camp Ritchie, MD, where he assisted in the joint American-British-Canadian Hill Project, processing captured Oberkommando der Wehrmacht (OKW) and Oberkommando des Heeres (OKH) documentary material between October 1945 and April 1946 in an attempt to improve Anglo-American intelligence organization and techniques in the context of a potential war against the Soviet Union. By the end of June 1946, all the GMDS hillbillies had been repatriated to Germany, where they were exempted from mandatory denazification and absorbed under amnesty into civilian society. At this point we again lose sight of Wagner, who probably returned to his native Cologne; it is possible that he subsequently worked for the Gehlen Organization.[15]

At Hans-Otto Wagner's office, the two young brothers were introduced to Gerhard Putz, and it was arranged that they should be granted visas for a one-month trip to Paris, purely for enjoyment. Returning from their holiday, now squarely in the Abwehr's debt, the brothers invited Putz and Wagner to visit them at their flat, and a purely social visit took place, still with no mention of secret work. Not until February 1942 was MHQ asked by Putz to help him screen some Persians in Germany who had volunteered to fight on the Russian front. From then on, gradually, subtly, and with far greater professionalism than Abw I L,

Putz and Wagner reeled the brothers in, flattering them, using them as consultants, and even involving them in interservice planning meetings with Kurt Schuback of the Amt VI Persia desk (though he appeared in mufti, deliberately obscuring his SS identity). In early May 1942, another one-month pleasure excursion to Paris was arranged, after which Putz and Wagner pressed home their advantage and asked the brothers to undergo military training – without taking the Hitler oath, which the brothers had previously baulked at – and they consented. After three weeks' basic training at Abwehr II's Hochwalde North Camp, Meseritz (now Międzyrzecz, Poland), they were commissioned as army lieutenants and sent in August 1942 to Lagow (now Łagów, Poland) for three further weeks of training. During this time, they visited the Freikorps Iran (FKI) in training at Meseritz (also meeting the Indian National Army [INA] commander, Subhas Chandra Bose), but they were never asked to join the FKI, as Putz and Wagner clearly had other things in mind for them. After that, the brothers were not required to perform any further military duties, and in September they resumed their hedonistic existence as Berlin playboys.[16] By now, Gerhard Putz had become their genuine friend; the brothers enjoyed all kinds of privileges, they were treated socially as royalty, and they were paid the princely sum of one million Reichsmarks.[17]

By the end of autumn, no doubt having become somewhat jaded by their idleness, the brothers' thoughts turned to Persia, and they resolved that MHQ should travel to Turkey in order to arrange for their return home. Putz made all the necessary visa and travel arrangements; MHQ departed for Istanbul at the end of November, returning to Berlin in early March 1943. But things had changed significantly for the Qashgai Brothers when MHQ encountered Parvis Wahabzadeh, a successful young Persian merchant and consular diplomat, in Istanbul in November 1942. Wahabzadeh was fundamentally pro-British, though disaffected since the 1941 invasion, and he had occasionally run errands in Turkey for the Abwehr. However, he was a strong advocate for tribal reconciliation and Persian unification. He had lived in England in 1936–39, had known the brothers there, and instantly advised MHQ that he and his brother should cease their pro-German activities and make an approach to the British passport control officer, Arthur Whittall (who was MI6 of course). Wahabzadeh recommended that the brothers should seek permission from Whittall to return to Qashgai territory, where they could help the British security forces maintain order amongst the tribes. This was of course shortly after the Allied victory in the Western Desert and shortly before the catastrophic German failure at Stalingrad: the writing was definitely on the wall, and Wahabzadeh clearly felt that the brothers were backing the wrong horse, and that it was high time for them to change sides, though he himself did not stop working for the Germans until August 1943. Not long after that, on his way ostensibly for business reasons from Ankara to Baghdad, Wahabzadeh was intercepted and detained at Aleppo, where he confessed his German allegiance under interrogation and furnished a great deal of information about the Qashgai Brothers and various Axis activities in Turkey. Notwithstanding his diplomatic status, the considerable pressure exerted on his behalf by the Persian government, and his generally cooperative attitude under interrogation, Wahabzadeh was detained until after the war.[18]

There was much shuttling between Istanbul and Berlin throughout 1943, which partially reflects the state of indecision about their loyalties in which the brothers found themselves. In January/February, and then in May, their two attempts to approach the British in the person of Arthur Whittall were rebuffed; consequently, disillusioned, they began to find themselves drawn into an unwanted, uneasy relationship with Heinz Gräfe and Kurt Schuback of Amt VI, now openly wearing their SS uniforms. Full of *Schadenfreude*, the two Amt VI officers had just completed their hostile takeover of Putz and Wagner's ANTON mission to the Qashgai, converting it into an SD sabotage operation, and they now desperately needed the brothers' tribal expertise. Courageously, the brothers did nothing to disguise their opposition to Gräfe's plan, as they realized it would cause trouble for their tribe. Meanwhile, Gerhard Putz, anxious to protect the brothers from Gräfe's clutches, willingly and efficiently cut all the red tape for them, enabling them to travel freely between Germany and Turkey. However, during the brothers' ultimate stay in the Reich between June and September/October 1943, Putz could protect them no longer. During a visit to Bohemia, they were arrested by the Gestapo and imprisoned in Karlsbad (now Karlovy Vary, Czech Republic) in a jail that was overcrowded with Czechs and other foreigners. The brothers prepared to face the worst, for they imagined that Nasir Khan had taken action against the ANTON group, and that they would be punished accordingly. After their release, probably achieved with considerable difficulty by Putz, the Abwehr colonel told the brothers that they were in great danger and must leave Germany as soon as possible, and they readily agreed. Gräfe now regarded them as hostages, and had instructed Putz to ensure that one brother always remained in Germany at any given time. Ignoring Gräfe's orders at great personal risk, Putz obtained exit visas for both brothers, permitting MHQ to escape to Turkey in September and MMQ in October 1943.[19]

It was a courageous act of defiance for which Gerhard Putz may well have forfeited his life,[20] though some have suggested that he may have been executed after 22 July 1944 because of his close friendship with Georg Hansen, the true architect of Stauffenberg's attempt to assassinate Adolf Hitler, yet Putz's name is not to be found among the lists of those executed in the wake of the failed coup attempt. Directly subordinate to and intimate with Abwehr II chief Erwin Lahousen, Gerhard Putz belonged to the loyal cadre of 'Canaris men' who carried out deliberate, systematic *Gegenarbeit* (resistance work) and *optimistische Irreführung* (optimistic deception) vis-à-vis Keitel's OKW, Jodl's Army General Staff, and Wehrmacht field commanders, as was expected and demanded of them by the admiral.[21] Certainly, at some time before the end of 1943, no longer protected at the Tirpitzufer by Lahousen, who had voluntarily transferred to the Russian front, Putz seems to have been posted from Berlin back to Vienna – where he had begun the war at the Abwehr station (Ast Wien)[22] – presumably at the instigation of the SD or possibly at his own request, as his family lived there. This transfer of course distanced Putz from the epicentre of the coup plot, which may have been to his advantage; however, no record can be found of Gerhard Putz's death, nor of where, how, or why he died, or whether he was even still alive in July 1944. All that we know for sure is that his name vanishes from the files in early 1944.

In mid-December 1943, Putz travelled most unexpectedly from Vienna to Istanbul for no apparent reason other than to ensure that all was well with his young Qashgai friends and to take them shopping. The fact that, at the same time, he informed them of Heinz Gräfe's presence in Turkey a few days earlier suggests that Putz genuinely feared that Gräfe was menacing the brothers, whom he wished to protect from the SS. Before the brothers had left Berlin, Putz had had to warn them not to do anything that might indicate their hostility to the Germans, such as revealing their intention to defect and return to Persia, as the SD would not hesitate to assassinate them.[23] This was the last time that the Qashgai Brothers would see their patron alive; to their subsequent regret, because they were already in negotiations with the British, they had felt embarrassed by Putz's visit and had refused to be seen with him in public. Such was their guilt about this behaviour that, after Putz's departure, they sent some Turkish chocolates to him in Vienna by way of apology. No doubt in deference to the colonel's advice that they keep a low profile in Turkey, it was not until January 1944 that the brothers, having finally severed their ties with the Abwehr, decided to make a renewed attempt to return to Persia, even cabling the shah himself about their predicament.[24] In mid-February, they received a letter through British diplomatic channels from their mother, Bibi Khanum Qashgai, in which she informed them of the arrangements she had made with the British authorities for them to return to Persia, where they would be left unmolested. The brothers immediately contacted Arthur Whittall, informing him of the letter and placing themselves under British orders. Doubtless acting on instructions received from MI6, Whittall raised no objections and granted them the necessary visas. The Qashgai Brothers finally left Istanbul for Persia on 16 March 1944, arriving in Aleppo two days later.[25]

Whilst the British had every intention of honouring the agreement DSO Persia had made with Nasir Khan and Bibi Khanum, they nevertheless submitted MHQ and MMQ not just to the routine SIME screening process at the Aleppo CEV described in Chapter 10, but they flew them to Cairo for detailed interrogation at Combined Services Detailed Interrogation Centre (CSDIC) Maadi. Interrogated separately, MHQ was found to be more informative than MMQ, probably because he had spent significantly more time in Germany than his brother; consequently, he seemed to know more about the Abwehr. However, once the interrogations had been completed, the brothers' evidence was found to be so consistent that only one report was needed to summarize the results. The verdict was generally positive, as the brothers appear to have been entirely cooperative, though perhaps a little cautious about the possibility of implicating themselves. They claimed that their only reason for remaining in Germany for so long and for cooperating with Abwehr II had been the bad relationship between the shah and their brother Nasir Khan. Soon after the brothers' arrival in Cairo, on 23 March 1944, Berthold Schulze-Holthus and the ANTON group were handed over to DSO by Nasir Khan, leaving the SIME interrogators a mere week in which to complete their detailed interrogation of the Qashgai Brothers.[26] On 31 March, after a 12-year exile, they arrived from Cairo in Tehran, where they were further interrogated by DSO for two days and were then released to rejoin their tribe on 3 April 1944.[27] When they reached Shiraz, they underwent a brief final interrogation by Major R. Jackson, the local ALO (who was probably also MI6), which added little to what they had already revealed in Cairo and Tehran.[28]

Once the brothers had originally reached neutral Istanbul, thinking that they had discovered an oasis of calm far from the Machiavellian emigré politics and relentless Allied air raids in Berlin, they found themselves instead catapulted into a hotbed of Nazi intrigue and international espionage.[29] They faced considerable pressures to prosecute both German and Allied causes, though their real interests lay simply in escaping Germany and returning to their tribe. Apart from the ministrations of Gerhard Putz – who had arranged their exit visas to the chagrin of Amt VI, promoting Abwehr II interests whilst acting supportively as a genuine friend – the brothers also had to resist at least two overtures from the Soviets. The first contact was made through one Moussa Sultanzadeh, who wanted the brothers to return to Persia via the Soviet-controlled northern route instead of through Syria. MHQ replied that, as his tribe was in southern Persia, he thought the idea impractical. The second approach, also rejected, with a similar offer of Soviet assistance, was made in January 1944 by Mohammad Vaziri, posing as Gholam Reza Abbassian. The brothers must have thought the offer curious, if not suspicious, coming from a self-declared SD agent.[30]

At first the brothers thought that Vaziri simply wanted money, but he was well dressed and wore gold. He talked a great deal about Franz Mayr and appeared to be very much against him, but paradoxically pro-German, asserting that Mayr had betrayed the German cause. Of course, this was typical of Vaziri, who seems to have been skilled at leaving people with the impression that he was not working for anyone other than the Germans.[31] After the war, some at DSO remained unconvinced about the genuineness of Vaziri's apparent conversion to the Stalinist cause – like Dick Thistlethwaite for instance, who thought that Vaziri was probably 'quadruple-crossing' everyone, though by then Thistlethwaite's was clearly a minority opinion, especially since Spencer's Russian counterpart, Grigori Asaturov, had officially claimed Vaziri as one of his agents as early as September 1943.[32] Not receiving any assent from the Qashgai Brothers, Vaziri called on them a second time, now accompanied by a blond German called Müller (probably Kunz Müller of Abw II SO, who also attempted unsuccessfully to recruit Vaziri's close associate, Firuz Khalilnia, and who was also presumably a Soviet agent),[33] and together they made a revised offer to the brothers. Vaziri said that he was forming a 'Persian Nationalist Society' in Istanbul and asked them to join. Both brothers hedged at this proposal, and declined Vaziri's subsequent offer to provide them with funds and introduce them to the German ambassador, Franz von Papen. From then on, whenever the brothers met Vaziri in the street, he would always wink at them, as if there were some secret understanding among the three. Eventually the brothers had to ask him to give up the habit, and that was the last they saw of Vaziri, who left Turkey for Switzerland and

Germany on 27 February 1944. Such, then, was the tenuous link that Joe Spencer was able to construct between the tribal and fifth-column channels, a link embodied only by the brief and nonproductive interface between the Qashgai khans and the man (Vaziri) who had once conceived and organized Franz Mayr's *Melliun*, but who had by late 1943/early 1944 hitched his wagon to Stalin's train, and whose duplicitous overtures the young brothers were wise to reject.

In January 1944, Joe Spencer noted a decline in Qashgai influence and a corresponding stiffening in the attitude of the Tehran government towards the problem of the tribes. He thought that the reason for this change in Qashgai prestige was probably that powerful interests in the capital and the provinces, who had formerly made good use of the Qashgai for their various intrigues, had now dropped them. However, another possible explanation was that the Qashgai Brothers had become better disposed towards the British, and their defection might have been considered regrettable in the eyes of those in Persia for whom pro-British sympathies were not a matter for congratulation.[34] Spencer also realized that the brothers were seriously compromised unless they could come to terms with him.[35] From at least as early as March 1943, he had possessed full knowledge of their history from childhood onwards, including their activities in England, Germany, and Turkey, right up to their current situation in Istanbul, where their movements, activities, and communications were under constant surveillance. Spencer was fully aware, for instance, that Gerhard Putz had twice met with the brothers during his surprise visit to Istanbul in mid-December 1943.[36] All that remained unknown was the nature of the instructions Putz had given them, for on 8 January 1944, the brothers made their move. They cabled the shah directly from Istanbul, as follows: 'We beg Your Majesty ... to issue necessary instructions so that we your servants may be able to return to our sacred country and serve Your Majesty under your care and orders'.[37]

The question remained: was this move in spite of their final meeting with Gerhard Putz, or because of it? Could it be that Putz, who – it must be remembered – was intimately associated with Abwehr resisters like Georg Hansen, in fact advised the brothers to stop working for the Nazis and defect to the British? Did Putz subsequently lose his life at the murderous hands of the SS, not just because – as has been suggested – he had originally allowed the Qashgai Brothers to leave Germany, but because he had actually connived at or even engineered their desertion to the Allied cause? One suspects that, had Gerhard Putz not had a family to support and protect from the Vienna Gestapo, he himself might have defected to the Allied side whilst visiting Turkey. Even more telling

Jm Namen
des
Deutschen Volkes
erteile ich

dem Major

Gerhard   P u t z

die Genehmigung zur Annahme

des Offizierkreuzes

des Königlich Ungarischen Verdienstordens.

Berlin, den   19.November 1941

Der Führer und Reichskanzler

Figure 4.2 Decorated spymaster: Gerhard Putz receives a medal from the Führer. Award of the highest Hungarian decoration for military service, signed by Adolf Hitler.
Source: Ms.47.92, Brown University Library.

is the strong possibility that Putz may have been a Jew, which would have made his position with the Abwehr (and that of his family) less and less secure after the departure of Erwin Lahousen for the Russian front in mid-1943 and with the increasingly vindictive stranglehold of Amt VI on Abwehr II planning and operations. At Brown University there exists a certificate awarding Major Gerhard Putz the Officer's Cross of the Royal Hungarian Order of Merit on 19 November 1941, together with the curatorial note: 'this was the last award given to a Jew before the purge'.[38]

Notes

1. United Kingdom, Naval Intelligence Division, *Persia*, Middle East Intelligence Handbooks 1943–1946, 5 (Gerrards Cross: Archive Editions, 1987), 338.
2. Ibid., 337–8. Enlightening information on contemporary indigenous perspectives and policies is to be found in Stephanie Cronin, *Tribal Politics in Iran: Rural Conflict and the New State, 1921–1941* (London: Routledge, 2006), 191–205. For specific information about the Qashgai, in addition to Schulze-Holthus, *Daybreak*, see Lois Beck, *The Qashqa'i of Iran* (New Haven, CT: Yale University Press, 1986); Oliver Garrod, 'The Nomadic Tribes of Persia Today', *Journal of the Royal Central Asian Society* 33, no. 1 (January 1946): 32–46, and 'The Qashgai Tribe of Fars', *Journal of the Royal Central Asian Society* 33, no. 3 (July 1946): 293–306; Pierre Oberling, *The Qashqa'i Nomads of Fars* (The Hague: Mouton, 1974), and 'Qashgai Tribal Confederacy', ELXAN (7 January 2004). For more about the Bakhtiari, see Gene R. Garthwaite, 'The Bakhtiyari Ilkhani: An Illusion of Unity', *International Journal of Middle East Studies* 8, no. 2 (April 1977): 145–60. An interesting contemporary photo-essay about the Qashgai is to be found in '*Life* goes on a Migration with Persian Tribesmen', *Life* 21, no. 6 (29 July 1946): 99–105. See also various index entries in *NSW*, 271–86.
3. See *NSW*, 177–9 about the DORA team with the Bakhtiari from 28 June 1943 until 29 August 1943 (Günther Blume [Waffen-SS] and Ernst Köndgen [Abwehr II]); see *NSW*, 182–9 about the ANTON team (Martin Kurmis [Amt VI], Kurt Piwonka, and Kurt Harbers [Waffen-SS]) with the Qashgai from 17 July 1943 until 23 September 1943 and subsequently with the Boir Ahmedi from then until March 1944, together with Berthold Schulze-Holthus [Abw I L]), who first joined the Qashgai in June 1942.
4. Unite Kingdom, Naval Intelligence Division, *Persia*, 337–8.
5. Ibid., 339–41.
6. *NSW*, 178.
7. KV 2/1485, TNA.
8. Anyone wishing to construct a more detailed narrative of Persian tribal affairs between June 1942 and July 1945 should consult the CICI tribal and political intelligence summaries in WO 208/1567–1569, TNA.
9. Defence Security Office, CICI Persia, Counter-Intelligence Summary No. 23, 13 April 1944, KV 2/1485, TNA.
10. Full details of the Qashgai Brothers may be found in SIME Report No. 3, Dates of interrogation: 22, 23–29 March 1944, KV 2/1941, TNA.
11. There exist numerous inconsistent spellings of their names in the records. The acronyms preferred here were formulated by DSO Persia, Conversation with Mohammed Hussein [*sic*] Qashgai, 23 August 1944, KV 2/1941, TNA.

12. Appendix C to SIME Report No. 4 on Parvis Wahabzadeh, 12 March 1944, KV 2/1941, TNA.
13. Ibid.
14. SIME Report No. 3, Dates of interrogation: 22, 23–29 March 1944, KV 2/1941, TNA.
15. See *NSW*, 163, For more about the Hill Project, see Derek R. Mallett, *Hitler's Generals in America: Nazi POWs and Allied Military Intelligence* (Lexington, KY: University Press of Kentucky, 2013), 140–67; for more about Hans-Otto Wagner, see ibid., 199; *NSW*, 49–54 passim.
16. SIME Report No. 3, Dates of interrogation: 22, 23–29 March 1944, KV 2/1941, TNA.
17. Extract from SIME Report No. 4 on Parvis Wahabzadeh, 12 March 1944, KV 2/1941, TNA.
18. See the Kew file on Parvis Wahabzadeh: KV 2/2640, TNA.
19. SIME Report No. 3, Dates of interrogation: 22, 23–29 March 1944, KV 2/1941, TNA.
20. See inter alia Wartime activities of the German diplomatic and military services during World War II, November 1949, US Army European Command, Intelligence Division, RG 263, Entry ZZ17, NARA.
21. See Bericht des Generalmajor Lahousen, Geheimorganisation Canaris, MSG 1/2812, Bundesarchiv-Militärarchiv, Freiburg-in-Breisgau (BArch-MArch).
22. Interrogation of Obstlt Fechner, 27 August 1945, 201692, CIA Research Tool (CREST), NARA.
23. Defence Security Office, CICI Persia, Counter-Intelligence Summary No. 23, 13 April 1944, KV 2/1485, TNA.
24. White to CICI Baghdad, 4 February 1944, KV 2/1941, TNA.
25. SIME Report No. 3, Dates of interrogation: 22, 23–29 March 1944, KV 2/1941, TNA.
26. Ibid.
27. Defence Security Office, CICI Persia, Counter-Intelligence Summary No. 23, 13 April 1944, KV 2/1485, TNA.
28. Interrogation Report No. 3, 7 April 1944, KV 2/1941, TNA. For more about Jackson, see Chapter 9.
29. See Barry Rubin, *Istanbul Intrigues* (New York: Pharos, 1992). But beware of Rubin's sole paragraph on Persia (*Intrigues*, 61), which is hopelessly skewed and inaccurate.
30. Extract from a report on a conversation with Mohammed Hussein Qashgai forwarded by DSO, CICI Persia, 23 August 1944, KV 2/1317, TNA; Vaziri correspondence, forwarded by DSO, CICI Tehran on 29 December 1944, KV 2/1317, TNA.
31. Extract from DSO Syria's Interrogation Report No. 1 on Firouz Khalilnia, 8 December 1945, KV 2/1317, TNA.
32. Thistlethwaite to Brodie, 4 January 1946, KV 2/1317, TNA; Soviet activities and the Vaziri case, Defence Security Office, DO/ASR/15, 6 August 1944, KV 2/1317, TNA; Thistlethwaite to Brodie, 4 January 1946, KV 2/1317, TNA; see also *NSW*, 114.
33. Intermediate interrogation report CI-IIR/44, 18 January 1946, RG 263, Entry ZZ18, Box 35, NARA. For the full narrative of Müller's attempt to recruit Khalilnia, see *NSW*, 90–91.

34. Extract from Security Summary No. 163, 5 January 1944, KV 2/1941, TNA.
35. Extract from SIME Quarterly Summary No. 163, 17 January 1944, KV 2/1941, TNA.
36. Ibid.
37. White to CICI Baghdad, 4 February 1944, KV 2/1941, TNA.
38. Adolf Hitler, Certificate awarding the Officer's Cross of the Royal Hungarian Order of Merit to Major Gerhard Putz, 19 November 1941, Ms.47.92, Hay Manuscripts, Brown University Library.

5
Quislings and Ordinary Persians

Not only had German agents organized a fifth column
from within, but the Abwehr and the Foreign Office in
the Reich itself had recruited a number of prominent
and dangerous Persian quislings in preparation for the
crossing of the Caucasus by the Wehrmacht. (History
of Combined Intelligence Centre Iraq and Persia)[1]

Of political intelligence pertaining to Persia, little may be learned from
this chapter. This is largely because the Abwehr and the SD ill-advisedly
concentrated their operational efforts not on the Persian polity itself,
but instead on an unruly handful of Persian emigrés within the Reich.
These exiles, mostly young students, spent the war squabbling over
their unrealistic dreams of governing Persia, encouraged by Berlin
spymasters whose aims seem to have been equally unrealistic. In this
chapter we will therefore seek to discover how and why the German
intelligence services came to waste scarce and valuable resources, for
years, on hypothesizing a regime change involving a small number of
ambitious but powerless men, out of touch with their occupied homeland, instead of establishing productive active-intelligence networks or
liaising effectively with their two agents in place, Franz Mayr (SD) and
Berthold Schulze-Holthus (Abwehr).

After the Allied invasion and occupation of Persia in 1941, the
Germans seem to have sustained little interest in fighting a secret war
on Persian soil, apparently because they had no residual vested interest
in the Persian state, the Persian economy, or Persian society. Indeed, up
to Stalingrad, Nazi interest was not in the Persian polity at all: it was in
subverting the Persian polity, which is something entirely different. After
Stalingrad of course, the Nazis lost sight of even that goal, as Franz Mayr

soon discovered when the FRANZ parachutists arrived in Tehran with only sabotage on their minds. True, there were some at the RSHA who thought it worthwhile to have Roman Gamotha and Amt VI C 14 dally with a handful of Persian quislings who could perhaps have formed some kind of ragtag opposition-in-exile, but there was no real prospect of their ever returning to Persia and forming a puppet government there, and the SD planners cannot have been so deluded as to have believed otherwise. Certainly not Gamotha himself, who very likely proposed the infeasible scheme disingenuously in order to justify his role as the Amt VI 'authority' on Persia, while of course squandering SD resources and postponing Operation NORMA indefinitely, to please his Soviet masters.[2]

Nevertheless, one of the Germans' most durable hypothetical operations, was the plan – using the tried and true Nazi paradigm of *Gleichschaltung* (forcible assimilation into pre-existing structures) – to designate and install a pro-Nazi quisling government in Persia. In Tehran, Joe Spencer was fully aware of the existence of the Berlin quislings and regularly kept Allied forces in the Middle East apprised of his awareness. He frequently reported on them in his periodic security summaries, generally under the rubric of 'The Persian Quisling Channel' (as opposed to 'The Tribal Channel' [i.e. Schulze-Holthus, Operation ANTON, and the Qashgai Brothers] and 'The Fifth-column Channel' [i.e. Mayr and the *Melliun* in Tehran]).[3] Faced with an amorphous mass of disparate Persian political groups, deconstructing the general security threat they posed into three distinct channels was a brilliant stroke. Having singled them out, far from being bemused by the farcical irrelevance of the quarrelsome quislings' political aspirations, Spencer rightly saw them as a specific potential security threat, were they to succeed in inserting a significant number of agents to set up active-intelligence networks, establish communications with Berlin, facilitate supply drops, sabotage infrastructure, or engage in political subversion – all measures that one might expect a serious revolutionary movement, backed by the German secret services, to take. However, as we shall see, only one or two Abwehr-controlled quislings managed to negotiate the frontier controls at Aleppo and reach Tehran; once there, they were unable to perform any of the above operational roles.

The grand revolutionary hypothesis was adopted originally by the Abwehr, and finally late in the war by the SD, long after any possibility of implementing such a scheme had expired. It is tempting to assume that the plan perhaps evolved through several clearly defined phases; however, largely because of the complex intrigues within the Persian diaspora in Germany, things were in reality very confused. No clear linear development of any one plan can be detected, but rather a number of disparate plans that cannot even be said to have formed a series. Why such planning was continued by the Abwehr after Stalingrad remains a conundrum; however, why Amt VI should have subsequently adopted a totally impractical quisling scheme at all is even more difficult to explain, except for the fact that it was Roman Gamotha, working against the RSHA, who appears to have invented or reinvented the plan and to have zealously promoted it – in his own best interests rather than in Persia's.

Early in 1944, immediately after the cancellation of the military sabotage operation codenamed NORMA, Gamotha was appointed by Schellenberg as head of a new Amt VI Persia desk (VI C 14) and was given the new task of forming within Germany a Persian shadow government-in-exile. In fact, there had been attempts to form a Persian shadow government from expatriates living in Germany since before the Anglo-Soviet invasion in 1941, the first being an initiative by the *Hizb Mille Iran* (Persian National Party [HMI]) led by Hassan Quraishi, Shahbahram Shahrukh, and the Qashgai Brothers. The aim of the party was 'to unite all Persians in Germany and form a free Persian government, recognized and supported by the Germans'. On the occupation of Persia by German forces this party would take over power and receive full support from the various high-ranking Persian officers and both the Qashgai and Bakhtiari tribes.[4]

In real terms, however, Joe Spencer at DSO Persia felt that few Persians realized what a German occupation would mean. According to him, the landowners and governing classes hoped that they would retain their privileged position and would be rewarded for rallying to Hitler's cause. The badly officered Persian army was smarting from the humiliation of the Allied invasion and occupation. Both the officer corps and the rank-and-file would probably satisfy their violent anti-Russian and less violent anti-British sentiments – as well as their general admiration for German military efficiency and past German successes – as soon as they felt that they could do so with impunity by actively opposing the Allies. The merchants and shopkeepers believed that a German occupation would mean a revival of trade. The very poor, who formed the majority of the Persian people, had 'been led to believe that the millenium would be at hand'.[5] At this stage in the war, few Persians (or British) were aware of the sheer horror of Nazi occupation as it was being experienced at first hand by the peoples of the southern Soviet Union, where (for instance) Crimean Tatars and Azeris were being summarily executed simply because, as Muslims, they were circumcised and were therefore ignorantly regarded by the SS and SD as Jewish. Stories of the Nazi rampage through the southern USSR and the maltreatment of Caucasians only began to reach the wealthier and better-informed Persian middle classes in the autumn of 1942. Little did ordinary Persians realize that not for long would their ideologically conceived 'pure Aryanism' offer any protection against the conditioned brutality and ignorance of such brainwashed Nazi occupiers.[6] But, as Spencer pointed out in March 1943, after the threat of German occupation had receded, 'not unnaturally those who wait for hours in bread queues and see well-fed British, Russian, Polish, and American soldiers prefer the Germans whom they have not yet seen'.[7]

By the summer of 1942, fence-sitting had become a national Persian pastime. With the German advances in southern Russia, pro-Axis feelings had begun to grow among ordinary Persians, at least in Tehran. Swastikas were chalked on walls, and some Persian men even began openly sporting little swastika badges on their lapels. On the other hand, now that a German invasion was within the bounds of possibility, and the prospect of Persia's becoming a battlefield had become more immediate, some who had scarcely concealed their pro-German feelings in the past were beginning to wonder whether a German occupation was perhaps so desirable. Having up to that point sympathized vaguely with the Axis, it slowly began to dawn on them that they might perhaps have something substantial to lose. Joe Spencer felt that, whilst further German pressure or success might lose the Allies some support, it might also thin the ranks of Axis supporters, up to a point, and might increase the numbers of those sitting uneasily on the fence awaiting the outcome of the campaign in Russia.[8]

Meanwhile, back in the German Reich, the quisling pecking order had been decided and announced by the *Hizb Mille Iran* as follows: MMQ (shah), MHQ (prime minister), Hassan Quraishi (foreign minister), Shahbahram Shahrukh (propaganda minister), and Ardishir Tarbiat (justice minister).[9] What was perhaps not apparent to the young rank-and-file HMI members, mostly students, was the extent to which they were being manipulated, and the fact that all the key personalities in the party were in the pay of the Abwehr. For instance, the HMI's original founder was Abwehr agent Hassan Quraishi, close business associate of the Qashgai Brothers, who liaised between Gerhard Putz and Hans-Otto Wagner of Abwehr II on the one hand and the young Persians on the other.[10] '[Quraishi] was in the habit of meeting all newly arrived Persians, and of obtaining any information from them which would be of use to the Germans. He passed this information to Putz and Wagner.'[11] Quraishi appears to have helped the Abwehr persuade various Persians to enlist in the German army; he also selected suitable Persians to work in the Persian department of Goebbel's propaganda ministry, headed by Shahbahram Shahrukh, another party leader. Shahrukh is described elsewhere as a discredited adventurer who was wanted in the Persian courts for embezzlement, and who had begun working for the Germans as early as 1939, when he was connected with the Siemens agency in Persia. It was there and then that he had first made the acquaintance of Werner Schüler of German naval intelligence (Abw I M). For some curious reason, Schüler came to trust implicitly the disreputable Shahrukh, who was known to have two German wives – one whom he married in Tehran, and one whom he married in Berlin – and came to depend heavily upon his advice in all matters concerning Persia. He even said of Shahrukh that he was 'an unusually gifted and ambitious man, who was better able to reconcile the mentality of the East with that of the West than any other Persian whom he knew'.[12] In Berlin, Shahrukh posed as an ardent nationalist in favour of a German victory, as he hoped in this way to realize his political ambitions in Persia.

The serious-minded Schüler, described as a normal, decent business-man, married with four children and 'not cut out for organizing espio-nage',[13] had been a carpet merchant in Tehran for seven years during the 1920s, and had been running the Abwehr naval-intelligence Orient desk since 1939. Consequently, Schüler seems to have felt that, as an old Persia hand and Farsi speaker, he was entitled to a preemptive, proprietary interest in Persian intelligence affairs. Consequently, he appears to have resented the sudden interest taken in Persia by Abw I L (Richard Bechtle) and Abwehr II (Gerhard Putz and Hans-Otto Wagner). The former because one of their officers, Berthold Schulze-Holthus, was marooned in Quashgai territory; the latter because the new Lend-Lease supply route from the Persian Gulf to the Soviet Union presented a tempting sabotage target. Because the tribal territory of the Qashgai was close to the main north–south railway (TIR), both Abw I L and Abwehr II wanted to make contact with the tribe. But Schüler felt that Persia was not suitable for active sabotage: the result would be negli-gible because there were insufficient opportunities for such acts. On the other hand, Abw I M were interested in establishing a naval active-intelligence service on the Persian Gulf, and even beyond.[14] The fact is that Schüler, who was also responsible for naval-intelligence operations in the Balkans, Turkey, and Italy, where he often went on field trips, seems to have taken very little interest in Persian operations, unless other branches of the Abwehr or Amt VI threatened to trespass on his territory or to become involved in quisling affairs.

Complicating this situation was the fact that Shahbahram Shahrukh saw himself as the future Shah and was disappointed with the HMI's appointments. Consequently, he founded his own *Iran Parastan* (IP) party in opposition to the HMI. Notwithstanding Schüler's complete confidence in him and reliance upon him for most of his valuable information on various Persian nationals,[15] the Qashgai Brothers maintained that Shahrukh would do anything for money and would turn to whomever could offer the most, even the Japanese 'if they were to come up with a dazzling enough offer'.[16]

However flawed their Persian protagonists and proxies, it certainly seems that the Abwehr had cornered this particular information and recruitment market to the exclusion of the SD. It was not until Roman Gamotha decided to breathe new life into the Free Persia movement early in 1944 that the Abwehr (and subsequently Mil D) lost the initiative. This explains why Gamotha quickly found himself in conflict with Werner Schüler of Abwehr naval intelligence (Abw I M), which had by then come to regard the Persian shadow government as its sole preserve.[17] Part of the problem for Abw I M, Abwehr II, and the SD was that they had great difficulty relating to the Persian psyche: the Persian expatriates thrived on political intrigue and drew the unsuspecting Germans into their tangled webs of nebulous and capricious ambition. Soon there were different factions all vying for plum positions in the future Persia. The conflicts among the expatriates were instantly transposed into corresponding conflicts within the German intelligence community, pitting one patron against another. In other words, far from manipulating the Persians, the Berlin spymasters were manipulated by them, or at the very least found it impossible to dominate their 'inferior' Persian proxies as they might have expected.

There were in fact significant numbers of young, unmarried Persian men living in Germany during the Second World War, most of whom wished to return to Persia. Some arrived in 1936, all of them orphans who had been brought up and educated at the Tehran Military School; another wave immigrated in 1940, sent to work and train in Germany by the Persian Ministry of Industry. For various reasons, both groups of young people ultimately became disillusioned and impoverished, making them easy prey for Nazi propagandists and recruiters who persuaded them that the Red Army was raping their mother country and that joining the German armed forces would guarantee their return to Persia and a chance to repel the Bolshevik invaders. When the ill-fated Freikorps Iran (Persian Free Corps [FKI]) was established in 1942, many young Persians enlisted, only to be discharged within nine months.

After Stalingrad, the German army had no further use for them, nor did they provide for them after the disbandment of the FKI. Consequently, many became unemployed, hungry, and increasingly desperate. The few who could return to Wehrmacht positions held before they joined the FKI were lucky; those who could return to their university studies also enjoyed some advantages. However, those who had left industrial jobs became destitute. It requires little imagination to realize that such men were potential Abwehr or SD recruits. And those who were politically engaged could be organized in a Free Persia movement such as Roman Gamotha apparently envisaged.[18] One Abw I M agent and former FKI volunteer, Ahmed Akbari, claimed that the FKI would never have existed had the Persian students not financed it themselves, which further explains their hardship after its dissolution.[19] One contemporary Tehran-based SOE officer commented not surprisingly that he viewed Persians who helped Germans not as criminals, but as dupes.[20]

Those originally designated to assume junior positions in a future Persian puppet government as envisaged by Abwehr II included certain Persians then living in Europe, most of them young men who had received or were currently receiving basic agent training (or special-forces training) from Abwehr II. In February 1942, Gerhard Putz read to MHQ a list of nine Persians who had volunteered to fight on the Russian front. In March 1943, those who still wanted to volunteer, after being told that they could not all expect to be officers, were sent to Meseritz for three to four months' training, along with 30 other Persians, 70 Germans, and 165 men of various Caucasian and central Asian nationalities, after which they were invited to continue with six months' further training, which would presumably be completed by January 1944.[21]

Planning for the SD quisling operation appears to have given Gamotha and his friend Pierre Sweerts, a Belgian Resistance plant at the RSHA, convenient excuses for travelling internationally, especially to Paris, where Gamotha had made contact with one Count Jean de Monçay of the so-called 'National Liberation Committee of Iran'.[22] The bogus 'count' was in reality none other than Reza Shah's exiled son-in-law, the highly intelligent, infinitely corruptible and criminal Muhammad-Husayn Ayrom, former Persian cossack and police commander, who had apparently paid cash for his grand title in neutral Switzerland or Liechtenstein, where he now lived in splendour.[23] In view of the SD duo's real, perverse reason for visiting Paris (black marketeering), it is probably significant that the general was himself a louche character: a notorious smuggler who had been forced to flee Persia and the wrath of

Reza Shah incurred by his large-scale smuggling operations.[24] After their Paris meeting in December 1943, Gamotha decided that Ayrom should head the SD quisling government, thus setting up a confrontation with Werner Schüler and his proposed shah, the equally flawed Shahrukh. Sweerts stated under interrogation at Camp 020 that both he and Gamotha were able to travel widely in Europe, providing them with ample blackmarketeering and smuggling opportunities, because after the cancellation of Operation NORMA they had 'little else to do'.[25] Possibly warned by Gamotha of the impending crackdown on their illicit activities, it was on one such trip to The Hague that Sweerts deserted to the Allies and was ultimately interrogated by MI5.[26] Certainly, it seems likely that Gamotha had no more need of Sweerts' help to run the Persian quislings, which must have become virtually a one-man operation of ever diminishing significance and relevance. It should be remembered that by the second half of 1944 Amt VI operations and the chain of command were already beginning to deteriorate and disintegrate. Officers were already preparing to run for cover; RSHA staff were generally becoming more and more preoccupied with the question of their own personal safety and welfare: how to survive the incessant air raids, how to protect their families, and how to find food and supplies. However, this also meant that Gamotha's quisling scheme and Gamotha himself became ever more dispensable. And, as soon as he had been spirited away in August 1944, under arrest and stripped of his rank, Gamotha's desk – and presumably his quisling operation – disappeared, as the 14 VI C desks were collapsed into four, including a new Near East desk (Amt VI C 3), which included responsibility for Persia.[27]

Of course, the question remains of why the SD leadership would have taken seriously Gamotha's assertion in the first place that it was necessary to establish a 'Free Persia' movement in Europe, when Germany was clearly no longer able to enter the region in force nor to influence Persian political affairs in any significant way. It is plain to see why Gamotha in his role as a Soviet agent might have wished to make mischief and hoodwink the SD or the Nazi leadership into accepting whatever preposterous schemes he could devise (or, in this case, resurrect). But why did Schellenberg and Kaltenbrunner, possibly even Himmler and Hitler, go along with it?

It is possible that Schellenberg – initially at least – saw the Persian quislings, especially the Qashgai Brothers, as potential factors in some future scenario involving British and/or Soviet interests in the region, and so he was disposed to delegate to Gamotha the task of surveilling and coordinating the unruly emigrés. At the time, Gamotha must have been desperate to find a project that would justify his continued presence at the RSHA. SD desk officers like him were all too aware that they could be transferred to the *Einsatzkommandos* or the eastern front at Schellenberg's merest whim. And, as a Waffen-SS officer with an impeccable military record, Gamotha may have felt more vulnerable than most. In his role as a Soviet agent, it was vital that he should remain close to the SD leadership, so the quisling scheme must have been all that Gamotha could find available to match his expertise and keep him in Berlin. As a measure of how defensive he had grown and how intense the debate about Persian quislings had become, it is worth noting that Gamotha went so far as to threaten Werner Schüler of Abw I M with arrest, simply because he was opposed to Gamotha's nominee, Ayrom, as quisling leader.[28] However, Werner Schüler resigned from his desk in June 1944 after what he himself described as 'a difference of opinion with the RSHA' and accepted a consular post in Turkey, not as far as we know as a direct result of Gamotha's threats, but because he had long considered the quisling plan to be ill-advised. Even before the mass arrests of Persian subversives in 1943 and 1944, Schüler considered that Gamotha's plans for a Free Persia movement in Europe would cause the German staybehinds and parachutists to lose all faith in a unified German policy on Persia.[29]

In fact, when interrogated by CSDIC in 1945, Werner Schüler maintained, perhaps disingenuously, that his original interest in exiled Persian nationalists was not political. With some support from the German Foreign Office, he had simply sought to recruit them as agents as part of his plan to establish a naval-intelligence service in Persia.[30] For example, some time in 1941–42, Schüler had been introduced to a Persian officer named Karagoezlu, who told him that he had been sent to Germany on behalf of a group of Persian officers to establish contact with the German military authorities. Karagoezlu, however, was hardly an ideal potential *V-Mann*: aged 60 already, he was more of a literary scholar than a soldier, controlled not by the Abwehr but by the German Foreign Office. Neverthelesss, once Schüler had acquired him and had obtained approval from his Abwehr superiors, he sent Karagoezlu on a relatively straightforward military active-intelligence mission to Tehran via the risky northern route through Azerbaijan and the Soviet zone in the summer of 1942 – despite objections from Shahbahram Shahrukh, who thought the plan too dangerous. Karagoezlu was to report back to Berlin (in person) after ascertaining whether German forces could count on the support of the Persian army if the Wehrmacht were to approach the northern border, and what Persian strength and equipment might be expected. Karagoezlu never reappeared in Berlin, and all contact with him was lost.[31]

The following year, Schüler made two further attempts to establish active-intelligence agents (Ahmed Akbari and Mohamed Akhundzade Salmassi) in Persia, but both men disappeared without trace. Schüler assumed that they had been intercepted and interned by the Allies somewhere between Aleppo and Tehran. In fact, Ahmed Akbari had found his way to Franz Mayr and had been sent by him with the SS DORA group to Bahktiari country, but never functioned as an effective Abwehr agent. He was arrested by DSO after their capture of Mayr. Salmassi, on the other hand, had indeed been intercepted by the British at Aleppo and was played back to Berlin as the notional agent KISS. The only other affair occurred in late 1943, when the Persian 'Black Eagle' nationalist movement contacted Shahbahram Shahrukh, seeking (unrealistically) German help to oust the Russians from Persian Azerbaijan. Schüler handed the matter over to Gerhard Putz of Abwehr II, who 'eventually dropped the affair'.[32]

From these failed initiatives, it seems clear that the relationship between Abwehr naval intelligence and the Persian quislings was military rather than political in nature. To this extent, Werner Schüler's clash with Roman Gamotha of the (political) SD over the question of Persian quisling leadership was doubtless caused because their interpretations of the fundamental purpose of cooperation with the exiles differed irreconcilably. It also provided Gamotha with an opportunity to be seen to be doing something useful – for once – in the interests of the SD, rather than procrastinating and dealing in the black market. The extreme nature of his threat to have Schüler arrested was probably deliberately calculated to attract as much attention as possible and to placate the SS. In other words, for Gamotha the quarrel with Schüler was probably nothing more than a smokescreen. Gamotha had no real interest in Persian nationalist causes; he was merely interested in prolonging his existence at Amt VI and saving his own neck. It is equally likely that Schüler's moves (claimed resignation from the Abwehr in the spring of 1944 and transfer to the Auslandsamt) were also contrived. They were probably not caused by Gamotha's threat at all but were deliberately staged by the Abwehr to mask Schüler's true role in Turkey as Kriegsorganisation Nahost (KONO) outstation head (with diplomatic cover as vice-consul in Izmir). It is even remotely possible that Schüler and Gamotha colluded in the deception.[33] Whatever his service status, Schüler admitted under interrogation at Camp 020 that whilst in Izmir he had undertaken active-intelligence work against the Allies (but not the Turks) for Erich Pfeiffer (head of KONO), thereby proving his disingenuousness.[34]

The very unsubstantiality of the quisling movement lent itself to Gamotha's purposes, for it enabled him to be seen undertaking an ostensibly grandiose scheme which he knew could neither be implemented nor have any material consequences. Gamotha clearly realized that it was no longer possible to recruit Persian agents within Persia, and that the only hope therefore of retaining some vestige of Nazi influence on political opinion in the region was to recruit agents outside the country, from within the Persian diaspora in Europe, to form a liberation movement, and to establish a shadow government, however ethereal. Perhaps he had convinced Walter Schellenberg that he could use the Persian expatriates as a subversive propaganda tool in some way – to bring pressure to bear on the occupying powers, especially the Russians, as they manoeuvred towards postoccupational realignment. Yet, cleverly, Gamotha seems to have convinced Schellenberg that such subversive objectives, probably best achieved through the newspapers and radio broadcasts, would necessitate another military mission, a successor to NORMA. Why else would the newly divorced Roman Gamotha have written in his marriage application of 22 March 1944:

> In mid-May, under orders of the Reichsführer-SS [Himmler], I am leaving as commander of *a special operation from which I shall be unable to return until the war is over*. I would, however, like to have a child with my future wife. I therefore request immediate approval, especially since General Dr Kaltenbrunner has also already agreed to officiate.[35]

In the absence of any further documentation concerning this new operation, only one hypothesis presents itself, namely that Gamotha was planning, as part of his cover, a mission that had little or nothing to do with the quisling plan – probably targeting the supply infrastructure in northern Persia, either the railway or the Caspian port installations. Had he not been removed from the RSHA, had he been able to continue with this scheme, one thing is certain: Gamotha would have used it as an opportunity to expend RSHA resources, and he would have done everything possible to prevent its actual implementation.

But what remains even more intriguing is the question of what motivated ordinary Persians to become involved and to choose sides in a war that had no intrinsic relevance to their daily lives in what was, technically at least, a neutral country – especially after Stalingrad, when it became abundantly clear which side was going to win. Sir Reader Bullard, who perhaps came to understand better than anyone what motivated Persians enduring the hardships of occupation and a wartime economy, wrote after the war: 'That all the Germans were eventually captured by the British Security Service reflects great credit upon Colonel E. L. Spencer and his officers.' Capturing German agents had given them nothing but satisfaction, but connected with it was a less pleasant duty: 'to prevent Persians, whether independently or in collusion with the Germans, from sabotaging the Allied war effort'.[36]

In this context of collusion, one contemporary Persian source, the Abwehr agent named Parvis Wahabzadeh, recruited by the Abwehr in December 1942, who later persuaded the Qashgai Brothers to desert the German cause and submit to British control, stated that Persians who worked to further the German cause did so for one or more of the following reasons: (1) financial gain; (2) privileges accorded to them by the Germans; and (3) idealism, usually found among students.[37] While the first and third reasons were universal and commonplace, the matter of privileges was unique to Persia and concerned favoured economic status and the granting of visas to Persian merchants, at least for as long as Persia (and Turkey) remained technically neutral. At a personal level, one of the most effective and least costly incentives was apparently the promise of permission to marry a German woman.[38] According to Gerhard Weinberg, Nazi racial policy actually prohibited marriage between (non-Aryan) Persians and (Aryan) Germans.[39] On the other hand, George Lenczowski, a former Free Polish diplomat in Tehran, wrote: 'To remove any causes for misunderstanding under the Nuremberg Racial Laws, a special decree of the Reich cabinet in 1936 exempted the Iranians as "pure Aryans" from their restrictive provisions.'[40] In other words, mixed marriages between pro-Nazi Persians and Germans seem to have been a 'grey' area that lent itself conveniently to pragmatic interpretation and manipulation by the secret services.

The possession of economic privileges facilitated the lucrative export of Persian goods (such as carpets) to Germany and all German-occupied countries. Under the Nazis, all imports were controlled by the Reichsstelle für den Aussenhandel (Reich Office of Foreign Trade [RfA]), which normally set both the import tax and the approved retail price. Any Persian exporter of course needed RfA authorization to do business with Germany; however, those with privileges, like the Qashgai Brothers, could obtain special RfA permits stamped *ohne Genehmigung* (without approval), allowing them to import and set their own prices freely, leading to huge profits. As citizens of a neutral, Allied-occupied country, transit (entry/exit) visas permitting entry to Germany or German-occupied countries were not normally granted to Persians, unless placed on the privileged list maintained by the German Foreign Office. The snag was that this list could not be accessed directly but only through the clandestine services: first, via the Abwehr; and then, the SD or, more specifically, the Gestapo (Amt IV). Thus, the German secret services were in a position to demand collaboration of any Persian who attempted to obtain such privileges. Finally, for the exceptionally privileged few, such as Wahabzadeh himself, was reserved the granting of a German diplomatic passport, but that only came to those who had, or claimed to have, strategic schemes to peddle. For instance, the Qashgai Brothers benefited more than any other Persian emigrés from their perceived influence in southwest Persia, their privileged status, their military rank, and their social position: both were Abwehr lieutenants and were addressed as *Fürst* (prince). Of course, their absurdly inflated 'royal' status belied the fact that Qashgai and Bakhtiari khans were more like feudal robber-barons than kings, but it permitted the brothers extraordinary access to high-priority military flights between Germany and Turkey whenever they wished. Thus they were able to escape the worst of the Allied air raids, flee to Turkey, and ultimately return to Persia, not as Nazi quislings but as princely prodigals and supporters of the Allied cause.[41]

The intriguing question of who was really deceiving whom or whose deception was the greater (that of the German secret services or that of the Persian quislings) remains moot. But both were undoubtedly eclipsed on a strategic scale by a handful of British officers in Cairo who formed a tiny clandestine military outfit called 'A' Force.[42]

Notes

1. The combatting of quislings, History of Combined Intelligence Centre Iraq and Persia, June 1941–December 1944, 15 December 1944, KV 4/223, TNA.
2. See *NSW*, 130–41, 204–8.
3. See Chapters 5, 4, and 3 respectively.
4. Information given by suspect enemy agent Tarbiat about his activities in Berlin during 1941–42 and his contact with Shahrokh [*sic*], enemy agent, and the Qashgai Brothers, also suspect, P1440, 14 April 1944, KV 2/1941, TNA.
5. Security Summary Middle East No. 85, 5 October 1942, WO 208/1561, TNA.
6. Bericht des Generalmajor Lahousen, Geheimorganisation Canaris, MSG 1/2812, BArch-MArch; Security Summary Middle East No. 81, 19 September 1942, WO 208/1561, TNA.
7. Appendix A to Security Summary Middle East No. 123, 19 March 1943, WO 208/1562, TNA.
8. Security Summary Middle East No. 67, 3 August 1942, WO 208/1561, TNA; Security Summary Middle East No. 71, 17 August 1942, WO 208/1561, TNA.

9. Information given by suspect enemy agent Tarbiat about his activities in Berlin during 1941–42 and his contact with Shahrokh [*sic*], enemy agent, and the Qashgai Brothers, also suspect, P1440, 14 April 1944, KV 2/1941, TNA.
10. For more about Quraishi (aka Gorechi, Goreshi, and Goreschi), see various reports in KV 2/1941, TNA.
11. Ibid.
12. Appendix D to FR 36, 28 January 1946, KV 2/2659, TNA.
13. According to Count Joseph von Ledebur, considered by CSDIC to be a walking 'Who's Who' of the Abwehr, in Personal characteristics of Schüler, Korvt-Kapt, Werner, KV 2/2659, TNA; for more about Ledebur as a reliable source, see R.W.G. Stephens and Oliver Hoare, eds., *Camp 020: MI5 and the Nazi Spies: The Official History of MI5's Wartime Interrogation Centre* (Richmond: PRO, 2000), 338–40.
14. Appendix D to FR 36, 28 January 1946, KV 2/2659, TNA.
15. Information given by suspect enemy agent Tarbiat, 14 April 1944, KV 2/1941, TNA.
16. CICI Counter-Intelligence Summary No. 23, 13 April 1944, KV 3/88, TNA. For more about Shahrukh, who was very influential in the Berlin diaspora but moved to Istanbul in 1943, see SIME Interrogation Report No. 3, 22, 23–29 March 1944, KV 2/1941, TNA.
17. CSDIC (WEA) BAOR final report on Gideon Richard Werner Schüler, 28 January 1946, KV 3/89, TNA.
18. CICI Counter-Intelligence Summary No. 23, 13 April 1944, KV 3/88, TNA.
19. Appendix A, CICI Counter-Intelligence Summary No. 24, 11 May 1944, KV 2/1485, TNA.
20. Christopher Sykes, *Four Studies in Loyalty* (London: Collins, 1946), 75. Extract reprinted by permission of Peters Fraser & Dunlop (www.petersfraserdunlop.com) on behalf of the Estate of Christopher Sykes.
21. SIME Interrogation Report No. 3, 22, 23–29 March 1944, KV 2/1941, TNA.
22. Extract from the MI5 Interim Interrogation Report on Pierre Marie Ernst Sweerts, 4 October 1944, KV 2/1492, TNA.
23. MI5 Interim Interrogation Report on Sweerts, 8 October 1944, KV 2/230, TNA.
24. For more about Ayrom (de Monçay) and his subsequent ill treatment by the SS, see Burke to Stephens, 9 August 1945, KV 2/272, TNA.
25. MI5 Interim Interrogation Report on Sweerts, 8 October 1944, KV 2/230, TNA.
26. Extract from interim report on Pierre Marie Ernst Sweerts, 4 October 1944, KV 2/1492, TNA.
27. Situation Report No. 8, Amt VI of the RHSA, Gruppe VI C, SHAEF Counter Intelligence War Room, 28 February 1946, RG 263, Entry ZZ17, Box 3, NARA.
28. See CSDIC (WEA) BAOR final report on Gideon Richard Werner Schüler, 28 January 1946, KV 3/89, TNA.
29. Ibid.
30. Appendix D to FR 36, 28 January 1946, KV 2/2659, TNA.
31. Ibid.; Appendix A to FR 36, 28 January 1946, KV 2/2659, TNA.
32. Appendix D to FR 36, 28 January 1946, KV 2/2659, TNA.

33. Appendix E to FR 36, 28 January 1946, KV 2/2659, TNA; cf. Extract from statements of Thomas Ludwig, 19 October 1945, KV 2/2659, TNA; War Room Summary on Korv. Kapt. Werner Schüler, Information given by Ledebur and Georgiades, KV 2/2659, TNA.
34. For more about Pfeiffer, see KV 2/267, TNA.
35. My italics. Verlobungs- und Heiratsgesuch, Roman Gamotha, Berlin-Grünewald, 22 March 1944, RS/B5043, Bundesarchiv Berlin-Lichterfelde (BArch).
36. Reader Bullard, *The Camels Must Go: An Autobiography* (London: Faber and Faber, 1961), 250.
37. SIME Report No. 4, 12 March 1944, KV 2/2640, TNA.
38. Appendix A, CICI Counter-Intelligence Summary No. 24, 11 May 1944, KV 2/1485, TNA.
39. Gerhard L. Weinberg, *Hitler's Foreign Policy: The Road to World War II 1933–1939* (New York: Enigma, 2005), 322–3.
40. George Lenczowski, *Russia and the West in Iran 1918–1948* (Ithaca, NY: Cornell University Press, 1949), 160.
41. SIME Report No. 4, 12 March 1944, KV 2/2640, TNA.
42. See *NSW*, 165, 223.

6
Strategic Deceivers

> The only purpose of any deception is to make one's
> opponent act in a manner calculated to assist one's
> own plans and to prejudice the success of his. In other
> words, to make him do something. ... Fundamentally
> it does not matter in the least what the enemy
> thinks; it is only what line of action he adopts as a
> consequence of his line of thought that will affect the
> battle. (Dudley Clarke)[1]

It has already been claimed in the Prologue that it was Archie Wavell who
provided the initial impetus for the organization of security intelligence in
the Middle East. It was also Wavell who first realized the vital contribution
that strategic deception could make to the successful conduct of military
operations in the Middle East and beyond. To this end, he appointed
Dudley Clarke to his Cairo staff in November 1940 to act as head of a
special section of intelligence for deception, which was constituted in
March 1941 as Advanced HQ, 'A' Force, a notional brigade of the Special
Air Service (SAS), which was at the time itself merely a notional force.[2]

By the summer of 1941, 'A' Force had assumed responsibility for
deception on the widest scale throughout the Middle East. This included
cover for troop and convoy movements, the creation and maintenance
of bogus units, and misleading information about British strength and
strategic intentions, using neutral Turkey as the principal channel for
contact with the Axis. In conjunction with the other agencies involved
in facilitating the passing of false information through double agents
(SIME [MI5] and ISLD [MI6]), the CHEESE source (which became the
codename for not one but a number of double agents) proved a particularly effective means of conveying deceptive intelligence to the

Germans between 1941 and 1945.[3] In fact, cooperation among the various agencies in the Middle East was exemplary: the misinformation passed through double agents was controlled, on the analogy of the Twenty (XX) Committee in London, by a number of 'Thirty (XXX) Committees' established throughout the Mediterranean and Middle East, increasing in number as Allied operations extended in scope. Eventually there would be 21 of them. Each consisted of a triumvirate, with an 'A' Force officer as chairman, an MI6 officer as secretary, and a third member from MI5. 'A' Force was responsible for general policy and for the text of the messages to be passed. As in Britain, MI5 ran the agents, providing case-officers and developing new channels. MI6 provided staff, communications, ciphers, and finance, and ran those agents who operated in territories not under the control of Allied forces. 'All these bodies worked as harmoniously together as could be expected.'[4]

It should be remembered that the Abwehr ENIGMA cipher was broken by Bletchley Park as early as December 1941.[5] The British were in fact reading both the Abwehr and the SD codes from 1941 onwards. The SD hand cipher was broken early in 1941 but was read less regularly than the Abwehr code.[6] From that moment on, 'A' Force (and SIME/CICI) were able to follow Abwehr planning and operations more or less on a daily basis. Astonishingly, they could identify and respond to the actions of any agent controlled by the Abwehr. As Tar Robertson, who spent the war at MI5, wrote long after the war to David Mure, who had served with Dudley Clarke:

> I have always said that we won the intelligence war in 1942. By having access to the thoughts of the Abwehr, the [German] armed forces, and even Hitler himself through ULTRA. ... The war was won by ULTRA and lost by the crass stupidity of Adolf. B1A and 'A' Force were just pawns, important ones, on a very large chessboard.[7]

Of equal importance was the fact that 'A' Force now had at their disposal a quality-control mechanism that permitted them to 'verify the credibility of their own double agents and see which of the messages they planted commanded credibility and which did not'. In other words, it was now possible to measure and exploit enemy fears and expectations fully and accurately.[8] Such knowledge of 'the trend of enemy anxiety' enabled 'A' Force 'to build up a fictitious and misleading structure and to represent Allied capabilities and intentions as very different from what they really were'. Thus, by March 1942, the notional order of battle in Persia had become an important component of a systematic plan for inflating

British strength throughout the Middle East. The overall scale of this comprehensive order-of-battle deception plan has been summarized as follows: 'A' Force created in 1942 one bogus armoured division (15th) and seven bogus infantry divisions (two of them Indian and one from New Zealand), as well as a bogus '25th Corps' headquarters. During the course of 1943 they were to add to this eight more infantry divisions (including two Polish and one Greek), three armoured and one airborne division, as well as a bogus army (12th) and another bogus corps headquarters (14th). Each formation had a real core in a training or line-of-communication unit. Careful records were kept, both in Cairo and in London, showing where each formation actually was, insofar as it was anywhere; where it was notionally supposed to be; the enemy's probable knowledge of the unit as gained from misinformation fed through strategic deception and through direct operational contact; and the conclusions he was known to have drawn through SIGINT or documents captured from him in the field. Such documents became available in quantity after the Battle of El Alamein. An analysis of them published by 'A' Force on 19 November 1942 showed that the existence of the greater number of their bogus units was now firmly credited by enemy intelligence. The armoured strength credited to the British forces was overestimated by 40 per cent and infantry strength by 45 per cent. These inflated figures were to remain in German intelligence estimates until the end of the war.[9]

Tenth Army was never a notional force on the scale of George Patton's First US Army Group (FUSAG), which was part of the strategic deception dubbed QUICKSILVER, and which played a celebrated notional role in the preparations for OVERLORD.[10] Nor was 10th Army a purely notional formation, which rendered it suitable for use as a component of Middle East strategy, being factually located within striking distance of various Axis operational theatres at various stages in the war (Southern Russia, Transcaucasia, North Africa, Syria and Palestine, Italy, and [notionally] Greece and the Balkans). Tenth Army was also factually below establishment, which meant that it could be notionally reinforced at any time without unduly arousing enemy suspicions.

Persia and Iraq Command (PAIC) began with only four or five under-strength factual divisions and a mass of heterogeneous base troops of the British Army, Indian Army, and Free Polish forces. The infantry divisions were deficient in artillery, engineers, and signals, while the sole armoured division lacked medium tanks.[11] On 1 October 1942, the factual 10th Army order of battle in Persia merely comprised 6th Indian Division, 5th Division, 10th Indian Motor Brigade, and 31st Indian Armoured Division.[12] However, as the war progressed, the enemy was induced to believe that PAIFORCE consisted of no fewer than 10 fighting divisions, and 'A' Force inflated 10th Army to become the strategic reserve for the whole of Middle East Command (MEC). By the autumn of 1943, it consisted of some genuine Polish training units and the following notional and seminotional formations at establishment strength: 31st Indian Armoured Division, 6th Indian Division, 12th Indian Division, 2nd Indian Division, 3rd Corps, and 22nd Indian Corps HQ. So convincing was the bogus order of battle that even Eisenhower and Alexander had to be persuaded that most of these forces were notional and therefore unavailable to them.[13]

What was extraordinary about the meticulously maintained bogus order of battle in the Middle East was the way in which it blended and balanced factual and notional information. The existence of three army headquarters was not pure fabrication: 9th and 10th were factual armies, while 12th was notional, based on the administrative forces known as British Troops in Egypt (BTE). However, the way in which all three were depicted was largely notional. At one point, 'A' Force HQ employed at least four PAIC battalions to do nothing but move around dummy tanks, regiments, and aircraft.[14] 'A' Force artfully manipulated such elements as factual and notional strengths and movements, real and simulated signals traffic, and all manner of signage in a credible yet infinitely subtle way, so that by the end of 1943 the factual or more frequently notional units had become so fixed in the enemy's mind that they were as real and menacing as any strictly factual buildup of Allied forces.[15] The key to such credibility was of course continuity, with each new cover plan dovetailing into the previous ones and rooted firmly in Dudley Clarke's original bogus order of battle, established when he first joined Wavell's staff in 1941. Thus, German intelligence ultimately became convinced that the Allies would invade Greece and the Balkans:

> The movement of forces away from Egypt and the build up of a great army, partly real and partly imaginary, in Persia and Iraq in turn was the basis of the movement back of General Wilson and his command which convinced Fremde Heere West [Foreign Armies West (FHW)] – the Abwehr was convinced in advance – that the invasion of the Balkans which they expected was about to begin.[16]

Of course, this conviction was reinforced in May 1943 by Operation MINCEMEAT, whose true significance is best appreciated in the wider context of 'A' Force strategic deception, rather than as an individual 'show', albeit a brilliant one.[17]

The extent to which the Abwehr and the SD may have been deterred from mounting covert operations in Persia by the notional threat of PAIFORCE in general and the notional strength of 10th Army in particular cannot be measured. Unfortunately, no documents appear to have survived which might indicate whether the deceptive intelligence successfully passed to Berlin from the Middle East by notional 'A' Force agents concerning the PAIFORCE order of battle was actually distributed to the Abwehr II or Amt VI operational planning staff. It has been suggested that, even if Schellenberg and other Amt VI (or Abwehr) officers had suspected strategic deception, they would never have revealed their suspicions, for they would have feared denunciation, posting to the Russian front, or even execution, had they exposed such widespread gullibility and incompetence in the German intelligence services.[18] However, it is surely reasonable to assume that the Berlin planners of sabotage and subversion may have been led by such false intelligence to view Persia in general as bristling with British forces and therefore as a far more hostile, discouraging operational environment for covert missions than it was factually. Consequently, in terms of Dudley Clarke's paradigm of thought translated into action,[19] the Abwehr and the SD may indeed have been deterred by Allied strategic deception from implementing most of their plans for clandestine operations, and – paradoxically – reacted with inaction. This assumption may at least go some way towards explaining why so few (only six out of 18) of their planned covert operations reached the implementation stage.

Notes

1. Dudley Clarke in CAB 154/2, TNA, also quoted in Howard, *Strategic Deception*, 41.
2. See Howard, *Strategic Deception*, 32–3.
3. Ibid., 36–7. For further details about CHEESE, see KV 2/1133, TNA.
4. Howard, *Strategic Deception*, 85. Cf. my comments on the dysfunctional interservice relationship between DSO and ISLD in Tehran in Chapter 7. In theory, there was a Thirty-four (XXXIV) Committee in Tehran; however, it never actually held a meeting and was instead subsumed under Thirty-two (XXXII) Committee in Baghdad. See Mure, *Practise to Deceive*, 49.
5. See Howard, *Strategic Deception*, 41.
6. Hinsley and Simkins, *British Intelligence*, vol. 4, 163.
7. Robertson to Mure, 28 October 1979, Private papers of D.W.A. Mure, 2194: 67/321/1-3, IWM.
8. Howard, *Strategic Deception*, 41.
9. Ibid., 43–4. With the creation of PAIFORCE under General Wilson in the summer of 1942, 'A' Force established a linked HQ in Persia. Ibid., 40.

10. See J.C. Masterman, *The Double-cross System in the War of 1939 to 1945* (New Haven, CT: Yale University Press, 1972), 223–31.
11. The history of the threat to the northern flank and the need for strategic reinforcements has been traced in Ian S.O. Playfair et al., *British Fortunes Reach Their Lowest Ebb*, vol. 3 (September 1941 to September 1942) of *The Mediterranean and the Middle East* (London: HMSO, 1960), 122–9, 362–77, 424–6.
12. Dharm Pal, *Campaign in Western Asia*, Official History of the Indian Armed Forces in the Second World War, 1939–45: Campaigns in the Western Theatre, ed. Bisheshwar Prasad (Calcutta: Combined Inter-Services Historical Section, India and Pakistan, 1957), 377.
13. Mure, *Practise to Deceive*, 43–4, 46, 126–7.
14. Report on visit to Egypt, 20.3.42–17.4.42 by Major T.A. Robertson, 7 May 1942, KV 4/234, TNA.
15. Mure, *Master of Deception*, 210.
16. Ibid.
17. For more about MINCEMEAT, the successful planting of a corpse carrying bogus plans for an Allied Balkan invasion, see the following files at Kew: CAB 79/60/26, CAB 146/442, CAB 154/112, HW 20/546, WO 106/5921, and WO 208/3163. See also inter alia Ewen Montagu, *The Man Who Never Was* (Philadelphia: Lippincott, 1954); Denis Smyth, *Deathly Deception: The Real Story of Operation Mincemeat* (Oxford: Oxford University Press, 2010); and Ben Macintyre, *Operation Mincemeat: How a Dead Man and a Bizarre Plan Fooled the Nazis and Assured an Allied Victory* (London: Bloomsbury, 2010).
18. Mure, *Practise to Deceive*, 202.
19. See epigraph.

7
Saboteurs and Spooks

> On the whole SOE activities in Persia were disappointing, because of the general nervousness among the British Foreign Office officials there, the lack of real first-class personnel, and complete lack of local material. (History of SOE in the Arab World)[1]

There is good reason for coupling the Special Operations Executive (SOE) and the Inter-Services Liaison Department (ISLD) under the same rubric in this book, for the work of the two services in Persia was inextricably intertwined and their identity possibly even coalescent, in the sense that ISLD appears to have used SOE in the region as a convenient proxy. What better cover can there be for a secret service than another secret service? Much of the discourse in *Nazi Secret Warfare* addressed issues of dysfunction in the German secret services, including problems arising from interservice rivalry. Whilst it has to be acknowledged that the British response to German threat in Persia was overwhelmingly concerted and effective, it is only fair to recognize that the British services in the region were themselves not immune to a certain degree of interservice rivalry and friction.[2] However, such instances were rare and were generally resolved in a timely fashion, so that no conflict was permitted to escalate to a point where it might actually impede operations. For instance, the relationship that existed between British counterintelligence and security intelligence in Persia, as represented by Joe Spencer's DSO Persia organization, and the British Secret Intelligence Service (MI6), thinly disguised in Asia as ISLD, was not a happy one.

The ultimate dysfunction of CICI–ISLD liaison in Persia is all the more noteworthy in the light of the optimism expressed about relations between the two organizations in the spring of 1942 by a senior MI5 officer, Tar Robertson, who visited SIME headquarters in Cairo and subsequently wrote: 'Finally there is the liaison between SIME and ISLD. This is undoubtedly the most striking feature of all.' According to Robertson, the closeness of contact between the two departments, both at the head offices and at the outstations, was remarkable especially over matters of counterespionage importance. This was partly due to the close friendship which existed between the heads of the two departments, together with the fact that the two offices were so closely situated. This liaison allowed for the smooth working of and the close cooperation between the two departments throughout the whole area (including Persia), and partly accounted for the fact that there was an ISLD presence in Turkey and everywhere else throughout the area. 'The result', Tar Robertson concluded, 'is that the interchange of information is free and the assistance which the departments give to each other is great. ... This is the only way satisfactorily to run intelligence work.'[3] Robertson even foresaw the establishment of a network of jointly controlled SIME and ISLD counterintelligence agents who would become staybehinds in the event of a German invasion of the region. In Persia, this notion never came to fruition. Instead, as we shall see later, it was the Indian Intelligence Bureau (IB) that created such a network of agents, under the sole control of their liaison officer in Tehran, Bill Magan.[4]

In theory at least, Robertson's optimism ignored the strong potential for animosity that lay in the fact that SIME and ISLD overlapped geographically and, partially at least, in their common pursuit of counterintelligence objectives. By 1943, Raymond Maunsell, head of SIME in Cairo, felt himself constrained to emphasize the necessity of whole-hearted collaboration with ISLD and the avoidance of friction, whilst warning that MI6 were taking 'more active measures' to establish themselves in counterintelligence in the Middle East. At the same time, however, Maunsell asserted that it was the duty of DSOs to direct counterintelligence in their areas, adding that, while the necessity for collaboration with ISLD was recognized, it had to be understood that the final responsibility for counterintelligence in the Middle East was SIME's, and it was the duty of DSOs, while doing their utmost to avoid friction, to make that clear.[5]

In fact, two years after Tar Robertson's positive report, CICI–ISLD relations in Persia had worsened to such an extent that the counterintelligence specialists at DSO Persia had come to view ISLD as – quite simply – parasitic. Their views found official expression, on the record, at the 1944 SIME conference held in Beirut. On that occasion, Joe Spencer stated that his relations with the local ISLD representative had deteriorated in the last year owing to a decline in the standard of their personnel. His statement appears slightly at odds with Maunsell's somewhat conciliatory perception, from his Cairo perspective, of 'the importance of good relations with ISLD owing to the powerful influence their organization enjoys and the value of the information they provide'.[6] Maunsell's view may have been influenced by the fact that at the headquarters level in London MI5–MI6 relations were generally good, at least insofar as the sharing of Middle East intelligence was concerned. Not so, however, with respect to counterintelligence operations.[7] According to CICI Baghdad and DSO Persia, the ISLD representative in Tehran was often asked by MI6 in London for reports on Axis activities in Persia and, as he had no information on the subject from his own sources, he habitually plagiarized the material in routinely received copies of DSO Persia's reports, rewriting them as his own. In doing so, he was of course pointlessly duplicating information which would already have been passed from CICI via MI5 in London to MI6 in the normal course of events.[8] Additionally, he may have been giving 'C' (Sir Stewart Menzies, head of MI6) the false impression that ISLD Persia rather than DSO Persia were doing all the responsible work there. This definitely appears to have been the case, for a signal was at one point received from MI6 by their Tehran representative, instructing him to send them the codes and equipment captured with the ANTON group, in the belief that he, not Joe Spencer, had been responsible for their capture. Chokra Wood was understandably indignant about this, while Spencer's comments on the actions of ISLD were apparently 'unprintable'.[9]

Upon learning of these unfortunate misrepresentations, Raymond Maunsell wrote:

> I sincerely hope that CICI may not fade out of Persia leaving MI6 alone to cover counter-intelligence. ... I fully support Wood ... and sympathize with the annoyance to both Wood and Spencer at this ridiculous duplication of work that has been carried out by the MI6 office in Tehran. In addition I may say that the little I have seen of that office did not impress me. I have, I must confess, never been able to understand the mentality which finds it necessary to justify its existence by poaching other people's game.[10]

Maunsell thought it particularly peculiar in view of the excellent work which Spencer and his unit had carried out in Persia in completely destroying the German intelligence organization there. 'It is my belief', he concluded, 'that in this work they received very little assistance from their MI6 colleagues.'[11]

It can have been of little reassurance to Chokra Wood to be told by his London superior, Sir David Petrie, that 'C' was well aware of 'the limitations in the scope of the work of MI6 in Tehran'.[12] Petrie, formerly a senior police and intelligence officer in India, was successful and popular as Director General of MI5 from 1941 to 1946. According to him, CICI served PAIFORCE, while the MI6 representative served the local British authorities. Their interests were mutual and to a certain extent 'must overlap and be closely integrated'.[13] And, as if foreshadowing the postoccupational realignment that was soon to come, already requiring less emphasis on Germany as the enemy and greater emphasis on the Soviet Union as the main intelligence target, Petrie added, in carefully chosen words: 'Spencer has a full-time job. The MI6 representative has probably less to do, but he must create and build up his position to meet long-term requirements. CICI knows the special interests of MI6 and should deal with MI6 as a separate department, but in the very closest collaboration.'[14]

The limited capability of the MI6 representative in Tehran was therefore at least partially attributable to the fact that he had no files to work with. ISLD had destroyed most of their records during the Rashid Ali coup, and he doubtless had little interest in the independent acquisition – from scratch – of intelligence on Nazi agents and sympathizers. The official record in fact shows that DSO Persia indeed 'assisted ISLD in building up fresh records'.[15] By mid-1944, whilst CICI's gaze remained constantly fixed upon German covert initiatives in the region, that of ISLD had undoubtedly become trained on Stalin's occupation forces and their newly perceived potential threat to British influence in the region after Germany's inevitable defeat. Thus, in a sense, ISLD were already fighting the Cold War in Persia well before the end of the Second World War. It is therefore hardly surprising that the two British services became increasingly at odds, simply because their strategic roles had diverged beyond reconciliation. Rather than standing shoulder-to-shoulder in Persia against a common foe, ISLD and DSO found themselves facing different enemies, back-to-back.

But the situation was further complicated by the presence in Persia of a third service (SOE), with which ISLD enjoyed a quasi-incestuous relationship of convenience, and with which DSO had little to do, greatly muddling the historical narrative. The principal difficulty for historians attempting to disentangle the complicated nexus of clandestine identities and roles is the almost total absence of SOE reports and personnel files in the existing accessible records, coupled of course with the inaccessibility of any relevant MI6 or ISLD records that might exist.

In order to ensure the widest possible yet most accurately targeted distribution of intelligence and counterintelligence product and analysis, the regional British security-intelligence formations (SIME, CICI, and DSO Persia) generated and sustained a monolithic corpus of regular and frequent reports throughout the war, which is a treasure-trove for the postwar intelligence historian. Conversely, however, SOE in Persia remained as tight-lipped and buttoned-up as ISLD, publishing virtually nothing, and ultimately destroying most of the documentation they had accumulated by the end of the war.

What we do know is that SOE work did not begin in Persia until shortly before the Anglo-Soviet invasion in 1941. To begin with, SOE's task was to create a secret oral propaganda organization, under Christopher Sykes [D/N11],[16] aimed at reaching all segments of the population, disseminating rumours, and distributing pamphlets and posters in an attempt to smear pro-German politicians, generate rumours, and inspire an anti-German spirit among the Persians. On instructions from Sir Reader Bullard, most SOE black propaganda was directed towards discrediting certain corrupt and undesirable deputies. SOE attacked them violently by means of clandestine leaflets – sometimes statements in their name denying that they wished to be elected, that they had a revelation from God which had made them devote the rest of their lives to religion, and other simple stratagems of that kind. SOE also confronted them in pamphlets signed by political parties, real or imaginary, accusing them of bribery, immorality, etc. In most cases the pamphlets stated the exact bribe offered, when, where, and to whom, or circumstantial evidence was offered pinning a deputy down to some horrible offence.[17]

At the same time, SOE sought to mobilize dependable pro-British elements, using them to form postoccupational cells to carry out sabotage, to murder local Nazi collaborators, to create strikes and slowdowns, and to otherwise cause general mayhem in the wake of a German invasion. Munitions dumps for use by these cells were also prepared, and communications networks were established. Two years later, after El Alamein and Stalingrad, all these clandestine measures, now suddenly rendered superfluous, had to be reversed. New issues, such as supply shortages, inflation, hoarding, political intrigue, corruption, and general war-weariness had to be addressed instead. SOE now had to counter ever-increasing dissatisfaction among Persians at the continuance of such repressive wartime measures as censorship, internment, and rationing.[18]

As the Germans were driven ever further from Persia by the Russian armies, SOE dissolved their sabotage teams and shipped their munitions and men to other theatres, leaving only a handful of Farsi-speaking officers in place, most with highly specialized knowledge and experience of Persia. Whilst fully trained in unarmed combat and all the other paramilitary skills required of serving SOE personnel, these few talented individuals spent their entire time engaged in one of two principal activities which could not be overtly associated with the British diplomatic representatives: (1) instigating and managing oral propaganda and other covert attacks targeting undesirable persons indicated by the Tehran legation, and (2) establishing clandestine contact with the tribes and other influential Persians. In the latter case, the legation staff obviously could not be seen overtly negotiating with the Qashgai or the Bakhtiari, as this would cut across the tribal policy of the central government. Behind such moves of course was the need to ensure the future security of the AIOC oilfields and the TIR within the tribal areas, especially that of the turbulent Boir Ahmedi, using methods for which SOE was peculiarly adapted.[19]

Kurdistan, astride the Persian-Iraqi-Turkish border and of potential strategic significance in the event of any German move against Persia, posed a unique problem. SOE were never able to penetrate the Kurdish region via neighbouring Soviet-occupied Persian Azerbaijan because it was felt that, if detected by the Russians, such activity would be difficult to deny and impossibly embarrassing. In 1941–42, however, John C.A. 'Johnny' Johnson (D/H302),[20] formerly ALO Sulaimaniya (Iraq), was able to do some penetration work in Persian Kurdistan and, in the event of a German invasion, planned to raise the Persian Kurds in a postoccupational revolt, together with the Iraqi Kurds he knew so well. Group Captain Johnson was particularly effective in the field because he was an acknowledged authority on Kurdistan who had developed a great facility with the Kurdish language, becoming a first-class RAF interpreter in 1935.[21] Even so, it was generally agreed that, in view of the non-Kurdish Persians' inability or unwillingness to mount any kind of defence against the Germans, they could at most be used in the Soviet-controlled northwestern region of Persia only as 'whispering and rumour' groups with wireless communication. To this end therefore, SOE trained mostly Persian Armenians as W/T operators and some even as saboteurs. Unfortunately, however, whilst avowedly anti-Soviet, these men also proved to be anti-British because they were upset by Britain's alliance with Stalin. SOE therefore deemed them unreliable, though they were of course never really put to the test because the Germans never crossed the Caucasus into Persian Azerbaijan.

SOE in Persia was under the overall command of Herbert Underwood (D/N9),[22] who, as military attaché at the legation (1938–41), had furnished Sir Reader Bullard in the first half of 1941 with the intelligence he needed on the Nazi diaspora to enable Churchill and Eden to justify the invasion and occupation of Persia (Operation COUNTENANCE). The story is that Bullard had to be persuaded gradually to condone covert activity to protect AIOC infrastructure and the TIR. Underwood first sought Bullard's permission to make contact with the dissident tribes, particularly the Bakhtiari, Qashgai, and Boir Ahmedi, initially to form sabotage parties, but later to create a nucleus for their postoccupational work. Unfortunately, Bullard and/or the British government were initially opposed to such contacts, not wishing to contravene the tribal policy of the Persian central government. With the ANTON parachutists by then posing an indefinite potential threat in Qashgai territory, SOE therefore took it upon themselves to raise sabotage/countersabotage teams clandestinely, together with a denial scheme elaborated in conjunction with the Transportation Directorate, which operated the TIR. Eventually, Bullard (or Whitehall) relented, enabling SOE to make what they described at the time as 'several excellent tribal contacts'. Thus, whilst nominally under the overall command of the former military attaché, SOE in Persia gradually and informally evolved into two loosely associated executive branches: sabotage, countersabotage, and tribal affairs under Underwood; and subversive propaganda now under Robin Zaehner (D/H141).[23] Working closely with DSO Persia, local ALOs, and with AIOC and railway officials, Underwood assumed responsibility for security throughout Khuzistan, especially in the oilfields around Masjid-i-Suliman (Masjed Soleyman).[24] However, as overall commander, Underwood's reach extended throughout the British zone, assisting the Persians to resist Russian encroachment, in conjunction with Bullard and Zaehner, by such covert means as providing financial assistance to the anti-Russian press, influencing members of the *Majlis*, and disseminating disruptive oral propaganda within the Tudeh Party.[25] One visitor to Tehran early in 1945, when the advisability of continuing the SOE role in the region was being scrutinized, found Underwood to be a charming man with a considerable circle of friends, particularly in the Persian army, through whom he could influence the decisions of the Persian government. However, the same source, who appears to have been sent out to Tehran to do a 'hatchet job' on the commander (if not on SOE as a whole), suggested that Underwood was a person who would hesitate to resort to ruthless methods if they were required, and would have difficulty in dominating his personnel when a fundamental issue was at stake.[26]

After his transfer to full-time SOE duties, whilst retaining the title of assistant military attaché for cover purposes,[27] Herbert Underwood was succeeded as military attaché at the Tehran legation by the extremely knowledgeable, experienced, and equally charming William A.K. 'Wak'

Fraser, IA, who had held the position once before (1924–28), having commanded the South Persia Rifles during the immediate postwar period (1919–21). Fraser was also Bill Slim's predecessor as commander of 10th Indian Division and Edward Quinan's predecessor as commander of IRAQFORCE. Working closely with Bullard, who was fortunate to have at his disposal an expert of Fraser's general rank and calibre, he served ably at the Tehran legation/embassy between 1941 and 1945, when he returned to Britain to resume the well-deserved retirement he had originally begun in 1941. Fraser helped Bullard especially with his realistic appreciations of Soviet activities in northern Persia and Kurdistan,[28] on which he kept a steady watch, no doubt in close cooperation with Joe Spencer at DSO Persia. Though Fraser reverted to the rank of lieutenant colonel for the duration of the war, everybody, even the Russians, always addressed him with the utmost respect as 'General Fraser'. He and his wife enjoyed the exceptional privilege of living in a large comfortable house in the summer-legation compound at the foot of the Alborz mountains amidst lovely scenery described by one visitor as reminiscent of the English Lake District.[29]

The problem for historians attempting to construct a cohesive SOE narrative is doubly difficult because, whereas the Germans allowed their rigid competencies and interservice rivalries – notably between the Abwehr and the SD – to impede their covert operations, the British in Persia preferred lively clandestine communication and cooperation among themselves, deliberately allowing a certain ad hoc blurring of service boundaries. At the lowest level, for example, civilian SOE recruits were often provided with instant service identities and ranks in various corps and regiments of the British Army; much favoured as cover were the Royal Artillery, the Royal Engineers, and the Royal Signals. Recruited for SOE by David Turkhud (D/N3)[30] in Tehran, for example, the Hungarian lawyer, nightclub musician, and part-time propagandist at the legation, Francis Shelton, after a brief meeting with Underwood, found himself suddenly and surprisingly a sergeant in the Royal Army Service Corps.[31] Such casual pragmatism and flexibility were almost unheard of in the bureaucratic German services, where any move towards interservice liaison or cooperation usually meant picking one's way warily through a minefield of jealously guarded political competencies and vested interests within one's own service, let alone beyond it.

In this context of close covert liaison and relatively fluid identities among the British services, it even became possible for one clandestine agency to provide cover for another (so-called 'cover within cover'), as for instance when an ISLD officer might work under SOE cover, whilst also officially functioning as a Foreign Office diplomat. Few on the legation staff would or could ever discover the true nature of his or her active-intelligence work, because even those with sufficient clearance to know that he or she was SOE would never guess that SOE was merely cover for a deeper espionage identity: not even the minister himself. Such was the case with the senior MI6 officer in the region, SOE propaganda chief Robin Zaehner and his assistant Norman Darbyshire (D/H923),[32] which makes the construction of Zaehner's particular narrative doubly difficult – though not his alone, for some of the other officers identified as SOE (for example, the field commander Underwood and his administrative officer Turkhud) may also have been working for ISLD, together with Mrs K.E. Sykes,[33] who was nominally Zaehner's secretary, and the Press Attaché, the redoubtable Ann Lambton, who was nominally Zaehner's boss, but who is only mentioned in the SOE records as 'an enthusiastic but discreet partner'.[34] Mrs Sykes certainly appears to have been much more than a mere secretary, assuming complete responsibility for Zaehner's work whenever he was in the field and writing 'very good' propaganda herself.[35] She and her husband Egerton, who was British Publicity Liaison Officer at the legation, and who in later life became a renowned Atlantologist, were apparently expert in working with (against?) the Russians, Poles, and Czechs, which strongly suggests their ISLD involvement. Their relations with the Soviet press attaché and the TASS correspondent (both of whom were concerned with political subversion) were excellent. The Egerton Sykes were said to be the only British in Tehran to have made any effort to break down the suspicions of the Russians.[36] Lambton, like Zaehner a learned Persianist, who would enjoy a long and distinguished postwar career at London University's School of Oriental and African Studies (SOAS), was probably also working for ISLD.[37] Remembering her after the war, Francis Shelton would describe Lambton, who was a devout Anglican, as 'large, bony, and dressed like a caricature of the proverbial vicar's wife'; she was also impressive and 'totally in command of herself in a stern and rather humourless manner – a very masculine, unsmiling old battleaxe'.[38] There is no actual proof that the formidable Lambton was MI6 and worked with Zaehner and Darbyshire for ISLD during the war, but it seems highly likely.[39] If so, it is of course also possible that one originally recruited the other and/or others. Together, all three would later collaborate in evolving a now notorious scheme for MI6 and the US Central Intelligence Agency (CIA) to topple the progressive Persian prime minister Mohammed Mossadegh (Operation BOOT/TPAJAX) and replace him with the duplicitous Fazlollah Zahedi.[40]

Working nominally under Lambton at the legation as part of his diplomatic cover, it is difficult to comprehend how Robin Zaehner managed his two layers of cover and three distinct service roles – assistant press attaché, head of SOE propaganda, and MI6 active-intelligence officer – without confusing them, as there must have been significant overlapping at times. His predicament, if he ever saw it as such, would have been equivalent to that of a triple agent, except that his three identities were all working in the same cause. Fortunately Zaehner was equipped with a formidable intellect, as is evidenced by his postwar academic career: he would later become – as Professor R.C. Zaehner – a distinguished, prolific scholar, teaching Persian and religion at Oxford University until his sudden death at the age of 61 in 1974. The son of Swiss immigrants, Zaehner was said to have had a brilliant mind and a prodigious gift for languages and, besides Farsi, was able to master such classical and ancient languages as Greek, Latin, Avestan, and Pahlavi, with a reading knowledge of Arabic, Sanskrit, and Pali.[41] Peter Wright, a senior MI5 officer who interviewed Robin Zaehner after the war concerning allegations that Zaehner had at some point worked for the Soviet Union[42] – a far-fetched notion, as it would have meant handling no fewer than four simultaneous roles – has described Zaehner's work under deep cover in wartime Persia on the basis of his personnel record as follows:

> He was responsible for MI6 counterintelligence in Persia during the war. It was difficult and dangerous work. The railway lines into Russia, carrying vital military supplies, were key targets for German sabotage. Zaehner was perfectly equipped for the job, speaking the local dialects fluently, and much of his time was spent undercover, operating in the murky and cutthroat world of countersabotage. By the end of the war his task was even more fraught. The Russians themselves were trying to gain control of the railway, and Zaehner had to work behind Russian lines, continuously at risk of betrayal and murder ... .[43]

How does Wright's description fit with DSO's view of Zaehner's 'parasitic' behaviour and derivative reporting, which had so angered Joe Spencer? First, it certainly seems consistent with the shift in ISLD's operational role from anti-German countersabotage to anti-Soviet counterintelligence and counterespionage from 1943 onwards. Second, it suggests that Zaehner was primarily interested in the Soviet zone of occupation in northern Persia, not in the British zone to the south, which might explain Zaehner's lack of any network of intelligence sources outside the Russian zone and his consequent need to 'poach' intelligence on southern Persia (where the Germans were) from DSO. Zaehner also worked closely with the British minister, Sir Reader Bullard, and enjoyed his full support as much as did Joe Spencer and the DSO staff. However, while no doubt fully aware of his SOE role, it is uncertain if Bullard was aware of Zaehner's work for MI6 – or at least the extent of it – nor of the possible involvement in active espionage of other members of the legation staff (e.g. Lambton, Darbyshire, and the Egerton Sykes), though he may well have had his suspicions.[44]

To the archival historian, Robin Zaehner's work for ISLD in northern Persia is of course distinctly opaque. All that is said in the SOE records is the veiled comment: 'It is difficult to explain in detail the full value of his work, but undoubtedly he has been of great assistance to the minister [Bullard], who is very keen for his work to continue.'[45] Whilst SOE were never able to penetrate the Russian-occupied zone,[46] Zaehner apparently had little difficulty in doing so, which leads one to wonder just how he succeeded. Apparently, the NKVD obstructed all efforts to appoint SOE representatives to Tabriz and Resht, which they regarded as a '"sinister" British move aimed at stealing a march on the Soviets for the postwar period'.[47] Presumably what made Zaehner exceptional in the first place was his mastery of Farsi and his knowledge of many regional dialects and minority languages. Also, the excellent relations established with the Russians by Egerton Sykes and his wife may have facilitated Zaehner's movements and contacts within the Soviet zone. However, as the war drew to a close, Zaehner faced a problem with one layer of his multiple cover. By 1945, SOE realized that they would need to arrange civilian cover for those British staff who chose – as Zaehner apparently did – to remain with the organization. Zaehner's solution (or was it MI6's?) was that he should persuade Oxford University to allow him to return to Persia to compile a modern grammar and dictionary of the Persian language. Zaehner appears to have informed SOE that he was confident he could make such an arrangement. Whether MI6 interceded on Zaehner's behalf in the common rooms of Oxford is not evident, but return he certainly did.[48]

In general, though, it can be safely assumed that Zaehner's task as an ISLD officer in wartime Persia undoubtedly had more to do with furnishing MI6 with intelligence and counterintelligence product about Soviet intentions and the perceived Soviet threat to postwar Persia and the Middle East than with the war against Hitler. And it was to Alex Kellar that the task fell of finding on behalf of MI5 an optimal solution to the vexed question of postwar counterintelligence compe-tences in the region. At issue was the question of whether to allow the formidable regional expertise developed by SIME to continue to function after the war under MI5 control, or whether control had to pass perforce to MI6, because of the SIS's traditional primacy in all overseas operations, whether of an active-intelligence or counterintelligence nature. It needs to be emphasized that the problem was centred on the specific question of responsibility for overseas counterespionage outside the British Empire (e.g. in Persia) and whether that particular remit would be surrendered by SIME to MI6 after the war, which it was. This potentially divisive interservice matter was entirely separate from the local tussle between Spencer and Zaehner concerning attribution of intelligence.[49] It was a thorny issue, and to resolve it Kellar visited the region three times, twice during the war (in March–May 1944 and February 1945) and once immediately after the war (May–June 1945). Yet the farsighted Kellar had already anticipated many of the security problems that subsequently arose in the Middle East in a report he filed as early as November 1943, before undertaking any regional field trips, in which he wrote: 'I consider our position in that part of the world will probably be most seriously threatened by Russia, whose penetration of the area, already evident in Persia, will perhaps present us with our most important and at the same time most difficult counterespionage problem.' Whatever the political conception of Russia's future status, British interests must, Kellar opined, be menaced, and no more so than in the Middle East where, in addition to the mineral wealth of Persia and Iraq, Suez and the Persian Gulf would give Russia sea-way to the Indian Ocean and beyond.[50]

After discussing the need to take into account realistically the US intelligence services as a potential postwar target, as well as a possible postwar resurgence of German interest in the region (realistic in 1943, no doubt), Kellar appealed for continued cooperation on counterintelligence between MI5 and MI6, whilst remaining vague as to who might ultimately control things. 'The problems', he wrote, 'are at any rate sufficiently complex and important to indicate that there can be little, if any, let-up in our counterintelligence activities in the area, and their integration under centralized direction would seem to be a necessary piece of rationalization.'[51]

Alex Kellar's desire for continued MI5–MI6 liaison and coordination was no doubt commendable, and his perception of the American OSS (later to become the CIA) as a latent if distant threat may even be considered visionary; however, that threat was actually more imminent than Kellar probably realized, unless MI6 had perhaps alerted him to egregious American activities in his region. The records clearly show that at least two OSS agents, both PGSC/PGC officers, were engaged in active-espionage operations (SI projects NE28A and NE28B) against Soviet occupation forces in the northern zone of Persia from August 1944 onwards (see Appendix A.5).[52] Unfortunately, there is nothing in the records to show unequivocally whether either MI5/SIME/CSIS/DSO (Kellar, Maunsell, Wood, Spencer, and Roger) and/or MI6/ISLD (Zaehner, Darbyshire, and Lambton) were aware of this clandestine American activity, which essentially had nothing to do with the Second World War and everything to do with a Cold War that was yet to come. According to Stephen Penrose, head of OSS SI Cairo, 'organization, liaison, and friendships' had definitely been established at the regional and possibly headquarters level with ISLD by September 1944.[53] Certainly, it is difficult to believe that a brilliant IO like Robin Zaehner would have been unaware of US agents operating in his area; sooner or later he would have come across them in the field, and probably did, though he may not have known just what they were up to. Alternatively, of course, likely through the personal friendship and excellent liaison maintained in the United States between Bill Donovan and William Stephenson of British Security Coordination (BSC), Zaehner's superiors at MI6 may have been fully aware all along of the active role played by OSS in the acquisition and analysis of military, political, and economic intelligence about the Russians in Persia during the final year of the war.

At any rate, Alex Kellar remained convinced that it would be necessary after the war for British counterespionage and counterintelligence in the Middle East to be directed centrally, because of the political, strategic, and economic importance of the region and the heavy burden of responsibility for security that the British secret services would continue to bear. Consequently, it would be necessary for a permanent solution to be found for the unsatisfactory overlapping of function between MI5 and MI6.[54] Clearly, any counterproductive rivalry between the services such as existed between Joe Spencer and Robin Zaehner in wartime Persia, however briefly and insignificantly, had to be prevented. The issue was not ultimately resolved until the Attlee Directive of 1948 and the Maxwell Fyfe Directive of 1952; however, in the case of India, MI5 did not cede competence to MI6 until the late 1960s.[55]

Precisely because, when compared with the organization's intense large-scale activity in occupied Europe, SOE did little and achieved little on its own cognizance in Persia between 1941 and 1945, one is tempted to see it as merely a convenient cover organization exploited by MI6 to mask their anti-Soviet espionage activities. But one needs to be careful not to distort things, for not all SOE officers worked for ISLD or against

Russia. Some officers were strictly SOE operatives working under 'single' diplomatic cover, the best examples being the distant cousins Christopher Hugh Sykes [D/N11] (see Figure 7.1) and Edward Molesworth Sykes [D/N4], who remained tirelessly engaged in anti-Nazi activity.

As a Territorial Army officer in The Green Howards since 1927, Sykes was commissioned in 1939 as a reserve officer in the regiment's newly formed 7th Battalion. He had by then already served as a junior diplomat in Berlin under Harold Nicolson, had travelled widely in Persia and mastered Farsi, and had published a definitive biography of the 'German Lawrence' of southern Persia, Wilhelm Wassmuss.[56] In June 1940, Sykes joined SO1 (later to become the Political Warfare Executive [PWE]), where he was personal assistant to Cudbert Thornhill, head of

Figure 7.1   Author and SOE propagandist: Christopher Sykes. Probably SOE's most talented propaganda writer, Sykes was a published author and friend of the novelist Evelyn Waugh. In 1943, finding his SOE career in the Middle East at a dead end, Sykes joined the SAS and fought courageously with the French Resistance.

Source: HS 9/1433/9, TNA.

SO1 (ME). In October 1941, after Thornhill had been sacked, Sykes was sent out to Tehran as SO1 Deputy Director of Special Planning (DDSP) under diplomatic cover (second secretary at the British legation) in the aftermath of the Anglo-Soviet invasion of Iran. There Sykes remained for a year until he was promoted and transferred to Cairo as DSP (ME). Soon out of a job because his department (G-2 Plans) had been wound up and its work transferred to PWE, Sykes found time to write a light novel, *High Minded Murder* (1944), a *roman à clef* set in wartime Cairo, in which he satirized the incompetence and infighting amongst the competing secret bureacracies of Cairo and targeted at least one prominent (thinly fictionalized) SOE personality.[57] There seems to have been a significant time lag between PWE's nominal takeover of the SO1 propaganda organization in August 1941 and its actual implementation at a far-flung outpost like Tehran and even in Cairo. Thus Sykes continued in his SO1 role until April 1943, a full 20 months after the formation of PWE. As a casualty of this seismic administrative shift, one can see how Sykes's considerable gifts were squandered in the name of empire-building and internecine rivalry, prompting one to wonder how many other highly talented individuals were wasted in such shuffles during the short but extremely troubled organizational history of SOE. Sykes would later describe the intrigues that prevailed at GHQ (ME) amidst an 'alphabet soup' of secret organizations in *A Song of a Shirt* (1953).[58] After failing to find any position as an intelligence officer in the Middle East, Sykes returned to the UK in May 1943, volunteered for the SAS, and was posted, along with his dear friend Evelyn Waugh,[59] to the Commando Training Depot at Achnacarry Castle, Invernesshire on 1 July 1943. As an SAS officer, Sykes, who spoke fluent French but could not pass as a native, then undertook extremely hazardous work with the French Resistance: an experience which he depicted in *Four Studies in Loyalty* (1946), along with some fragmentary memoirs of Persia.[60] It is probably safe to say that Christopher Sykes spent his entire eventful war fighting Nazis, without any involvement in MI6 anti-Soviet activity. Meanwhile, Edward Sykes, together with his Farsi-speaking assistant D. Scott [D/H509], was based at Isfahan under diplomatic cover as vice-consul with responsibility for propaganda in southern Persia and among the Bakhtiari. Like Christopher, Edward Sykes does not appear to have had any MI6 role, though his close association with Underwood, who did, might suggest otherwise.[61]

Initially, until the autumn of 1942, under threat from the Nazis advancing ever further south, SOE potentially had a significant sabotage and countersabotage role to play in the region, though a difficult one. According to the official war diary, 'Persia was a hostile country, our control was precarious, and the position was deteriorating. Such conditions made SOE work extremely difficult.'[62] However, from 1943 onwards, SOE undoubtedly struggled to justify their continued presence in Persia, once the threat of a large-scale German military invasion from the north had evaporated, and since their responsibility for subversive propaganda had been assumed not long after the Anglo-Soviet invasion by PWE, though Tehran-based propaganda operations remained essentially in the hands of the same SOE (and diplomatic) personnel. Consequently, whilst generating and disseminating propaganda, and monitoring the tribal regions, there would be no more SOE 'bangs' in Persia. Therefore it seems only natural that, because they had linguistic talents and numerous Russian contacts, some SOE officers and agents would have gravitated towards ISLD, particularly as the Soviet Union replaced Nazism as the new target of British (and American) active espionage. The only career alternatives for SOE personnel who did not migrate to ISLD were transfers to Cairo, Delhi, or London, and an uncertain future. This is precisely what happened in November 1942 to a disillusioned Christopher Sykes, who had worked long and hard to build up an efficient SOE propaganda organization in Persia and the Middle East, only to see it handed over to PWE. An innocent victim of fierce 'bloody-minded' rivalries, one can imagine Sykes' anger and frustration immediately before the takeover when, in the summer of 1942, after setting up a clandestine Farsi broadcasting station in Palestine, he discovered that a diplomat at the Tehran legation had broken security and had informed the Persian prime minister all about Sykes' initiative, forcing closure of the station.[63] Sykes did not wish to risk repeating such an experience by joining any SOE propaganda unit in India or elewhere.[64] Only by leaving SOE and volunteering courageously for operational duty with the SAS was Christopher Sykes able to prolong his military career until war's end.[65]

By contrast, the relationship between SOE under Underwood and DSO Persia under Spencer and Roger was unambivalent and clearly delineated. Notwithstanding Spencer's own SOE provenance, security officers aboard his tight ship did not normally perform dual roles for SOE or ISLD (with the possible exception of R. Jackson in Shiraz). DSO's clearly defined remit was the acquisition and analysis of counterintelligence and security intelligence in full cooperation with CICI, SIME, and MI5, not sabotage, subversion, or active espionage in cooperation with SOE or MI6. Furthermore, DSO officers were tasked to confront the manifest Nazi threat, not to anticipate a hypothetical Soviet one. Even so, Tehran was a relatively small circus; liaison among the various British services and the diplomats under Sir Reader Bullard remained close and amicable throughout the occupation, with the possible exception of the acrimonious relationship between Joe Spencer and Robin Zaehner.

Notes

1. History of SOE in the Arab World, September 1945, HS 7/86, TNA.
2. For an interesting and well-informed account of the evolution of effective working relationships among various British intelligence organizations in the region, see Adam Shelley, 'Empire of Shadows: British Intelligence in the Middle East 1939–1946' (PhD diss., Cambridge, 2007), 144, 147–57.
3. Report on visit to Egypt (20.3.42–17.4.42) by Major T.A. Robertson, 7 May 1942, KV 4/234, TNA.
4. Curry, *Security Service*, 272–3. See also Chapter 9.
5. Minutes and notes on the meeting of SIME representatives held at Beirut 12–13 Feb 43, KV 4/420, TNA.
6. Minutes of the SIME Annual Conference, held in Beirut 2–4 April 44, KV 4/234, TNA.
7. Hinsley and Simkins, *British Intelligence*, vol. 4, 187–9.
8. Wood to Petrie, 8 May 1944, KV 4/223, TNA.
9. Ibid.
10. Maunsell to Petrie, 7 June 1944, KV 4/223, TNA.
11. Ibid.
12. Petrie to Wood, 26 May 1944, KV 4/223, TNA.
13. Ibid.
14. Ibid.
15. History of Combined Intelligence Centre Iraq and Persia, June 1941–December 1944, KV 4/223, TNA.
16. SOE symbols 6, HS 8/971, TNA; see also HS 9/1433/9, TNA.
17. Memorandum on SOE activities in Arab Countries, Persia, Egypt and Cyprus, HS 7/85, TNA.
18. Ibid.
19. Ibid.
20. SOE symbols 6, HS 8/971, TNA.
21. Air Ministry Announcements, *Flight*, 10 October 1935, 383. Johnny Johnson's pioneering anthropological and lexicographical work on the Kurds is still considered significant today. In addition to Kurdish, Johnson spoke several Indian and Middle Eastern languages, including Arabic and Farsi. See also: Air Commodore J.C.A. Johnson (16247), *Air of Authority: A History of RAF Organisation*, http://www.rafweb.org/Biographies/Johnson_JCA.htm.
22. SOE symbols 6, HS 8/971, TNA.
23. Memorandum on SOE activities in Arab Countries, Persia, Egypt and Cyprus, HS 7/85, TNA.
24. Ibid.
25. History of SOE in the Arab World, September 1945, HS 7/86, TNA. Underwood was subsequently provided with permanent diplomatic cover as political adviser in Khuzistan. See HS 7/285, TNA.

26. Ibid. The source was L.J.W. Richardson, who spent five days in Tehran in March 1945; his subsequent report in the Kew file has been severely redacted.

27. Ibid.

28. See, for example, Fraser to Way, 11 December 1944, WO 208/3085, TNA.

29. Private papers of E.N. Sheppard, 509, IWM. I wish to thank the Trustees of the Imperial War Museum for allowing access to this collection held in the IWM Sound and Documents Section.

30. See HS 9/1491/4, TNA. The file indicates that one of Turkhud's responsibilities was the 'local recruiting of Joes'.

31. Private papers of F. Shelton, 13556, IWM; Dr Francis Shelton, interview by author, London, 11 April 2014.

32. SOE symbols 6, HS 8/971, TNA.

33. Iran, March 1945, HS 7/86, TNA.

34. Ibid.

35. Memorandum on SOE activities in Arab countries, Persia, Egypt, and Cyprus, HS 7/85, TNA.

36. Ibid.

37. For evidence of Lambton's scholarship, see Ann K.S. Lambton, 'Persia', *Journal of the Royal Central Asian Society* 31, no. 1 (January 1944): 8–22.

38. Private papers of F. Shelton, 13556, IWM; Dr Francis Shelton, interview by author, London, 11 April 2014.

39. Cf. Stephen Dorril, *MI6: Inside the Covert World of Her Majesty's Secret Intelligence Service* (New York: Touchstone, 2002), 561, 850n7, who suggests that Lambton's position as press attaché was typical MI6 cover.

40. See Martin Kramer, 'Miss Lambton's Advice', *Middle East Strategy at Harvard (MESH)*, 20 August 2008, http://blogs.law.harvard.edu/mesh/.

41. A.F. Judge, 'Special Duties and the Intelligence Corps, 1940 to 1946', unpublished MS, Military Intelligence Museum and Archives, Chicksands, Bedfordshire. Cf. Robin Zaehner's predecessor in Tehran and fellow Oxonian, Christopher Sykes, who wrote after the war obliquely and perhaps peevishly, albeit without direct reference to Zaehner: 'To speak many tongues with grace and fluency is not necessarily a mark of intellectual distinction; it is a gift which the laughing gods often bestow upon dullards' (*Four Studies in Loyalty*, 49. Extract reprinted by permission of Peters Fraser & Dunlop [www.petersfraserdunlop.com] on behalf of the Estate of Christopher Sykes). According to Dorril, *MI6*, 563, Zaehner was known familiarly as 'Doc Zaehner'; however, I can find no archival evidence of this, though he was frequently referred to as 'Dr Zaehner' (or even 'Dr Z') in reports. Dorril also provides an unflattering depiction of Zaehner's appearance and personality as perceived by Queen Soraya and others: 'pebble glasses, squeaky voice and "mad professor" eccentricities'; 'slippery as an eel' and playing a 'sinister role' at court. Ibid., 563, 850nn14–15. Reprinted with permission of The Free Press, a Division of Simon & Schuster Inc., from *MI6: Inside the Covert World of Her Majesty's Secret Intelligence Service* by Stephen Dorril. Copyright © 2000 by Stephen Dorril. First published in the UK by Fourth Estate Limited. All rights reserved.

42. It is worth noting that, after meeting him, Wright quickly became convinced that Zaehner had remained loyal. In fact, Wright felt bitter and angry about

the accusation against Zaehner. See Peter Wright, *Spycatcher: The Candid Autobiography of a Senior Intelligence Officer* (New York: Viking, 1987), 244–6.

43. Ibid., 244–5.
44. Ibid.; History of SOE in the Arab World, September 1945, HS 7/86, TNA.
45. Memorandum on SOE activities in Arab countries, Persia, Egypt, and Cyprus, HS 7/85, TNA.
46. History of SOE in the Arab World, September 1945, HS 7/86, TNA.
47. Saul Kelly, 'A Succession of Crises: SOE in the Middle East, 1940–45', *Intelligence and National Security* 20, no. 1 (March 2005): 136.
48. Future cover for British staff, Summary of activities, March 1945, HS 7/86, TNA. For an interesting though far from conclusive discussion of MI6–SOE relations in London and the Middle East, see Nigel West, *Secret War: The Story of SOE, Britain's Wartime Sabotage Organisation* (London: Hodder & Stoughton, 1992), 250–2. A similar discussion of MI6–SOE relations in (mainly southeast) Asia is to be found in Richard J. Aldrich, 'Britain's Secret Intelligence Service in Asia during the Second World War', *Modern Asian Studies* 32, no. 1 (1998): 179–217.
49. Regarding the MI6 counterespionage remit, cf. Andrew, *Defence of the Realm*, 442–3; Howard, *Strategic Deception*, 32.
50. Note on future security problems in Mid-East, November 1943, KV 4/384, TNA.
51. Ibid.
52. History of the Near East Section, OSS, Cairo, 22-25, Document No. 11384/004, RG 226, Entry 210, Box 261, NARA.
53. Ibid.
54. Report of visit by Mr A. J. Kellar to SIME and CICI organizations, May 1944, KV 4/384, TNA.
55. See Andrew, *Defence of the Realm*, 443.
56. Christopher Sykes, *Wassmuss: The German Lawrence* (London: Longmans Green, 1936).
57. Christopher Sykes, *High Minded Murder* (London: Home & Van Thal, 1944); West, *Secret War*, 55, 278n6.
58. Christopher Sykes, *A Song of a Shirt* (London: Verschoyle, 1953); West, *Secret War*, 56, 278n8.
59. Aside from his informed literary analysis, Sykes's biography of Waugh (Christopher Sykes, *Evelyn Waugh: A Biography* [London: Collins, 1975]) may be read as an interesting factual account of clandestine warfare seen through the prisms of military, intelligence, and social history.
60. Christopher Sykes, *Four Studies in Loyalty* (London: Collins, 1946).
61. Memorandum on SOE activities in Arab countries, Persia, Egypt, and Cyprus, HS 7/85, TNA; Judge, 'Special Duties and the Intelligence Corps, 1940 to 1946'.
62. SOE War Diary, November/December 1942, HS 7/267, TNA; also in Kelly, 'Succession of Crises', 135.
63. History of SOE in the Arab World, September 1945, HS 7/86, TNA.
64. Cipher telegram received from Cairo, 8 May 1943, HS 9/1433/9, TNA.
65. D/HV [Pearson] to D/HX [Nixon], 22 May 1943, HS 9/1433/9, TNA; Declaration on termination of agreement, 22 June 1943, HS 9/1433/9, TNA.

8
Operation PONGO

An unconfirmed source of unknown reliability has reported that General Zahedi, the suspect Persian GOC Isfahan, is obtaining a portable W/T transmitter, allegedly for the use of his children, who are apparently to receive instruction in Morse. (SIME Security Summary)[1]

In the absence of any reported offensive SOE actions – so-called 'bangs' – on Persian soil between 1941 and 1945, mention needs to be made here of a unique PAIFORCE covert operation (codenamed PONGO) which marked the special-operations debut of Fitzroy Maclean, who would subsequently distinguish himself as a prominent SOE commander (D/H178)[2] with Tito's partisans in Yugoslavia. According to Maclean, who planned the Persian operation himself without any formal sanction by SOE, to whom the task would normally have fallen, he was given a free hand by Sir Reader Bullard and Jumbo Wilson's chief-of-staff, Joseph Baillon, in the matter of the arrest of the powerful southern Persian malcontent Fazlollah Zahedi, governor-general of Isfahan (see Figure 8.1): 'Only two conditions were made: I was to take him alive and I was to do so without creating a disturbance.'[3] According to Jumbo Wilson, the decision to arrest Zahedi was his and achieved its goal: 'the possibility of others being treated in a like manner put a complete damper on any further activities of the plotters'.[4] Although Zahedi was in clandestine contact with the Germans, and his arrest removed a significant security threat, there was no security-intelligence (CICI/DSO) involvement in Operation PONGO. It was essentially an independent military special operation carried out on 7 December 1942 by regular infantry soldiers (Seaforth Highlanders) with negligible commando training under GHQ

Figure 8.1 Surgically removed: Fazlollah Zahedi. The malignant Persian general was spirited away to internment by Fitzroy Maclean and his Seaforth Highlanders in a clinical commando operation
Source: Wikipedia Commons/PD.

Baghdad (PAIFORCE) command. However, PONGO did not encroach upon the competence of DSO, which had yet to be fully established, nor upon that of SOE, since it did not involve sabotage or subversion. This does not mean that CICI were not responsible for obtaining and analysing the intelligence that alerted Bullard and Baillon to the dangers inherent in allowing the deceptively charming Zahedi to pursue unchecked his malevolent intentions, which included 'liquidating' the British consul in Isfahan and hoarding so much grain that Persians throughout the country would starve.[5] On the contrary, the operation was entirely dependent on accurate intelligence supplied by DSO to CICI, which was then relayed to PAIFORCE.

As a neutral country under the aegis of British interest, yet outside the Empire, Persia could in no way benefit from the imperial 'benevolence' experienced in difficult times by such colonies as India. Consequently, when economic conditions became desperate, as they did in 1942 when 20 people were killed and 700 wounded during bread riots in Tehran,[6] the average Persian could expect nothing but deprivation and neglect, for good governance under wartime occupation seems to have been beyond the competence of the young Shah's governments and officials. The frailty of the Persian polity and economy under British and Russian occupation seems merely to have aggravated the nation's susceptibility to systemic corruption and mischief of all kinds, together with a widening of the social divide between immensely rich, powerful, but unscrupulous villains like Zahedi and the destitute general population. Given acute food shortages, crop failures, inflation, and civil unrest throughout 1942, it is understandable that Zahedi's criminal intentions with respect to the food supply were taken very seriously by the British security forces, as they could have had far-reaching political and social consequences. However, Zahedi was a prime target for CICI mainly because he was deeply implicated in the subversive activities of Franz Mayr and the *Melliun Iran* movement, on the basis of hard evidence acquired on 2 November 1942.[7] Additionally, the catalyst for action against Zahedi was his callous attitude and that of the military governor of Feridun, Sadiq Khan Feruhar (NIAZMAND) (another known pro-German fifth columnist), towards the shocking Harris–Griffiths triple murder on 3 August 1942.[8]

A vacationing 11-year-old Australian schoolboy (Ian Griffiths), his medical-missionary father (Dr Leslie Griffiths), who had lived and worked in Isfahan since 1938, and his close personal friend (R.C. Skipworth Harris), a British consular official working for SOE (D/N14)[9] under diplomatic cover, were travelling in Lorestan (tribal territory then under Persian army occupation). There all three were shot to death in cold blood by a band of 200 Bakhtiari tribesmen (under Zahedi's military control and probably bribed by Feruhar on Zahedi's orders to ambush the British agent).[10] The day before, the three expatriates, accompanied by five Persian guides, had visited the site of a downed Soviet aircraft in the Zagros Mountains – amidst some of the finest mountain scenery Persia has to offer, below the perpetual snows of the spectacular Oshturan Kuh range (over 4000 m), about 48 km east of Dorud – no doubt to provide some adventure for young Ian Griffiths.[11] There they had examined the crash site, had buried the bodies of the Russian airmen, and had collected all the documents they could find, including some 'red-coloured papers', which were probably classified documents that Harris had been instructed to retrieve. After a night under canvas with the nomadic Hivedi tribe of the Chahar Lang Bakhtiari, the party set off on horseback in the direction of Zazb and Mahru, having hired a 50-year-old local Hivedi guide named Sayyid Murad Zahrai for the journey. At about 09:00 hrs, the group entered a defile, with Harris riding in front, followed by Dr Griffiths, and Ian Griffiths behind his father. The remaining members of the party were walking much further back with the eight pack-donkeys, perhaps deliberately because they knew what was about to happen. Suddenly a shot rang out from above, and a bullet hit Harris in the leg, passing through his leg into the horse. Both fell to the ground. Griffiths raised his rifle and fired a shot which ricocheted off a stone. Immediately afterwards a second shot from the 'bandits' hit Griffiths in the stomach or hip and killed him. Harris meanwhile sat up and was trying to draw a pistol from his pocket when Zahrai seized Griffiths' rifle and shot Harris through the mouth with it, presumably killing him instantly. While this was happening, Griffiths' small son jumped off his horse and scrambled under a bush. That was the last that witnesses saw of him.[12]

Some 12 days later, under the protection of a large cavalcade of heavily armed horsemen, John D'Aeth, then ALO Isfahan (later to become vice-consul at Hamadan), accompanied by Grigore 'Gregory' Banquei of the Imperial Bank of Iran (a personal friend of the victims), entered the desolate valley where the victims' corpses, including that of the Griffiths boy, lay rotting in the summer heat, badly disfigured and partially devoured by desert scavengers. The scene was as pitiful as it was hideous. Dr Griffiths' hands and feet were missing. The skin of his stomach was drawn up to his chest, and some parts of his body appeared to have been eaten by bears. His false teeth had fallen to the ground. A few paces further on, Harris's body was found in similar condition. The top part of his head was missing, apparently as a result of the bullet fired by Zahrai. Harris's thigh bone was found to have been broken when his horse fell. Ian Griffiths' knitted pullover was also found with plenty of blood hardened on it, together with his chest, ribs, arms, and leg bones, but no head. 'We searched for the other remains of the boy, but nothing more could be found.'[13]

It is not known how Ian Griffiths perished, for up to the time that his remains were discovered, it was generally thought that he might still be alive. Presumably, his father's killers had dragged the terrified boy from his hideaway beneath the bush, and had cruelly murdered him. Ultimately, all three victims were laid to rest in the New Julfa Armenian cemetery in Isfahan after official postmortem examination at the Isfahan Church Missionary Hospital on 20 August 1942, which concluded that all three deaths were 'due to gunshot wounds'.[14]

As prominent representatives of the British consulate and the Church Missionary Society (CMS) respectively, both Skipworth Harris and Leslie Griffiths were well known in Isfahan to Persians and British expatriates alike. Consequently, the grisly, ruthless murders caused shockwaves throughout the region. This created a serious problem for the British diplomatic and military authorities, because, whilst the records show their genuine desire to apprehend the culprits and compensate Griffiths' widow and Harris's family, the last thing they wanted was for attention to be drawn to Harris's clandestine activities. One Isfahan consular official wrote to the Foreign Office:

> We should avoid saying openly that it was Harris's own fault. I myself think that he *was* rash. He went unescorted into a dangerous area and he went with a few arms which were no doubt, on the face of it, one of the immediate causes of his death. But we don't need ... to say publicly that it was his own fault. In any case, for his work in gathering information about tribes, an escort of Persian military would be the very last thing he could desire, because it would most certainly prevent him obtaining information and would only probably (but not necessarily) keep him safe, especially as the man who would have supplied it would have been Feruhar, who is our enemy.[15]

Whilst many initially felt that Skipworth Harris had been headstrong and negligent, it seems unjust that some continued to hold him responsible for the tragedy after it had been established that the ambush was planned rather than provoked. According to the British consulate in Isfahan, Harris had been warned by local tribesmen not to venture into the Oshturan Kuh area because it was dangerous, but he had evidently disregarded these warnings because he felt that his SOE assignment, not only to retrieve secret documents from the Soviet aircraft but also to investigate reports of Germans hiding nearby, took precedence. In fact, the British consular officials originally considered it possible that the ambush might have been laid by fugitive Germans. However, it subsequently became clear that there were no Germans in the area, and that the instigators were no doubt none other than Zahedi and Feruhar. Later, Sir Reader Bullard would describe Skipworth Harris as 'an able and sensible man' and 'an officer with special qualifications' who got himself killed in circumstances which reflected very seriously on his judgement, and which were causing the legation 'serious embarrassment'.[16] But Bullard's view seems unjustified, unless he was unaware of the true nature of Harris's remit, and the fact that he was working for SOE.

But what was Harris really up to in Lorestan, and for whom was he really working? It is certainly clear from SOE records that Harris was SOE (D/N14),[17] and certain facts and circumstantial evidence in the Foreign Office files might suggest that Harris was merely under diplomatic cover in Isfahan rather than a bona-fide vice-consul. In the days immediately following the retrieval of the bodies from the desert, the Foreign Office requested details from the legation 'as Harris had consular cover',[18] to which the military attaché, Wak Fraser, replied vaguely and evasively: 'Harris assisted Consul, Isfahan, and furnished valuable information on conditions in Bakhtiari, which he knew well. HM Minister and Military Attaché and others frequently consulted him on Bakhtiari matters.'[19] In fact, the records clearly show that Harris was not merely under consular cover but was a genuine consular official, having been gazetted as a Colonial Office Eastern Cadet in 1930.[20] Yet he was equally clearly acting under the command of Herbert Underwood, head of SOE in Persia, for Underwood claimed after the murder that Harris 'had misunderstood his instructions'.[21] A few days later, Underwood also stated that 'Harris was actually carrying out three months' old instructions of the GOC ... reconnoitring the western part of his area towards the railway'.[22] Additionally, the Foreign Office correspondence speaks of Harris remotely, as if he were a member of some other organization beyond their control – obviously SOE. As to the underlying cause of the barbaric attack, Wak Fraser was under no illusion as to the identity of the real perpetrators. He wrote to the Foreign Office: 'Harris's movements were always closely watched and even hampered by local military authorities (especially Colonel Feruhar, military governor of Feridun) many of whom are openly pro-German. There are good grounds for suspicion against them. Harris knew too much about their oppressive measures and pro-Germanism for their liking.'[23]

Joe Spencer was equally convinced of Feruhar's guilt and by association that of Zahedi too. Feruhar of course was Zahedi's close companion and enjoyed the general's protection at all times. Before the vile murders, on 1 June according to Spencer, Zahedi was reported as saying that it would be a good thing if Skipworth Harris were killed in Bakhtiari country, and about the same time he had expressed both verbally and in writing his annoyance at British agents' going to Feridun without his permission. Spencer concluded: 'as in the case of Feruhar, a very strong suspicion exists in the minds of almost everyone who has been investigating the murder of Harris, Griffiths, and his son that Zahedi is at any rate indirectly involved'.[24] Much was made at the time of how unwise and provocative it was for Skipworth Harris to have travelled armed in a tribal area. However,

Harris was an experienced agent who undoubtedly knew exactly what he was doing; it seems clear that he was deliberately targeted as part of Zahedi's personal vendetta against the staff of the Isfahan consulate.

In his official report on the tragic incident, the Kurdish expert John C.A. 'Johnny' Johnson (also SOE), now under diplomatic cover as vice-consul in Isfahan, wrote to CICI that the whole of Isfahan was already waiting to see what would happen as a result of the affair, and that, unless very strong action were taken at once, it would be highly detrimental to British prestige, and would probably result in other attempts to kill British people.[25] No doubt Johnny Johnson was ultimately gratified, for Fitzroy Maclean and his Seaforths successfully executed a daring covert raid on General Zahedi's home on 7 December 1942 (Operation PONGO), kidnapping the general more or less without incident.[26] After Zahedi's arrest and internment, for the duration of the war, CICI assessed the significance of PONGO in words that directly addressed Johnson's concerns:

> This removal of one of the main obstructions to British efforts to improve the economic conditions and the security position in Isfahan is one of the most important security measures taken in Persia since the Allied occupation, and should serve as a deterrent to similar undesirable persons who have hitherto relied on their position to protect them in their subversive activities. There have been no visible reactions to this effective counterstroke except for the congratulations offered to the British authorities by certain leading Persians on the arrest of Zahedi. It is likely however that other Persian obstructionists will not fail to take warning from the fact of Zahedi's arrest, the effect of which should assist in maintaining our prestige, and improving our security throughout Persia.[27]

Certainly, the British consul in Isfahan, Charles Gault, was delighted that the general had been surgically extracted from his territory. He wrote at the time: 'Zahedi was a man who had an iron in every fire, however small it might seem, and that was the cause of unrest in Isfahan.'[28] The general's clique of wealthy Isfahanis ('some dozen men, all rascals') had been taken aback and were greatly subdued. They were at the same time the richest merchants in the bazaar and the biggest factory owners and landowners; and, according to Gault, Zahedi clearly had had them all in his pocket.[29]

It is of course scandalous and deeply ironic that, barely ten years later, after overthrowing the democratically elected government of

Mohammad Mosaddeq in a now notorious coup orchestrated jointly with the CIA, essentially to protect Anglo-American oil interests, the British Secret Service (MI6) nominated none other than the murderous, anti-British Fazlollah Zahedi to succeed Mosaddeq as Persian prime minister.[30] Equally ironic is the high likelihood that the original architects of Mosaddeq's downfall were none other than the two orientalist dons at the wartime Tehran legation – Robin Zaehner and Ann Lambton – who reputedly cooked up their sinister scheme (Operation BOOT) for MI6 (which culminated in the progressive prime minister's callous victimization and execution) some time after they returned from Tehran to the common rooms of Oxford and London.[31] And we know without doubt that it was Zaehner's assistant in Tehran, Norman Darbyshire, who worked (as the MI6 representative) with the American Persianist Donald Wilber (as the CIA representative), to elaborate the Machiavellian plan as Operation TPAJAX for CIA purposes.[32] Both men had doubtless first met during the war, when Wilber was working under cultural cover for the OSS.[33]

Almost as an omen of things to come in the next decade, the only negative reaction to Operation PONGO came from Washington – not surprisingly, for the State Department was briefed on the operation by the ever-hostile US minister, Louis G. Dreyfus Jr. Ultimately, it was this American opposition that prevented DSO from carrying out any further arrests of Persian officers implicated in the subversive plotting that emanated from the circle around Zahedi. In fairness, it has to be added that it was not only the odious Dreyfus who raised objections to further British action: the US adviser to the Persian army also felt that the arrest of an officer like Feruhar might have the undesirable effect of lowering morale among the Persian officer corps in general, and DSO seem to have accepted his view.[34] Ultimately though, SOE never really succeeded in overcoming American resistance to their presence and subversive activities in Persia. One SOE officer who served in the region felt that the Americans were simply not 'in favour of having any fifth columnists for fear of disturbing friendly relations between the Allies and the Persians'.[35] In postwar retrospect and whilst acknowledging the difficulties inherent in waging coalition warfare, at least one American historian who studied the security situation in Persia felt uneasy with what he saw as the 'criminal' naivety of the American position.[36]

The verdict of history may restore the good name of Skipworth Harris, for the archival record shows beyond a shred of doubt that the terrible human tragedy of August 1942 was not provoked by him, but planned by Persian malcontents. In December 1944 and March 1945, the Tehran embassy, under direct instructions from the Foreign Office, filed memoranda with the Persian Ministry of Foreign Affairs roundly chastizing the Persian central government for failing to take any action against the Hivedi tribe, who had murdered Harris, Griffiths, and Griffiths' son 'in circumstances of the greatest barbarity', and demanding immediate steps to apprehend the murderers and bring them to justice.[37] These *démarches* had the desired effect, for by the autumn of 1945 two men had been tracked down and arrested in connection with the murders and despatched to Tehran for trial by military court.[38] By October, a third suspect had been committed for trial.[39] Some time during the next couple of months, the staff of the Tehran embassy were informed that the accused – the guide Sayyid Murad Zahrai and two elderly men (Haidar Zamani and Ali Barani)[40] – had been tried, found guilty, and sentenced to death, whereupon they had immediately appealed their sentences.[41] It took over two years for the Court of Appeal to reduce the sentences from death to two years' solitary confinement – by then already served – at which point the Foreign Office (FO), dissatisfied with the leniency of the court, instructed the embassy to demand an explanation, especially in view of the extreme brutality of the murders.[42] The explanation duly came, four months later, providing the astounding news that the accused had never actually been sentenced to death for murder by the court of first instance, but only to 15 years' hard labour for banditry; consequently, the reduction in their sentences could not be considered lenient. Furthermore, the noncapital sentence had been additionally justified by implausible and contradictory witness statements which had allowed the accused to portray themselves convincingly as mere bandits out for plunder, not participants in the murders.[43] It took until 1950 for the embassy to obtain from the Persian Ministry of Foreign Affairs a copy of the judgement by the appeal court,[44] indicating insufficient proof of murder, at which point the FO apparently decided to drop the case.

Sadly, under the Persian legal system, justice was neither done, nor seen to be done. However, in a mere two or three years, Fazlollah Zahedi would become the unlikely darling of the British and US intelligence services and would have the mantle of central power thrust upon him. One cannot be blamed for wondering if MI6, possibly at the behest of the CIA, pressured the FO to withdraw their advocacy for the murdered trio in order to appease Zahedi and smooth the way to Mossadeq's downfall. One should not forget how extraordinarily upset the Americans had been about Operation PONGO and the original internment of Zahedi some eight years earlier. But should one really be surprised at Washington's (or Langley's) unerring ability to select the ugliest of political personalities to prosecute its causes?

Notes

1. Security Summary Middle East No. 86, 10 October 1942, WO 208/1561, TNA.
2. SOE symbols 6, HS 8/971, TNA.
3. Fitzroy Maclean, *Eastern Approaches* (London: Jonathan Cape, 1949), 214. Extract reprinted by permission of Peters Fraser & Dunlop (www.petersfraser-dunlop.com) on behalf of the Estate of Fitzroy Maclean. An unillustrated version of Maclean's autobiography was also published in the United States as *Escape to Adventure* (Boston: Little Brown, 1950). For more about Zahedi, see Milani, *Eminent Persians*, 495–505.
4. Wilson, *Eight Years Overseas*, 146.
5. See Stephen L. McFarland, 'Anatomy of an Iranian Political Crowd: The Tehran Bread Riot of December 1942', *International Journal of Middle East Studies* 17, no. 1 (February 1985): 51–65.
6. Ibid.: 51.
7. Plan for breaking the German fifth column in Persia, 11 August 1943, KV 2/1477, TNA.
8. First reported in Security Summary Middle East No. 79, 14 September 1942, WO 208/1561, TNA.
9. SOE symbols 6, HS 8/971, TNA.
10. Most of the details about the Harris–Griffiths murder case are to be found in FO 799/8, TNA. Also see isolated documents in FO 248/1411, FO 371/31386, FO 371/31387, FO 371/31418, FO 371/31419, FO 371/35068, FO 371/45502, FO 371/52764, FO 371/62059, FO 371/62077, FO 371/68742, FO 371/82392, FO 799/11, FO 847/177, and FO 921/3, TNA; as well as 'Persian Brigands' Crime', *The Times* (12 August 1942); 'Aust. Missionary Killed in Persia', *The Courier-Mail* (13 August 1942); 'Australian Missionary Killed by Brigands in Persia', *The West Australian* (13 August 1942); 'General Cables', *Townsville Daily Bulletin* (13 August 1942).
11. Johnson to CICI Baghdad, 8 August 1942, FO 799/8, TNA.
12. Isfahan to Hankey, 25 August 1942, FO 799/8, TNA.
13. Ibid.
14. Postmortem certificate, Church Missionary Hospital, Isfahan, 20 August 1942, FO 799/8, TNA.
15. Isfahan to Hankey, 25 August 1942, FO 799/8, TNA. Original italics.
16. Legation minute (annotated 'Col Underwood for action'), 29 August 1942, FO 248/1411.
17. SOE symbols 6, HS 8/971, TNA. For more on Skipworth Harris and SOE, see SOE War Diary 43, Middle East and Balkans, July–August 1942, 106–9, HS 7/266, TNA; SOE War Diary 44, Middle East and Balkans, September–December 1942, 367, HS 7/267, TNA.
18. London to Tehran, 16 August 1942, FO 248/1411.
19. Tehran to FO, n.d., FO 248/1411.
20. *London Gazette*, no. 33659 (7 November 1930), 7072.

21. Isfahan to Hankey, 25 August 1942, FO 799/8, TNA.

22. Underwood to Gault, 31 August 1942, FO 799/8, TNA.

23. Tehran to FO, n.d., FO 248/1411.

24. Spencer to Bullard (via Fraser), 30 August 1942, FO 248/1411, TNA.

25. Johnson to CICI Baghdad, 8 August 1942, FO 799/8, TNA.

26. See Appendix D to Report on the Methods of Ensuring Security of the Road Bushire-Shiraz-Isfahan, 10 January 1943, WO 201/1400A, TNA; Maclean, *Eastern Approaches*, 212–21; Frank McLynn, *Fitzroy Maclean* (London: John Murray, 1992), 113–16.

27. CICI Security Intelligence Summary No. 48, 15 December 1942, WO 208/3089, TNA.

28. Isfahan Consulate Diary, 16–31 December 1942, FO 799/11, TNA.

29. Ibid.

30. For more in general about the Mossadeq coup, see *Mohammad Mosaddeq and the 1953 Coup in Iran*, ed. Mark J. Gasiorowski and Malcolm Byrne (Syracuse, NY: Syracuse University Press, 2004); also Davies, *MI6*, 224–7; Kermit Roosevelt, *Countercoup: The Struggle for the Control of Iran* (New York: McGraw-Hill, 1979), passim.

31. See Hugh Wilford, *America's Great Game: The CIA's Secret Arabists and the Shaping of the Modern Middle East* (New York: Basic Books, 2013), 163–8; specifically regarding Lambton's role in the Mossadeq coup, see Kramer, 'Miss Lambton's Advice'.

32. TP was CIA code for Iran; 'Ajax' was a popular American household scouring agent (equivalent to 'Vim' in Britain). Full documentary evidence of the coup, including the role of MI6, has been assembled and published by The National Security Archive (an independent non-governmental research institute and library located at The George Washington University), including Wilber's after-action report written in March 1954 and originally published by the *New York Times* in 2004 (http://www.nytimes.com/library/world/mideast/041600iran-cia-index.html). See 'The Secret CIA History of the Iran Coup', *National Security Archive Electronic Briefing Book No. 28* (Washington: The National Security Archive, 2000). Wilber appends the original operational plan to his report, including a 'Summary of Preliminary Plan Prepared by SIS and CIA Representatives in Cyprus'. See also Donald N. Wilber, *Adventures in the Middle East: Excursions and Incursions* (Princeton, NJ: Darwin, 1986) passim.

33. For more about Wilber's wartime OSS role, see Chapter 13.

34. Minute, 30 December 1942, E7561; FO to Tehran, 4 January 1943, FO 371/31387, TNA.

35. SOE War Diary, January/March 1943, HS 7/268, TNA.

36. See the correspondence between Ladislas Farago and Sir Reader Bullard in GB 165-0042-3/11, MECA. As far as I can tell, Farago never published any of his extensive research on Persia, which is unfortunate, for he was a pioneering investigative intelligence historian – though not an academic – with a nose for buried archival treasure, who wrote extremely readable books. His contribution would no doubt have been valuable and stimulating. He is the only historian I know of who has shown any sustained interest in Persian covert operations. His best-known work is Ladislas Farago, *The Game of the Foxes: The Untold Story of German Espionage in the United States and Great Britain*

during World War II (Toronto: Bantam, 1973), which disappointingly makes no mention of the foxy games played in Persia. For a critical view of Farago's reliability as a researcher, see Gerold Guensberg, 'Abwehr Myth: How Efficient Was German Intelligence in World War II?' *Studies in Intelligence* 21, no. 3 (Fall 1977): 39–40.

37. Lascelles to Intizam, 15 March 1945, FO 371/45502, TNA.
38. Monypenny to Bevin, 13 September 1945, FO 371/45502, TNA.
39. Somers-Cocks to FO, 16 April 1946, FO 371/45502, TNA.
40. Enclosure 1 to Tehran Chancery letter No. 165/1/4/50 of 11 January to Eastern Department, FO 371/82392, TNA.
41. Somers-Cocks to FO, 1 December 1946, FO 371/45502, TNA.
42. FO to Tehran, 21 May 1948, FO 371/68742, TNA; Creswell to Isfandiari, 8 June 1948, FO 371/68742, TNA.
43. Persian Ministry of Foreign Affairs to British Embassy, 25 September 1948, FO 371/68742, TNA.
44. Tehran to FO, 11 January 1950, FO 371/82392, TNA.

9
Secondees from India

> We were seated on rough tribal rugs on the floor of a small tent, one side of which was raised to form a sort of marquee, and through which we had a charming view of the Qashgai camp under the white trunks of a grove of poplar trees, with the wide plain and high mountains in the background. (Bill Magan [MI5])[1]

Until the Second World War, the Government of India (GOI) had always tended to regard most of eastern, southeastern, and central Persia as its sphere of influence and had assumed responsibility for diplomatic representation and intelligence gathering in that region. Personnel manning consular posts in Ahwaz, Kerman, Meshed, and Seistan, for example, were traditionally drawn from the Indian Civil Service, the Indian Political Service, and the Indian Army, whereas the Tehran legation and consulates in other Persian regions (for example, in Isfahan, Kermanshah, Khorramshahr, Resht, and Shiraz) were staffed by the London-based diplomatic and consular services. A traditional rivalry and a rather cumbersome reporting system evolved, according to which intelligence was transmitted by the predominantly Foreign Office posts to the FO in London, whence copies were sent to the India Office, and relevant information was then forwarded by them to Delhi. Conversely, GOI posts reported directly to Delhi, whence copies were sent to the India Office in London, for onward transmission to the FO.[2]

In practice, early in the war, the FO routinely consulted Delhi before implementing policy in Persia, including any proposed measures to counter Axis intelligence and other secret activities. Shortly before the Anglo-Soviet invasion, the FO, alarmed at the proliferation of German agents and the growth of German influence in Persia, suggested fighting fire with fire: recognizing the GOI's interest and strong representation in the region, they proposed to Delhi a mass infiltration of British agents into Persia under commercial or even religious cover 'more or less on the German model' and sought Delhi's input. Not unnaturally, the GOI appear to have been almost as alarmed at Whitehall's proposal as at any Nazi intrigues and showed little enthusiasm for the bold plan. Consequently, they sought to delay it, after various substantive objections had been raised by, among others, the political resident in Bushire. Fortunately perhaps for both Whitehall and Delhi, the dispute was effectively neutralized by the decision to stage a full-scale military invasion and occupation of Persia (Operation COUNTENANCE).[3]

A flurry of correspondence in the records shortly after the Anglo-Soviet invasion reveals something of the background to the secondment of William M.T. Magan early in 1942 from his Indian Army cavalry regiment (Hodson's Horse) to DSO Persia, overtly to liaise between CICI and Delhi, but covertly to establish a network of underground staybehind agents in Persia to resist the enemy behind German lines, should the Wehrmacht break through Transcauscasia.[4] This correspondence is interesting inasmuch as it shows how, after the invasion, in late 1941, it was ensured that all security-intelligence organization and operations in Persia would come under the CICI umbrella, without interference from Delhi, yet without upsetting the GOI. The supportive, no-nonsense attitude of the British minister in Tehran, Sir Reader Bullard, clearly helped the C-in-C India and the C-in-C Middle East to get the policy approved. It seems that the GOI was facing an extreme shortage of manpower at the time. However much it might have wished to 'maintain influence' and retain control of political intelligence operations in eastern Persia, including those concerning tribal affairs, the GOI was not in a position to provide sufficient numbers of consular political officers to do so. Ultimately, it was compelled in some areas to rely upon the assistance of DSO Persia's ALOs for the acquisition of political intelligence. Seconding a single IO (Magan) to Tehran to liaise with DSO was therefore a simple solution to what had become a daunting problem. And it was of course an appointment that suited Magan nicely and enabled him to carry out his covert role without being detected.[5]

Referring in late October to various proposals relating to intelligence organization in Persia, the FO declared that Bullard's staff had the situation well in hand, and that Bullard had suggested that the GOI appoint their own special officer to Tehran (presumably to handle liaison with Delhi). The FO continued: 'There has been a large increase in the staff at Tehran, with a consequent tendency to unwieldiness and duplication, and Bullard's view ... is that further additions to staff should be made only for objects with which the present staff cannot adequately deal.'[6] A little over a week later, the FO cabled with heightened urgency: 'Commander-in-Chief India and Commander-in-Chief Middle East consider that establishment of security and intelligence organization in Persia under CICI is essential in order to watch future attempts by enemy to develop subversive activities which must be expected after the present setback to their plans, especially if German forces draw nearer to Persia. The present opportunity of penetration by security service may not recur.'[7] The suggestion that CICI should include an 'intelligence organization' appears to have rather unnverved Indian Political Intelligence (IPI), ostensibly at least, for they minuted in late November that they were somewhat worried by the use of the term 'intelligence' alone, as opposed to 'security and intelligence'. However, it had become clear that the new organization was intended for 'security intelligence' only, and IPI were grateful to the India Office for confining themselves to this term.[8]

Nevertheless, when Bill Magan was summoned to Delhi in January 1942 to confer with Sir Denys Pilditch, Director of the Indian Intelligence Bureau (DIB), it was clear that, with the Germans at the gates of Transcaucasia, the absence of any British intelligence organization in Persia was the truly unnerving circumstance. Pilditch told Magan that, if the commander-in-chief of the German forces in south Russia were to succeed in breaking through the Caucasus into Persia as a prelude to attacking India, they did not want to be caught in a situation like Malaya. Pilditch asked Magan if he, as a Persian speaker and having knowledge of the country from having lived there for a year, would go into south and east Persia and try to form a staybehind organization to provide intelligence from behind the German lines in Persia, if the Germans should succeed in getting there. Pilditch went on to say that the Germans had left their own staybehind organization in Persia which had gone underground, and that PAIFORCE was trying to mop it up. Magan felt that he clearly could not refuse Pilditch's request to carry out the Persian operation. Recognizing that he was the only person with both Persian knowledge and experience and the required relationship with the GOI Intelligence Bureau (IB), to which he would be reporting in Quetta, Magan decided to set up his base there, as it was ideally located on his direct route through Baluchistan into eastern and southern Persia.[9]

So, after establishing a Quetta support base and recruiting a Farsi-speaking Hazara police driver from the Quetta police, Sergeant Ibrahim

Khan – a First World War veteran who became his trusted companion – Magan set about establishing various forms of cover ideal for his projected activities. First, he got himself appointed 'temporary military vice-consul' at the British consulate in Kerman, engaged upon road and other reconnaissance; second, he attached himself to the Royal Engineers repairing the access roads leading from the Indian border into Persia and played multiple roles with the sappers as adviser, as liaison officer between them and the Persians, and as a general reconnaissance officer making advance preparation for the arrival of British and Indian forces. Quickly and methodically Magan assembled his network, travelling immense distances across southeastern Persia while doing so. It is interesting to note that in this remote region, by contrast with other parts of the country, there was little support for the Germans. As Magan noted, the people of southern and eastern Persia had traditionally maintained very close trade links with British India; consequently, they were appalled at the prospect of coming under the heel of Hitler's Germany. This meant that the area as a whole was well disposed towards the British and welcomed their interest in frustrating the German advance there.[10] Magan's accurate perception is never echoed in any of the German records. The Nazis' simplistic interpretation of contemporary Persian political opinion saw the majority of Persians throughout the country as pro-German. From the 1930s onwards, this fundamental error of judgement led Berlin to make false political assumptions about Persia and very poor operational decisions, which cost them dearly over the course of the war. Typically, a German naval-intelligence (Abw I M) agent noted, 'There is no doubt that the mass of the Persian people have an extremely hostile attitude towards the Allies.'[11]

Magan then moved on to Tehran to establish his final cover as Indian Intelligence Bureau (IB) liaison officer with what he referred to as the 'small PAIFORCE security intelligence organization': in other words, DSO Persia.[12] Here Magan was reunited with his old friend from the IA, Alan Roger, who was ADSO. It is unclear whether Magan improvised his position with DSO as he had created his cover in Kerman, or if he was formally attached to DSO by the IB. He certainly appears to have been required to coordinate his plans with PAIFORCE and to keep the British legation fully informed of his plans and undertakings. This suggests that his appointment was official. Whilst fully realizing that his expertise as a regular-service IO could be put to good use in mopping up fugitive Germans, it was equally clear to Magan that his first priority was to prepare for a possible German breakthrough from the Caucasus, and that he had to get on with the job of recruiting a large network of intelligence agents in central, southern, and eastern Persia. As Magan saw the situation when he was given the assignment, the Germans, in January 1942, were bogged down in south Russia by the winter, but would be on the move again when the spring thaw came and might, by Magan's calculations, get through the Caucasus by the early autumn of 1942.[13]

He could not afford to risk blowing his cover by recruiting agents personally. Therefore Magan delegated the task to three assistants: an American carpet dealer in Isfahan, an Indian police officer serving as vice-consul in Yezd, and a Greek carpet merchant in Kerman. Magan's job was also greatly facilitated by the fact that the IB assumed full responsibility for agent training. Once recruited, agents were sent across the frontier at Zahidan and on to the IB in Quetta. The tradecraft insisted upon by Magan, especially his personal use of cutouts, reveals the professionalism that marked his approach to any operation; it stands in contrast to the absence of policy and tradecraft among German stay-behinds and other operatives in Persia. In Magan's own words:

> I insisted that no potential agent was to be approached without my explicit permission. I also insisted that nothing was to be recorded on paper which could reveal details of the operation. We also wrote no letters. All communication must be oral, which was one reason for the immense amount of travelling I had to do, because I also insisted on visiting my subordinates rather than them visiting me. ... I did not meet any of the agents we recruited, and none of them ever knew of my existence.[14]

After six months of very hard work, Magan had finished: he had nine trained agents stationed on the strategic routes leading from Persia to India. They were well paid by the Indian government and were promised significant bonuses if they ever had to work behind the German lines. But this was of course never to be. Sooner than anticipated, Magan had to deal with the dual questions of whether and how to wind up his organization in the event of a German defeat in southern Russia, which is of course what ultimately happened.

After Stalingrad, Magan did not return to India but stayed on at DSO Persia, maintaining liaison between Tehran and Delhi, to watch outside leakage channels on behalf of India, with a view to building up channels for Indian deception material and to operate them when and if they opened up, while ensuring that any material disseminated followed the general strategic deception policy of the 'A' Force organization. As has

already been shown in Chapter 6, 'A' Force was an inter-services deception organization created by Wavell in 1940 and ultimately absorbed in
the Middle East under the command of Dudley Clarke into MI9. At the
same time Magan helped Joe Spencer out as much as he could, bringing
his considerable professional expertise to the task of smoking out and
capturing enemy agents – what Magan called 'rat catching':[15]

> I was not a member of the Tehran security office. I had two special
> missions to carry out for the Government of India. But the security
> people kindly put me up in their nest and allowed me free access to
> their records. And because I was there and they were short-handed,
> and I was the only regular soldier, I muscled in and took part in all
> their physical operations, mopping up German staybehinds and
> parachutists.[16]

Perhaps Magan's most valuable contribution to the work of DSO was
the final, tricky negotiations that he and R. Jackson (ALO and vice-
consul Shiraz) conducted with Nasir Khan Qashgai and his mother Bibi
Khanum Qashgai in February–March 1944 for the release into British
custody of Berthold Schulze-Holthus and the ANTON group, who had
been held captive by the Qashgai and the Boir Ahmedi in tribal territory
since September 1943.[17] Magan described his initial meeting with the
Ilkhan's mother as historic: 'I was introduced to an elegant and digni-
fied middle-aged woman and a bony middle-aged man who was her
secretary and confidant. She was Bibi Khan[um].' Clearly Bibi ruled the
tribe, she had an intellect and character 'as hard and sharp and clear
as a diamond'. In the next room her 16-year-old daughter was cough-
ing her heart out dying of consumption, but Bibi Khanum showed no
emotion. 'And her secretary was just such another. It was impossible
not to compare them with Elizabeth and Will Cecil.' Magan could not
remember for how many days he argued with them, but at length Bibi
Khanum gave in. She told Magan that, if he was prepared to go out into
the mountains to the tribe, Nasir Khan would arrange to hand over the
Germans.[18]

Not knowing quite what to expect, Bill Magan duly followed Bibi
Khanum's instructions and set out with Jackson to meet the tribe.
Magan's description of his crucial meeting with the *Ilkhan* is memorable:

> Nasir Khan has the strongest personality of any Persian I have met
> other than the notorious General Zahedi. He is a big, hard man ...
> nervous in manner, obviously highly strung, perhaps even hysterical,

but in his meeting with us he was open and direct, and there was nothing obsequious about him. ... After the usual compliments, and a minimum of introductory small talk, we got down to hard business. ... For six solid hours we battled with Nasir Khan, ... [who] probably believed he was fighting a preliminary round for high stakes and was bent on wasting as little time as possible on the traditional courtesies. It was hard for us to frame our tactics as the meeting went on, as Major Jackson and I had very little opportunity to talk together alone.[19]

However, they had set themselves one firm objective before starting, which was to get written instructions from Nasir Khan for the handing over of the Germans, and in that they succeeded.[20]

After the war, Alan Roger, who found Bill Magan's account of the part he played 'a little modest', summarized Magan's contribution to the ANTON capture. According to Roger, Magan's offer to go to Shiraz and negotiate with Bibi Khanum and Nasir Khan was accepted by DSO with enthusiasm, because of his 'very good Persian' and his profound understanding of the way the Persian mind worked. 'Also we had a great respect for his diplomatic skill,' Roger added.[21] However, Jackson's motivation as a negotiator is less transparent; indeed, 'Major R. Jackson MBE', a phantasmal figure who would be expelled from Persia in the early-1950s, together with Robin Zaehner, at the insistence of Mohammed Mossadeq shortly before his downfall,[22] is difficult to trace in any organization's records. At the time of the ANTON capture, Jackson, likely an MI6/ISLD counterintelligence officer keeping watch on Abadan and oilfield security throughout Khuzistan, was operating under consular cover at the Shiraz consulate and under military cover-within-cover as one of Joe Spencer's ALOs. Typically for an MI6 operative, Jackson's profile is extremely low: there is scarcely a mention of him in either the FO or CICI files, and 'Jackson' may even be an assumed name.[23] He was certainly not SOE, for no trace of him is to be found in their records. Beyond this, Jackson's pairing with Zaehner as *personae non gratae* in 1952, as well as Magan's astonishing total exclusion of Jackson from his 'approved' (i.e. sanitized) postwar account of the Qashgai negotiations,[24] strongly suggests that Jackson was indeed SIS. Certainly Mossadeq was gunning for him and publicly denounced him as an MI6 officer; the subsequent denial issued by the Foreign Office is unconvincing.[25] It is understandable that DSO (Magan) should have willingly shared responsibility with ISLD (Jackson) for striking a deal with Nasir Khan, for they had divergent – though complementary – operational and political agendas. The former desperately wanted to interrogate Schulze-Holthus and the ANTON parachutists, who had eluded capture for so long,[26] and who potentially possessed the answers to a long list of key security questions. The latter would clearly have sought to bring the most powerful Persian other than the shah over to the Allied side, thereby pacifying his large armed tribe, with a positive knock-on effect on the overall tribal situation, and guaranteeing the security of oil supply to the Allies from southwestern Persia.

Bill Magan was not entirely alone in Persia as a representative of the Indian security forces. Early in 1943, the GOI sent Major G.A. Naqvi, formerly of the Indian CID, to study the Indian community in Persia with special reference to anti-British and pro-Axis activities. As a result of Naqvi's report on his return to India, eight Indian suspects were arrested under the Defence of India Act as they crossed the Indo-Persian frontier, according to Sir Reader Bullard. Whether or not these malcontents were actively engaged in German covert operations remains unknown; however, the lack of any reference to them in the security-intelligence records suggests not, though they were probably aiding the enemy in some support role, possibly associated with the establishment of W/T communications with Abwehr II in Berlin on behalf of Subhas Chandra Bose and the Indian National Army (INA). Subsequently, according to Bullard, Naqvi was permanently attached to the British legation in Tehran as Indian chargé d'affaires to continue his work, with an official mandate to 'cultivate the better types of Indian' and to consider in what ways they could best be helped – whether in trade matters, army contracts, or in any legitimate grievances they might have against Persian officials or others.[27] In operational terms, however, this was merely a rather elaborate cover; according to MI5, Naqvi was actually seconded to DSO as IO (Indian suspects), using his legation position during the occupation purely as diplomatic cover.[28] Whether he continued after the war to play some kind of clandestine role remains unclear.

In June 1944, Sir Olaf Caroe of the Indian External Affairs Department and the DIB, Sir Denys Pilditch, visited Tehran for a week to discuss problems of mutual interest with the British authorities. Unfortunately, however, their visit coincided with the height of Soviet obstructionism; consequently, the Russians refused them permission to visit Meshed (in the Soviet zone), where the GOI had always had extensive interests. It is not possible to find any further information about IB interest in or concern about wartime Persia in the records, which is hardly surprising, since the British had the security situation firmly under their control.[29]

Notes

 1. Extract from a report by Major W.M.T. Magan of the Military Security Dept, Tehran, 12 April 1944, FO 371/40180, TNA.
 2. See 'British Intelligence on Persia (Iran), c. 1900–1949: Secret and Confidential British Intelligence and Policy Files', in A.J. Farrington, ed., *British Intelligence and Policy on Persia (Iran), 1900–1949: India Office Political and Secret Files and Confidential Print* (Leiden: IDC, 2004), 3–5.
 3. The relevant correspondence is to be found in IOR/L/PS/12/3517, BL.
 4. Magan, *Middle Eastern Approaches*, 16–17. The publication of Magan's memoirs, upon which much of this section is based, has been sanctioned by MI5, which is fortunate because I was not surprisingly unable to find any trace of Magan's covert work in the records. See also 'Brigadier Bill Magan (Obituary)', *The Telegraph* (22 January 2010).
 5. See GOI External Affairs Department to Secretary of State for India, 18 December 1941, E 8443/42/34, FO 371/27161, TNA.
 6. Caccia to Peel, 28 October 1941, E6813/3326/24, IOR/L/PS/12/656, BL.
 7. FO to Tehran, 7 November 1941, E7150/3326/34, IOR/L/PS/12/656, BL.
 8. IPI minute, 26 November 1941, 6341, IOR/L/PS/12/656, BL.
 9. See Magan, *Middle Eastern Approaches*, 16–17, 19.
10. See ibid., 22–3.
11. Betr. Iran, 14 May 1943, RW 5/317A, BArch-MArch.
12. See Magan, *Middle Eastern Approaches*, 23.
13. See ibid., 24.
14. Ibid., 26.
15. Clarke to Kenny, 27 July 1943, WO 201/?853, TNA.
16. Magan to Pilditch, 3 February 1981, GB165-0199, MECA.
17. Magan to Spencer, Events related to the capture of the ANTON group, 29 March 1944, KV 2/1484, TNA. One should not be misled by Magan's prefatory disclaimer: 'This is not a comprehensive factual report of the events which led up to the capture of the ANTON group.' In fact, Magan's eleven-page report is as close to an accurate account as we are ever likely to get, although he modified the narrative in postwar correspondence, attributing greater significance to the role of Bibi Khanum in tribal affairs and for some reason – probably official redaction – excluding Jackson from his account. For the full story of Schulze-Holthus and the ANTON parachutists, see also *NSW*, 144–57, 182–90.
18. Magan to Pilditch, 3 February 1981, GB165-0199, MECA.
19. Bullard to Baxter, 12 April 1944, FO 371/40180, TNA. Attached to this memorandum is an interesting lengthy portrait of Nasir Khan by Captain A. Garrod, RAMC, OC 12 Indian Division Mobile Dispensary, which facilitated his access to Qashgai tribal territory.
20. Ibid.
21. Note by Mr Alan Roger, MBE, n.d., GB165-0199, MECA.
22. 'British Plead in Vain to Keep Consuls in Iran', *Chicago Tribune*, 14 January 1952. Jackson is described as 'embassy secretary'.
23. All I can find are the following sources: FO 248/1531 and KV 2/1484, TNA.
24. See Magan, *Middle Eastern Approaches*, 79–80, cited in *NSW*, 187 and mentioned above.

25. See Dorril, *MI6*, 570; Ali Rahnema, *Behind the 1953 Coup in Iran: Thugs, Turncoats, Soldiers, and Spooks* (New York: Cambridge University Press, 2014), xvii, 237–8.
26. Schulze-Holthus had been fugitive since Sptember 1941; the ANTON group since their landing in July 1943.
27. Bullard to Eden, 20 March 1944, E 2135/189/34, IOR/L/PS/12/3472A, BL. Naqvi, alternatively described as Indian Affairs Attaché, is identified in a group photograph of legation staff taken in Tehran on 27 April 1946: Photo 920/2(41), Skrine Collection, IOR, BL. To corroborate Naqvi's diplomatic cover, see IOR/R/15/1/720, BL.
28. Appendix IX, Security: Persia, 16 February 1943, KV 4/240, TNA.
29. Bullard to Eden, 9 March 1945, E 2050/31/34, IOR/L/PS/12/3472A, BL.

10
Interrogators and Custodians

> It was agreed that ... bumping off should be the
> exception rather than the rule. We all felt that it was
> far preferable to keep these people as reference books
> since we never knew when they might be useful or
> when some further piece of information might turn
> up which would render interrogation desirable. (Guy
> Liddell [MI5])[1]

Largely as a consequence of extensive experience acquired with German
prisoners-of-war during the First World War, British POW policy was
fundamentally humane during the Second.[2] It certainly used to be a
popular notion that spying was treason and that the inevitable penalty
for such treachery was death. Consequently, influenced no doubt by
their own regime's savage practices, most captured German operatives probably believed this during the Second World War and were
extremely fearful under interrogation that they would ultimately face a
British firing squad, which of course made the interrogator's job easier.
However, these Germans were generally unaware that official British
policy had by then evolved to a point where a living spy was usually
considered more valuable than a dead one. Thus, of the 440 men interrogated at Camp 020 between 1940 and 1945, only 14 were actually
executed for espionage.[3] Lest it be thought that British policymakers
and executives were motivated primarily by empathy or compassion in
not sending spies to trial, it needs to be recognized that in reality their
main objection to placing German agents before the courts lay in the
perceived risk of failure to secure a conviction and the death penalty.
Certainly in cases where there was no material evidence, where agents
had been successfully turned and doubled, or where prisoners had been

captured outside the United Kingdom, no capital proceedings were ever launched against them, nor were their lives ever really threatened.[4]

When Dick White of MI5 visited the Middle East in January–February 1943, one of his six proposals for the reorganization and reform of SIME – the one which caused him 'the most labour and time to achieve' – was that proper machinery should be established for examining new arrivals in the Middle East area and 'that a proper interrogation centre should be set up for handling spies and major suspects'.[5] It seems that, rather than arriving with a set agenda, White came to Cairo with an open mind and reached his conclusions during his trip. The need for an interrogation centre was brought home to him by the way in which an important German spy was handled while he was in Cairo. There being no proper facilities for the man's interrogation, he was kidnapped and hidden in a villa belonging to SIME. While there, certain drugs were apparently used to induce him to confess. The extraction of a confession took a fortnight and was, even then, not fully and satisfactorily achieved. With this example before him, White suggested to all the officers concerned that this was not the best way to interrogate a spy. 'I pointed out the necessity for method and discipline in the work of interrogation, the corollary to which was the possession of a proper interrogation centre, staffed by trained interrogators,' White concluded.[6]

White then managed to broker a deal between Raymond Maunsell, head of SIME, and Gustaf Rodd, head of CSDIC, for the establishment of a special SIME section of the Maadi Prisoner-of-War Interrogation Centre. By the time the arrests of German parachutists and agents in Persia began in mid-1943, it was to the 20 SIME cells at Maadi that they were brought and thoroughly interrogated by the staff of 12 SIME interrogation officers, according to a methodical and disciplined procedure, before being interned in Palestine. Maadi, under the overall command of a SIME officer, was reserved for the most serious cases, where detainees were known or strongly suspected to be enemy agents. In addition, for less serious cases, there was a large villa at Heliopolis with an additional 25 cells and four interrogation rooms; in the autumn of 1944, CSDIC handed over the entire Maadi camp to SIME.[7]

Three methods were employed to extract intelligence from German prisoners: direct interrogation, hidden microphones, and stool pigeons.[8] According to the direct method – the most effective means of obtaining operational information – prisoners were questioned by SIME specialists primarily in order to elicit information about their personal and service histories; their units, unit strengths and command structure; and details about tactics, callsigns, weaponry, training, previous missions, and new technology. Of secondary interest were prisoners' political beliefs, their views of the war situation, and their attitudes towards their officers and political leaders.[9] Although eavesdropping by means of concealed microphones was perhaps the least demanding way of accumulating intelligence, it was also the most time-consuming and least productive method, often rewarded with nothing more than many hours of banal conversation or, worse yet, silence. Its advantage over the other two methods lay in its potential for revealing obscure subjective intelligence: prisoners' likes, dislikes, ambitions, and fears. While eavesdropping involved no risk, the third method – described in May 1944 as 'increasingly successful' – of using two captured German spies as stool pigeons planted within the prisoner population was an extremely dangerous business, sometimes leading to severe beatings and even deaths.[10] Yet these plants were generally considered merely a means of obtaining 'important supplementary information which was used to corroborate that gleaned from interrogations and microphoning'.[11] However, such corroboration was an essential component of the total evaluation process: none of the three acquisition methods was intended to be used in isolation and seldom, if ever, was. The entire system depended on the meticulous comparative analysis and crossreferencing of *all* assets and product: captured documents, intercepted signals, and direct interrogation transcripts, as well as the information yielded by eavesdropping and plants.

Raymond Maunsell himself has given us some idea of what a captured agent, 'frightened and with morale at a low ebb', might have expected upon arrival at Maadi: (1) first and foremost a cup of tea and a cigarette; (2) clothes and belongings removed and searched; (3) inspection by medical orderlies for vermin; blood and urine specimens taken; (4) a hot bath and shower; (5) medical inspection by Royal Army Medical Corps (RAMC) doctor (some 70% of 'intake' had venereal infections for which they were thankful to be treated); (6) issue of clean clothes and cigarette ration; return of harmless effects; and (7) a hot meal.[12]

If the prisoner responded to this initial 'softening up' process, his whole background and story would gradually emerge and a decision would have to be reached whether to employ him as a stool pigeon, or – if he had a radio – to 'work him back', or to send him for trial, probably on some minor charge that would ensure his imprisonment. If a prisoner were German he would tend to be difficult at first. The Maadi interrogators then usually approached him along the lines that they were sorry for him, as he had been thoroughly let down by his bosses from the safety and comfort of their offices, for the British knew he was coming and already had quite a bit of information about him. 'Not one of our German prisoners eventually failed to cooperate with us,' wrote Maunsell.

> It is a fact that every German, once he had persuaded himself that his masters had carelessly thrown him into the danger line without taking the proper precautions, came over to us. I cannot recall how many so-called agents agreed to work for us, but I should say at least a dozen.[13]

It is not without significance that not a single German escaped from Maadi or attempted to do so.

It is noteworthy that, according to Maunsell, as a strict rule, no SIME interrogator ever blackmailed a prisoner with the threat of torture or execution; however, the legitimate threat of court martial was sometimes used 'if a captured suspect was troublesome or obdurate'.[14] In Persia too at Sultanabad (Arak), captured subversives and saboteurs were treated well: 'we never received any complaint from them directly, in fact a number of them stated how kindly they had been treated and used to send flowers and other small tokens to our own officers after their release from internment'.[15]

As historians, our interest today in wartime interrogations largely concerns the issue of their reliability. The information they yield certainly needs to be approached with a certain degree of scepticism; however, we also need to use a healthy dose of common sense to get us beyond the doubts. Certainly, some German prisoners like Franz Mayr (after stubborn initial resistance) simply threw in the proverbial towel after capture, perceiving themselves quite accurately to have been neutralized and their war to be over, whereas others remained still in some sense fighting the war and engaged with service politics, seeking to lay the blame for their failure elsewhere. As Franz Mayr's principal interrogator noted after initially questioning the SD officer,

> what the agent says about the [rival] Abwehr's inefficiency, due to lack of organization, red tape, dearth of adequate materials, and lack of manpower, may be true to a certain degree. His statements may, however, be exaggerated. It is possible that the stress he has laid on [the] Abwehr's inadequacy may be provoked by his annoyance at the inconveniences caused to his own group, on the one hand, and by his desire to divert the attention of the British from his Abwehr comrades to SD activities and expeditions on the other. It certainly

seems plausible that he should seek to minimize the importance of Abwehr activities by making out that the SD missions are much better organized and more successful.[16]

With the luxury of hindsight and crossreferencing, we now know of course that the scepticism shown by some interrogators towards statements by Abwehr or SD officers in the context of their fierce interservice rivalry was perhaps unwarranted, and that the picture of the German intelligence services painted by such officers was relatively realistic and accurate. Consequently, the interrogators' view of Abwehr and SD efficiency and operational potential was sometimes slightly skewed. And this surely is the point: that the effect of the prisoner's information on British intelligence and security *at the time* is what matters, not its effect on the historian. Modern historians have adequate technical tools with which to defend themselves against inaccuracies in interrogation reports; the interrogators themselves had few. And sometimes the most subtle inaccuracies are to be found not so much in the prisoner's statements as in the interrogator's interpretation of them. Fortunately for the interrogators of the two main groups featured in this book (FRANZ and ANTON), their task was greatly facilitated by the fact that they were dealing with groups rather than lone individuals; by isolating group members from each other under interrogation, it was always possible to play them off against each other to arrive at the common truth.

It is, however, the interrogation of the young Abwehr major (Gottfried Müller) who led the MAMMUT group, which never actually reached Persian soil, though Persian Kurdistan was unquestionably one of its targets, that proved most productive for Maadi interrogators, not least because Müller provided them with a comprehensive list of all the Abwehr and SD covert initiatives planned against Persia up to the time of his capture on 28 June 1943. In most respects, Müller's interrogation was relatively straightforward. The facts he yielded may be crossreferenced satisfactorily with other sources in the archival files and with general knowledge about Abwehr covert operations, but this information was not extracted from him without a great deal of difficulty in the early stages of the interrogation process, before he was broken, which gave rise to no fewer than 13 interrogation reports between June and October 1943. In addition, Müller's interrogation was interrupted and consequently slowed down by the temporary absence of the interrogating officer, who was seconded to Tehran to assist in the interrogation of Franz Mayr and the FRANZ/DORA group after their capture in August and September. This hiatus, however, ultimately proved useful, for it enabled the interrogating officer to crossreference many of Müller's statements about previous expeditions with those made under interrogation by Mayr and his group.[17]

When Gottfried Müller was first interrogated at CSDIC, he lied about certain matters (not specified in the archival file), whilst insisting that, as a German officer, he could never make a false statement. However, once the interrogating officer had proved to Müller that his lies were self-evident, he was quickly broken when told that he was not protected by the Geneva Convention because he was a spy (from which Müller inferred that he could therefore be summarily executed). His interrogator also felt that the fact that Müller was 'utterly devoid of imagination and completely lacking in any sense of humour' (unlike Franz Mayr, who had a ready wit) played into his hands. After he had been broken, Müller actually apologized to his interrogator for 'unwittingly telling minor untruths'. He went on to say that 'he had become so adept at lying over the ... past four or five years that occasionally force of habit prevailed upon him to deviate from the truth, while in reality he was most anxious to avoid falsehood'. Müller's sincerity seems to have been borne out by the fact that he subsequently rectified all his erroneous verbal and written statements. Consequently, when the full report on his many interrogations was released, it was assumed by CSDIC to represent reliable information.[18]

Social class-consciousness was also thought by the staff at CSDIC to have played a key role in the acquiescence of both Gottfried Müller and Franz Mayr. Both men had come from relatively humble origins and in early youth had nurtured a common ambition to become not mere soldiers but military officers. Müller's family had been so poor that he had had to leave school at age 13 and become an apprentice. When Müller and Mayr were admitted, entirely on their merit, to what they perceived as an exalted and select caste, they seemed somehow convinced – yet reluctant to admit – that they were in some sense not regular members of it, and thus to doubt themselves. Such doubts were intensified when, shortly before his mission, Müller had vaulted from lieutenant to acting major, whilst the other members of the MAMMUT team had jumped from other ranks to acting second lieutenant. This Abwehr practice of promoting agents shortly before their missions, accompanied by the promise that the promotion would be confirmed if the mission was successful, tended only to undermine rather than buoy the men's self-confidence. This curious kind of inferiority complex led to a certain insecurity and lack of resolution in both Müller and Mayr which proved to be their undoing in the interrogation room.[19]

What probably also contributed to Müller's stricken conscience about lying under interrogation was his upbringing and the spiritual crisis he was experiencing at the time: Müller's father was a Lutheran clergyman, Müller had grown up in a highly religious atmosphere, and, after his release and repatriation, he would devote the rest of his life to the international religious organization he founded in Stuttgart in 1957.[20] Müller has always contended that he experienced a personal epiphany in his 'death cell' in Egypt which changed the rest of his life. What this meant for his interrogators was that they were dealing not with a Nazi fanatic but with a conflicted and irresolute young man who was therefore malleable and potentially informative. And, in response to their expert questioning, Müller sang like a canary.

The result is one of the most important documents ever produced by CSDIC: a 140-page interrogation report, together with six illustrated appendices, describing in meticulous detail not just the planning, preparation, and execution of an Abwehr *Ferneinsatz* (long-range operation), but also the organization and general activities of the Abwehr espionage and sabotage services, their sabotage and W/T training centres, the rivalry between the Abwehr and the SD (about which little detail was known but much was suspected by the British at the time), Abwehr–Luftwaffe cooperation, Abwehr special forces, and a list of over 300 personalities known to the prisoner.[21]

The question of how such valuable intelligence was to be distributed was a tricky one. Generally, it was essential (1) that it be disseminated as quickly as possible, before it became degraded, and (2) that it be correctly targeted at those agencies and organizations which could use it or further distribute it most effectively. It was also important not to release information indiscriminately when it might endanger ongoing tactical operations, cause blowback in other theatres, or upset Stalin. Among the Allies there was an underlying spirit of cooperation with regard to intelligence sharing, but it could never become a routine process, so high were the stakes and so great the potential rewards. However, by 1944 a relatively secure, flexible system had evolved whereby the Allies could submit questionnaires to each other, requesting specific information yet permitting the interrogating agency to retain full control over the selection and distribution process.

Sometimes the Allies would even broker intelligence on each other's behalf, as can be seen from correspondence between the commanding general of the US Military Mission to Moscow and the head of OSS, essentially enabling the acquisition on the Russians' behalf of product generated by British interrogations at Maadi. In this instance, the NKVD requested that certain questions about Persia be put to members of the Abwehr who had been taken to Cairo concerning the extent of German espionage from Turkey into Persia, including its director, composition and location of operational points, name of agency, assignments given to such agencies in Persia, and methods of communication from Persia to German intelligence headquarters in Turkey.[22] One might think perhaps that the NKVD could have made a direct approach to the British at one of their regular meetings with Joe Spencer in Tehran, who could have then forwarded the Russian request via Chokra Wood in Baghdad to Raymond Maunsell in Cairo. However, the principle in operation here seems to have been similar to that applied consistently by the SOE Security Directorate to establishing outside official contacts: go as high as possible on the working level and then be as forthcoming as possible.[23] Thus the veteran Russian spymaster Gaik Ovakimyan, head of the American Department of the First Directorate (disguised as the notional 'Major General Aleksandr P. Ossipov', for he had previously been deported from the United States as a spy),[24] clearly realized that the sensitivity of the information he sought required an even higher level of authority than CICI, SIME, or Alex Kellar at B Branch, and so he routed his request through Moscow and Washington. Such was the constructive nature of the OSS–NKVD relationship, attentively fostered throughout the war by Bill Donovan, and such was the sophistication with which Allied intelligence sharing was generally conducted.

By the time Kellar visited Cairo, Baghdad, and Tehran on his first of three tours of inspection in March–April 1944, he found the Tehran interrogation arrangements to be generally satisfactory. DSO had by then acquired a private villa for housing and interrogating enemy agents and suspects. There was, however, no intention to supersede SIME's interrogation centre at Maadi. The procedure followed was for DSO to interrogate satisfactorily on local matters and then pass on any important cases to SIME for further investigation.[25] Also of vital significance and concern for DSO – but entirely beyond their control – were the severely underresourced interrogation facilities of the Anglo-French CEV at Aleppo, the last important station on the Baghdad Railway from Turkey before it entered CICI territory, for it was only here that enemy agents destined for Persia could be intercepted. Fortunately the French commandant, who had little interest in such cases, was only nominally in command; the centre was actually run by one beleaguered SIME officer with a wholly inadequate staff of three Greek examiners and one administrative officer. The volume of travellers was extraordinarily high; for instance, in the one-month period between 21 February and

20 March 1944, 2,135 refugees and travellers passed through Aleppo, every one of whom had to be documented and interrogated. If the examining officer was satisfied with their credentials, passengers for Persia and Iraq were allowed to proceed by the same train; if not, they were held at Aleppo until their position had been clarified, after their particulars had been sent to SIME in Cairo for further examination. In fact, even though there was no routine examination of passengers travelling in the reverse direction from Syria to Turkey, the CEV was so understaffed that personnel from DSO Syria had to be conscripted to process travellers. All exits at the railway station had to be guarded; no one was allowed to leave the station unless in possession of the red card issued after satisfactory examination.[26]

In addition to this, arrivals claiming to be employees or agents of British intelligence organizations had to be accommodated on special premises at Aleppo while instructions as to their disposal were awaited from Cairo. Special arrangements existed with the other British secret services (SOE and ISLD) to expedite the processing of their personnel or personalities in whom they were interested. However, this was clearly the riskiest screening process of all, where the stakes were high and mistakes had to be avoided. Consequently, the procedure was unforgiving and unhurried. In all but the limited number of cases where SIME was satisfied that the individual for whom exemption was claimed was a fully accepted and guaranteed agent, interrogation took place as usual, even though the individual was subsequently to be handed over to the interested organization.[27]

In general, one of the most difficult questions facing SIME throughout the Middle East was the disposal of suspects. Enemy agents, including Franz Mayr, Berthold Schulze-Holthus, and the parachutists of the FRANZ and ANTON missions, were detained in military custody at the Emmaus (Imwas) internment camp staffed and controlled by SIME in Palestine. Emmaus was the Colditz Castle of the Middle East: a specially adapted, isolated hilltop monastery (Our Lady of the Seven Sorrows, Latrun), from which escape was virtually impossible (see Figure 10.1). However, no accommodation was made for the large number of minor suspects, political agitators, criminals, and others who flocked to the region during the war. Most enlisted in the Allied forces, ended up in refugee camps, or were simply released into civilian society, where they disappeared without trace.[28] Within Persia, of course, there was 50 Internment Camp at Sultanabad (Arak), which Joe Spencer considered the 'biggest debit entry' of the war, along with the forces required to guard it.[29] Yet it was Sultanabad that differentiated Spencer's jurisdiction

Figure 10.1 Colditz of the Middle East: Emmaus (Imwas) Internment Camp. At this hilltop monastery in Palestine (now Israel) important enemy agents were detained by SIME for the duration of the war, including Franz Mayr, Berthold Schulze-Holthus, the FRANZ and ANTON parachutists, and Fazlollah Zahedi
Source: Wikipedia Commons, 'The Trappist Monastery at Latrun' by Bukvoed, used under CC-BY-2.5, desaturated and resized from original.

from the rest of the Middle East, in that it enabled DSO Persia to isolate subversive elements and other dangerous malcontents, holding them locally and preventing them from being passed to other regional centres where they would be less available for further interrogation, vanishing into the Persian street, or attempting to reach German contacts in neutral Turkey.

Notes

1. Diary of Guy Liddell, 3 February 1941, KV 4/187, TNA.
2. See Mallett, *Hitler's Generals*, 2.
3. Camp 020 prisoners mentioned elsewhere in this study include Ernst Kaltenbrunner, Joseph Ledebur, Franz Mayr, Gottfried Müller, Erich Pfeiffer, Walter Schellenberg, and Pierre Sweerts. All survived the process, though Kaltenbrunner was later executed at Nuremberg.
4. See Curry, *Security Service*, 228–9.
5. Report on visit to the Middle East by Lieutenant Colonel D.G. White, 22 February 1943, KV 4/240, TNA.

6. Ibid.
7. See undated handwritten annotation in Appendix A (SIME Interrogation Section, 25 April 1944) of Report on visit by Mr A.J. Kellar to SIME and CICI organizations, May 1944, KV 4/384, TNA. CSDIC has recently been thoroughly investigated by Falko Bell in his doctoral dissertation: 'Wissen ist menschlich: Der Stellenwert der Human Intelligence in der britischen Kriegsführung 1939–1945' (PhD diss., Glasgow, 2014).
8. See inter alia Kent Fedorowich, 'Axis Prisoners of War as Sources for British Military Intelligence, 1939–42', *Intelligence and National Security* 14, no. 2 (Summer 1999): 168.
9. Ibid., 169.
10. The identities of the stool pigeons remain unknown. Report on visit by Mr A.J. Kellar to SIME and CICI organizations, May 1944, KV 4/384, TNA.
11. Fedorowich, 'Axis Prisoners': 170.
12. Private papers of R.J. Maunsell, 4829:80/30/1, IWM. Shelley, 'Empire of Shadows', 159–63, includes a brief but interesting discussion of rendition and the generally benevolent treatment of prisoners of war at Maadi.
13. Ibid.
14. Ibid.
15. Spencer to Bullard, 5 October 1959, GB165-0042-3/7, MECA.
16. First detailed interrogation report on Mueller, Agt by Major Edmund Tilley, C7(d)(ii) Abw II/OR, 27 October 1943, WO 201/1402B, TNA.
17. First detailed interrogation report on Mueller, Agt by Major Edmund Tilley, A1 Preamble, 27 October 1943, WO 201/1402B, TNA.
18. Ibid.
19. Ibid.
20. The Bruderschaft Salem, a non-denominational Christian non-profit welfare organization, carries out charitable work in global hotspots to help people in difficult situations regardless of their beliefs or nationality. See http://www.saleminternational.org for further details.
21. First detailed interrogation report on Mueller, Agt by Major Edmund Tilley, 27 October 1943, WO 201/1402B, TNA.
22. Deane to Donovan, 3 March 1944, RG 334, Entry 310, Box 50, NARA.
23. Note by Commander John Senter, RNVR, 16 July 1945, HS 7/31, TNA.
24. See Vadim J. Birstein, *The Perversion of Knowledge: The True Story of Soviet Science* (Boulder, CO: Westview Press, 2001), 413–14.
25. Report on visit by Mr A.J. Kellar to SIME and CICI organizations, May 1944, KV 4/384, TNA.
26. Ibid.
27. Ibid.
28. Ibid.
29. Appendix A, CICI Counter-Intelligence Summary No. 24, 11 May 1944, KV 2/1485, TNA.

11
Ruskies

> Russian attempts to penetrate us do not surprise or
> alarm us in the least. ... We have always operated for
> the most part in the open, and this is probably what
> puzzles them most of all. (Alan Roger [ADSO Persia])[1]

Of vital importance for Joe Spencer's 'ratcatchers' was liaison work with
other British and Allied agencies in the region, namely 10th Army HQ
(PAIFORCE); the British legation; the Secret Intelligence Service (MI6),
operating locally as the Inter-Services Liaison Department (ISLD); the
Special Operations Executive (SOE); US Persian Gulf (Service) Command
(PGSC/PGC), including the field-security forces of the US Counter
Intelligence Corps (CIC); and, last but by no means least, the security
forces of the Soviet Union (NKVD). In order to ensure tight occupa-
tional security, Spencer realized from when he first arrived in Tehran at
the beginning of 1942 that the maintenance of effective liaison between
the occupying powers was crucial, and that internal security could only
be effective if the competent authorities in both zones regularly discussed problems of mutual interest and concern. As Sir Reader Bullard
noted in 1945, notwithstanding American 'inexperience' and Russian
'ill will', Persia was the one country where British, American, and
Soviet civil and military authorities met on a broad land front, and the
necessary contacts at the various technical levels proceeded reasonably
smoothly and efficiently, in spite of difficulties in the political sphere.[2]

However, trilateral relations were by no means uniformly successful. For instance, so heartfelt was the Russians' appreciation of
Spencer's liaison work with them that they unfortunately refused to
have any dealings with the Americans on security matters, claiming
that their relationship with Spencer was sufficient.[3] Since the British

were technically responsible for security throughout Persia (outside the Soviet zone), the Russian refusal had no diplomatic repercussions. Nevertheless, in practical terms, it represented an unwelcome extra demand on the already meagre resources of DSO Persia as an intermediary, and it meant that Spencer's liaison with the Americans had to be as effective as that with the Russians.

While the Nazi enemy of course remained the prime concern of British security forces in Persia (DSO) between 1941 and 1945, one can observe a growing awareness of the Russian presence in the region as a potential threat to British interests and a gradual return to the mentality of the Great Game.[4] After the immediate improvement in Anglo-Soviet relations in the region between June and September 1941, following operations BARBAROSSA and COUNTENANCE play was essentially suspended while Russia fought for its life and had little time for pursuing foreign policies not directly connected with the war effort. Then, after Stalingrad, as Russians started to feel more confident of victory and their own strength, the old rivalry began to re-emerge during the summer of 1943. Russia adopted a more vigorous line beyond its own frontiers

Figure 11.1 August 1941 invasion: Red Army troops enter Tabriz. Tankmen of the Soviet 6th Armoured Division with their T-26 battle tank and infantry in the background, late August 1941
Source: Wikimedia Commons/PD.

and entered the struggle for oil concessions with all the resourcefulness of an experienced capitalist oil combine.[5] It became apparent that
the increasingly assertive attitude of Soviet officials conflicted with
British interest in safeguarding the status of Persia as a buffer state and
in protecting its regional oilfields, pipelines, and refineries, which the
Russians had originally targeted in early 1941, before BARBAROSSA and
the subsequent thaw in Anglo-Soviet relations. In other words, as early
as mid-1943, with Germany's ultimate defeat still a long way off but
more or less a certainty, Britain and the Soviet Union began to align
themselves in preparation for the resumption of postwar play. Thus the
continuity of the Great Game in central and western Asia – begun in
the early 19th century – was really only interrupted for a relatively brief
spell of two years between June 1941 and July 1943.[6] However, both
occupying powers in Persia fortunately recognized that this strategic
rivalry did not diminish the need for cooperation between their security
services. On the contrary, Joe Spencer and Alan Roger noticed, no doubt
to their relief, that cooperation in one field was not made impossible
because of friction in another. Though the British did not approve of
the Soviet attitude on the question of Persian oil, this did not in any
way affect cooperation between DSO and the NKVD.[7]

It was not the task of DSO to obtain information about Soviet intelligence by undercover methods; that was the job of ISLD under Robin
Zaehner. Nor would the use of such methods have been consistent with
DSO's need to remain on cordial terms with the Russians in order to
carry out effective security liaison. Spencer and Roger therefore preferred
to concentrate on fostering cooperation; the acquisition of intelligence
about Soviet operational methods ensued from such cooperation incidentally rather than intentionally. Spencer was interested purely in
the security of the country when he opened up liaison with his Soviet
colleagues; he never received any directive to gather information about
the Russians.[8] After all, CICI was a security-intelligence formation, not an
active-intelligence agency. However, Roger felt that much could be
accomplished by working in contact with Russian intelligence with
proper reserve and eyes 'well open'. It would afford far better opportunities for learning all about it than by 'peering through keyholes' or
relying entirely on 'delicate and highly placed sources which must not
be compromised', and which are therefore often uncheckable.[9]

It was learned, for instance, that the Russians probably used censorship as their principal means of selecting and recruiting Persian agents,
that Persians permitted to cross the sealed Soviet-zone borders without
hindrance were probably combining trade with espionage, and that

Persians interned and subsequently released (or otherwise given preferential treatment) were probably Soviet spies. Such lack of subtlety in Russian methods of recruiting and running agents enabled DSO to identify various Persians as agents of Moscow with relative ease and probably without the Russians' knowledge. The British also derived from their cooperation over time with the Russian security officers in Tehran (Captain Guterman, Grigori Antonovich Asaturov, Nicolai Fedorowich Zemskov, and Major Sosnin) a general picture of the NKVD in Persia, which appears to have been embedded within the Soviet censorship administration.[10] With the exception of Sosnin, these officers had at some time or other had an office in the Anglo-Soviet-Persian Censorship; moreover, DSO thought that their censorship duties had not merely been a cover, but that they had in fact regarded their censorship work as an integral part of their general security task.[11] Reluctantly perhaps, Spencer and Roger were forced to acknowledge that the Soviet system of combining censorship, frontier control, and the running of agents and double agents under one roof – and of employing only Soviet citizens to coordinate these measures – was far more effective than the British system of compartmentalizing such tasks as censorship, travel control, and the investigation of counterintelligence cases – and of hiring non-British nationals as censors, who were inefficient and generally unaware of the importance and sensitivity of some of the documents they were required to process.[12] Yet, with the arrival of Sosnin as Soviet security officer in 1944, the Russian system seemed to undergo a significant change, for the likeable Red Army interrogator appeared to have no censorship function at all; paradoxically, Roger even felt that it was possible that the NKVD had decided from observation that the decentralized DSO system was superior and had adopted it.

DSO's perception of the links between Soviet security and the active-intelligence role played by the Soviet embassy in Tehran remained rather more speculative. It was certainly clear that a link existed between the two; however, Alan Roger could only point with confidence to the spymaster role obviously played by the ambassador himself, Mikhail Alexeyevich Maximov, a hard-line Stalinist. Joe Spencer, on the other hand, hypothesized under Maximov a homogeneous organization responsible for such varied aspects of intelligence work as espionage, counterespionage, censorship, arrests and kidnapping of anti-Soviet personalities, and subversive activities in general – the whole being carried out in line with central policy formulated by Moscow.[13]

In the closing months of the war, Alan Roger compiled a definitive summary of DSO's cooperation with the Russian security authorities, tracing its history from early 1942, 'when it was difficult to distinguish between a Russian officer and a Russian private', to a time when the Soviet intelligence machinery in Persia had become so extensive that it needed an official with ambassadorial rank to be its director.[14] To be more specific, Soviet intelligence used the occupation of Persia to establish its largest known presence beyond the USSR, with nearly 40 residencies and sub-residencies. The main residency in Tehran had 115 operations officers, whose principal task was the identification, abduction, and liquidation of those whom Stalin considered 'anti-Soviet' elements.[15]

However superficially cordial, Anglo-Soviet cooperation was not at all synonymous with joint operations: apart from the KISS double-cross,[16] which necessitated some degree of cooperation and coordination between DSO and Soviet security, and the Vaziri case, which included an informal intelligence-sharing agreement, operations within the Soviet and British zones were conducted for three years separately and without significant mutual disclosure. In the case of Mohammad Vaziri, Spencer's patient and persistent approach paid significant dividends. By maintaining a cordial atmosphere in which Moscow Centre could admit without losing face that they had recruited and run Vaziri, Spencer caused them to hand to DSO 'on a platter' a complete cross-section of their methods of intelligence, including such things as the types of agents used (mostly Persian Azeris who were interrelated), their names, the amounts they paid, and the quality of the weapon they had forged. Without realizing it, the Russians even revealed some of the grave mistakes they had made.[17]

The general policy adopted by Spencer was to force cooperation by breaking down suspicion and by making the Russians acknowledge their own responsibilities. Initially, Russian suspicion of British motives was considerable, not because of any questionable moves by DSO but rather because life under Stalin naturally engendered deeply ingrained distrust. For instance, it took years before Russian security officers would sign receipts for documents or suspects handed over to them by DSO, because they simply did not wish to put their names on paper. Actual discussions took place quite frequently. On routine matters, Spencer's Russian specialist, D.R. Caird, a former Indian Army officer who had served in the White Russian army during the Russian civil war,[18] would simply visit his Russian counterpart and submit his requests orally, which were never answered immediately. On more important questions, the Soviet security officer would visit Joe Spencer at his home, where things would usually be set down in writing. It would sometimes take months before queries were answered and issues resolved, suggesting that all matters had to be referred by the Russians to Moscow Centre for decision, whereas Spencer of course made most decisions on the spot, without any reference to MI5 in London, SIME in Cairo, or CICI in Baghdad. In fact, for the benefit of the Russians, Spencer studiously maintained a pose of being completely autonomous and ignorant of what was happening elsewhere in order to avoid taking the Russian point of view against any British organization. This proved necessary because the Russians clearly found it difficult to understand why DSO did not have the same power over British institutions as the NKVD over organs of the Soviet state. 'They have ... expressed dismay and shown irritation that we do not come to a decision ... when it conflicts with high British policy, instead of acting first and "telling the diplomats what to do" afterwards.'[19]

Despite such occasional misunderstandings, mutual respect and trust evolved over the years, and Anglo-Soviet security collaboration in Persia grew progressively more intimate and more effective. It needs to be remembered, however, that Anglo-Soviet cordiality was by no means synonymous with openness, particularly with respect to signals intelligence. It has been asserted that MI5's greatest single wartime handicap was its lack of Soviet SIGINT; GC&CS (Government Code and Cipher School) did not decrypt the communications of Soviet intelligence agencies.[20] Consequently, MI5 was as a matter of course in no position to pass any decrypts of Soviet intelligence to Tehran, regardless of whether or not they would have been willing to share such intelligence with Joe Spencer. Whilst any question of how much this may have handicapped Spencer in his dealings with the Soviet security forces remains speculative, it is not known how much SIGINT material was passed locally and more or less informally to DSO by the Soviets.

The main vehicle of Stalinist propaganda in Persia during the Anglo-Soviet occupation was a political party: the Tudeh Party.[21] Founded shortly after the 1941 invasion, it actually represented the culmination of a Marxist revolutionary movement begun in the early 20th century which used the liberal Persian press to attack Tsar Nicholas and promote radical views. After the 1917 Bolshevik revolution in Russia, Marxist activity in Persia intensified, and in 1920 a Soviet 'Republic of Gilan' was proclaimed, to be followed by a communist uprising in Tabriz. However, when Persia signed a treaty of friendship with the Soviet Union in 1921, these early revolutionary initiatives collapsed. After his accession to power in 1923, Reza Shah pursued a vigorous anti-Marxist policy, ultimately jailing 50 labour leaders in 1929. However, by less than a decade later, left-wing Persian radicals included not only

Soviet-trained revolutionaries but also significant numbers of Marxist intellectuals from the universities and the professions. In 1937, Reza Shah moved against them, arresting a number of prominent intellectuals led by a university professor of German named Tagi Erani, most of whom were subsequently sentenced to lengthy terms of penal servitude after the so-called Trial of the 53, where they were convicted of 'receiving funds from the USSR and of communist activity'.[22] As is so often the case when revolutionaries are incarcerated, their imprisonment merely enabled them to regroup, rethink, and reinvent their communist cause, endowing it with better discipline and better intelligence. And so, when released in 1941, these prison-trained activists immediately organized, establishing the Tudeh, 'recruiting members, establishing a party press, and setting up connections with the labour movement and other front organizations'.[23] By early 1943, they were publishing three daily newspapers in Tehran, had brought about the establishment of the Central United Council of Trade Unions (CUCTU), and were ready to put up candidates for the *Majlis*. For the remaining period of the occupation, their elected members in the Persian parliament – officially nine, although seven additional members were probably covert Tudeh supporters – proved to be very effective in obstructing the legislative process.[24] Thus the Soviet occupiers had no need to establish in Persia an elaborate internal propaganda apparatus, for the Tudeh functioned adequately on their behalf as a proxy purveyor of communist propaganda firmly situated within the Persian polity. The party consistently parroted the Stalinist line, and there was every indication that it enjoyed direct command liaison with the Soviet Union.[25]

In the field, within the British zone of occupation, the Russians needed watching, for Red Army officers would occasionally stray into Joe Spencer's territory. Neither the British nor the Americans seem to have known quite what the Russians' motives were, though it appeared superficially that they were merely seeking to exercise a measure of control over the flow of Lend-Lease war materiel from the Persian Gulf to the Soviet zone. Yet, the suspicion clearly lingered that, however ingenuous such Russian incursions seemed, they were probably spying: assessing the strengths and weaknesses of the British and US forces policing the TIR and guarding the southwestern oilfields, refineries, and ports. Besides, the British FSS were very aware that it would not be difficult for fifth columnists to dress as Russian officers, who were initially not even required to carry identity papers when travelling outside their own zone, unlike British and American service personnel.[26] The Russians may also have nurtured an espionage interest in the tribal situation. To increase its political influence in the region with a view to postoccupational realignment, the Soviet Union undoubtedly needed to know as much as possible about the relationships between such powerful tribes as the Qashgai and the Bakhtiari, and about the state of the tribal leaders' political relations with the central government.

Even in the south of Persia, Russian consular staffs were on the large side, and the members of these staffs toured a great deal in their areas. Each man appeared to have been chosen as an authority on, say, agriculture, minerology, or industry, and to be competent to collect and assess information on his particular subject. It was therefore considered likely that each consulate had on its staff at least one intelligence specialist. The Russians had a habit of sending these officers in parties or individually to move about the south and even into Iraq, blandly ignoring the fact that the Iraqi and Soviet governments had no diplomatic relations. The Soviet parties which toured within the British zone usually had some scientific, semi-scientific, or even cultural cover, but there was little doubt that a great deal of other information (topographical, for instance) was being carefully collected.[27]

Typical incursions into southern Persia occurred in the summer of 1942. For example, on 12 June, a pass was granted to a Soviet naval rating to proceed to Bandar-i-Shahpur.[28] On 22 July no fewer than nine Red Army officers and 12 ORs arrived unannounced at Khorramshahr to guard munitions being unloaded.[29] In the same month, three Red Navy officers were granted six-month passes to visit the Gulf ports and inspect Soviet ships, though their remit was even more extensive: they were to take up posts at Khorramshahr, Bandar-i-Shahpur, Bushire, and Basra to deal with Russian ships and generally to keep an eye on the onward transit of all goods destined for Russia.[30] Clearly, 10th Army HQ were not happy about the fact that the Tehran legation had granted these *laissez-passer* without informing them; the Senior Naval Officer Persian Gulf (SNOPG) was also upset at the apparent interference with his status and authority. That no accommodation was available, that none of the Soviet personnel could speak English, and that no interpreters had accompanied them were seen as additional irritants.

The use of Soviet forces personnel to spy on the British and the Americans alongside their regular service responsibilities cannot have been viewed by Russian security as the ideal method of recruiting, deploying, and controlling agents, especially as they had ample other means at their disposal. DSO were fully aware of Soviet methods of recruiting talent, the most obvious being the use of censorship to compromise and manipulate potential assets. Other instruments were the selective issuing of visas and other travel documents, the equally selective granting of release from internment, an appeal to Marxist ideological conviction or national sympathy, and lastly the inspiration of sheer terror. Interestingly, bribery does not appear to have been included in the inventory taken by Joe Spencer; however, it was undoubtedly also widely used. It was the transfer of large sums of money from Persia that first alerted DSO to the possibility that Mohammad Vaziri was working not only for the Germans, but also as a Soviet double agent in Turkey. However, for DSO the identification of Soviet agents was another matter – a formidable task, in fact. According to Alan Roger, there were far too many people who asserted that any bookseller with a Russian book in his shop, any Armenian who gave money to Soviet charities, or any of the many orange sellers outside Soviet-occupied buildings were all dangerous Soviet agents likely 'to appear from underneath the pillow to strangle the unfortunate patriot'. As there were doubtless many genuine Soviet agents in the country, such panic reports made their identification all the more difficult, and their investigation one of considerable delicacy. What worked to DSO's advantage, in the case of both Russian agents and pro-German fifth columnists, was the fact that they were usually densely interconnected by family or tribe, which meant that the firm identification of one single agent often led to the unmasking of many more. Ultimately, the best way to identify an agent was of course getting the Russians to admit that they were running him, which is what happened with both Vaziri and Hamburger.[31]

Only one Soviet espionage case – that of Rudolf Hamburger – was actually solved by the Counter Intelligence Corps (CIC), with a surprising outcome. In his quest for intelligence, Hamburger attempted to bribe an American PGC officer, who immediately reported the approach. Suspecting that Hamburger was a German spy, CIC placed him under surveillance, arrested him, and interrogated him, only to discover that he was in fact working for the Russians and was actually a Marxist political refugee from Nazism. Hamburger was immediately passed on from CIC to DSO, who returned him to the Russians, instructing them in no uncertain terms 'to get him out of town'.[32] The handover took place at dead of night on a lonely road surrounded by all the mystery of the most dramatic spy film. Originally recruited in 1943 by the Russians in Switzerland for secret intelligence work in Persia, when he returned to Moscow from Tehran Hamburger was tried for unknown reasons on bogus charges and was imprisoned in a Ukrainian labour camp. On his release in 1952, he moved to Dresden (East Germany), where he resumed his former career as an architect and died aged 77 in 1980.[33]

The Vaziri case revealed to British security one major mistake that the Russians had made in handling double agents. It was always difficult to know in such cases how much to mix the factual with the notional, but the Russians tended to make their cases excessively factual. Alan Roger felt that this was because they were trained highly, but only for factual operations, including such direct methods as kidnapping or blackmail. Consequently, Soviet intelligence officers usually lacked the imagination required for notional cases. When Vaziri needed a false passport, apparently having no counterfeiting department themselves, the Russians used no fewer than six real agents to procure one, and – embarrassingly – in their attempts all were arrested as fifth columnists. When Rudolf Hamburger needed one, they had to go to great lengths to obtain a Honduran passport. When the Russians were told about the KISS transmissions to Berlin, they had great difficulty in believing that KISS was not a factual W/T operator. Another identified weakness besides lack of ingenuity was that Soviet security were unable to run notional agents in Persia because they lacked accurate records, at least locally. Time after time, they would ask DSO for information about a certain person without apparently knowing his full name. As Alan Roger noted, 'it is perfectly obvious that one cannot run notional cases unless one's records are absolutely accurate'. However, as Roger was quick to point out, the inaccuracy of Soviet records should not be taken to mean that the Russians were technically inefficient in other fields. They had for instance an excellent and speedy photographic service, which DSO often used, and an excellent signals system.[34]

One of the few Persian narratives concerning Anglo-Soviet intelligence relations to have received some attention from intelligence historians and other scholars[35] in recent years is that of the KISS double-cross: an elaborate and sucessful W/T disinformation operation that featured the notional playback of a factual Abwehr operative, who was impersonated in transmissions by a dedicated DSO case officer, S.D. Shearman.[36] So convincing were the notional KISS's messages, which were transmitted between 22 March 1944 and 3 May 1945, that he fooled even the wily Berthold Schulze-Holthus (no longer SABA, but now codenamed MAJOR), called in to authenticate KISS, into accepting them as genuine. From late March 1945 onwards, it was clear from the nature of the requests for action that Schulze-Holthus himself was controlling some of the traffic.[37] In fact, the operation was a relatively insignificant side-show that occurred late in the war and that probably had little effect on the German war effort – and even less on Persia. Shearman himself concluded that 'if nothing else, certain German officers were kept busy.

No deception was attempted, the value of the information given was small; it merely reached Berlin more quickly than through their usual channels such as travellers, newspapers, and broadcasts.'[38] The Amt VI or MilAmt officers in Berlin who received KISS's messages were probably dissuaded from sending further missions to Persia, perhaps even Roman Gamotha's planned mission to Mazanderan, because they came to accept that their link with KISS was sufficient, or the best that they could hope for.

The details of the case are as follows. An Abwehr naval-intelligence asset, a former Siemens electrical engineer named Mohamed Akhundzade Salmassi,[39] under the control of Werner Schüler of Abw I M, was sent out to Persia from Berlin in October 1943. He was supposed to take possession of a previously delivered W/T set, to use it to notify Berlin before the end of March 1944 of his safe arrival, and then to transfer its operation to an experienced Abwehr signaller named Hans Georg Georgiades (DRILLIG), who was to join Salmassi in Isfahan or Tehran in the spring of 1944. (Georgiades was in fact never sent to Persia; after Schüler's transfer to Turkey in June 1944, the Persian mission was never mentioned to him again.[40]) After that, Salmassi was to carry out unspecified espionage activities for Schüler. Later, during the summer of 1944, it would become clear to SIME that Schüler's mission for Salmassi was actually quite specific. He was to gather information as to the quantity and type of military and nonmilitary supplies from Anglo-American sources transiting Persia to Russia; on the relationship between the Russians and the Anglo-American authorities in Persia; on Russian and Anglo-American dispositions and strengths; on shipping in the Persian Gulf; and on points at which supplies to Russia could be disrupted.[41]

Once in Istanbul, Salmassi contacted the Persian Abwehr officer who had originally introduced him to Schüler – without knowing that he was an important MI6 double agent codenamed BLACKGUARD[42] – and informed him that he had no intention of working for the Germans in Persia. Continuing his journey, Salmassi was intercepted by officers of DSO Syria at Aleppo on 20 November 1943, where he resisted interrogation for three days but then broke down. He made a full statement to his interrogators about his Abwehr mission, and, having signed a declaration promising to remain silent and not to work against the Allies, was released, arriving in Tehran on 29 December 1943, where he found employment in a Russian-controlled arsenal.[43]

Meanwhile BLACKGUARD, acting under instructions from SIME, covered Salmassi's tracks by informing the Abwehr that he had not been compromised in Aleppo. Now that Salmassi, codenamed KISS, had been effectively neutralized, he was interrogated further on general matters and

Abwehr personalities, and was even sent to Maadi for detailed technical interrogation by SIME about his W/T training and his codes. The plan to use KISS was such that he had to remain quite ignorant of the operation. The British case officer who was to impersonate him had to absorb KISS's transmitting style and at later stages of the operation even his character. Salmassi was then released in Tehran and placed under surveillance; however, the British were entirely confident that he had no wish to continue working for or against any intelligence service and granted him unrestricted freedom. On 22 March 1944, contact was established, initiated by Berlin (MARQUIS), with KISS's impersonator deliberately sending poor Morse style and communicating only low-grade intelligence that the Germans could have easily obtained by other means.[44]

Without knowing it, the Russians became involved in the playback case from the moment when, on 20 May 1944, MARQUIS started asking questions about Soviet activities in Persia. The notional KISS stalled, claiming that money was needed to bribe the Russians for such information. The Abwehr then sent BLACKGUARD the sum of £2000, which he immediately appropriated, and for which the notional KISS thanked MARQUIS! Then, on 29 June 1944, the Russians informed DSO that they had intercepted a transmitter operating from the house in which the KISS operation was taking place factually. This was awkward, as it was not felt that Joe Spencer's instinctive response – that the address in question was a British officers' mess – would fool the Russians for long.[45] Consequently, it was decided that they had to be brought in on the case. However, it took seven months to resolve the question of Russian assistance and approval, which had to be referred by Joe Spencer to Alex Kellar at MI5, whence the matter proceeded through channels to Moscow. Meanwhile, KISS continued to transmit chicken-feed to MARQUIS until even that 'foodstuff' became seriously depleted.[46] Suddenly, after MI5 had abandoned all hope of Soviet cooperation, for no apparent reason other than that they might wish to penetrate DSO, the Russians supplied a positive response in December 1944, offering complete collaboration on the KISS case. So, cautiously, on 17 January 1945, Alan Roger met with Major Sosnin and provided him with factual details and information about the KISS case, together with a cover story fabricated to safeguard BLACKGUARD. Cooperation proceeded, though it proved difficult at times because of the Russians' need to consult Moscow Centre before making any decision, even about minor amendments to KISS's messages.[47]

Very late in the game (on 24 January 1945), MARQUIS unexpectedly enquired about the possibility of a second 'Big Three' Tehran conference. Amt VI wished to know whether Stalin would attend, openly indicating that the question was of the highest importance.[48] If seeking sensation, it would perhaps be tempting – but of course quite wrong – to assume that this inquisitiveness indicated that Amt VI were considering an assassination attempt. However, for that to be the case one would have to ignore, for instance, the fact that Roman Gamotha's Operation NORMA had been cancelled a year earlier, that his Persia desk (VI C 14) had been closed in August 1944 and his expert team dispersed, and that Kurt Schuback, the RSHA 'desk jockey' who headed the newly formed VI C 3 desk (the unit in contact with KISS), was for many reasons totally incapable of mounting such a 'black op'.[49] But of course, British intelligence knew little about Amt VI and nothing of the almost total dysfunction and incapacity of the RSHA, whose officers were by early 1945 more interested in personal survival than in lunatic schemes to assassinate Stalin. The Russian authorities originally wanted KISS to report that the conference was expected to take place in Tehran, and that the embassies were making discreet preparations. DSO pointed out to them that to send such a message would risk blowing KISS, and the Russians acquiesced. So, the notional KISS replied vaguely that, whilst he was aware that the Shah had offered the Allies his hospitality, he had no other information about the matter. On 2 February 1945, KISS also told MARQUIS that he could find out nothing more about the conference, though he had tried hard. He also expressed his personal anxiety about the situation on the Eastern front. It was a shrewdly concocted mixture of credible operational incapacity and personal frailty. This exchange appears to have been the only moderately challenging event during the entire KISS operation, requiring an imaginative response agreed upon cooperatively by the British and the Russians.

About three weeks later, on 21 February 1945, Sosnin abruptly informed Alan Roger that he (i.e. Moscow Centre) was no longer interested in KISS. Roger pointed out that DSO had received questions from Berlin relating essentially to the Soviet zone, but Sosnin maintained that the British should send whatever answers they thought best. He even refused to accept copies of past traffic.[50] It seemed fairly clear to Roger that the Russians had decided to discontinue their collaboration owing to the final question put by MARQUIS as to what the Russians were up to in Azerbaijan. 'As they are up to all sorts of monkey tricks,' Roger told Guy Liddell during a visit to MI5, 'including propaganda for the inclusion of Persian Azerbaijan in the USSR, the question is clearly an awkward one.' The Russians apparently had no objection to DSO's continuing the case since they (the Russians) had the cipher keys.

Liddell also noted at the time that relations (with the Soviets at the Tehran level) were perfectly friendly, though somewhat tentative.[51] So, KISS notionally continued to pass interesting but low-grade information to MARQUIS, and to avoid awkward questions while requesting more money. On 1 May 1945, obviously struggling under extreme difficulties, MARQUIS sent a message to KISS hinting at the intention to close down, stating that he would transmit at a later date. On 3 May 1945, two days before the final surrender, MARQUIS said goodbye (in English) and gave call signs, in case it were possible to make contact again.

During the approximately 13 months of transmissions, DSO undoubtedly learned more about the organization and methods of the Russian security authorities than they did about the German intelligence services. It quickly became clear that the Russians were no strangers to the operation of double agents and other kinds of special cases like KISS, that they knew a lot more about DSO's personnel and installations than had been realized, and that they had a greater interest in Turkey (to secure access to the Mediterranean) and Abadan (to secure access to oil) than had been previously imagined. Such strategic considerations aside, beyond its contribution to the intelligence war with Germany, the KISS operation is significant mainly because it enabled DSO to obtain a more accurate keyhole view of Soviet security methods:[52] information that would prove valuable for MI5 and MI6 postoccupational operations and would do much to bolster the postwar career prospects of former DSO officers like Joe Spencer, Alan Roger, and Dick Thistlethwaite, who quickly became acknowledged experts on Russian counterintelligence and security intelligence.

It had been a remarkable period of *rapprochement* and inspired cooperation at the tactical level among a handful of security personnel responsible for safeguarding wartime Persia. For a brief while all their ideological differences were muted and transcended, but it was not to last. Sir Thomas Rapp, former British consul in Tabriz (in the Soviet zone), wrote after the war that the Soviet authorities were clearly looking ahead to the situation that would exist at the end of hostilities against Germany, when they could again show open enmity towards British interests, 'an enmity they had never in their hearts ceased to feel'. That the British were for the time being their allies was quite clearly a matter of convenience, involving no loyalties that did not suit Stalin's purpose. 'We are your friends now,' the head of the NKVD told Rapp's daughter at a Tehran party, 'but [we] won't be in three or four years.'[53]

Shortly after the war, with CICI about to close its Tehran office, Alan Roger wrote his final report on what had been an extraordinary four-year experiment in liaison and cooperation between DSO and the NKVD. In it Roger observed that, since the war against a common enemy had ended, there were fewer and fewer topics on which he and his staff could consult the Russians. The opportunities for observing their reactions therefore also became fewer. Nevertheless Roger considered the experiment to have been well worth trying. He and his officers had acquired a good idea of how the Russians worked and of the sort of people they employed, even if they did not know exactly how they were organized. They now knew for example that Russian IOs were not usually specialists in any one branch of intelligence; they knew the way their minds worked, and generally what to expect from them. They had learned too that Soviet intelligence seemed to be moderately efficient, but by no means the terrifying instrument it was sometimes thought to be. The Russians Roger had dealt with, including Sosnin, had often been remarkably clumsy in putting over a plant or trying to conceal something. 'It is the ruthlessness of the Soviet state behind the intelligence which is fearsome, rather than the intelligence itself', Roger concluded.[54]

Notes

1. Cooperation with Russian security, Supplementary Report No. 3, 30 August 1945, KV 4/225, TNA. Apart from the (moderately redacted) KISS files (KV 2/1281–1285), the most informative files at Kew on relations between CICI and the Soviet security authorities in Persia are KV 4/224–225.
2. Bullard to Eden, 9 March 1945, E 2050/31/34, IOR/L/PS/12/3472A, BL.
3. Report on visit by Mr A.J. Kellar to SIME and CICI organizations, May 1944, KV 4/384, TNA.
4. An excellent introduction to the Great Game as it was played in Persia, including German subversive activities in the region during the First World War, is Antony Wynn, *Persia in the Great Game: Sir Percy Sykes, Explorer, Consul, Soldier, Spy* (London: John Murray, 2003). See also Karl E. Meyer and Shareen Blair Brysac, *Tournament of Shadows: The Great Game and the Race for Empire in Central Asia* (Washington, DC: Counterpoint, 1999). On the Great Game and Persia during the 1930s and 1940s, see Miron Rezun, 'The Great Game Revisited', *International Journal* 41, no. 2 (Spring 1986): 332–6.
5. Cooperation with Russian Security, 28 December 1944, KV 4/224, TNA.
6. For a detailed study of Anglo-Soviet relations and the Great Game in the region during the Second World War, see Harold J. Kosiba, 'Stalin's Great Game: Anglo-Soviet Relations in the Near East, 1939–1943' (PhD diss., Indiana, 1991).
7. Cooperation with Russian Security, 28 December 1944, KV 4/224, TNA.
8. Ibid.
9. Roger to Spencer, 5 August 1944, KV 2/1317, TNA.
10. Information about Russian intelligence methods in Persia derived from cooperation between DSO Tehran and the Russian security authorities, 7 March 1945, KV 4/224, TNA. According to Donal O'Sullivan, *Dealing with*

the Devil: Anglo-Soviet Intelligence Cooperation during the Second World War* (New York: Lang, 2010), 197–8, Asaturov's real identity was I.I. Agayants, and Sosnin's was P.M. Zhuravlev.
11. Ibid.
12. Cooperation with Russian Security, 28 December 1944, KV 4/224, TNA.
13. Information about Russian intelligence methods in Persia derived from cooperation between DSO Tehran and the Russian security authorities, 7 March 1945, KV 4/224, TNA.
14. Cooperation with Russian Security, 28 December 1944, KV 4/224, TNA.
15. See Christopher Andrew and Vasili Mitrokhin, *The World Was Going Our Way: The KGB and the Battle for the Third World* (New York: Basic Books, 2005), 169.
16. See KV 2/1281–1285, TNA.
17. Soviet SIS activities and the Vaziri case, Defence Security Office, DO/ASR/15, 6 August 1944, KV 2/1317, TNA.
18. See WO 372/25/3232, TNA. Caird's promotion from 2nd Lieutenant to Lieutenant is announced in *London Gazette* 31123 (14 January 1919), 720; and his retirement from the Indian Army Reserve of Officers (IARO) four years later in *London Gazette* 32814 (13 April 1923), 2731. It would therefore appear that Caird was, technically at least, a reserve officer in the IARO while serving in Russia; the precise nature of his soldiering there is unknown and may well have included military and/or political intelligence work. It is of course possible that Caird volunteered for the White Army spontaneously; however, it seems more likely that he was inserted as a field operative by some British or Indian agency.
19. Cooperation with Russian Security, 28 December 1944, KV 4/224, TNA.
20. Curry, *Security Service*, 21.
21. *tudeh* = masses.
22. The best immediately postcontemporary source on the history of the Tudeh Party is a CIA appreciation written in 1949 entitled 'The Tudeh Party: Vehicle of Communism in Iran', CIA-RDP80R01731R001300060066-4, CIA Research Tool (CREST), NARA.
23. Ibid.
24. Ibid.
25. Ibid.
26. Goff to British Military Attaché, 8 July 1942, WO 201/1314, TNA.
27. Dewhurst to Hankey, 22 July 1944, FO 371/40172, TNA.
28. Hankey to GHQ 10th Army, 9 July 1942, WO 201/1314, TNA.
29. Underhill to British Military Attaché, 25 July 1942, WO 201/1314, TNA.
30. Hankey to GHQ 10th Army, 9 July 1942, WO 201/1314, TNA; de Fonblanque to GHQ MEF, 23 June 1942, WO 201/1314, TNA.
31. Cooperation with Russian Security, 28 December 1944, KV 4/224, TNA.
32. Information about Russian intelligence methods in Persia derived from cooperation between DSO Tehran and the Russian security authorities, 7 March 1945, KV 4/224, TNA; Security Summary Middle East No. 134, 29 May 1943, WO 208/1562, TNA.
33. Report on cooperation with Russian security, 28 December 1944, KV 4/224, TNA. For Hamburger's own fascinating and moving account of his years

in exile, see Rudolf Hamburger and Maik Hamburger, *Zehn Jahre Lager: Als deutscher Kommunist im sowjetischen Gulag* (Munich: Siedler, 2013).

34. Ibid.

35. Most notably O'Sullivan, *Dealing with the Devil*, 205–13; Süleyman Seydi, 'Intelligence and Counter-Intelligence Activities in Iran during the Second World War', *Middle Eastern Studies* 46, no. 5 (September 2010): 733–52; Calder Walton, *Empire of Secrets: British Intelligence, the Cold War and the Twilight of Empire* (New York: The Overlook Press, 2013), 70–1. Unfortunately, whilst Seydi's synoptical skills are impressive, he cannot seem to master the fine details, repeatedly misspelling Franz Mayr's name (and several others) and getting many elementary facts wrong.

36. The main files at Kew on the KISS operation (KV 2/1281–1285, TNA) are in themselves sufficiently comprehensive and detailed to support a separate monograph.

37. See miscellaneous DSO Persia cables of March and April 1945 indicating Schulze-Holthus's involvement in the KISS traffic, e.g. Tehran (Carstairs) to London (Kellar), 31 March 1945, KV 2/1285; see also *NSW*, 231.

38. Brief summary of KISS case, September 1945, KV 2/1285, TNA.

39. Extract from SIME Report No. 1 on Mohamed Achundzade Salmassi, 2 February 1944, KV 2/1318, TNA. Salmassi has also been painstakingly identified on the basis of an academic transcript by Donal O'Sullivan, *Dealing with the Devil*, 211, though he might have spared himself considerable effort had he examined the Kew file (KV 2/1318) on Hans Georgiades (DRILLIG), which identifies Salmassi.

40. SIME Report No. 1 on Hans Georg Georgiades, 9 January 1945, KV 2/1318, TNA.

41. Copy of telegram from SIME, 20 June 1944, KV 2/1281, TNA.

42. He has been identified, unconvincingly and without evidence, as the prominent Persian quisling and propagandist Shahbahram Shahrukh by Seydi, 'Intelligence and Counter-Intelligence', 734n9.

43. Brief summary of KISS case, September 1945, KV 2/1285, TNA.

44. Ibid.

45. Robertson to SIS, 25 August 1944, KV 2/1281, TNA.

46. O'Brien to Robertson, 6 January 1945, KV 2/1281, TNA.

47. Information about Russian intelligence methods in Persia derived from cooperation between DSO Tehran and the Russian security authorities, Summary of salient points in DSO Tehran's Supplementary Report No. 1, 13 March 1945, KV 4/224, TNA.

48. Thirty Committee Meeting, 30 January 1945, KV 2/1285, TNA.

49. See *NSW*, 208, 231–2; see also Chapter 5 about the possibility that Gamotha might have planned a sequel to NORMA.

50. Cooperation with Russian security, Supplementary Report No. 2, 3 April 1945, KV 4/225, TNA.

51. Diary of Guy Liddell, 5 March 1945, KV 4/196, TNA.

52. Cf. Walton, *Empire of Secrets*, 70.

53. Persia 1943–44, Sir Thomas Rapp Collection, GB165-0234, MECA.

54. Cooperation with Russian security, Supplementary Report No. 3, 30 August 1945, KV 4/225, TNA.

12
'Operation LONG JUMP'

> The Russian security authorities may have invented the story because they wished to magnify their own importance, and perhaps because the whole credit for breaking up the German organization in Persia had deservedly gone to DSO. (SIME Security Summary)[1]

> Since 1965 many espionage stories have appeared in the Soviet Union depicting the amazing achievements of good Soviet citizens. It is easy to see the hand of the Soviet propaganda apparatus in such fabrications. (Berthold Schulze-Holthus)[2]

It is seldom possible to identify parachute missions to Persia specifically from the existing records. This is true, for instance, of a number of unidentified aircraft and parachute sightings mentioned either in the archival records or in other literature,[3] or even in internet forums and blogs, where scholarly sourcing is seldom found. As the war progressed and Allied operational intelligence grew in volume, depth, and accuracy, the degree of speculation and the number of rumours diminished. Conversely, however, after the war they increased, as the hard intelligence that could have adjusted and corrected them remained closed to the public, and unfettered sensationalist writers quickly sought to fill the void with grossly inaccurate operational accounts based on nothing more than rumour and anecdote. Had the official records been available, such explosive narratives could easily have been discredited by hard archival intelligence. Instead, with no correction from government sources, unfounded and/or conflated scenarios were permitted to proliferate, leaving today's historians to pick their way gingerly through a minefield of misinformation and disinformation, hopefully in an attempt to set the record straight.

It is always necessary to distinguish between contemporary speculation and postwar sensationalism. The former process was an essential integral constituent of purposive intelligence analysis during the war, especially in the earlier phases of security-intelligence work in Persia, before a significant number of Axis or pro-Axis agents had been captured and interrogated, and the information obtained from them had been collated, cross-referenced, and corroborated. The latter phenomenon, on the other hand, is generally associated with the literature of neofascist or antifascist historical revisionism, particularly when authored by less than scholarly writers who have often employed the internet to propagate unsourced (or inadequately sourced) myths about the performance of Nazi agencies and agents in the region. An example would be the attribution to the Abwehr of a mythical parachute operation codenamed 'BAJADERE', together with a mythical narrative according to which 100 soldiers of the FKI entered India through Persian Baluchistan in January 1942 and carried out successful covert action on Indian soil. There is no basis for this operation in the records.[4] Quite apart from the logistical infeasibility of such a long-range operation, the FKI was not mustered and sworn in until August 1942, only reaching its full strength of trained soldiers in mid-1943.[5] Equally fictional is the operation codenamed 'AMINA',[6] which supposedly saw large numbers of marauding German special forces roaming around northern Persia (and even as far south as Abadan) in the aftermath of the Rashid Ali Gailani coup failure in May 1941 and before the Anglo-Soviet invasion in August 1941.[7] Such narratives generally have in common an absurdly inflated operational scale, involving hundreds of participants. Contrast such fictions as 'BAJADERE' and 'AMINA' with the typically more modest, factual attempts by the Abwehr to insert officers singly, such as the Gräwer initiative in February 1941[8] or the deployment a few months later of the former First World War agent Oskar von Niedermayer to Persia (under the alias Otto Normann) in the summer of 1941, which was cut short by the Allied invasion. Niedermayer was at the time attached to Sonderstab F (Hellmuth Felmy's special-operations staff) in Athens; he was to be sent via Turkey on a reconnaissance mission 'of great significance for any military operations in the region, with particular reference to road conditions'.[9]

Thus, the neglect of occupied Persia by serious Western scholars for 70-odd years has permitted certain conflated, sensational narratives of mass-landings by German parachutists and Nazi 'black ops' to achieve folkloric stature in the popular imagination. Most of such fables have validity only as propaganda: they seek variously and disingenuously to glorify either Nazi or Soviet heroism. However, one extraordinary American memoir, penned improbably by Stanley Lovell, the former head of the Research and Development Branch of OSS, and published as a work of nonfiction, strives to apotheosize the deeds of a mythical 'Agent C-12', who supposedly led a group of witless Nazi saboteurs from their dropzone in Kurdistan to Tehran, where they allegedly planted high-explosive charges beneath the streets to be used by the Big Three attending the Tehran Conference in 1943. In his defence, it must be said that throughout his narrative Lovell repeatedly casts doubt on the veracity of his own tale, yet he ends it with the paradoxical statement: 'My tale has no more confirmation than Horatio at the bridge or Theseus and the minotaur, but I choose to regard it as one of the outstanding exploits in the history of OSS.'[10] In reality of course, Lovell's tale is utter nonsense – a partial conflation perhaps of Operations MAMMUT and FRANZ[11] – and his 'choice' unjustified.

An entirely different but equally nonsensical assassination narrative, also published as nonfiction, which needlessly conflates and exaggerates the achievements of British security intelligence, comes from the pen of the police detective responsible for Winston Churchill's safety at the Tehran Conference. According to Walter H. 'Tommy' Thompson, during the two nights preceding the conference about 60 German parachutists landed in two separate drops south of Tehran. They were then hidden, disguised, and supplied with weapons and plans – by whom Thompson does not say. As they floated down, however, many were caught by 'Joseph' [*sic*] Spencer's agents. The remainder, lured by Spencer to a rendezvous with their captured leader, were rounded up one-by-one at gunpoint.[12] It is not clear if this fantasy – obviously a garbled conflation of the FRANZ drop and the Mayr, FRANZ, and DORA arrests – is purely Thompson's invention, or if it is based on hearsay, probably originating from the NKVD, though the naming of 'Joseph' Spencer could hardly have been a Russian idea. However, the mythical nature of the narrative should certainly place Churchill scholars on alert, prompting closer scrutiny of the rest of Thompson's sensational memoirs, not least the 'unexpurgated' version discovered by his great-niece after his death, published in 2003,[13] and then featured in a bafflingly naive 2005 television series.[14] According to Linda Stoker, on the basis of her great-uncle's papers, Churchill survived two Nazi assassination attempts: the first at the Windsors' home in France in 1939, and the second in Cairo (not Tehran!) in November 1943, neither of which is supported by any archival evidence.[15]

One of Canaris's biographers, the journalist and newspaper editor Ian Colvin, son of a celebrated *Morning Post* leader-writer, told Winston Churchill in 1951 that the former head of Abwehr II, Erwin Lahousen, had recently informed him that OKW chief-of-staff Wilhelm Keitel had ordered Canaris to have Churchill killed by (deniable) Spanish Moroccan agents at Casablanca in January 1943. It is peculiar that no mention appears to have been made in this context of Roosevelt. Keitel had probably received a direct order from Hitler, but Canaris did not pass it on to Lahousen, whose department would have been responsible for its execution, and who anyway considered such an operation to have been technically infeasible.[16] Colvin, who enjoyed Churchill's complete confidence, is undoubtedly a credible source. Before the war he was Berlin correspondent of the *News Chronicle* and had regularly fed Churchill valuable intelligence gathered from clandestine relationships established with various senior German military officers, like Lahousen, and other influential anti-Nazis who saw that Hitler's accession to power would mean the ultimate ruin of Germany and Austria.[17] Of course, we will never know which scheming sycophant planted the idea of assassination in the Führer's (or his field marshal's) mind. However, we do know from Lahousen's own testimony that, while Hitler may have wanted Churchill dead, and various Nazis may have dreamed up ways of dispensing with the indefatigable British leader, no assassination plan was ever formally implemented by the Abwehr because Wilhelm Canaris simply would not allow it. According to Lahousen, Canaris always insisted on the primacy of the 'absolute prevention or failure to follow orders for kidnapping, assassination, poisoning, or similar actions'.[18] Furthermore, according to Canaris's most prominent biographer, the *Spiegel* journalist Heinz Höhne, it was precisely around the time of the Casablanca Conference that Canaris became particularly anxious to establish a liaison with the Allies by capitalizing on the personal friendship between Paul Leverkuehn of the Abwehr's Istanbul station and Bill Donovan, chief of OSS.[19] Under such circumstances, Keitel's Casablanca murder scenario would obviously have been anathema to Canaris's peacemaking initiative. However, it remains the only Nazi assassination scheme to target Churchill that has been reliably documented – though unofficially, informally, and eight years after the fact. All the others are fantastical.

The ongoing problem of postoccupational Russian revisionism and the deliberate distortion of Second World War history aimed at placing Stalin's achievements and – as recently as 2007, Russian achievements in general – in a favourable light is something far more serious than the muddle caused by careless British publishers and filmmakers in search of sensation. It is particularly difficult to contend with narratives describing nonexistent Nazi covert operations like 'AMINA', concocted presumably for propagandistic or political ends, for it is hard enough to find sufficient documentary evidence to prove the existence of factual German operations in Persia. Disproving notional ones can be extremely challenging, especially when they are sanctified by the extant Russian secret services, and when – disappointingly – no counterclaims are lodged by the British services, who no doubt have access to relevant records and sufficient *gravitas*. But there seems to have been (and there continues to be) simply no political will in the West to debate the much-abused major issue of security at the Tehran Conference and to set the record straight. So, let us exploit this study of Allied security in occupied Persia, largely based on archival evidence, as an ideal platform for exposing those responsible in Russia (and elsewhere, but mostly in Russia) for distorting the Tehran security situation on the basis of little more than hearsay or pure invention and for promoting a fatuous assassination scenario which simply never happened.

'Operation LONG JUMP' (or 'WEITSPRUNG' in German) is the most obvious hoax: a notional SD 'black op' of which there is no mention in the British, American, or German archives, probably authored by the NKVD (or possibly the Glavnoye Razvedyvatel'noye [GRU]) and perpetuated by the Komitet Gosudarstvennoi Bezopasnosti (KGB) (and latterly by the Federal'naya sluzhba bezopasnosti Rossiyskoy Federatsii [FSB] or Sluzhba vneshney razvedki [SVR]). Not only did Russian propagandists succeed in fooling an American president into believing that German assassins were lurking in Tehran at the time of the Big Three conference in 1943,[20] worse still they succeeded in bamboozling no fewer than four postwar Western historians who should have known better into accepting their preposterous version of events.[21] In view of the general inaccessibility of Soviet secret files to Western scholars during the Cold War (and indeed even today), it is difficult to see how these authors could have based their suppositions on primary archival sources researched at first hand in Russia.[22] Of necessity, whatever their personal or political motivations for embracing the Soviet mythology of Tehran, they can only have derived their narratives from published (as opposed to archival) accounts supplied by the tightly controlled, official or semiofficial purveyors of Russian propaganda to the West, parroting without criticism the rogue literature available to them.

Pre-eminent among the four is the respected Second World War specialist John Erickson, and at the centre of the historiographical storm is the 'factional' novel *Assassinat au sommet* published in 1968 by an obscure French journalist named Laslo Havas.[23] As if conscious of the limitations placed on his work by Soviet heavy-handedness, Erickson even included in his celebrated *oeuvre* on the war in Russia a 'Note on Sources and Materials Relating to the Soviet-German War (1941–45)', from which it is clear that he had no access to anything but Soviet-controlled literature: mainly official histories and published memoirs.[24] The only archival records at Erickson's disposal were German military documents, where he would of course have found no evidence of 'Operation LONG JUMP'. Yet, it is clear that much of Erickson's uncharacteristically derivative account of events in Tehran was taken either directly from a slim but thoroughly misleading monograph on Persia by Miron Rezun[25] or from some common source shared by both scholars, probably Havas. It is puzzling and problematic that such competent historians as Erickson and Rezun, both with solid reputations as archival sleuths, should have accepted a secondary narrative unsupported by sound archival evidence and supplied indirectly by a regime notorious for disseminating propaganda in lieu of history. Such is the phoney Havas novel, which seeks to score points for Russia at the expense of Britain and the United States, falsely depicting a time when Anglo-Soviet liaison in Persia was actually at its most effective and led directly, well in advance of the Big Three summit, to the factual round-up of all remaining pro-Nazi agents in the Tehran area. None of them was a would-be assassin; the conference site was in fact wholly secure, and any notion of a Nazi 'threat' wholly fantastic.

According to DSO, the high spot of Anglo-Soviet liaison was actually achieved in August 1943, three months before the Tehran Conference, when British and Russian security-intelligence staff combined forces to compile a list of the Persian fifth column for arrest, which was then presented jointly by the British and Soviet ambassadors to the Persian government. At that particular time, their collaboration could hardly have been closer, and in many cases the evidence brought against suspects was even compiled jointly in the DSO office by Joe Spencer and the Russian Security Officer.[26] At the time, personal relations between various officers and organizations in PAIFORCE and their Soviet opposite numbers were extremely cordial, and a great show of goodwill was more often than not made by the Russians quite independently of the amount of real cooperation given. The records show that the most notable overt demonstrations of friendship by the Russians towards the British were immediately after the Tehran Conference: fraternizing between Russian and British officers took place in the form of an apparently spontaneous outburst on the part of the Russians.[27]

Most far-fetched among the fictitious narratives of a Nazi plot is perhaps the notion that Wilhelm Canaris and the Abwehr originated a 'LONG JUMP' scheme, to which end the admiral himself supposedly even visited Tehran as early as 1941 – before the Big Three even existed in anyone's imagination.[28] Subsequently, the plan is said to have passed from the Abwehr to Walter Schellenberg and Amt VI, although 'black ops' were never part of their remit. The SD may have had no scruples about the use of mass murder for racist or ideological reasons, but the assassination of a head of state was never considered by Himmler – or even less by Canaris – to be an acceptable operational method, perhaps because the Reichsführer-SS, who had been horrified by Reinhard Heydrich's fate, envisaged himself as a future statesman and potential target. Also, the absence of any confirmation of such an Abwehr plan by Erwin Lahousen, whose department would have been responsible for its execution, even after his transfer to the Russian front in mid-1943, until the creation of the Militärisches Amt in mid-1944, renders the notion highly suspect. Lahousen was generally regarded after the war as one of the most reliable, cooperative, and forthcoming of captured enemy intelligence officers, not least because of his valuable testimony for the prosecution at Nuremberg and his provision of many important documents secretly abstracted during the war on orders from Canaris. Had there been any Abwehr assassination plan (besides the embryonic, nonviable Casablanca scheme mentioned earlier), either Lahousen, his successor Freytag von Loringhoven (also a dedicated Canaris man), or his close associates Wolfgang Abshagen and Kurt Fechner would surely have documented it in the Abwehr II *Kriegstagebuch* (War Diary), and it would have been one of the many matters of record mentioned by Lahousen in his postwar conversations on the basis of the War Diary.[29] Regrettably, however, a specious rogue literature – highly suitable for journalism and dramatization, as propaganda often is – has emanated from the Russian propaganda mill and has endured almost unchallenged until the present day.

There has even been a lame attempt to associate the identity of the (factual) staybehind air-intelligence officer Berthold Schulze-Holthus with that of Havas's notional Soviet agent named 'Ilya Svetlov' (aka 'Walter Schultz'), whose equally notional wife 'Anna' – hardly to be confused with the real, formidable Gertrud Schulze-Holthus – was supposedly not his wife at all but a Nazi agent planted on him by Schellenberg (with whom, as an officer in the Luftwaffe not the SD, Schulze-Holthus in fact had no dealings until he was repatriated to Germany in 1945). This legend, worthy of a juvenile comic-book, seems to have come unstuck mainly because 'Svetlov' would have been notionally active in the Tehran area when the real Schulze-Holthus was factually far to the south in Qashgai territory. To his credit, the author of the travesty, Laslo Havas, acknowledged that the real Schulze-Holthus could not have been in Tehran during the conference.[30] Yet, this was by no means the only disqualifying anachronism in Havas's book. He sought to inflate his story with as many Nazi leaders as possible, even though most had in reality never paid any attention to Persia. In an orgy of name-dropping, he populated his narrative with a surfeit of characters or personalities, some devoid of any connection with wartime Persia (such as Somerset Maugham and Ian Fleming!), and numerous invented spies, agents, and *femmes fatales*, whom Havas represented as authentic, and whose photographs he even falsified. He littered the book with places, events, and documents that either had little bearing on contemporary Persia or – more frequently – had no factual basis at all. And, like so many postwar authors, Havas ascribed to the odious and overrated Otto Skorzeny abilities and influence far beyond the man's actual reach.

Although it strays beyond even the mythical storyline created by Havas, one commercially successful film has been made on the basis of his book: *Tegeran 43* was a joint Soviet-French-Swiss coproduction made by Mosfilm, Mediterraneo Cine, and Pro Dis Film, and directed by Aleksandr Alov and Vladimir Naumov.[31] Essentially Soviet propaganda, the film won the Golden Prize at the Moscow International Film Festival in 1981. In the United States, the film was alternatively entitled *Assassination Attempt*, whilst the West German distribution title was *Killer sind immer unterwegs*. The success of the film is no doubt largely attributable to the fact that it starred such famous actors as Curd Jürgens and Alain Delon and featured one of Charles Aznavour's most celebrated songs, 'Une vie d'amour', sung for the soundtrack by Mireille Mathieu, for in other respects it is barely watchable. It has a perplexingly ornate plot, with no basis in history; the characters are stereotypical; and the multilingual dialogue is muddled by inconsistent and unreliable subtitling. An earlier, less successful Anglo-Italian film, *Teheran*, depicting a Nazi time-bomb attack on the Big Three, predates the Soviet propaganda campaign; however, its content too is decidedly pro-Russian.[32] It was directed by William Freshman and Giacomo Gentilomo, and was released in 1946. A 1994 made-for-TV film, *World War II: When Lions Roared* (alternatively entitled *Then There Were Giants*), directed by Joseph Sargent, depicts the strategic relationships between Churchill, Roosevelt, and Stalin, culminating in the Tehran Conference; however, it thankfully makes no mention of 'LONG JUMP'.[33]

Eleven years later, in 2005, 'Operation LONG JUMP' was featured in a 13-part British 'documentary' television series narrated by Denis

Waterman and entitled *Churchill's Bodyguard*.[34] Here the storyline has clearly been adapted from the work of Laslo Havas: White Russian paratroopers are despatched to Tehran by Otto Skorzeny (who else?). Immediately upon landing, they turn themselves in to the Soviet embassy (which seems an absurdly elaborate way of deserting the Vlasov cause). German stormtroopers accompanying the Vlasov men then prepare to attack the Allied leaders under cover of a civilian riot, but they are ultimately killed when led into a trap by a local German agent doubling for the British. Of course, no attempt has been made to 'document' the narrative: the wholesale acceptance and conflation of the Havas scenario without any attempt to corroborate or verify it is absurd. Such mischief should have exposed the producers to accusations of collusion with the neo-Stalinist propaganda machine, were Western critics (and historians) not so lamentably ill-informed about what really went on (or did not) at the Big Three conference. Instead, these 'documentary' filmmakers were let off Scot-free, their reputations unimpeached, and their dreadful travesty continues to dupe viewers into accepting their baseless epic as history.

Worse still, in Philip Kerr's gratuitously violent political novel from the same year (2005), *Hitler's Peace*, Qashgai tribesmen ['of northern Iran' (*sic*)] are used by the Abwehr in an operation ('LONG JUMP') aimed at assassinating the three Allied leaders at the Tehran Conference. Betrayed to the Soviets, the Qashgai are executed by the NKVD. Kerr has evidently plundered Kew, mentioning Operation FRANZ and the Abwehr/Amt VI rivalry, and employing Schellenberg as a protagonist and the initiator of 'LONG JUMP', but Kerr's book remains a misleading muddle of fantasy, inaccuracy, distortion, and speculation that abounds with Nazi stereotypes and is of no historical value whatsoever.[35]

Two years earlier, in 2003, Gary Kern, an American translator and researcher, had tried to come to grips with such nonsense and expose the mythological events that had been added by the Russians to embellish what is in reality a simple narrative of practical security measures taken to protect the lives of three statesmen in the face of subsequently disproven rumours of an assassination attempt.[36] In his study, which deals primarily with the issue of the 'bugging' (by Stalin) of Roosevelt's quarters during the summit, Kern lists – and indicts – the published literature on 'LONG JUMP', which he identifies as having been actively promoted by the KGB in the press.[37] Unfortunately, Kern appears to have been unaware that – 34 years earlier – none other than Berthold Schulze-Holthus, incensed at having his identity (and parts of his autobiography) hijacked and manipulated by the Russians, had already addressed the matter. However, because Schulze-Holthus's debunking of Havas's 'factional' novel, which the (real) German spy dubs 'a grotesque falsification',[38] was never widely published but appeared only in *Die Nachhut* (the limited-circulation house organ of the Abwehr veterans' organization, Arbeitsgemeinschaft ehemaliger Abwehrangehöriger [AGEA]),[39] the former Abwehr officer's version of events remained unread by a larger public.

Seething with resentment, Schulze-Holthus wrote that the answer to the question of why 'this most important secret operation in all history' was not revealed until 1968 was extremely simple: it never took place and only emerged in 1968 as a creature of Laslo Havas's imagination. The publishers evidently believed that they could point to a certain camaraderie or conspiracy among the secret services as the cause of this 'failure to elucidate the historical truth'. Schulze-Holthus was referring here to the apparent fact that both OSS and the 'British intelligence service' had refused to confirm the accuracy of Havas's 'revelations'. According to Schulze-Holthus, however, this had nothing to do with any 'conspiracy', for how could those intelligence services, who knew very well what really occurred in Persia in the late autumn of 1943, possibly confirm something that had never happened?[40]

Schulze-Holthus went on to accuse Havas of having tricked his readers into accepting his 'spy novel' as authentic historiography, endowing it with the semblance of sound scholarship by absorbing into it Schulze-Holthus's own relatively accurate and verifiable account of events in Persia up to the summer of 1943.[41] At this point, however, Havas's account had departed from history. He introduced at least half a dozen fictitious characters and described twenty fictitious parachute drops connected with the assassination plot. Had these parachute drops actually taken place, Schulze-Holthus would undoubtedly have been interrogated about them by DSO when he was arrested four months later, yet he was not. Furthermore, whilst in captivity in Palestine, Schulze-Holthus had had many conversations with Franz Mayr and the German parachutists who had actually been dropped into Persia, Kurdistan, and Palestine, during the course of which no mention had ever been made of 'LONG JUMP'.[42] When, after his repatriation to Germany in January 1945, Schulze-Holthus was interrogated 'very thoroughly' by the SD, including Schellenberg himself, there had also been no mention of any Tehran operation nor of any of the 38 SS members and 60 Vlasov Russians conjured up by Havas. Furthermore, Schulze-Holthus was unable to confirm the existence of Havas's central character, the Swiss double agent 'Ernst Merser'. Schulze-Holthus was thoroughly briefed in

1941 and in 1945 on the names of all German operatives in the region; no 'Merser' was to be found on any of the Abwehr or SD lists.[43]

Even the few factual characters featured by Havas were falsified. The 'second coming' of Roman Gamotha for instance was pure fiction. In reality, when he returned to Germany from Persia in March 1943, Gamotha's poor health (he suffered from severe bouts of recurrent malaria) would have rendered him too fragile to lead any 'black op' eight months later. This is why Gamotha was given a comfortable desk job at Amt VI, once he had recuperated sufficiently to return to full-time paper-work. In early 1945, the head of VI C 3, Kurt Schuback, briefed Schulze-Holthus fully on Gamotha's factual doings, and Schulze-Holthus met Gamotha himself at the latter's home near Vienna days before the end of the war, just prior to Gamotha's final defection to the Russians. During these conversations neither Schuback nor Gamotha made any mention of a return to Persia, which they would of course have done, had it ever happened. Schulze-Holthus also talked to Theodor Staisch, who had fled Persia with Gamotha in 1942, and Hassan Quraishi, the Qashgai Brothers' private secretary, who is a character in Havas's version of the plot;[44] neither man ever mentioned 'LONG JUMP'. Unconvincingly, Havas adds in a disclaiming footnote that his character 'Gorechi', who is killed during his version of 'LONG JUMP', is not Quraishi the secre-tary but 'one of the most influential Qashgai politicians', which merely compounds the fiction. The real Quraishi was in fact a concentration-camp prisoner at the time of the Tehran Conference, while Staisch corroborated the official SD account of Gamotha's career already given to Schulze-Holthus by Schuback, which of course excluded any assas-sination plot.[45]

The capture of Franz Mayr and the FRANZ/DORA group by DSO was also falsified by Havas. According to Schulze-Holthus, the quarrel in Isfahan between Mayr and his Armenian agent Moses Gasparian (MUSA), which was the initial incident in Mayr's downfall, had had nothing to do with money, as Havas suggests, but had been about Gasparian's demand that Mayr should get Hitler to make a binding declaration guaranteeing Armenian independence.[46] Besides this, the handing over of a suitcase containing the addresses of Mayr's Persian collaborators and political friends to the British consul in Isfahan (in November 1942) was obviously not the immediate catalyst for the arrest of Mayr and the FRANZ parachutists in Tehran (in August 1943). In fact, for weeks after the handover, Mayr had carried on business as usual. The arrests were actually a direct result of the arrest on 14 August 1943 of young Werner Rockstroh, one of the FRANZ parachutists, who 'sang like a canary' when captured. All these informative factual details about the suitcase and the arrests were obtained by Schulze-Holthus directly from Mayr himself and the FRANZ/DORA group during their shared internment in Palestine.[47] Significantly, Schulze-Holthus's version of events is corroborated by the CICI and DSO records, to which he of course had no access.[48]

Schulze-Holthus also discusses the acute shortage of air transport at the time of the Tehran Conference, specifically the lack of large long-range aircraft capable of flying missions from Crimea to Persia and back. By August 1943, only one suitable aircraft remained, which the Luftwaffe and the SKL insisted on retaining for North Atlantic reconnaissance flights in support of maritime (U-boat) operations. Besides, as Schulze-Holthus points out, any flight over neutral Turkey would have required Hitler's personal approval, which was never given.[49]

In the next edition of *Die Nachhut*, in a contribution supporting Schulze-Holthus's review of Laslo Havas's book, the editor of the serial, Franz Seubert, identified three of the authors on Gary Kern's list (Alexander Lukin [whom Schulze-Holthus had cited as Havas's inspiration], Victor Yegorov, and Laslo Havas himself) as purveyors of Stalinist mythology, with Havas singled out for having plagiarized Lukin's articles, reproducing and compounding Lukin's falsehoods in a lengthy work of fiction that masqueraded as fact.[50] According to Seubert, Yegorov had actually attacked Lukin for pretending to have first-hand knowledge of the events in Tehran, while in fact possessing only hearsay evidence. Yet, Yegorov himself was also the source for some of the false information in Havas's book: Yegorov's descriptions were even more improbable and more like a novel than those of Lukin. Seubert stated flatly that Yegorov's book was pure propaganda; the *Sunday Times* had called it a 'farrago'.[51] In fact, the *Sunday Times* had published a somewhat ambivalent article shortly after the appearance of Yegorov's account, comparing it with Lukin's narrative and severely criticizing both contradictory Soviet 'works of fiction'.[52]

However, ill-advisedly, the *Sunday Times* had called upon the worst possible source, the notoriously self-serving and unreliable Otto Skorzeny, the so-called Waffen-SS 'commando ace', to provide a German view of 'LONG JUMP' ('WEITSPRUNG'). The story was that Walter Schellenberg had appointed Skorzeny, barely two months after his kidnapping/'rescue' of Benito Mussolini in Italy in September 1943, to lead a death squad into Persia to kill the Big Three. True to character when interviewed by the press, Skorzeny was quick to absolve himself of any complicity in a 'black op', yet he claimed to have been asked by Schellenberg to lead one (something never subsequently acknowledged by Schellenberg), which he (Skorzeny) 'bluntly' refused to do.[53] Thus Skorzeny achieved his (typically) disingenuous intention of portraying himself in the British press positively as a discerning special-forces professional, whilst shifting the responsibility for any skullduggery (or failure) to Schellenberg. Skorzeny must have pleased Moscow greatly by perpetuating their mythology. Unfortunately, on the basis of such spurious, uncorroborated evidence, the unsigned *Sunday Times* article came to the erroneous conclusion that 'there *was* a German plot to kill the Big Three as they met'.[54] Needless to say, there is not a shred of documentary evidence to be found in support of this narrative in the British, American, or German archives. In this context, incidentally, one may witness a most peculiar alliance of convenience between Hitlerite and Stalinist propagandists, with both camps seeking to apotheosize their 'heroes of Tehran': the thoroughly overestimated Skorzeny and the thoroughly flawed NKVD.

Yet, the same newspaper also interviewed former US ambassador to the Soviet Union Averill Harriman, who had worked closely with Molotov on security during the Tehran Conference, and Sir Kenneth Strong, who was at the time of the conference Ike Eisenhower's Assistant Chief of Staff for Intelligence (G-2) at Allied Force Headquarters (AFHQ), and a German specialist besides. Shortly before the conference, according to the President's Log for 28 November 1943, Harriman appears to have been completely duped by Molotov, emphasizing to FDR that the city of Tehran had been under complete German control only a few months before, and that the risk of assassination of Churchill and Stalin while coming to visit Roosevelt [at the US embassy] was very real.[55] Harriman's assertion about 'complete German control' is plainly absurd, and would have been ridiculed by DSO, had they learned of it. It is likely that Harriman was parroting what he had heard from NKVD officers, possibly at the earlier Cairo conference from Andrej Vyshinski (Soviet Assistant Commissioner for Foreign Affairs), or from Molotov himself. FDR's security boss, Mike Reilly, also heard from the NKVD that Nazi parachutists had jumped in the Tehran area the day before but had not been apprehended.[56] However, when interviewed by the British press, Harriman back-pedalled, giving his story a different spin:

> Molotov never mentioned specific evidence of a specific plot. He simply warned me, in strong terms, that there were a lot of German agents in the area. He said he was afraid there *might* be a plot. That was all. And, when the conference was over, I specifically asked Molotov if there had been a plot. He said they had taken precautions because of rumours. He never said there was a specific plot.[57]

Kenneth Strong's response, on the other hand, was unequivocal:

> I never heard about a plot, and I am pretty sure I would have been
> told if there was any evidence ... . I still assume that the Russians
> wanted precisely what they got. They used the plot to persuade
> Roosevelt to move into a villa in the compound of the Russian
> embassy in Teheran. And you may be sure that was well bugged.[58]

And then there is the issue of the German propaganda broadcasts before
the conference. On 22 November 1943, an article appeared in the *New York
Times* claiming that the Germans had used radio stations they controlled
in Finland and France to announce that there was to be a Big Three meeting in Tehran at the end of the month.[59] Had they actually been planning
to assassinate or kidnap the participants, why would they have made such
an announcement, alerting the security authorities to their interest in the
event? The German-controlled broadcasts are just additional proof that
nothing could have been further from the Germans' minds than an attack
on the Big Three. In the popular media, doubtless in an attempt to drive a
wedge between the Big Three, the Nazis always tended to give the impression that they knew better than the Allies themselves what the Allies were
up to. In this vein, the broadcasts announcing the Tehran meeting were
merely routine propagandistic posturing, and not related in any way to
the actual security situation in Tehran, about which, with no active agents
remaining in the area, Berlin knew little or nothing.

Ultimately, it is the British, who were responsible for counterintelligence and security in Tehran at the time of the Big Three
conference, whose records tell the true, anticlimactic story of the circumstances underlying the notional Operation 'LONG JUMP'. In postwar correspondence, one of Joe Spencer's most reliable officers, Dick
Thistlethwaite, by then a senior MI5 official, stated unequivocally that
CICI knew of no German agents in the Tehran area at the time.[60] One
month after the conference, Joe Spencer heard of Roosevelt's jocular
reference (greeted with general laughter) to 'a German plot': 'of course,
in a place like Teheran there are hundreds of German spies, probably,
around the place, and I suppose it would make a pretty good haul if
they could get all three of us going through the streets'.[61]

Spencer reacted quickly, issuing a 'most secret' summary for general
internal distribution throughout the Middle East, in which he wrote:

> While agreeing with Mr Roosevelt that the assassination of the three
> leaders would have been 'a pretty good haul', it must be pointed out

that, as far as this office is aware, there is no truth whatsoever in the reports given in the press or on the radio. Both the President of the United States and the *Daily Mail* correspondent were probably referring to some garbled form of the Mayr plot. Such careless reporting and broadcasting is harmful and more so when the facts can easily be checked on the spot.[62]

And in the next SIME quarterly summary, the following note appeared:

The favourable course of the war and the arrest of Franz Mayr and his associates ... have caused a great improvement in the security situation, which is probably now better than at any time since the beginning of the war. It is unfortunate therefore that President Roosevelt should have given much publicity to the groundless Russian story of the presence of 100 German agents at Tehran.[63]

Around the same time, Spencer also pointed out that the Russian security authorities may have invented the story because they wished to magnify their own importance, and perhaps because the whole credit for breaking up Mayr's organization had deservedly gone to the British. However, neither before nor during the conference had the Soviets breathed a word about any Nazi 'plot' to the British legation staff or to DSO, though they had apparently filed a vague report with C-in-C PAIFORCE.[64]

Twenty years later, Sir Reader Bullard wrote privately that he was convinced at the time, and was still convinced, that there was no Nazi plot.[65] And in his published memoirs he had this to say:

Molotov declared that a plot to kill one or other of the Big Three had been discovered by the Soviet Secret Intelligence. Now for Roosevelt to stay in security in the place where the meetings were held and not risk his invaluable life in the streets was sensible, but the 'plot' was too much. After the conference British security officers ragged their Soviet opposite numbers about it. The poor Russians apparently put on a look of helplessness mixed with an appeal for sympathy, as though to say: 'You know what it is: if Molotov says there's a plot there is a plot.'[66]

Three years on, after correspondence with authors Ronald Seth (who subscribed to the Russian story evidently on the basis of Lukin's account) and E.H. Cookridge (who claimed that he had treated Russian and American versions of what happened in Tehran 'with utmost caution'), Bullard wrote to the American historian Ladislas Farago, who rejected the Russian version, describing it as 'an escapade in Bolshevik propaganda':[67] 'The story rests upon the bare allegation by Molotov: all reports, whether from Churchill or Harry Hopkins or others, go back to that allegation, which in my opinion was put forward as an additional argument for the removal of President Roosevelt from the United States legation to the Soviet embassy.'[68] Thus Bullard's view is identical to that expressed by Sir Kenneth Strong. Moreover, the elaborate 'LONG JUMP' scenarios, even if truly contemplated by Berlin, would have been entirely unnecessary. According to Joe Spencer, Churchill himself pointed out during the conference — sardonically, no doubt — that, since the FRANZ/DORA parachutists had been flown to Persia from Germany, it would have been possible to disrupt the conference with

Figure 12.1 Notional, not national heroes: Gevork and Goar Vartanyan. Two Soviet foreign-intelligence operatives who helped to conflate a garbled narrative of Operation FRANZ and the state of heightened security at the Tehran Conference into the myth of 'Operation LONG JUMP'
Source: RIA Novosti.

a single suicide plane flying from Germany and bombing the embassy. 'I think our nearest air defence at that time was based in Cairo', Spencer added.[69]

Yet the Russian propaganda apparatus – long after the passing of the NKVD and the KGB, who probably originated and sustained the myth of 'LONG JUMP' – persists even into the 21st century in disseminating that myth. In 2003, for instance, the official Kremlin International News broadcast an absurd press conference with a panel of veterans of the Russian Foreign Intelligence Service to commemorate the 60th anniversary of the Tehran Conference and to promote the publication of a book by one of the 'veterans' present, Yuri Lvovich Kuznets, entitled *Teheran-43 or Operation Long Jump*. Also in attendance were Gevork Andreyevich Vartanyan and his wife Goar Vartanyan (see Figure 12.1) – both described as 'veteran spies, veterans of the external intelligence service', and it is Vartanyan who, claiming to have served in Persia throughout the war (1941–45), blustered:

> Many say that no such [assassination] attempt had been made. All this is rubbish. An attempt had been made, and we provided the security of the conference and we knew what was going on. Actually, there had been an attempt and you know from history that six radio operators had been seized and made to defect and they worked under the control of our intelligence services from Berlin.[70]

According to Vartanyan, there was no doubt that there was a conspiracy; however, there were unfortunately some self-styled writers who distort history. Before long they would be claiming that there was no Great Patriotic War or that Russia was a mere participant. Gradually, credit was being ascribed more and more to the Americans and the British, while the Russians were being quietly sidelined. 'And I think it is your duty,' Vartanyan continued, 'the duty of printed and electronic media, to provide more historical facts on the air so that the people know and do not forget the services that the Soviet Union has made to the whole world.'[71]

The moderator of the 2003 event promptly conflated the mythology by suggesting that British intelligence had claimed the credit for foiling an attempt on the Tehran *troika*. At this point, he passed the microphone to Vladimir Alexeyevich Kirpichenko, whom he described as a former Deputy Chief of the KGB First Main Directorate (Foreign Intelligence) who had access to archival materials. Whilst asserting that there was very good cooperation between the British and Russian intelligence services in Persia and that Kuznets' book was 'strictly docu-mentary', Kirpichenko then started to propagandize: 'There is endless discussion on whether there was a LONG JUMP or not. I want to say that there were preparations for the assassination of the heads of three states ... . The assassination had been prepared and there is no doubt about that.'[72]

What follows is sheer nonsense: Kirpichenko enumerates the same fictitious events and characters created by Lukin, Yegorov, and Havas, concluding: 'I don't see any flaws in the book. Everything is perfect. It provides valuable material for a person who studies the history of intel-ligence.'[73] Questions are then put to the panelists, such as 'Are there any secrets left concerning the Tehran Conference?' And 'If there are still such secrets in documents and archives, when will they be disclosed?' to which no clear answer is given. At this point, the author himself, Kuznets, volunteers evasively that he does not think any intelligence service in the world will open up the last document even to scholars, not to mention the broad public. Kirpichenko adds fantastically that the Russians foiled the Nazi plot partly because 'our Cambridge Five from London' [sic] provided us with genuine documents on the eve of the Tehran Conference. Even Otto Skorzeny himself was supposedly dropped near Qum to reconnoitre 'the sites he was interested in'. (How he could possibly have then been extracted from Persia and returned to Germany is not mentioned.)[74] Reiterating Skorzeny's notional role, 'Hero of the Soviet Union' and 'legendary Soviet spy' Gevork Vartanyan subsequently gave at least two interviews – one as recently as 2007 – about his work in Persia in which he is said to have prevented the murder of Stalin, Roosevelt, and Churchill.[75] Relentlessly and repeat-edly, the Russian television organization TV-Novosti (RT International) has continued to pitch the phoney Vartanyan story to a global viewer-ship. In May 2008 and again in May 2009, a documentary programme aired depicting 'the legendary spy ... who actually saved the lives of the Big Three' and featuring interview with Vartanyan, who was only 19 years old in 1943, having apparently become an NKVD officer at the unlikely age of 16. And in January 2012 Vartanyan's death was marked by a seven-minute newscast on RT International. Even Russian president Dmitry Medvedev expressed his condolences to Vartanyan's friends and relatives, saying:

> Gevork Vartanyan was a legendary intelligence agent, a genuine patriot of his country, a bright and extraordinary person. He took part in splendid operations, which went down in the history of the

Russian foreign intelligence service. His death is an irretrievable loss to his family and all those who knew and highly appreciated the legendary man.[76]

Unquestionably, the NKVD played a major role in the successful maintenance of law and order in Persia, specifically within the northern provinces, which they controlled absolutely and exclusively, allowing neither interference nor incursions by the British and Americans. In that sense the Soviet service contributed significantly to the overall success of the Allied security forces in the region. However, that was the limit of their contribution. Any attempts to make the Western Allies 'eat crow' by comparing the NKVD's performance with that of DSO and the American CIC must be discounted, because the Russians have never permitted – and still do not permit – access to the relevant official records, if any still exist. Furthermore, their respective remits are not comparable. NKVD operations were limited to the relatively small Soviet occupation zone north of the Alborz Mountains and adjacent to the Caspian, whilst DSO were responsible for policing the major cities of Tehran, Isfahan, and Shiraz, as well as the vast hinterland of Persia with its extensive oilfield and transportation infrastructure. For their part, the Americans bore no formal security responsibility beyond the maintenance of internal security and order among US personnel, within US installations, and on the US-managed Lend-Lease supply routes.

It needs to be emphasized that all the Russian fabrications, including the oral excurses, are marked by conceptual imprecision and a curious lack of narrative focus or rigour, which is of course attributable to the fact that they are not based on concrete documentation but are born of imagination. An example would be the tendency of the propagandists to view German espionage and special operations as monolithic, with no clear distinction between the Abwehr and the SD, or the competence of Canaris as opposed to that of Schellenberg. They also clearly assume that their audience has no knowledge of the archival records, which may be a safe assumption within Russia, but not beyond. What is less clear is why the Putin-era intelligence services should find it expedient to resurrect and promulgate a baseless and obscure Stalinist myth set in wartime Persia. It seems that the motivation is broadly nationalistic, and that the impetus may have come from KGB veterans in an effort to bolster the significance of their careers, their service to the Soviet/Russian state, and the continuance of their pensions and comfortable Moscow apartments.

Thankfully, and at long last, one Western author has recently written a carefully researched, accurate, highly readable novel based on the archival narrative to rival the Laslo Havas myth. It is to be hoped that Patrick Clark's self-published book will reach a wide enough readership to eclipse Havas' nonsense and finally set the 'LONG JUMP' record straight, at least in the popular imagination.[77] However, the real historiographical task remains: professional war historians, especially intelligence historians, need to come to grips with and address the fact that, had it ever been seriously mooted at the Berkaerstrasse HQ, 'Operation LONG JUMP' would have been far beyond the conceptual and logistical capability of Amt VI in late 1943. Neither Walter Schellenberg nor Otto Skorzeny would ever have been capable of mounting so challenging a 'black op', even if the department's resources had allowed them to do so. Whilst undoubtedly very able in his self-serving way ('a priggish little dandy ... [who] played the skin-saving game with foppish elegance'),[78] Schellenberg was too ignorant of the region to execute such an undertaking. And his only adviser on Persian affairs, Roman Gamotha, was a Soviet plant who constantly misinformed him and would have done everything in his power to sabotage any 'LONG JUMP', as he did the factual Operation NORMA. As for Skorzeny, no Nazi's reputation as an operational leader and influential personality has been more grossly inflated by postwar authors, historians among them. In reality, Otto Skorzeny was but a ruthlessly ambitious, boorish bully who alienated most of those with whom he had contact, even within the SS, and whose lack of intelligence led him to depend heavily on his adjutant, Karl Radl, to do his hard work for him.[79] And, of course, neither man had any independent knowledge of Persia.

Those who have written subjectively about the 'LONG JUMP' scenario appear to have been motivated by one of three causes: Stalinism, Nazism, or sensationalism. It has to be regretted that so far few writers have championed the Allied cause, ignored the rogue literature, studied the files, and embraced objectivity and accuracy in this matter. But the archival records speak for themselves: they say unequivocally that 'LONG JUMP' was never seriously conceived, never planned, and never executed.

Notes

1. Security Summary Middle East No. 161, 22 December 1943, WO 208/1562, TNA.
2. 'Eine groteske Fälschung', *Die Nachhut: Informationsorgan für Angehörige der ehemaligen militärischen Abwehr* 7 (9 April 1969): 26, MSG 3/667, BArch-MArch.
3. Prior to the Tehran Conference, during the most aggressive phase of German covert operations in the region, namely the summer of 1943, no fewer

than 34 unidentified aircraft sightings were reported and officially documented by the Allies. See Unidentified aircraft over Persia and North Iraq, 17 June–11 September 1943, WO 208/1588A, TNA. Most mysterious is the following report of sightings in southwest Persia, at the extreme limit of any German aircraft's fuel range: 'On two or three occasions in the quarter-moon, unidentified aircraft have flown over Abadan. ... I think we can take it that these were German aircraft on reconnaissance ...'. See Extract from Enclosure 1A to M.O.5/BM/1700 Encl. 'A', Iran I.6.g, WO 208/1588A, TNA.

4. There was a factual unit named 'Sonderkommando (SK) Bajadere' (see *NSW*, 63, 88, 164, 175, 200, 252); however, I have been unable to trace any mention of an operation by that name in the archival records. Had it existed, it would no doubt have been planned by Hans-Otto Wagner of Abwehr II, who had dealings with INA leader Bose, and it would therefore normally have been mentioned in connection with Wagner or Bose. Not surprisingly therefore, there is no mention of any such aerial deployment on Indian soil in Adrian Weale's archives-based essay on the FKI in *Renegades: Hitler's Englishmen* (London: Pimlico, 2002), 199–201. According to Weale, the men of the FKI saw active duty only in the Netherlands (building coastal defences), France, and Germany. Apart from the odd skirmish with the French Resistance, they appear to have done no fighting at all. In fact, the Germans seem to have been anxious to keep them as far as possible from any direct confrontation with British forces.

5. See Weale, *Renegades*, 200.

6. Aminah bint Wahb was the mother of the prophet Mohammed.

7. 'Operation AMINA' (June–July 1941), which some sources describe as two or three separate operations, is not to be found in the archival records. Even though the Abwehr records would probably have been destroyed, had it/ they occurred on the scale described in the rogue literature, the operation(s) would surely have been described in surviving Allied documents. The main rogue sources on 'AMINA' are the self-published Klaus Benzing, *Der Admiral: Leben und Wirken* (Nördlingen: Klaus Benzing, 1973), 135–6; Franz Kurowski, *The Brandenburgers: Global Mission*, trans. David Johnston (Winnipeg: J.J. Fedorowicz, 1997), 124–6; and recently Chapay A. Sultanov, *Would the Allies Have Won without Baku Oil?* (Baku: Nurlar, 2008), 147–51. Benzing hardly inspires confidence as a source of any information, for he was ostracized by his fellow former Abwehr officers for falsely claiming to have found a copy of Canaris's missing diary in East Germany (see Gerold Guensberg, 'Intelligence in Recent Public Literature,' *Studies in Intelligence* 21, no. 3 [Fall 1977]: 47–9). Kurowski's book is one of the worst popular histories I have ever read: the sections entitled 'The Operation in Iran' (123–33) and 'The Role of the Brandenburgers in Operation TIGER' (137–9) are littered with errors, contradictions, and exaggerations. The source of some of Kurowski's misinformation appears to be David Littlejohn, *Foreign Legions of the Third Reich* (San Jose, CA: Bender, 1987), another popular work to be approached with great caution. In keeping with other published Russian accounts of Persian operations, Sultanov's narrative is muddled, vague, and dubiously sourced.

8. *NSW*, 84.

9. See Mansfeld to Krummacher, 7 August 1941; Grobba to RAM, 19 August 1941; Grobba to Krummacher, 26 August 1941, GFM 33/463, TNA.

10. Stanley P. Lovell, *Of Spies and Strategems* (New York: Pocket Books, 1964), 110.

11. See *NSW*, passim.

12. Walter H. Thompson, *Assignment: Churchill* (Toronto: McLeod, 1955), 283.

13. Walter H. Thompson, *Beside the Bulldog: The Intimate Memoirs of Churchill's Bodyguard* (London: Apollo, 2003).

14. *Churchill's Bodyguard*, produced by Jonathan Martin et al., directed by Jonathan Martin and Philip Nugus, Nugus/Martin Productions Ltd, 2005.

15. Regarding the genesis of the *Churchill's Bodyguard* television series, see Tom Hickman, *Churchill's Bodyguard* (London: Headline, 2005), vii–viii. Confusingly and without any indication of his source, Hickman asserts that Erwin Lahousen testified in 1950 that Hitler had ordered an assassination attempt in Tehran. Not surprisingly, I have been unable to corroborate Hickman. See ibid., 297n6.

16. See Ian Colvin, *Chief of Intelligence* (London: Gollancz, 1951), 164–6; 'Riddles, Mysteries, Enigmas', *Finest Hour* 1, no. 15 (Summer 2002): 13; correspondence between Colvin and Churchill about Lahousen in CHUR 2/168A/135–6, CAC.

17. See Winston S. Churchill, *The Gathering Storm*, vol. 1 of *The Second World War* (London: The Reprint Society, 1950), 81.

18. V/48/F8 to V.F., Reports by Generalmajor Lahousen, 15 December 1945, KV 2/173, TNA.

19. Heinz Höhne, *Canaris*, trans. J. Maxwell Brownjohn (New York: Doubleday, 1979), 482–3.

20. See 'The Nine Hundred and Twenty-seventh Press Conference (Excerpts). December 17, 1943', in *The Public Papers and Addresses of Franklin D. Roosevelt*, 1943 Volume, *The Tide Turns* (New York: Harper, 1950), 549–53; 'Stalin Bared Plot against President', *New York Times*, 18 December 1943.

21. 'Richard Deacon' (Donald McCormick), 'Nigel West' (Rupert Allason), John Erickson, and Miron Rezun. See Richard Deacon, 'Ilya Svetloff Foils the Nazis', in *A History of the Russian Secret Service* (London: Frederick Muller, 1972), 392–403; Nigel West, *Historical Dictionary of World War II Intelligence* (Lanham, MD: Scarecrow Press, 2008), 140–1; John Erickson, *The Road to Berlin: Stalin's War with Germany*, vol. 2 (London: Weidenfeld and Nicolson, 1983), 149–54; and Miron Rezun, *The Iranian Crisis of 1941: The Actors: Britain, Germany, and the Soviet Union* (Cologne: Böhlau, 1982), 57–63 (also available in *The Soviet Union and Iran: Soviet Policy in Iran from the Beginning of the Pahlavi Dynasty until the Soviet Invasion in 1941* [Alphen aan den Rijn: Sijthoff & Noordhoff, 1981], 358–65). While Deacon became notorious during his career in historical journalism for 'gilding the lily' whilst in search of sensation, West, Erickson, and Rezun are surely made of sterner stuff as professional historians and archival scholars, which makes their gullibility all the more astonishing and alarming. Lacking archival access, Rezun rightly makes no attempt to cite Russian primary sources; however his stated reliance on 'an anonymous researcher in Eastern Europe who has copies of the relevant NKVD records' (99n190) is ill-advised and methodologically unsound, as is his lengthy footnote (101n203) protesting (a little too much) at Western debunking of the 'LONG JUMP' myth. Rezun's sarcastic assertion that critics of the scenario are 'mostly German of course' is offensive and unworthy of a professional historian.

22. The Russian military records on the Soviet invasion and occupation of northern Persia remain classified and firmly closed. Alex Statiev, email message to author, 14 August 2014.
23. Laslo Havas, *Assassinat au sommet* (Paris: Arthaud, 1968). The English version of this elaborate fabrication is Laslo Havas, *The Long Jump*, trans. Kathleen Szasz (London: Neville Spearman, 1967). Having misread a magazine article by Canaris's biographer Heinz Höhne ('Selten Skrupel', *Der Spiegel* 41, 8 October 1979: 252–7), ignoring a crucial possessive apostrophe (rare in German), Miron Rezun twice carelessly names the author for whom he advocates 'Laslo Havas Mär' (see Rezun, *Iranian Crisis*, 101n203), wrongly interpreting Höhne's use of the archaic form *Mär* (= *Märchen* [fairy-tale]) and including it in the French author's name.
24. Erickson, *Road to Berlin*, 789–92.
25. Rezun, *Iranian Crisis*.
26. Response to questionnaire on Russian counterintelligence and security drawn up by Counter-Intelligence Planning Section for Austria, AFHQ, 1945, KV 4/225, TNA.
27. Russian relations and activities in Persia since September 1941, KV 4/224, TNA.
28. Cf. Rezun, *Iranian Crisis*, 46–7, 96n151, 101n203.
29. Special interrogation report, SIR 48, 18 November 1946, KV 2/173, TNA.
30. See Havas, *Long Jump*, 123; Rezun, *Iranian Crisis*, 56–63.
31. *Tegeran 43*, produced by Georges Cheyko et al., directed by Aleksandr Alov and Vladimir Naumov, Mosfilm, 1981.
32. *Teheran*, produced by John Stafford and Akos Tolnay, directed by William Freshman and Giacomo Gentilomo, Industrie Cinematografiche Associate Internazionali, 1946.
33. *World War II: When Lions Roared*, produced by Bruce M. Kerner et al., directed by Joseph Sargent, Gideon Productions, 1994.
34. 'Suicide Attack in Tehran', *Churchill's Bodyguard*, produced by Jonathan Martin et al., directed by Jonathan Martin and Philip Nugus, Nugus/Martin Productions Ltd, 2005.
35. See Philip Kerr, *Hitler's Peace: A Novel of the Second World War* (New York: Penguin, 2005).
36. Gary Kern, 'How "Uncle Joe" Bugged FDR: The Lessons of History', *Studies in Intelligence* 47, no. 1 (2003), https://www.cia.gov/library/center-for-the-study-of-intelligence/csi-publications/csi-studies/studies/vol47no1/article02.html. In addition to Kern, Donal O'Sullivan has recently published a common-sense appreciation of the 'LONG JUMP' scenario, concluding that it likely never happened. See 'Casablanca East: Joint Anglo-Soviet Counter-Intelligence in Iran', in *Dealing with the Devil*, 195–204.
37. The works cited by Kern are: Alexander Lukin, 'Operatsiya "Dal'nayi prizhok" [Operation Long Jump]', *Ogonek*, no. 33 (1990), 15 August 1965, 25, and no. 34 (1991), 22 August 1965, 25–27; Kyril Tidmarsh, 'How Russians Foiled Nazi Plot to Kill Teheran Big Three', *The Times*, 20 December 1968; Victor Yegorov, *Zagovor protiv 'Evriki': broshenny portfel* [The Plot against 'Eureka': The Lost Portfolio] (Moscow: Sovetskaya Rossiya, 1968); Pavel Sudoplatov and Anatoli Sudoplatov, *Special Tasks: The Memoirs of an Unwanted Witness, a Soviet Spymaster*, with Jerrold L. and Leona P. Schecter (Boston: Little, Brown,

1994), 130–1; and Havas, *Long Jump*. The publication of Lukin's articles did not go unnoticed in the West; see 'Soviet Says It Foiled Plot to Kill Roosevelt', *New York Times*, 25 August 1965.

38. See 'Eine groteske Fälschung', *Die Nachhut: Informationsorgan für Angehörige der ehemaligen militärischen Abwehr* 7 (9 April 1969): 18–26, MSG 3/667, BArch-MArch.

39. *Die Nachhut: Informationsorgan für Angehörige der ehemaligen militärischen Abwehr*, MSG 3/667, BArch-MArch. During my research at the Bundesarchiv-Militärarchiv in Freiburg, I found in MSG 3/667 a complete bound volume of *Die Nachhut*, an obscure, unpublished serial circulated between 1967 and 1975 among (and with contributions by) former members of the Abwehr. As far as I know, the only other available copy in existence is to be found at Stanford University.

40. Schulze-Holthus, 'Fälschung': 18–26, MSG 3/667, BArch-MArch.

41. Ibid., 19.

42. Ibid., 23.

43. Ibid., 23–6.

44. See Havas, *Long Jump*, 218n10.

45. Schulze-Holthus, 'Fälschung', 24–5, MSG 3/667, BArch-MArch.

46. *NSW*, 110.

47. Schulze-Holthus, 'Fälschung', 25, MSG 3/667, BArch-MArch. My dates, based on archival records, in parentheses.

48. See Narrative of arrest of Franz Mayr and a group (Gruppe FRANZ) of German parachutists who landed in the Siah Kuh area, 121 km southwest of Tehran on 22 March 1943, WO 208/1588A, TNA. For further details about the arrests, see *NSW*, 118–21.

49. Schulze-Holthus, 'Fälschung', 24, MSG 3/667, BArch-MArch.

50. Franz Seubert, 'Vernichtende Urteile über das Machwerk "Assassinat au Sommet"', *Die Nachhut: Informationsorgan für Angehörige der ehemaligen militärischen Abwehr* 8 (15 September 1969): 12–14, MSG 3/667, BArch-MArch.

51. Seubert, 'Vernichtende Urteile', 13, MSG 3/667, BArch-MArch.

52. 'How Gallant Comrade Schultz Foiled Nazis', *Sunday Times*, 22 December 1968.

53. Rezun, *Iranian Crisis*, 101n203.

54. See 'Gallant Comrade'.

55. United States Department of State, *Foreign Relations of the United States Diplomatic Papers: The Conferences at Cairo and Tehran, 1943* (Washington: USGPO, 1943), 463.

56. Kern, 'Uncle Joe'.

57. See 'Gallant Comrade'.

58. Ibid.

59. 'Big Three Meeting Still Open Guess', *New York Times*, 22 September 1943.

60. Thistlethwaite to Bullard, 11 July 1952, GB 165-0042-3/7, MECA.

61. Roosevelt, *Public Papers*, 552.

62. Counter-Intelligence Summary No. 16, Defence Security Office CICI Persia, 20 December 1943, KV 2/1480, TNA. The *Daily Mail* correspondent in Cairo had apparently written that German parachutists had landed in Persia during the conference with the intention of rousing the tribes against the Allies.

63. Extract from SIME Quarterly Summary for the months Sept–Dec inclusive, SIME GHQ MEF, 17 January 1944, KV 2/1480, TNA.
64. Security Summary Middle East No. 161, 22 December 1943, WO 208/1562, TNA.
65. Bullard to Seth, 10 September 1963, GB 165-0042-3/11, MECA.
66. Bullard, *Camels*, 255.
67. Seth to Bullard, 14 September 1965; Cookridge to Bullard, 15 November 1965; Farago to Bullard, 26 October 1966, all in GB 165-0042-3/11, MECA. 'Edward Henry Cookridge' was actually the Vienna-born Edward Spiro (1908–1979), a journalist and historian who also authored supposedly true spy stories, using several additional aliases including Peter Leighton, Peter Morland, Ronald Reckitt, and Edward H. Spire. He is perhaps best known for his interesting and useful biography of Reinhard Gehlen: E.H. Cookridge, *Gehlen: Spy of the Century* (New York: Random House, 1972). Spiro claimed to have fought with the Czech resistance and to have been imprisoned at Dachau and Buchenwald, though the circumstances remain murky. It has been suggested that he was actually MI6.
68. Bullard to Farago, 22 October 1966, GB 165-0042-3/11, MECA.
69. Spencer to Bullard, 5 October 1959, GB 165-0042-3/7, MECA.
70. Press Conference with Veterans of the Russian Foreign Intelligence Service, *Official Kremlin International News Broadcast*, 18 November 2003, http://www.fas.org/irp/world/russia/teheran43.html.
71. Ibid.
72. Ibid.
73. Ibid.
74. Ibid.
75. *Axis Information and Analysis*, 4 May 2006, http://www.axisglobe.com/print_news.asp? news=8421; 'Tehran-43: Wrecking the Plan to Kill Stalin, Roosevelt, and Churchill', *Russian News and Information Agency Novosti*, 16 October 2007, http://en.rian.ru/analysis/20071016/84122320-print.html.
76. 'The Soviet Spy Who Saved Stalin, Roosevelt and Churchill', Spotlight (RT telecast), 8 May 2008 and 8 May 2009; 'Spy Who Saved Allied Leaders from Nazi Assassination Plot Dies at 87', *Prime Time Russia* (RT telecast), 12 January 2012. Medvedev's eulogy is reproduced in 'Legendary Spy Dies Aged 87', *RT News*, 12 January 2012, http://rt.com/news/prime-time/gevork-vartanyan-passed-away-539/.
77. Patrick Nolan Clark, *A Strange Murder in the Persian Corridor* (North Charleston, SC: CreateSpace, 2014).
78. Stephens and Hoare, *Camp 020*, 365.
79. Liquidation Report No. 13, Amt VI of the RHSA, Gruppe VI S, SHAEF Counter Intelligence War Room, 28 November 1945, RG263, EZZ17, B3, NARA; *NSW*, 95.

13
Yanks

> Iran is a very interesting field in which to observe British and Russian systems. (History of the Near East Section, OSS Cairo)[1]

> To gather information about Iran in Iran is an extremely difficult, thorny, and delicate task. (P.D. Panchesa [US Steel])[2]

The Americans' political paradox in Persia, typical of US involvements in the Middle East and elsewhere even into the 21st century, rendered some Americans almost as tricky for British security to deal with as the NKVD. The now familiar contradiction lay in the Americans' frequent attempts to embrace the moral high ground with great zeal on the one hand, especially in the face of what they perceived as the menace of British or Soviet 'imperialism', and their own decidedly utilitarian quest of protecting US corporate and economic interests (epecially in oil) on the other. These interests were generally neither any less acquistive nor any more intrinsically ethical than those of the two Great Powers with a long history of self-serving involvement in the region: the British and the Russians. From these Great Game players' viewpoint, the hypocrisy of the Americans was self-evident. Washington had intentionally and transparently acquired influence over key sectors of the Persian state that it sought to control by disingenuously sending a series of 'missions' to support and reform them. Thus, by infiltrating and installing US advisers to reform the financial system, the food and supplies distribution system, the armed forces, the police, and the gendarmerie, the Americans had joined the Great Game, adding their own peculiar brand of neoimperialism to the mix. Thus, because of its own tacit complicity and cupidity, Washington was required by the other players to play by the rules and was in no position to indulge in denial or to lay claim to any measure of moral authority. And so, when dealing with representatives of the two 'senior' powers, some Americans became noticeably insecure, touchy, and defensive about their role in Persia, all the more because they were clearly conscious of being perceived as neophytes in the region, and because none of their missionary ventures proved successful. Fortunately for the British security authorities, these difficult men were for the most part civilian diplomats from whom DSO Persia were relatively distanced and reasonably insulated. On the other hand, the US Army officers with whom Joe Spencer frequently had to liaise tended to condone British influence in the region and generally welcomed British expertise in dealing with the complexities of military occupation, reciprocating with their own generous offers of material support. For example, in their opposition to what they saw as British and Soviet 'imperialist aggression', the State Department's openly anti-British Jack Jernegan and Louis Goethe Dreyfus Jr, US minister-plenipotentiary in Tehran, manifested empathy with German expansionism, choosing to overlook the appalling aggression of the Nazis just across the northern border, notwithstanding the latter diplomat's Jewish origin. By contrast, the US military commander in Persia, Donald H. Connolly, was always a staunch supporter of British interests and causes – but more of this later.

Lest one be accused of anglocentrism, it must be said that some measure of the scale of Dreyfus's anti-British acrimony may be gauged from reading a relatively objective, benign account by Simon Davis, a New York-based diplomatic historian, of Dreyfus's choleric perceptions, including his personal antipathy towards Sir Reader Bullard, and his hostile manoeuvres aided and abetted by the equally anglophobic Jernegan, before and after the Anglo-Soviet invasion, right up to the time of Dreyfus's transfer to Reykjavik after the Big Three conference.[3] If one strips the diplomatic veneer from such a narrative of ostensible, frequently feigned high-mindedness, it becomes clear that the distemper of Dreyfus, Jernegan, and the envoy Patrick J. Hurley was really all about advancing US strategic interests (in Saudi oil, for example) and maintaining a balance of power in the Persian Gulf region, which Britain and Russia were seen by some (but not all) in Washington to threaten. Such strategic considerations were of course less evident to those charged with maintaining security at the tactical level; thus cooperation was far closer among Allied security officers than among diplomats at the three Tehran legations.

After the Japanese attack on Pearl Harbor in December 1941, the Americans began to engage earnestly with the issue of how best to configure and deploy their intelligence forces in the Middle East. Initially, the intention was clearly to cooperate with the British, whose *savoir-faire* and influence in the region could only benefit the relatively inexperienced Americans. However, it is important to understand that, in early 1942, whilst the Americans recognized that Persia lay within the sphere of British strategic responsibility, all reports received by them also indicated that the British were distrusted there and that there was a general pro-Axis feeling among Persians, intensified by German propaganda and stimulated by German military successes in North Africa and southern Russia. Thus, initially at least, Washington made the same generalized (false) assumptions about Persian political opinion as Berlin. It also needs to be understood, however, that the Americans were repeatedly misled, whether disingenuously or not, by their man in Tehran, Louis Dreyfus, whose reporting was often highly subjective. At the same time, Washington seems to have been convinced, naively perhaps, of the existence of a decidedly pro-American feeling in Persia, which may or may not have been heightened by Dreyfus's perceptions.[4] Whether groundless or not, this sunny optimism, coupled with seductive overtures from the Persians themselves, prompted the Americans to send a series of missions to Persia during the Second World War. According to Sir Reader Bullard, British minister in Tehran, it was the British who originally suggested to the Persian government in February 1942 that they should engage American advisers.[5] By contrast, an unidentified confidential informant told a US CIC agent that it was none other than Louis Dreyfus who was himself largely responsible for the (second) Millspaugh mission to Persia.[6] In his postwar memoir, Arthur Millspaugh certainly wrote of Dreyfus in glowing terms, nevertheless reserving most of his praise for Dreyfus's wife, Grace, who seems to have earned the approbation that eluded her husband. She achieved great popularity among the disadvantaged of Tehran for her charitable works, which no doubt helped to delay until after the Tehran Conference her husband's inevitable dismissal from his post and banishment to Iceland.[7] A British visitor to wartime Tehran described one of Grace Dreyfus's lavish charity balls as a tremendous affair held in a magnificent ballroom and attended by at least 200 people, the men in white ties and tails, and the women in lovely and gorgeous dresses.[8]

The initial mission to facilitate the supply of Lend-Lease materiel to the Soviet Union (the Wheeler mission) was followed during the summer and autumn of 1942 by five subsequent missions – to reform the

Persian economy (the Millspaugh mission), the food and supplies distribution system (the Sheridan mission), the Persian armed forces (the Greely/Ridley mission), the Persian police (the Timmerman mission), and the Persian gendarmerie (the Schwarzkopf mission [GENMISH]) – all of which proved to be unmitigated failures – as well as two additional advisers on agriculture and public health.

At the local diplomatic level Anglo-American relations got off to a poor start. The US legation frequently caused problems for the British authorities in Persia, not least because Louis Dreyfus (see Figure 13.1), proved to be most undiplomatic and fundamentally anti-British. During his lengthy State Department career, Dreyfus, a native of Santa Barbara, CA, served as US consul in Budapest, Paris, Palermo, Dresden, and Copenhagen; as US minister to Afghanistan, Iran, Iceland, and Sweden; and as US ambassador to Afghanistan. Sir Reader Bullard described Dreyfus as a 'somewhat tortuous character ... whom the Persians frequently tried to influence against us. ... Mr Dreyfus generally avoided supporting our representations on questions of general importance to the Allies and left [me] to bear the whole burden of unpopular

Figure 13.1   Anglophobe extreme: Louis Goethe Dreyfus Jr.
Source: Harry S. Truman Library and Museum, courtesy of Stock Montage M99018, accession no. 99–358.

representations to the Persian government'.[9] Indeed, there is evidence that Dreyfus was even pro-German and actually fostered relationships with various Nazis and Nazi sympathizers. When, for instance, the United Kingdom Control Commission (UKCC) attempted to rationalize Persian road transport in the summer of 1942, Dreyfus deliberately wrecked their plans. When Operation PONGO was carried out in November of that year, resulting in the arrest of Fazlollah Zahedi,[10] Dreyfus saw to it that the US government lodged a formal protest with Britain. By year-end, Bullard had had enough and wrote that if more cooperation had been forthcoming from the American minister in pressing the Persian government to take the measures which were essential to solve the urgent problems of 1942, 'much less trouble would have been experienced and, incidentally, we should not have had to bear all the odium of them. This might have had an appreciable effect on our relations with Persia.'[11]

Even American historians have found Dreyfus to have been something of a national embarrassment. For instance, Ladislas Farago wrote to Bullard after the war that, in the course of his research, he had read the published telegrams of Dreyfus and had consulted the papers of the American legation in Tehran.

> To be entirely frank, I was struck, not merely by Mr Dreyfus's somewhat strange concept of Anglo-American cooperation in Iran during a war which our countries fought together against the common enemy, but especially by his rather deprecating and sceptical attitude toward your concern about Allied security in Persia and by his failure to appreciate your efforts to rid the country of Nazi agents.[12]

Farago was actually appalled by the tone and substance of Dreyfus's despatches, even more so in the light of postwar revelations which proved Bullard right and Dreyfus wrong.

Farago went on to suggest that Dreyfus's opinions and prejudices were shaped by Jack Jernegan, one of the State Department's leading young Middle Eastern experts, while the latter was serving as third secretary at the Tehran legation. A native of Los Angeles, who may well have been on familiar terms with Dreyfus before serving under him in Persia, John Durnford 'Jack' Jernegan ultimately rose to become US Assistant Deputy Secretary of State after the war and served as US ambassador to Iraq and Algeria. Farago discovered that, 20 years after the war, Jernegan still considered the policies of the Tehran legation to have been 'proper, prudent, and right', even going so far as to say that 'whatever security problems there were in Persia were either invented or magnified by the British authorities for selfish purposes'.[13] And then Farago dropped a bombshell, stating that he believed he had stumbled upon extraordinary material to bear Bullard out completely and to place Dreyfus's handling of the situation in even worse light. It seems that Farago had found several reports of the German minister (and SS brigadier), Erwin Ettel, to his superiors in Berlin in which he described his friendly relations with Dreyfus, who was aiding him with advice and information virtually to the bitter end in 1941 (i.e. Ettel's expulsion from Persia). In a report dated 30 August 1941, Ettel went so far as to say that, notwithstanding the hostile attitude of Roosevelt, 'Mr Dreyfus is a real friend and in full sympathy with Germany.'[14]

Bullard's response to these Ettel disclosures about a time at which America was not yet in the war was that he could imagine Dreyfus saying, 'I was only trying to be neutral, which the British were not', but that the US minister's behaviour after Pearl Harbor was unjustified. Roosevelt had seen a world danger rising and invented a quite new policy to meet it. Dreyfus seemed to have opposed that, both before the Anglo-Russian invasion and afterwards also, even when the United States had become a belligerent.[15]

According to Farago, there were even some officers among the US security forces of PGSC who were fundamentally anti-British in their attitudes. On one occasion he was treated to a lengthy dissertation against the British security forces, with George P. Hill Jr, Provost Marshal of PGSC, giving the impression that the Nazis in Persia were 'all very nice and harmless people, the unfortunate victims of British perfidy and Russian terror'. Farago thought that under the circumstances it had wider implications to point out how naïve – 'to put it charitably' – the US representatives in Persia really were, and how seriously they interfered with 'urgent and farsighted efforts to secure this important hinterland of the war from German machinations'.[16]

Hill held a highly responsible and sensitive position requiring him to liaise effectively with the British and the Russians. Fortunately, the PGSC commander, Donald Connolly, was by no means anti-British and was consequently able to offset some of the ill effects of Dreyfus's influence. Equally fortunately, Dreyfus was not taken seriously by President Roosevelt, who, for instance, barred him from attending Churchill's dinner party at the Tehran Conference in 1943, presumably in order to avoid any embarrassment in Stalin's presence.[17] In what amounted to a further presidential snub, three months later Dreyfus found himself transferred from Tehran to Reykjavik.[18] For his part, Connolly cooperated with British security whenever possible, and relied on them for favours, which could sometimes place them at a disadvantage. Sir Reader Bullard revealed after the war that Connolly at one point asked him to secure the arrest of over 30 Persian employees on the railway, otherwise Connolly would not accept responsibility for the railway system which it was his job to run. Bullard acted on this immediately, as a good ally: the suspects were all arrested and placed under Anglo-Persian internment. As a result, according to Bullard, 'doubtless the British had all the blame, whereas our intelligence people were not consulted as to the suspicions against the accused'. Did it advance the interests of the British as opposed to the Allies? Indeed, did any arrests that DSO effected or caused to be made do the British any good? On the contrary, Bullard concluded that 'it aroused discontent against us, the British'.[19] But Bullard also wondered what criticism the British would have incurred from the United States if they had allowed all the Persian suspects to go free and damage the railway or the oil industry.[20]

However, Louis Dreyfus in no way restricted his acrimony to the British. On the contrary, he appears to have been equally unpleasant towards any American outside his own particular State Department clique, including John N. Greely, who headed the original US military mission to the Persian army in April 1942. Indeed, Dreyfus succeeded in perversely marginalizing and paralysing the Greely mission to such an extent that Greely eventually had to be withdrawn. He was replaced by Clarence S. Ridley, who took up his Tehran post at the end of 1942, armed with a brand-new remit designed to neutralize Dreyfus and ensure mission success.[21] A man of Dreyfus's distemper had naturally garnered for himself some powerful opponents in Washington during the course of his consular and diplomatic career, including the President himself and his ebullient Undersecretary of State, Sumner Welles. With characteristic enthusiasm, Welles advocated for the immediate resumption of the Greely mission under Ridley's command on the grounds of the perceived need to correct the poor morale and pro-German sentiment in the Persian army, as well as to combat the work of Nazi agents in the theatre.[22] At the same time, Welles concurred with the Operations Division of the War Department (OPD) that no miraculous transformation of the Persian army into an effective Allied fighting force could be expected.[23] At most, American advisers might be able to reorganize it into a small, efficient force capable of maintaining the internal security of the country, which Ridley himself stated would be 'desirable to the British from the standpoint of operations and ... advantageous to the US from the viewpoint of supplying Russia'.[24]

Very differently from Dreyfus, the leader of the US mission to the Persian gendarmerie (GENMISH), H. Norman Schwarzkopf and his deputy Philip T. Boone, proved to be most helpful to Sir Reader Bullard and British interests. Boone even became Bullard's close friend. At some point of course, each of the American missions was bound to give rise to security and intelligence issues. It is simply not possible to deploy any team of experts and advisers with executive powers, essentially engaged in a sophisticated process of technology transfer, halfway around the world without raising intrinsic concerns as to the security of their mission and without creating opportunities for the acquisition and analysis of intelligence. Conscious of this, in February 1942, whilst overseeing the establishment of the initial US military mission to Persia, the US Chief of Staff, George C. Marshall, wrote to the senior British military representative in Washington, Colville Wemyss: 'Considering intelligence activities, it has been my observation, wherever a mission operates, unless specifically directed otherwise, the tendency is to absorb intelligence personnel in that vicinity, who then find their primary responsibility is to serve that particular mission.' According to Marshall, this crippled their effectiveness as immediate sources of military information for the War Department, by imposing 'echelons of delay' between them and the General Staff.[25]

Marshall's perceptions led to an arrangement whereby it was agreed that the division of responsibility for intelligence gathering would, in the case of Persia, remain with the professionals, either under diplomatic cover (e.g. military attachés at the Tehran legation) or as part of PGSC (i.e. G-2 or X-2 staff). As a consequence of this agreement, Connolly, the PGSC commander, was issued with clear instructions on military-intelligence personnel and procedures which stated that the selection, location, transfer, and administration of all US War Department intelligence personnel in Persia would remain under the control of the WD. This did not, however, deter OSS from placing their own intelligence officers, nominally under army command, under diplomatic cover with the civilian Millspaugh mission.[26] Up to the time of Marshall's letter, there is no mention in the WD planning documents of intelligence operations or the use of intelligence personnel in the Persian theatre. The overriding concern was how best to supply Russia with Lend-Lease material as rapidly as possible, in order to thwart any German offensive through Turkey or through Transcaucasia. To that end, such technical issues as the construction of port, transportation, and storage facilities; the supervision of the supply, assembly, and maintenance of American equipment brought into the Persian theatre; and the daunting logistical problems presented by the prospect of operating in a topographical and climatic environment as hostile as Persia overwhelmed and eclipsed any consideration of intelligence and security issues. It is significant that an experienced engineering officer was selected to head the Persian initiative. Raymond A. Wheeler of the US Army Corps of Engineers (USACE) was designated mission chief effective 27 September 1941, barely a month after the Anglo-Soviet invasion.[27] He was quick to obtain the expert assistance of J.A. Gillies, former General Manager of the Santa Fe Railway, to study the truly mammoth task of expanding and modernizing operation of the TIR.[28]

This then was the focus of the initial US mission to Persia: to coordinate and supervise an engineering project of enormous scale.[29] In the early stages of the project, matters of intelligence – whether to do with espionage, counterespionage, security intelligence, sabotage, propaganda, or subversion – were given scant consideration. Later, after the establishment of PGSC in August 1942,[30] when the Americans decided to deploy the field-security forces of CIC in Persia, their decision was logically prompted by the need to secure their strategic project by safeguarding the vital lines of communication and supply between the Persian Gulf and the Soviet Union. Less logical, however, would seem their decision to send to Persia OSS active-espionage and counterintelligence agents, particularly in a theatre where a moratorium on positive intelligence operations existed – mutually agreed between the British and the Soviets. In fact, if there was any logic at all, it was to be found in the Americans' somewhat self-righteous sense that they had an intelligence role to play in Persia *by default*. Even the normally equanimous Stephen Penrose, head of OSS Near East Section, thought that by mid-1943 the situation in Persia had become more acute from an intelligence point of view precisely because General Connolly had been prevailed upon by the Russians to withdraw all military intelligence. The British too had been instructed by the Foreign Office to do no intelligence work in Russian-occupied areas. 'That leaves us holding a sack and bearing a considerable responsibility', Penrose wrote.[31] Clearly, he was unaware at the time that ISLD (MI6) officers were active in Persia.

It was of course against the Soviets rather than the Germans that OSS covert operations were directed. Consequently, the Americans appear to have been anxious to conceal the true extent of their activities from British security intelligence, anticipating that they would be vehemently opposed by Chokra Wood at CICI, whom they described as 'an old Indian officer, of a type which is apt to view civilian activities of this sort with considerable disapprobation'. Shrewdly, the Americans therefore decided to completely expose a single OSS officer (Tom Allen) to Wood, to give him the impression that no other representatives were operating in Persia and Iraq. In response, Wood agreed to allow Allen to continue operations, and friendly relations were established between CICI and OSS.[32] Instructions were actually received by Wood 'from higher authorities' to work in the closest collaboration with members of OSS. The relevant directive went so far as to state that Wood was to take the Americans into his confidence 'on practically any of the many ramifications of his security work'.[33] Initially, the Americans fully understood the reciprocal nature of this relationship; in time, however, as they gained in experience and confidence, there was less candour. CICI noted that their records section was placed completely at the disposal of OSS, and OSS were careful to have their reports checked by Wood before despatching them to Washington. Later, however, it became clear that OSS were carrying on certain activities about which they preferred CICI to remain ignorant. These activities seemed not altogether disconnected from postwar commercial ambitions. Apart from this, cooperation left nothing to be desired and was 'of mutual benefit to both services'.[34]

The precise nature of American positive-intelligence (SI) work in Persia varied considerably with the passage of time. In the autumn of 1942, with few OSS agents yet deployed in the field and German forces nearing the Persian border, early efforts were devoted to recording and reporting on those installations which would be useful to the Germans, and which therefore constituted potential bombing targets. Then, as the threat of invasion receded, emphasis was placed throughout 1943 on drawing up detailed reports on the Persian polity, industry, and infrastructure in an attempt by OSS to acquire and analyse intelligence which had not been collected previously by any other agency. Initially tasked with these reporting duties for the whole of Persia were only two young archaeologists under cultural diplomatic cover at the Tehran legation: from September 1941 onwards, Joseph M. Upton, a naval reserve officer from the Metropolitan Museum of Art; and Donald N. Wilber, an expert on Persian art and architecture from the Iranian Institute who joined OSS in May 1942 and arrived in Tehran a year after Joe Upton.[35] At this stage in the war, before SI was fully coordinated by OSS Cairo, the initiative for reporting remained with the individual field agents. Joe Upton, for instance, reported his activities and observations simply by writing personal letters directly to Bill Donovan, head of OSS, in Washington.[36] By late 1943, however, requests for specific information were prioritized and cleared in Cairo before being conveyed to agents working in Persia. In the reverse direction communications between

Tehran and Cairo apparently remained far from perfect throughout the war. A primary problem was the slowness of communication with the Cairo office. Reports were turned in at specific times set by the cooperative and helpful officials of the US embassy. These should have gone out by pouch and in a Cairo-bound plane within a few hours, but the normal time for delivery at the Cairo office was from six to eight days. Naturally such delays lessened the value of 'spot material on the rapidly changing political scene'.[37]

There were also difficulties with the accessibility and security of records. To maintain full security, all papers and notes had to be be kept at the US embassy. This meant that it was difficult to consult back material and nearly impossible to keep expanding and up-to-date files on a variety of important subjects. Furthermore, the physical effort of noting and then typing material was often a severe tax on the time of the individual who had to maintain security while such work was in progress. The only apparent solution to these difficulties seemed to be the establishment of a cover within the embassy or facilities for work within the embassy buildings.[38]

As the war progressed and the Americans gained experience in the unfamiliar region, so too their policy towards Persia mutated and evolved. By early 1943, the Near Eastern Affairs Division of the State Department had begun to appreciate the true significance of the country – 'its value as a supply route to Russia, its strategic location, and its vast production of petroleum products'.[39] Persia was seen as a 'buffer ... protecting [US] oil interests in Saudi Arabia' from Stalin's covetous gaze.[40] More importantly, however, Washington was beginning increasingly to turn its own gaze towards the Soviet Union as a potential antagonist. According to State's perspective, for considerably more than 100 years Russia had been pressing down upon Persia from the north, repeatedly threatening new annexations of territory, repeatedly attempting in one way or another to dominate Persia. Three times in the 20th century alone Russian troops had entered Persian territory against the will of the Persian people. 'We should be fully alive to the character of the present Russian occupation of the northern provinces', State Department policy planners wrote.[41]

Thus Washington began to contemplate with anxiety such Soviet moves in the north as the restriction of the Persian police and gendarmerie, the immobilization of the Persian army, the manipulation of the restive Kurds, and the propagandization of the general population. The strained relations between the Russian and British authorities also concerned the Americans, as well as the apparent attempt by Stalin to weaken British influence by forcing Britain to bear the brunt of Persia's economic problems. Increasingly, the Americans became convinced that the time had come for them to assume a Great Power role in the region, co-equal with Britain and Russia. The very fact that Persia had been a 'sphere of influence' in dispute between two Great Powers made it all the more desirable that a third, disinterested [*sic*], power should be called in to eliminate the dispute. Both Britain and Russia would be relieved of an anxiety and constant source of friction if each could be assured that the other would have no special position in the area, and it was not inconceivable that both would regard this assurance as worth whatever ambitions might be given up. In this connection, it seemed hardly possible that either could suspect the United States of having imperialistic designs in a country so far removed from North America, and where they could never hope to employ military force against an adjacent Great Power.[42]

This not-so-subtle – disingenuous rather than 'disinterested' – shift of emphasis in US policy on Persia towards the contemplation of postwar scenarios undoubtedly influenced the decisions made by the United States on the deployment of covert agents and the configuration of intelligence and security forces within Persia during the final two and a half years of the Second World War. While the employment of 'military force' might have been discounted, the use of covert agents clearly had not, for OSS posted their assistant to the chief of the Near East Desk in Washington, Stephen B.L. 'Binks' Penrose Jr (see Figure 13.2), to Cairo on 15 May 1943 as head of Near Eastern Secret Intelligence (SI), with instructions to establish intelligence-gathering services in the Middle East, including Persia. Despite handicaps such as lack of assistance and supplies and the necessity for coordinating plans and activities with those of his British counterparts (SIME, CICI, ISLD, and SOE), Penrose was able to lay a firm foundation for OSS intelligence work in the Middle East. His prior knowledge of the area, gained during three years as a professor at the American University of Beirut (of which he would become president after the war), during which he travelled extensively throughout the Near East, and subsequently as assistant director of the Near East College Association,[43] was of inestimable value to OSS in recruiting future representatives who were to operate in countries like Persia where strong religious, political, and racial differences existed. Penrose succeeded in placing some 20–30 key officers under various types of cover, responsible to and directed by him and his successors, who in turn employed or accepted the services of nearly 300 informants or 'secondary representatives'. Of all the Middle Eastern

Figure 13.2 Penetrating one's Allies: Stephen 'Binks' Penrose Jr.
Source: AUB Photo Collections, Archives and Special Collections, Jafet Library, American University of Beirut.

countries, Penrose was most successful in establishing his operatives in Persia, where relations with the Russians were most delicate and where German agents were active. Penrose was ultimately awarded the Bronze Star Medal (BSM) for his wartime OSS service.[44]

The purpose of Penrose's Near East Section was to secure secret intelligence on conditions and trends in a region which, although not occupied by the enemy, was home to large numbers of Nazi sympathizers and many enemy agents actively engaged in securing intelligence, disseminating rumours, and otherwise conducting psychological warfare or organizing subversive movements and sabotage. The stability of the region was seen by Washington to be threatened by the existence of dissatisfied religious minorities, nationalist political movements, and imperialistic spheres of influence. One important but limited American objective was the acquisition of intelligence about strategic infrastructure, such as as ports, refineries, pipelines, roads, telephones, etc. While counterintelligence was not a direct responsibility of SI, inevitably intelligence about hostile agents and suspicious characters was secured and passed on to X-2 Branch. But Near East Section's primary role was to keep the US government informed about political, economic, and social developments and trends in the region.[45]

When he first arrived in Cairo, instead of being able to devote his time to the work of the section, Penrose found it necessary to take on the additional duties of reports officer, registry officer, and central files head, without any secretarial or clerical assistance. He was joined a month later by Archie S. Crawford, whose Near Eastern experience proved to be of great help in originating intelligence material and in criticizing and processing reports turned in from the field. Crawford was also able to help materially in the establishment of new field contacts and the recruitment of personnel. Many acute field problems arose (and were successfully solved) during the first year of operation: relations with State Department officials; security and cover of agents; security of communications; reindoctrination and retraining of established agents; implementation of new procedures and directives; the need to recruit new agents to cover vital spots; and the establishment of a subagent system to allow for accurate evaluation and analysis of reports.[46]

In January 1944, Penrose was promoted and took over Middle East SI, with the dependable Crawford succeeding him as Near East Section Chief, and the lively Lewis Leary as Crawford's assistant. At this time, the six major problems to be dealt with were seen by the section as follows: (1) *The handling of agents.* A great deal of time and energy was constantly devoted to personal problems and matters of morale, cover, communications, relations with representatives of the State Department, Army, and other government agencies. (2) *Improvement in the quality and volume of reports.* This involved constant attention to working up and dispatching specific directives and requests for information to all individuals in the field, reporting to them evaluations of their reports, advising them as to possible improvements in technique, and suggesting possible additional contacts which might prove of value to them. (3) *Expanding field coverage.* This involved consideration of possible new agents, with consequent problems of cover and communications. Effective field agents for work in the Near East were few and far between, and the matter of their cover required detailed and cautious attention. (4) *Cover.* In the Near East area the cover of field representatives was a problem of major importance. Unlike certain other areas where cover could be superficial, in the Near East it had to be real and a vital part of the representative's operation. Continual attention had to be given to maintaining and improving the cover of men who were already in the field to prevent their exposure to real physical danger. (5) *Office personnel*. The Near East Section had from the time of its organization been handicapped by a lack of competent personnel to handle the work successfully. Ideally, each agent would hear from the section at least once a week, and constant attention would be given to the individual problems of each man. This required a heavy burden of correspondence and organization of material for it. In addition the heavy volume of intelligence reports (running as high as 148 reports per month) demanded long hours of editing, criticizing, evaluating, and preparing for dissemination. It was a burden too heavy to be efficiently carried. (6) *Speed in processing reports*. The section felt that one of its major functions was to transmit intelligence received from the field with the least possible delay. Under the circumstances, there was danger of failure in this regard, although the record to date had been astonishingly good.[47]

In fact, at the operational level, the Cairo office solved its problems largely by modelling itself on the paradigm of the central clearinghouse or hub whose spokes radiated throughout the region and which was connected umbilically with Washington. At the extremity of each spoke, each field representative was assigned an animal codename (e.g. TIGER) for use on reports which came from him or from the subsources of the network he had established, for which he in turn became a hub. When teamwork was called for, some representatives (like Upton and Wilber, for instance) were revealed to each other; others were kept isolated and unaware of other OSS field men operating in their area. Subsources were chosen for their geographical distribution, strategic position for securing intelligence, and discretion. Remarkably, most subsources were unpaid, so their friendship had to be maintained through a judicious and very limited granting of gifts, such as cigarettes, cigarette lighters, pens, professional apparatus, hearing aids, and various American publications. Communication between Cairo and agents in the field was carried out by means of letters, cables, visits of Cairo office personnel, and visits by field representatives to Cairo. Letters from Cairo were addressed – usually on a regular weekly basis – to codenames (like 'Richard Lowe', who was actually Joe Upton) and sent by diplomatic pouch to the appropriate US minister or consul who had – in theory at least – been informed confidentially of the true identity of the recipient, who would collect his mail in person. The reverse process was employed for messages from the field. Each field representative was assigned a double-transposition cipher poem and a range of numbers for cables in both directions. The most challenging aspect of servicing field personnel was arranging for them to avail themselves of the various military support services (such as transport, vehicles, and fuel) to which they were entitled and needed without compromising their deep cover.

General US diplomatic interest in Persia and specific OSS intelligence activities in the region were two entirely different things: unrelated, uncoordinated, subject to different priorities, and often hopelessly at odds. Not only did the representative agencies frequently clash over jurisdictional and procedural issues, both significant and petty, but so too did such representative personalities as Binks Penrose (OSS), Donald Connolly (US Army), and the peevish Louis Dreyfus (State). Clearly, the entire system of covert communication, supply, and finance of course depended very much on the maintenance of goodwill and good relations between OSS, the US Army, and the State Department, and on the guaranteed discretion of the latter two. Unfortunately, the cooperation of State's diplomatic representatives at their overseas missions was sometimes grudgingly given, and the reputation for uncooperativeness acquired by some seems to have been as inexplicable in wartime as it was well deserved. Iraq, Syria, Palestine, and Saudi Arabia were rated highly as cooperative missions; Afghanistan was considered hostile; and Persia was considered neutral or indifferent.

Unfortunately, Louis Dreyfus, who ran the Tehran legation, was in fact inquisitive and anything but cooperative. To get things done effectively in Persia, Penrose had to rely heavily on the good offices of the largely consenting and compliant PGSC/PGC commander, Donald Connolly. In fact, the US minister to Egypt, where Binks Penrose's Near East Section was based, adopted the extraordinary position that Egypt was simply 'not a field for our intelligence activities'.[48] The main problem with hostile, indifferent, or even inquisitive diplomats was of course that of security. For a time at least, some ministers demanded copies of all OSS reports and paraphrases of OSS cables routed through their legations. Once in their clutches, these highly sensitive documents were not always controlled securely, thereby seriously jeopardizing the cover effectiveness of Near East Section agents. Also, the real identities of agents sometimes became known to legation personnel.[49] Identities were also leaked when OSS connections were revealed on passenger lists, travel orders, baggage tags, and bills of lading. In view of what was at stake, it is difficult to understand why OSS, which was technically under Army command, did not use military channels of communication rather than diplomatic ones, as was suggested by one

Cairo officer.[50] Perhaps it was because, initially at least, most of the OSS agents in Persia were civilians under civilian cover with no access to military staff.

It is all the more curious because, when Penrose had visited Tehran on a troubleshooting mission in August 1943, he had indeed resolved the security problem – permanently he thought – with characteristic common sense and decisiveness by arranging for all highly classified OSS documents to be transmitted by sealed Army pouch within the State Department bag. Until then, the practice of the legation had been to transmit OSS reports by pouch, but to require that a copy be left for the legation. However, this was not only expensive, in view of the high cost of paper in Tehran, but it was definitely insecure, for the minister, Dreyfus, did not handle the reports himself, and OSS agents felt no assurance that they were not left carelessly lying around. As a result, agents hesitated to prepare materials of an exceedingly sensitive nature. Penrose therefore proposed to the military attaché that in especially confidential or secret cases the reports might be transmitted to Cairo in his pouch, which was not seen by the legation, though it was transmitted in the regular diplomatic bag. To this the attaché readily agreed, having had personal experience with the lack of security in the legation.[51]

Somehow, some time later, perhaps because of a subsequent change in legation staff, the procedure established by Penrose appears to have been terminated, and the security problems returned. Given the extreme latitude granted by State to its ministers abroad, it is quite possible that the reversal of policy was purely capricious in nature, for relations between OSS and State were never good, with many diplomats appearing to exploit every opportunity to make the clandestine field work of OSS as difficult as possible. Later in the war, some – if not all – OSS communications between Cairo and field representatives in Persia and Iraq appear to have been routed via CICI Baghdad and the US military attachés at the Baghdad legation, no doubt because OSS relations with Chokra Wood had by then become extremely cordial, enabling Penrose to transmit documents via British security directly to the attachés (Colonel Baker and Major Robert Rigg), effectively bypassing State.[52] Penrose was certainly delighted with the new arrangement, for he wrote: 'We have absolute confidence in Rigg, ... and all feel that this new route will be both more secure and more time-saving'.[53] Another OSS ruse was to transmit important intelligence in letters (which were not normally read or copied by State) rather than in reports (which were). That the intransigence of State officials should have been allowed to force such elaborate procedures on OSS seems extraordinary; how-ever, it must be remembered that, had Penrose objected, precious cover might have been compromised.

For some reason that OSS officers could never grasp, State officials seemed to resent their secrecy on principle and would go so far as to jeopardize enterprises of national importance on the merest whim or as a result of pure negligence. The potential for open confrontation was never far from the surface, as can be seen in the anger of the nor-mally unflappable Penrose, trying to get a valuable OSS representative (Dr Hans Hoff) accredited at the Baghdad legation but thwarted by State officials. Penrose was infuriated at the arrogant obtuseness of the State Department in refusing to assist in any way a man who not only assumed considerable risk for the service of the US, but voluntarily entered work which might cost him the chance of obtaining his highly desired citizenship because he felt the urgency of getting at his job as quickly as possible. Hoff simply could not understand a government in time of war which was willing to permit a point of peacetime procedure to stand in the way of helping its own wartime cause. Penrose could not understand it either, saying: 'I don't like to be ashamed of my govern-ment. I am filled with righteous indignation.'[54]

The quintessential function of the Near East Section was to receive and disseminate intelligence reports, which varied greatly in qual-ity. Between June 1943 and October 1944, a total of 228 reports from Persia were issued by Near East Section.[55] Some agents who had better acquaintance with the local situation produced complete reports on a particular subject. Others would submit more or less unconnected items which then had to be woven into one or more reports. In all cases, how-ever, the material was checked in Cairo for reliability. It was then edited, codenamed, and evaluated on the basis of the reputation and qualifica-tions of the source. In general, the section tended to err on the con-servative side and leave to Washington any upward re-evaluations. With respect to the degree of dissemination, sound judgement was called for, so that the security of the source was always protected. In certain cases, where reports contained such secret information about officials or policies that no local dissemination was possible, they would be sent directly to Washington where they might be handled with requis-ite discretion. Likewise, counterintelligence or security-intelligence information was sent directly to X-2 Branch without dissemination. Occasionally, field agents were permitted to cable particularly 'hot' material directly to Washington, but only after the assignment of a so-called G-number to prevent duplication.[56]

Inconsistent quality was a major problem. Some agents would provide necessary background information for perspective, correct names of individuals or entities, and logically reasoned work. Others, however, would submit a mass of miscellaneous items and minor isolated facts, the significance of which was lost because no logical relationship was shown. They usually did this because they had many contacts but lacked the knowledge of conditions in their area which would have enabled them to weave these separate items into a cohesive, well-rounded report. The section staff were thus forced to attempt a synthesis of such scrappy intelligence without being able to verify its accuracy. At the same time, it was seen as important not to criticize field agents unduly but to give them encouragement and advice. While relaying critical comments to sources, it was essential to bear in mind the feeling of loneliness, isolation, and discouragement to which every field operative is constantly subjected. Every effort had to be made to maintain morale and to stimulate interest and effort by generous doses of praise and encouragement. The Cairo staff always tried to show their representatives that their efforts were appreciated and were 'serving the constructive values which the whole organization was created to produce'.[57] This fundamentally humane approach to agent management was essentially of Penrose's making. His policy contributed incalculably to the maintenance of high morale among a widely dispersed force of field men, most of whom worked in stressful isolation and a demanding physical environment.

How were Near East Section's representatives recruited, selected, and trained? Local recruitment in the Near East was very limited due to the absence of suitable candidates with reasonable cover; however, a small number of US Army personnel were secured locally. Most OSS agents were initially recruited and trained in the United States rather than in-theatre, including those who had prewar experience in the Middle East. Even so, upon arrival in Cairo, they had to be thoroughly briefed in terms of the problems they would face in the field. They also had to be warned of the difficulties of maintaining their cover. Good cover was deemed by Near East Section to be the ultimate priority in any circumstances. Wartime restrictions on travel and manpower meant that a good cover job was difficult to conceive and equally difficult to maintain. The section succeeded in placing archaeologists, teachers, businessmen, doctors, lawyers, civil servants, and forces personnel in quasi-official or regular positions, but always where the cover best suited the individual, and that took some effort. Cover had to be plausible, and the agent had to fill it and live it in such a natural way that his OSS identity was never known or suspected.

In addition to its regular 'representatives', OSS Near East Section also took advantage of every opportunity afforded by its location 'in one of the large political centres and on the geographical periphery of the Middle East' to secure intelligence through 'special' or 'temporary' missions (or through informants not in contact with one of its regularly approved projects). One such special mission was CUB, an American employed by the Persian government, who was described as 'a special contact (i.e. direct subsource [close friend] of a Near East Section officer) ... who had been able to supply occasional authentic economic material'. Typically, CUB's remit was to supply intelligence on local economic and agricultural matters, indicating a distinct lack of focus by OSS SI on the struggle with Hitler and the general military situation, at least in the case of such 'special' missions. However, in most cases OSS were no doubt simply fulfilling requests for information submitted by any number of Washington clients, who of course set the priorities.[58]

In contrast with such special missions, there were for most of the occupation period six long-term or 'regular' missions or 'projects' in Persia, whose profiles provide a valuable insight into the qualities esteemed so highly by Near East Section. Individually, the OSS officers who executed these missions were exceptional – scholarly or military men with unique talents – yet all were required to possess one common qualification for their diverse roles: 'good cover'. Most prominent were two 'old Persia hands', the archaeologists Joseph M. Upton and Donald N. Wilber, who were capable of moving effortlessly among Persian high society and around the Persian provinces. Joe Upton (cover-named 'Richard Lowe' [TIGER]) was considered the senior OSS representative in Tehran, having been recruited in Washington in 1941; he had previously resided for many years in Persia, engaging in intellectual pursuits. Upton was a Harvard man from the Metropolitan Museum of Art whose cover job was supervising a major archaeological excavation for the Persian government at Nishapur in the vast northeastern province of Khorasan. His archaeological activities, which involved frequent trips to remote regions under Soviet control, were so natural that he was not suspected of belonging to the secret world even by Americans who had known him for many years, and certainly not by the Russians. Upton knew the language, history, and customs of the country and was considered by Near East Section to be an efficient and tireless worker. He also happened to be a reserve naval officer, about which he apparently felt very conflicted until he was advised by Binks Penrose not to reveal his OSS role to the Navy.

Joe Upton's junior, Donald Wilber (cover-named 'Eliot Grant' [TAPIR]), was a highly regarded authority on Persian art and architecture; he was

a graduate of Princeton, where he had also taught archaeology before
the war, subsequently working for the Iranian Institute in New York.
Wilber's initial cover in Tehran was as assistant to the director of The
Asia Institute, which brought him into contact with many interesting and important sources of intelligence. In February 1943, however,
after befriending PGSC commander Donald Connolly, Wilber became a
special assistant in the US Army Office of Technical Information (OTI),
under the nominal supervision of the military attaché at the Tehran
legation, who had no knowledge of Wilber's connection with OSS,
though the collaborative Connolly may have been tacitly aware of his
covert role. Together, these two scholars and close associates controlled
a network of no fewer than 34 registered subsources and informants in
the field. Upton co-operated closely with his fellow New Yorker, both
travelling extensively throughout the country, reporting on roads, economic conditions, and popular feelings and prejudices, with increasing
emphasis on Soviet rather than Nazi activities.[59] Controversially, it is
interesting to note that, according to the official OSS record, Upton
also reported (i.e. spied) on the British, though there is no indication
of precisely which British activities or services he targeted. He may well
have been keeping a wary eye on fellow Persianist Robin Zaehner of
ISLD, whom he probably encountered in Tehran, if not in the Russian
zone, and with whom he would have had much in common intellectu-
ally. One should remember that, ten years later, Zaehner and Upton's
colleague Wilber would be jointly complicit in the MI6–CIA scheme to
overthrow the Mossadeq government. According to Near East Section,
both Upton and Wilber were – like Zaehner – scholars rather than spies,
but the accuracy of Wilber's observations and the strategic importance
of his sources made many of his reports 'very solid'.[60]

A third Tehran-based operative was the influential and prolific author
Harold Lamb (TIMUR, LION), recruited in Washington in 1943, who
had become very popular throughout the region, and who consequently
had access to leading personalities in Persia and Iraq. Unlike Upton and
Wilber, Lamb was a celebrity and therefore had no need for a cover
name (nor was he assigned one). His real name was actually the key to
his success as a penetration agent, facilitating his access to close-knit
social elites. He exploited his literary reputation and unusual opportunities to probe the minds of political leaders and to observe the plans
and projects of their governments. The only cover Lamb used for his
OSS secret-intelligence work in Tehran was his freelance journalism for
Saturday Evening Post and the *Ladies' Home Journal*. Thus he succeeded
in penetrating the very highest echelons of Persian society, numbering

the young Shah among his close personal friends. Considered the most talented of the nine US agents in Persia, Lamb's covert role was never revealed by Near East Section to CICI, nor to the US legation staff, including the minister himself. In fact, Penrose decided that Lamb was so valuable a source that he kept him covered to everyone in Tehran except Upton and Wilber, through whom Lamb communicated with Near East Section in Cairo.[61]

One young officer, Thomas B. W. Allen ('Calvin Warne' [KANGAROO]), well acquainted with the languages of western Persia, was recruited and trained in the United States, arriving in Persia in July 1943. His first cover activity proved rather thin, but he managed within three months to secure a position as a Persian civil servant in what Near East Section described as 'an area of major interest and difficulty of access', namely the cereals and bread section of the US (Millspaugh) Mission to the Persian Department of Finance, where his immediate superior happened to be Archie Crawford's brother, J. Forrest Crawford. However, early in his posting, whilst operating as something of a lone maverick among isolated frontier districts of northern Iraq and northwestern Persia, Tom Allen incurred the displeasure of numerous individuals, not least several influential British officers, and had to be reprimanded severely for his wayward behaviour by Binks Penrose. Of course, the last thing Penrose wanted was for Allen to attract the attention of British security, known in section parlance as 'our friends (or cousins or brethren) across the river'. But it turned out that CICI were already well aware of Allen's presence and the nature of his work, which was quite dangerous and highly effective. According to Penrose, Allen had to proceed with great caution, for the Russians were filtering down into his area, and they would undoubtedly have created a 'rather painful situation' if they had picked Allen up. 'This trans-border stuff can be pretty ticklish', Penrose wrote.[62] Eventually, Allen seems to have received enthusiastic support from 'the Colonel and the Squadron Leader' (Wood and Dawson-Shepherd), who readily dismissed any allegations against Allen, granting him 'blanket approval' to come and go as he pleased anywhere that his job naturally took him. Of Chokra Wood's cooperative attitude, Allen wrote: 'I go with his blessing and the full support of his organization.'[63] Soon after, Allen was posted by the Millspaugh Mission to Tabriz, where he settled nicely into his cover work, furnishing J.F. Crawford with detailed reports on the local economy whilst becoming a productive agent for OSS, providing Near East Section with valuable intelligence on Persian Azerbaijan and Persian Kurdistan, which were rapidly becoming areas of primary interest to the Soviet Union. Allen's solid intelligence was of course shared generally with CICI and especially benefited Joe Spencer, who welcomed such exceptional product from a reliable source within the Soviet zone.[64]

All these OSS personalities present the historian bent on ascertaining their true identities with an intriguing problem.[65] Without any clear consistency Near East Section tended to supply their representatives with cover names and their senior representatives even with alternative cover names (in addition to their cryptonyms) which were often (but not always) exchanged for their real names in correspondence and reports, possibly leading the archival researcher to conflate the number of agents in play. Also thrown randomly and confusingly into this mix were such clear nicknames and short forms as 'Binks' or 'Steve' (Stephen Penrose), 'Tom' (Thomas Allen), and 'H' (Harold Lamb), together with such descriptive phrases as 'the old lion' or 'the king of beasts' (also Lamb). One might well ask: why bother with such trivia? The answer is of course that this is no trivial issue. Only by accurately identifying his field men and their extra-service backgrounds, knowledge, skills, and achievements can we gain full measure of the impressive extent and depth of the talent at Penrose's disposal. Besides, identity is often a crucial absolute in secret warfare; an agent's safety often depends greatly upon it or upon its concealment, which is precisely why OSS training placed such great emphasis on the establishment of feasible cover and the associated protection of identity. Within the service, security was scrupulously observed; however, the occasional lapse was bound to happen. For instance, it was possible for the author to establish the true identity of an otherwise fully covered and extremely important field man in Iraq ('Henry Ibsen' [BUNNY]), an eminent physician with contacts in the highest echelons of Iraqi political life, as none other than the renowned Austrian psychiatrist Hans Hoff, simply because of a single mention in clear of his wife's name by the section chief.[66]

Whatever their true names and identities, Near East Section recorded that by the end of the war they controlled at least eight positive-intelligence officers in Persia,[67] for whom three priority remits had clearly emerged: (1) the interpretation of internal politics with repeated attempts to forecast future developments; (2) the study of Soviet activities within Persia and an attempt to define their ultimate aims; and (3) the study of what the Americans perceived to be British interference in Persian politics and British efforts to dominate the postwar markets in Persia. Clearly, even at the operational level, Germany was no longer a factor for OSS, and German intentions merited no consideration whatsoever.[68] This is evidenced by the posting to Persia in 1943 of T. Cuyler

Young (possibly codenamed 'Roger Black' [cryptonym unknown]) under diplomatic cover as a public affairs officer at the US legation – yet another Persianist with Harvard and Princeton connections – whose OSS work appears to have targeted the Tudeh Party. After the war, Young would join Donald Wilber in operations culminating in the 1953 Mossadeq coup.[69]

Penrose's section was not the only OSS formation operating in Persia and Iraq. On 1 March 1943, Bill Donovan created the Counterintelligence Branch of OSS (X-2), and plans were immediately laid for representation in the Middle East including Persia, where X-2 worked independently of SI Near East Section. On 15 June 1943, a new order was issued awkwardly renaming the branch the 'Counterespionage Branch of the Intelligence Branch of the Intelligence Service of OSS' and (thankfully) stating that it should be referred to by OSS members in conversation and in communications simply as 'X-2 branch'.[70] As with any counterespionage formation, the internal secrecy with which X-2 shrouded its activities and personnel arose from the particularly sensitive nature of CI work, which called for the use of penetration, surveillance, and double agents, as well as 'dealing directly with the enemy intelligence machine a great deal of the time'.[71] Consequently, in a neutral capital like Tehran, it was decided that X-2 should maintain an organization separate from the rest of OSS (i.e. SI) because its cover, activities, and liaisons might differ greatly from those of other branches. The function of X-2 was seen by OSS as involving the acquisition and evaluation of three different types of counterintelligence (or 'protective' intelligence): military, economic, and political. However, the OSS charter made it clear that X-2's remit was limited to the protection of OSS activities and personnel, including SI, leaving the responsibility for protecting such strategic assets as the Lend-Lease route across Persia to CIC. In practice, this meant that, when X-2 came across military intelligence of use to others, they were required to disseminate it to all other counterespionage agencies (e.g. CIC/PGSC and CICI/DSO) and even to any civilian agencies with no means of protecting themselves that might benefit from the knowledge of it (e.g. the US legation).

It is important to note that, from the very beginning, X-2's remit in the Middle East was not confined to action against the Axis. In the area of military intelligence, for instance, it included the 'detection of and protection against all enemy *or hostile* intelligence systems, agents, and activities'.[72] This meant that not only were German saboteurs and fifth columnists fair game, but also (among others) rebellious Persian tribes, the British, and, most importantly, the Russians. The priorities were clearly enunciated in an OSS X-2 planning document of January 1944: 'The main task here is the detection of German agents operating among the wild tribes in the western half of the country, *reporting on the activities of friendly agents (Russian, British, etc)*, and penetration of an enemy system which has been operating from Iran.'[73] There is even anecdotal evidence of minority anti-British sentiment among some OSS officers. One wrote in the autumn of 1944: 'I am glad to see ... that there is control over material passed on to the British. They seem to be enemy No. 1 over here. They are dead against any American interests coming into Iran.'[74]

However, X-2's assigned priorities led the counterintelligence branch into areas of potential conflict with SI, especially where nonmilitary (i.e. political and economic) intelligence was concerned. But, yet again, non-Axis targets were included – 'political bodies have long afforded excellent cover for German, Italian, *Russian, and many other* agents'[75] – and postwar realignment was already being considered a significant factor. According to SI, there was at the time no other American organization taking a really active interest in these bodies, excepting the State Department. However, diplomatic personnel could not penetrate these potentially subversive groups because of the very fact that they were representatives of the US government, and could not endanger the diplomatic relations for which they were responsible. In the Middle East, where political unrest promised to be prevalent during the post-war period, it was extremely important that the US government be kept informed of the latest developments. Here again, X-2 had to be careful not to conflict with any SI operations directed toward the same end, but had to cooperate closely with that branch.[76]

And cooperate they did. By the close of 1943, Archie Crawford of SI could write:

I have just had a talk with the young man out here running X-2. He said that if they ran across any positive intelligence, he would tell us, under very confidential restrictions, which might confirm dope we had had from other sources, or give us a lead for something to look into. I liked him. Drake by name, I believe. But he said he would cheerfully deceive us as to the source, so I gather that he takes his job conscientiously.[77]

By the end of the war, such casual cooperation between Near East Section and X-2 Branch had been placed on a more or less formal reciprocal basis. A similar arrangement had been made with the Chief of X-2 for use and distribution of materials of an SI nature obtained by representatives of X-2, to which was added a reciprocal arrangement whereby all reports of X-2 nature acquired by SI operatives were turned over to that branch for exclusive handling.[78]

So much for the positive-intelligence operations of OSS in Persia. On the defensive side, the deployment of US military security forces sprang from different roots. In July 1942, CIC Operations Division in Washington first decided to send a total of four officers and 33 special agents (Casual Detachments 6615-RRR and 6614-SSS) to the Middle East; however, it was not until five months later that one officer (Edward P. Barry) was detached from Cairo and sent to Tehran to set up a CIC field office to cover Persia and Iraq, which he opened the following February. Barry was then joined by another officer (Edward A. Tobin) and 13 ORs.[79] Much later (in 1944), for his outstanding security work during the Tehran Conference in late 1943, the able Edward Barry was awarded the Legion of Merit, promoted to major, and transferred to OSS.[80] Ultimately under the command of John T. McCafferty, who was transferred from Cairo in October 1943, the Persia and Iraq CIC detachment was responsible for physical security and criminal investigations throughout the PGSC/PGC area, including the Lend-Lease route, but it was hampered by having no authority to gather operational intelligence, for which it was forced to depend to a considerable extent on SIME (in practice, DSO Persia). However, as is evident from certain British operational narratives (for example, the arrest of Franz Mayr and the FRANZ parachutists),[81] the Persia unit of what would later (in August 1944) become 400th CIC Detachment soon found it necessary to disregard PGSC/PGC policy and mount its own undercover operations, as a result of which counterintelligence information began to flow in both directions between the two Western Allies, though the American contribution remained comparatively small. CIC certainly became the normal channel of communication between SIME and all other American intelligence organizations, and SIME held the corresponding position with respect to CIC contacts with British intelligence (DSO), an arrangement which met with Raymond Maunsell's wholehearted approval.[82] In Persia of course, because of the regional devolution that characterized Maunsell's organization, this meant that the interface between SIME and CIC at the highest level became a matter for the British minister Sir Reader Bullard and the PGSC/PGC commander Donald Connolly, both masters of the art of constructive (and civilized) liaison.[83] But more of this a little later.

When DeVere Armstrong visited the region in late 1942 on behalf of CIC Operations Division, he came to some specific conclusions regarding the internal-security situation and its effect on the Lend-Lease supply route from the Persian Gulf ports to the Soviet Union. The problem of security for the TIR had not been solved. Considering the serious food situation and the continuing sabotage and pilferage of Lend-Lease supplies (conservatively estimated to be 10–15 per cent), it was essential that corrective steps be taken. Jumbo Wilson had told Armstrong personally that he did not have the means to carry out his primary military mission and to provide adequate security at the same time for the TIR. The Russians had indicated that they *would* guard the railway if the British or Americans did not.[84]

In fact, in September 1942, the US War Department and the Foreign Office had hammered out an unequivocal bilateral agreement concerning the division of responsibilities with regard to security in the Persian supply corridor, according to which security for the routes was a 'primary responsibility' of the British military authorities, who agreed to furnish the necessary military protection to ensure adequate security of the railways, roads, and harbour facilities against the threat of sabotage and Axis air, ground, and sea operations. At the local level, American and British responsibilities were subsequently defined in a joint agreement between PAIFORCE and PGSC, which was in turn based on a Combined Chiefs of Staff (CCS) directive on control of movements in Persia dated 7 April 1943.[85] However, in September of that year, the PGSC commander reported that security conditions in his area were not satisfactory. He added that, while British commanders were doing an excellent job with the means at their disposal, additional means were necessary if adequate military protection were to be provided for the PGSC area.[86]

When the Americans were elaborating their plans for the establishment of PGSC, they do not appear to have envisaged security problems of this nature. They certainly recognized that any German successes in the Caucasus would likely increase the danger of civil unrest and acts of sabotage against Persian infrastructure, and that appropriate protective measures would have to be introduced. However, they felt that the extent of such anti-sabotage protection could not be predicted. There were several hundred bridge and tunnel structures on the TIR alone, yet the American plan called for the deployment of only one military-police battalion (727th Military Police Battalion: 29 officers and 720 ORs) and one military-police company (259th Military Police Company: 5 officers and 170 ORs)[87] – fewer than 1000 men – for routine interior guard and police duties throughout the entire theatre, including ports and other installations. According to the American plans, US military police could not be used to provide security for structures on the lines of communication or for other critical installations. Engineer railroad units and other military elements had to be trained to defend themselves against marauders, and, in case of attack, to give a good account of themselves with the limited weapons at their disposal. The performance of their technical duties would, however, preclude their use for the protection of lines of communication. Security and anti-sabotage precautions were therefore apart from the intended uses of US troops. It was assumed that since Persia was within the British area of responsibility, the necessary security of these supply routes and critical installations would be provided by the British.[88]

For their part, the British argued the technical point that certain security measures against sabotage of the TIR, for instance, could only be implemented by trained railway-operating personnel (i.e. American troops). Consequently, compromises frequently had to be made in practice, and close cooperation between British and American commanders at the local level usually solved the problem.[89] Such cooperation was very important to DSO, for their special railway intelligence unit was experiencing considerable difficulty penetrating the tight security with which Franz Mayr's highly disciplined railway-espionage and railway-sabotage cells were protected. Consequently, DSO needed all the railway expertise and intelligence the Americans could provide.[90]

Even so, in response to formal American complaints, an official investigation into the troublesome situation in the form of a tour of inspection and a thorough review of security arrangements in the PGSC area was conducted by 'a high official of the Security Service' on behalf of the British Chiefs of Staff during the summer of 1943. As a result of this review, much was done 'to improve general security measures'.[91] Meanwhile, at the highest executive level, Donald Connolly stuck doggedly to his original terms of reference, which stated unequivocally that US troops under his command were responsible solely for the transport of supplies through the Persian corridor and not for internal security. In order not to be seen to compromise his position, he is even said to have refused to provide US soldiers to guard the US legation in Tehran, as a result of which the building was repeatedly robbed. In contrast, the British legation was continuously guarded by a considerable contingent of British troops.[92] But by the end of 1943, Connolly was able to state to a visiting general that security arrangements within PGSC/PGC were satisfactory and that no further action was necessary, and none was taken.[93]

Generally, the duties of CIC fell into the following five categories: (1) loyalty investigations; (2) disaffection investigations in the military establishment; (3) espionage; (4) sabotage; and (5) the detection and curtailment of black marketeering. Most of the 600 (minimum) loyalty investigations conducted by CIC in the Middle East consisted in the routine vetting of potential officers prior to their admission to officer-candidate school. Loyalty checks were also carried out on personnel whose assignment to duty in cryptographic sections was anticipated and on candidates for naturalization. From time to time CIC were required to investigate reports of possible disaffection and potential disloyalty to the United States. In a few cases, for instance, the literary interests of servicemen in pro-Nazi publications aroused suspicion; however, none was ever charged.

In matters of sabotage, because of the obvious vulnerability and supreme importance of the supply routes, CIC maintained an extremely close watch for signs of trouble; however, there were only individual acts of sabotage to deal with, rather than any concerted campaign. Occasionally, vehicle radiator hoses were cut; obstructions were laid across railway lines; points, fuel tanks, and brake boxes were tampered with. Yet all these cases were essentially internal-security problems – isolated instances of the manifestation of personal grievances on the part of tribesmen, civilian employees, or military personnel – rather than the result of concerted enemy action. No one type of incident was repeated often enough to warrant the establishment of extra precautions, nor was anyone ever found guilty. Of course, had Franz Mayr not been captured by DSO, the story might have been very different. Thanks to their development of a useful informant circle, CIC were perhaps most successful in fighting black-market crime in Khuzistan, where most illegal commercial activities were run by Azeri Turks and Arab brigands operating in the Khorramshahr area.[94]

Since PGSC/PGC policy precluded any gathering of positive intelligence by CIC, the corps was somewhat restricted in its scope when it came to the first-hand acquisition of political or military intelligence that might have some bearing on issues of security. Consequently, it had to settle more often than not for whatever crumbs fell from the British table. However, nothing could prevent CIC from closely monitoring political events, demonstrations, and trends, particularly of the potentially explosive kind so common in Persia. Thus CIC studied the Persian polity and cultivated informants whose possible knowledge of events affecting American personnel was considered valuable. Such activity was deemed permissible where potential harm to US personnel, damage to installations, or delay of operations were identified.[95] While OSS and the British mostly succeeded in recruiting officers with solid cultural and linguistic expertise, CIC was significantly hindered in political-intelligence gathering by the fact that no one in the Tehran detachment could speak or write fluent Farsi, forcing investigators to rely on the disparate, often indifferent skills of the mostly not Persian, but Armenian interpreters available to them, who were known sometimes to bring their own subjective, minority issues to the workplace and to allow their politics to 'colour' their translations.[96]

In practice, with only a limited number of in-theatre CIC and field-security personnel available and in view of the wide dispersal of US forces over the vast desert tracts of southern and central Persia, the Americans wisely decided to introduce a decentralized countersubversion (CS) system to protect the Lend-Lease supply routes and depots. According to this system, all military units and establishments assumed responsibility themselves for measures to be taken against subversive or criminal activities, the abuse of trust by military or civilian personnel, and constant checks on troop morale. The desired ratio of security operatives to personnel was at least 1:30, and preferably 1:15. Since most American officers and ORs were busily engaged in their primary job of delivering war materials to the Soviet Union, every effort was made to ensure that investigative activities and paperwork were minimized. Beyond this, the Americans benefited greatly from the fact that it was DSO which shouldered the primary burden of responsibility for CS response, at least in cases where it could be demonstrated that the delivery of war materials was affected. Even in other cases, where US personnel were implicated in subversion or crimes, the Americans usually had the option of dealing with the matter themselves or reporting it to DSO for further action.[97]

For their part, DSO seem to have done everything possible to accommodate and facilitate CIC operations in the region. In late August 1943, SIME released a paper setting forth certain principles to guide the 'intimate' association with their American counterpart which indicated the closeness of the cooperation between the two organizations. According to SIME, the American intelligence services had an important role to play in the Middle East area, not only on behalf of the US government, but indirectly on behalf of the British and Allied governments as well. In particular, as far as SIME was concerned, the activities of CIC were to be assisted in every possible way and its officers treated with the same degree of confidence as the officers of SIME. It had to be borne in mind that CIC officers were valuable colleagues, who were in a position not only to assist British security-intelligence officers in their activities, but also to provide them with objective and independent information of value.[98]

Even so, it was Joe Spencer's DSO Persia organization that bore the main responsibility for internal security. Notwithstanding the tendency of their legation's diplomats to resent rather than acknowledge the extent of British expertise and resources in the region – the culmination of centuries of imperial management experience – CIC officers came to admire and rely upon British expertise in all security matters. At the regional level, for instance, SIME selectively shared with the Americans intelligence product resulting from interrogations at CSDIC Maadi.[99] Specific American CI and CS measures depended heavily on the effectiveness of the cooperative relationship with DSO and the efficiency of British security, and in this respect, by the end of 1943, the British Chiefs of Staff were able to report that the Persian declaration of war on the Axis, the arrest of a number of Axis elements and of doubtful railway employees in Persia, the opening of negotiations with hitherto recalcitrant tribesmen, and the general tightening up of security measures, particularly at Abadan, had combined to cause a noticeable improvement in the situation and had greatly decreased the likelihood of damage on the Aid to Russia routes and in the oil areas.[100]

By the spring of 1944, however, an element of distrust had entered into Anglo-American intelligence affairs: for instance, a 'Guard' stamp was introduced by the British for documents to be kept from American eyes. Whilst MI5 and SIME remained anxious that the cordiality of the Anglo-American relationship should be preserved, they felt that they would have been failing in their duties if they had omitted to take the precaution of covering American intelligence activities that militated against British interests, of which there was increasing evidence in the region. Furthermore, the exchange of information between SIME and CIC had grown very one-sided, with the Americans receiving considerably more intelligence than they gave in return, although this may have been simply because CIC operated in the Middle East on a smaller scale than either the British or OSS.[101] As Guy Liddell observed in general reference to MI5's relationship with the FBI, 'I recognized that the flow of information from East to West would always be greater than from West to East.'[102]

Of greatest significance perhaps, not for the joint occupation of Persia and the concerted struggle against Nazism, but for the realignment and reconfiguration of the Allied secret services as they moved towards post-occupational roles, was the insertion of active OSS espionage agents in August 1944 tasked exclusively with the acquisition of military, political, and economic intelligence on the Soviets in northern Persia. Edwin 'Ed' Wright (TIMBER WOLF) and Arthur "Art" Dubois (TEDDY BEAR) were US Army officers recruited together and trained in Washington, and, after some time in Cairo, deployed to Persia in August 1944, where they were assigned as cover to the staff of PGC in accordance with an agreement struck between Bill Donovan, head of OSS, and Donald Connolly, commander of PGSC/PGC, whose association with OSS was, initially at least, entirely clandestine. After the war, Binks Penrose wrote: 'The general would have had a conniption fit if he believed that USAFIME [United States Army Forces in the Middle East] was informed of his collaboration with us.'[103] Both Wright (a former missionary, archaeologist, and avowed anticommunist) and Dubois had previous experience in Persia and were considered to be of the highest possible calibre. Their military cover permitted them to travel widely throughout the country without impediment. There was clearly never any intention of employing these officers against the Germans. Ed Wright in particular seems to have targeted the Russians, submitting what Cairo described as 'exceedingly valuable reports'. A Russian speaker and extremely influential within OSS, Wright had previously served the US government in the Soviet Union and was considered well able to concentrate on economic intelligence and 'observe developments of the Russian programme in Iran'.[104] And so it was that the intelligence Cold War actually began in Persia in the long hot summer of 1944, for it was uniquely there and then that the Americans and the British faced the Russians directly, with no barbed wire or barricades between them, and covertly spied on each other whilst still overtly friends and allies.

Notes

1. History of the Near East Section, OSS Cairo, from 15 May 1943 to 15 September 1944, RG 226, Entry 210, Box 261, NARA.
2. Panchesa to Wolf [Head of US Steel Export, favoured OSS commercial cover], 16 August 1941, RG 226, Entry 210, Box 334, NARA.
3. Simon Davis, *Contested Space: Anglo-American Relations in the Persian Gulf, 1939–1947* (Leiden: Nijhoff, 2009), 63–77, 86–100, 128–31, 142 passim.
4. Handy to DCOS, 28 August 1942, RG 165, Entry 421, Box 109, NARA.
5. See Bullard, 'Persia', 15; *Camels*, 244.
6. Schroeder to OIC, 6 April 1944, RG 226, Entry 120A, Box 22, NARA. Both the first Millspaugh mission (1922–27) and the second (1942–45) implemented some reforms to the Persian economy, but ended in failure.
7. Arthur C. Millspaugh, *Americans in Persia* (Washington: The Brookings Institution, 1946), 49–50; Badi Badiozamani, *Iran and America: Re-Kindling a Love Lost* (San Diego, CA: East-West Understanding Press, 2005), 28.

8. Private papers of E.N. Sheppard, 509, IWM.
9. Bullard to Eden, 29 April 1943, E 2450/239/34, IOR/L/PS/12/3472A, BL.
10. See Chapter 8.
11. Bullard to Eden, 29 April 1943, E 2450/239/34, IOR/L/PS/12/3472A, BL.
12. Farago to Bullard, 12 October 1966, GB165-0042-3/11, MECA.
13. Farago to Bullard, 26 October 1966, GB165-0042-3/11, MECA.
14. Farago to Bullard, 16 November 1966, GB165-0042-3/11, MECA.
15. Bullard to Farago, 22 November 1966, GB165-0042-3/11, MECA.
16. Farago to Bullard, 26 October 1966, GB165-0042-3/11, MECA.
17. Bullard to Farago, 31 October 1966, GB165-0042-3/11, MECA.
18. Schroeder to OIC, 6 April 1944, RG 226, Entry 120A, Box 22, NARA.
19. Bullard to Farago, 1 November 1966, GB165-0042-3/11, MECA.
20. Bullard, *Camels*, 251.
21. Lindsay to Maddocks, 11 January 1943, RG 165, Entry 421, Box 109, NARA.
22. Welles to Stimpson, 21 August 1942, RG 165, Entry 421, Box 109, NARA.
23. Handy to DCOS, 28 August 1942, RG 165, Entry 421, Box 109, NARA.
24. Ibid.; Memorandum, 4 January 1943, RG 165, Entry 421, Box 109, NARA. Importantly, the memorandum indicates that Dreyfus agreed with Ridley's comments.
25. Marshall to Wemyss, 19 February 1942, WPD 4511-62, RG 165, Entry 281, Box 251, NARA.
26. See Strong to Connolly, 21 October 1942, RG 165, Entry 421, Box 581, NARA.
27. See Crawford to Wheeler, 26 September 1941, WPD 4596-1, RG 165, Entry 281, Box 259, NARA
28. Wheeler to Stettinius, 26 October 1941, WPD 4596-14, RG 165, Entry 281, Box 259, NARA.
29. For a map of the Lend-Lease supply network, see Appendix A.4.
30. Persian Gulf Service Command (PGSC) was renamed Persian Gulf Command (PGC) in December 1943.
31. Penrose to Warne, 8 July 1943, RG 226, Entry 217, Box 1, NARA.
32. Preliminary report of trip of S.B.L. Penrose, Jr, Aug–Sept 1943, 21 September 1943, RG 226, Entry 215, Box 3, NARA. The identity of the revealed officer was not recorded.
33. History of Combined Intelligence Centre Iraq and Persia, June 1941–December 1944, KV 4/223, TNA.
34. Ibid.
35. Wilber, *Adventures*, 101, 105, passim.
36. See RG 226, Entry 210, Box 334, NARA.
37. Field report of Eliot Grant, 11 July 1945, RG 226, Entry 210, Box 58, NARA.
38. Ibid.
39. Memorandum on American policy in Iran prepared by the Division of Near Eastern Affairs, Department of State, 23 January 1943, RG 165, Entry 421, Box 197, NARA.
40. Operations Division to Roberts, 31 October 1944, 334.8 (Iran), RG 165, Entry 421, Box 222, NARA.
41. Memorandum on American policy in Iran prepared by the Division of Near Eastern Affairs, Department of State, 23 January 1943, RG 165, Entry 421, Box 197, NARA..

42. Ibid.
43. Halsey to Loud, 25 April 1942, Series 8 (OSS), Box 5, Folder 8, Penrose Papers (PP), Whitman College and Northwest Archives (WCNA), Walla Walla, WA.
44. Toulmin to USAFIME, 11 November 1944, Series 8 (OSS), Box 5, Folder 8, PP, WCNA. For more about Penrose's work in Cairo and that of Cairo station, see Wilford, *Great Game*, 35–41.
45. History of the Near East Section, OSS Cairo, from 15 May 1943 to 15 September 1944, RG 226, Entry 210, Box 261, NARA.
46. Near East Section report, 15 April 1944, RG 226, Entry 210, Box 261, NARA.
47. Ibid.
48. History of the Near East Section, OSS Cairo, from 15 May 1943 to 15 September 1944, RG 226, Entry 210, Box 261, NARA.
49. Ibid.
50. McBaine to Toulmin, 20 May 1944, RG 226, Entry 210, Box 261, NARA.
51. Preliminary report of trip of S.B.L. Penrose, Jr, Aug–Sept 1943, 21 September 1943, RG 226, Entry 215, Box 3, NARA.
52. See, for example, Penrose to Rigg, 4 May 1944; Donor to Warne, 5 May 1944, RG 226, Entry 217, Box 1, NARA. The fact that the minister-resident in Baghdad, Loy Henderson, was probably OSS may also have contributed to the successful adoption of this method.
53. Penrose to Warne, Letter No. 7, 3 May 1944, RG 226, Entry 217, Box 1, NARA.
54. Penrose to Loud, 28 July 1943, RG 226, Entry 215, Box 3, NARA.
55. Preliminary report of trip of S.B.L. Penrose, Jr, Aug–Sept 1943, 21 September 1943, RG 226, Entry 215, Box 3, NARA.
56. Ibid.
57. Ibid.
58. History of the Near East Section, OSS, Cairo, 22-25, Document No. 11384/004, RG 226, Entry 210, Box 261, NARA.
59. Cf. Wilber, *Adventures*, 97–147; Wilford, *Great Game*, 38.
60. Cf. Wilber, *Adventures*, 101, 105, passim.
61. Preliminary report of trip of S.B.L. Penrose, Jr, Aug–Sept 1943, 21 September 1943, RG 226, Entry 215, Box 3, NARA.
62. Penrose to Loud, 25 October 1943, Box 5, Folder 4, PP, WCNA.
63. Warne to Art [Arthur Dubois?], 25 February 1944, RG 226, Entry 217, Box 1, NARA.
64. Allen has become a shadowy figure. For someone described after the war (*Nevada State Journal*, 22 March 1952) as a 'noted authority on conditions in the Middle East and well-known lecturer, historian, and educator' there is strangely little trace of him left today.
65. These OSS agent profiles have been compiled on the basis of evidence found in the following specific records: History of the Near East Section, OSS, Cairo, 22-25, Document No. 11384/004; McBaine to Toulmin, Report on Trip through the Middle East, 3–18 May 1944, 20 May 1944, Document No. 11397/019; Crawford to Penrose, Near East Section SI, Period 1 January–30 June 1944, 22 June 1944, Document No. 11383/002, RG 226, Entry 210, Box 261, NARA. Also generally in RG 226, Entry 215, Box 3, NARA and Series 8: OSS, Box 5, Folder 4, PP, WCNA.
66. Leary to Loud, 13 January 1945, RG 226, Entry 215, Box 3, NARA.

67. See Notes on representatives in Iran and Iraq based on field trip made by Gordon Loud, November 11–24, 1944, RG 226, Entry 210, Box 261, NARA.
68. Field report of Eliot Grant, 11 July 1945, RG 226, Entry 210, Box 58, NARA.
69. See Mark J. Gasiorowski, 'The CIA's TPBEDAMN operation and the 1953 Coup in Iran', *Journal of Cold War Studies* 15, no. 4 (Fall 2013): 10; K. Allin Luther, 'In Memoriam: T. Cuyler Young, 16 August 1900–31 August 1976', *International Journal of Middle East Studies* 8, no. 2 (April 1977): 268; Wilford, *Great Game*, 38.
70. 'General Order Establishing the Counter Espionage Branch of the Intelligence Branch of the Intelligence Service of OSS', 15 June 1943, *A Counterintelligence Reader*, ed. Frank J. Rafalko, vol. 2 (Washington, DC: National Counterintelligence Center, 2004), 159–60.
71. Proposed plan of operations for X-2 Branch, USOSS Cairo, Egypt, 25 January 1944, RG 226, Entry 210, Box 261, NARA.
72. Ibid. My italics.
73. Ibid. My italics.
74. Scott to Crawford, 25 September 1944, RG 226, Entry 215, Box 3, NARA.
75. Ibid. My italics.
76. Ibid.
77. Crawford to Loud, 10 December 1943, RG 226, Entry 215, Box 3, NARA. The 'young man' referred to is R.G. Drake, then acting chief of X-2 in Cairo.
78. Report by Near East Section for 1–15 January 1945, RG 226, Entry 215, Box 3, NARA.
79. Historical report CIC, PGSC, December 1942 to January 1945, 16 May 1945, RG 226, Entry 120A, Box 22, NARA; History of the Counter Intelligence Corps in the Middle East: September 1942 to May 1945, 20 May 1945, RG 319, Entry 134A, Box 17, NARA.
80. History of the Counter Intelligence Corps in the Middle East: September 1942 to May 1945, 20 May 1945, RG 319, Entry 134A, Box 17, NARA. At the Tehran Conference Barry actually had one of his men (Robert S. Wraugh) 'double' for FDR to provide additional security for the President (Counter Intelligence Corps [CIC] Chronology of World War II [September 1939–September 1945], History of the Counter Intelligence Corps, Volume II, RG 319, NARA).
81. See *NSW*, 119–20.
82. Maunsell to Toulmin, 3 June 1944, History of the Counter Intelligence Corps in the Middle East: September 1942 to May 1945, 20 May 1945, RG 319, Entry 134A, Box 17, NARA.
83. See *NSW*, 121–4.
84. Armstrong to Chief, Strategy and Policy Group, OPD, 12 January 1943, RG 165, Entry 421, Box 357, NARA. Original italics.
85. Connolly to Marshall, 1 November 1943, RG 218, Geographic File 1942–45, Box 176, NARA.
86. Handy to Secretary, JCS, 16 September 1943, RG 165, Entry 421, Box 581, NARA.
87. Plan for operation of certain Iranian communication facilities between Persian Gulf ports and Tehran by US Army forces, 3 December 1942, RG 218, Geographic File 1942–45, Box 176, NARA. This plan is one of the most useful contemporary geographical reference sources in the archival literature.

88. Ibid.
89. Security conditions in Persian Gulf Service Command, 9 November 1943, CCS 349/1, RG 218, Geographic File 1942–45, Box 176, NARA.
90. Plan for breaking the German fifth column in Persia, 11 August 1943, KV 2/1477, TNA.
91. I am unable to confirm who the official was – possibly Dick White or Lord Rothschild.
92. Berle to Leahy, 15 October 1943, RG 218, Geographic File 1942–45, Box 176, NARA.
93. Sommerville to Secretariat, CCS, 2 December 1943, RG 218, Geographic File 1942–45, Box 176, NARA.
94. Historical report CIC, PGSC, December 1942 to January 1945, 16 May 1945, RG 226, Entry 120A, Box 22, NARA.
95. Ibid.
96. Ibid.
97. Operating of the CS system, 17 August 1943, RG 226, Entry 120A, Box 22, NARA.
98. Quoted in Report of visit by Mr A.J. Kellar to SIME and CICI organizations, May 1944, KV 4/384, TNA.
99. Cf. Mallett, *Hitler's Generals*, 6.
100. Security conditions in Persian Gulf Service Command, 9 November 1943, CCS 349/1, RG 218, Geographic File 1942–45, Box 176, NARA.
101. Report of visit by Mr A.J. Kellar to SIME and CICI organizations, May 1944, KV 4/384, TNA.
102. Diary of Guy Liddell, 30 July 1943, KV 4/192, TNA.
103. Penrose to Loud, 1 June 1944, RG 226, Entry 215, Box 3, NARA.
104. History of the Near East Section, OSS, Cairo, 22-25, Document No. 11384/004; McBaine to Toulmin, Report on Trip through the Middle East, 3–18 May 1944, 20 May 1944, Document No. 11397/019, RG 226, Entry 210, Box 261, NARA. See also Wilford, *Great Game*, 39, 43, 46–7.

14
Standing Down

> The PGC is melting away before our eyes like the snows of winter. Lewis Leary (OSS)[1]

At 10 o'clock in the morning of 8 January 1945, the commanders of PAIFORCE (Sir Arthur Smith) and PGC (Donald P. Booth) met to discuss the drawing down of British and American forces in Persia. Smith stated that, as soon as Lend-Lease functions ceased, only British security troops and a few disposal agencies would remain in Persia. Booth replied that the only US forces to remain would be certain supply troops, personnel to evaluate US property, and disposal personnel. The two men affirmed that British forces would not be required to provide security 'within the fence' of American installations. It would take until the end of the year to complete the withdrawal of all American forces from Persian soil, but finally, on 30 December, the USS *General W.P. Richardson* cleared the port of Khorramshahr, carrying the last GIs homeward.[2]

OSS took a rather pessimistic view of what would happen to their IOs after the war and regretted that the lack of any definite constructive plan would no doubt hasten the day that their most valuable undercover representatives would leave them:

> Most of our field men, at least the civilians among them, have been drawn from long-established professions to which they intend to return. Many of them have been separated from their families for considerable periods, living under certain difficulties and privations, and even hardships. In spite of all the efforts of the Washington and Cairo offices, such widely separated field men sometimes find it difficult to believe in the value of their services. All these factors combine to build up a desire to go home.[3]

By the end of 1945, DSO Persia, replaced by 'Persia Section', had been virtually stood down. Staffed in Tehran by only two officers and one NCO (Captains Wickens and Watson, and one corporal-clerk seconded from CICI Baghdad),[4] it had in its final months been reduced to the status of an *adresse de convenance*. As such, it was intended to facilitate the sorting of mail in CICI Baghdad registry in the weeks immediately following the transfer in August–September 1945 of all DSO's records from Tehran to Baghdad. At that time, despite shrinking volume, a considerable amount of outstanding correspondence begun in Tehran still had to be processed by CICI Baghdad, so the retention of a Tehran address ensured correct rerouting of mail. Consequently, while Persia Section could no longer by late 1945 be regarded as an active and officially established component of CICI, it was necessary for the two remaining Tehran officers to be completely intimate with the DSO records, as indeed they were. One of them described their situation as follows: '[We] are … in no sense officially running a "live" Persia Section capable of answering queries on events in present-day Persia'.[5] No new reports concerning Persian affairs were being added to Persia Section records. 'We are both in daily expectation of repatriation to the UK,' added George Wickens,

> and it was simply decided to profit by our presence here in the interval to achieve the final organization of Persia records into a neat library of reference complete to about September 1945. We have also been able to give pertinent, personal counsel on cases primarily of interest to CICI Baghdad or other organizations, where Persians or former foreign residents in Persia were concerned, but again purely fortuitously.[6]

Perhaps the best indication of the special character of Persia Section was the fact that the date of its liquidation was likely to be determined not by considerations of security but by the ultimate repatriation of the two officers theoretically composing it. Apart from the operational case files, which formed the bulk of the DSO material transferred to Baghdad, the records included a massive card index containing some 61,000 names. The outgoing Defence Security Officer, Alan Roger, felt at the time of the transfer that it would be useful for MI5 to card the names, in case they should disappear 'into the maw of MI6's records'. Should MI6 in future have 'become sticky' about producing material originally compiled by DSO, then MI5 would at least be in a position to say that they knew the material existed. Roger also arranged at the time to have a subject list made, in case it should ever be necessary to refer to a particular matter with which DSO might have dealt.[7]

At various times during 1945, most of the PAIFORCE Field Security Sections that had supported the work of DSO were disbanded where they stood, rather than being transferred to other theatres. Their FSOs departed, leaving the section WOs to wind operations down and lead the men out of the country, which they did by various routes. One of the largest sections, 73 FSS, augmented by a merger with 402 FSS, remained in Khuzistan until February 1946,[8] presumably to help protect the strategic regional assets of the AIOC from possible Soviet threat. Following the disbandment of DSO, it is not clear from whom these last British forces on Persian soil took their orders. The last Russian troops left Persia in April 1946.

The postoccupational and postwar careers of those who operated what was arguably the Allies' most successful security-intelligence response to German provocation are difficult to trace, for security protocol demanded of those former British officers nothing less than total secrecy and silence. Of Chokra Wood, for instance, we know little beyond the fact that he was rewarded for his administrative work as head of CICI with the OBE in 1943.[9] After the war, Wood finally retired from the second (intelligence) phase of his distinguished career in the Indian Army – like his father as an honorary colonel – and returned to the UK, resuming his prewar administrative duties at the Royal National Orthopaedic Hospital, Stanmore, Middlesex, now as House Governor.[10] It is said that during his tenure Wood made many unsuccessful attempts to rebuild the RNOH, which was still largely housed in wartime emergency buildings and was in a deplorable state. He died in 1961 at Lymes Farm House on the RNOH estate, which had been his family home since 1937. After Wood's death, the house was converted into residential quarters for female staff; the building was ultimately demolished in the 1970s. In June 1963, the RNOH 'Ward Block Boys' was renamed 'Colonel Wood Ward' in his honour; sadly however, in the mid-1990s that commemoration was erased by a subsequent renaming.[11]

By 1944, as a result of his unique face-to-face experience with the Russians, Joe Spencer had become recognized as Britain's foremost expert on Soviet counterintelligence and security intelligence and was widely consulted on liaison matters, earning him a splendid reputation which no doubt led to his successful postwar career in MI5. Spencer's liaison experience with the US forces of PGSC/PGC also stood him in good stead. After returning home from Persia, Spencer was posted to the European theatre where, between February and May 1945, he served successively as Assistant Chief of Staff, G-2 (British), HQ Berlin District and as chief of British counterintelligence in occupied Germany until shortly after the cessation of hostilities. At that time the Americans awarded Spencer the Legion of Merit (LOM), commending him for being of invaluable assistance in organizing the intelligence staff of US and British officers in occupied Germany on an integrated basis. 'His broad knowledge of the intelligence field and of enemy intelligence systems enabled him to assist materially in completing the outline and later the detailed plans.'[12] It was claimed that Spencer contributed much to the cordial Anglo-American relationship and mutual under-standing, reflecting great credit upon himself and his service.[13] By September 1946, now back in London with the Security Service, Spencer had become MI5's military adviser and the head of B1A, which was B Branch's subsection for left-wing subversive activities, under B Branch director Roger Hollis (about whose possible treachery opinions remain divergent, and who ultimately succeeded Dick White as service chief).[14] After receiving the OBE and retiring from MI5 in 1954, Spencer became De Beers' chief illegal diamond buying (IDB) investigator, thus convinc-ingly completing the transition from 'amateur' in 1942 to thoroughly professional security expert in 12 eventful years. He died in 1976 at the age of 74.

His second-in-command, Alan Roger, remained with SIME for some time after the war, reluctant to leave the army life he loved, serving as DSO Hong Kong, after which, decorated with the MBE and demobilized, like Joe Spencer with the rank of lieutenant colonel, Roger disappeared into civilian life in the Scottish highlands with little trace. It was said that he would always evade talking about his achievements, dismissing them as nothing. Blessed with a large family fortune, Roger devoted his time during the postwar years to collecting art and gardening – about which he was passionate – in the beautiful walled garden he created on a grand scale at his 33,000-acre estate in Wester Ross. Nevertheless, he also found time to serve as a judge for the Royal Horticultural Society, vice-president of the National Trust for Scotland, a director of the National Galleries of Scotland (among other directorships), and a council member of the Contemporary Arts Society. Alan Roger died in 1997 aged 88.[15]

Fellow 'ratcatcher' and IB Liaison Officer Bill Magan, who had estab-lished a network of staybehind agents in Persia in 1942, also rose to become a very senior MI5 officer, together with another skilled Tehran IO, Dick Thistlethwaite, and the brilliant Alex Kellar – all members of a group known at MI5 as the 'First Eleven' – a self-deprecatory term which of course belied their professionalism, as if security intelligence were really nothing more than a public-school game of cricket. Bill Magan received the CBE in 1958, retired ten years later from MI5, and died forty-two years after that aged 101. Thistlethwaite succeeded Kellar on his retirement in 1965 as Director of F Branch, retiring himself in 1972.[16] Alex Kellar rose to become the first civilian head of SIME in 1946, succeeding Raymond Maunsell. Apparently in delicate health, six months after taking over in Cairo, the 'eccentric' Kellar had to be relieved of his post and invalided back to Whitehall, having suffered a nervous breakdown caused by overwork and suspected amoebic dysentery.[17] He was succeeded as head of SIME by the 'far more robust' Bill Magan.[18] After this unfortunate episode, Kellar was sent out to Singapore for a year as head of Security Intelligence Far East (SIFE).[19] He then played a prominent role as MI5's security expert on Zionism and the Palestine Mandate, as well as in the negotiations leading to decolonization in the Far East and in Africa. It was during this period in his career that he is said to have foiled at least one potentially devastating, UK-based Irgun terrorist campaign about to be launched against British troops returning home from Palestine.[20] Kellar served as director of F Branch (communist subversion) from 1953 to 1958, and of E Branch (countersubversion) from 1958 to 1962. After retirement from MI5 in 1965, decorated with the CMG and OBE, Kellar worked for a while for the Scottish Tourist Board, and he died in 1982 at the age of 78. He was interred with his parents in their family grave at St Mary the Virgin, Friston on the South Downs.[21]

One of the most prescient documents that Kellar has left us in the official records is his classic security appreciation of November 1943 – which should be required reading for all students of intelligence history – in which he summarized the counterintelligence problems likely to continue in the Middle East after the war.[22] The greatest threat he saw was Soviet penetration of the region, already evident in Persia, not necessarily by means of actual occupation, but merely by eliminating British influence and establishing governments well disposed towards Moscow. Crucially and correctly, Kellar perceived that it would be immaterial from the security point of view whether Russia was viewed as remaining true to the principles of international communism or as having abandoned those for an aggressive nationalism aimed at imperialist domination. What mattered was Soviet access to the mineral wealth of Persia and Iraq, and to the Indian Ocean. What mattered too was how Washington would respond to such developments. It seemed to Kellar that US commercial interests would probably cause the Americans to operate an intelligence network in the region, which the British would be required to counter.[23] When Alex Kellar returned from a two-month visit to Cairo, Baghdad, and Palestine in February 1945, he wrote yet another definitive report which demonstrates the lucidity and accuracy of his perceptions of the new age that was dawning in both the political and the secret worlds. He found the Middle East no less interesting or important because Axis espionage in the area was on the decline. Quite apart from the Arab–Zionist problem, Kellar felt that there would be much to do in countering the designs of allies who were already indicating that they would be tomorrow's enemies in the field of intelligence. Problems were arising out of this new situation that were already becoming 'complex and delicate'. In this, Kellar was certain, MI5 would have a vital part to play.[24]

The remaining DSO Persia officers – Wickens the don, Carstairs the schoolmaster, and Caird the professional soldier – eventually returned as far as we know to civilian life, no doubt with many a tale to tell, yet never to be told. From his humble beginning as an FSS sergeant, George Michael Wickens – the 'last man standing' in Tehran – would evolve after demobilization into a distinguished and prolific Persian scholar, teaching at the universities of London, Cambridge, and Toronto, where he became founding chair of the Department of Islamic Studies in 1961.[25] Of Carstairs and Caird and the other officers, ORs, and civilians of DSO Persia there is no trace. Without betraying or compromising the enforced silence of those who performed covert roles for the Allies in Persia so successfully, may this book and its companion lend them some shape and substance, and extend to them the posthumous recognition they deserve, whilst filling a significant lacuna in Second World War intelligence history. Theirs was not a savage war of noise and bloody death; it was a patient, cerebral struggle against a formidable enemy rarely glimpsed. Theirs was a war of potential strategic threat on an unimaginable scale: of Nazi plans and plots and treachery, lit by menacing twilight, with long shadows cast by alien personalities only they could identify, define, apprehend, and ultimately defeat.

Notes

1. Leary to Loud, 24 February 1945, RG 226, Entry 215, Box 3, NARA.
2. T.H. Vail Motter, 'American Port Operations in the Persian Corridor', *Military Review* 29, no. 6 (September 1949): 12.
3. History of the Near East Section, OSS, Cairo, 33, Document No. 11384/004, RG 226, Entry 210, Box 261, NARA.
4. Wickens to Kellar, 19 November 1945, KV 4/223, TNA.

5. Ibid.
6. Ibid.
7. Roger to Kellar, 29 August 1945, KV 4/223, TNA.
8. A.F. Judge, 'The Field Security Sections of the Intelligence Corps, 1939 to 1960', unpublished MS, Military Intelligence Museum and Archives, Chicksands, Bedfordshire. The original rationale for the retention of Allied forces in Persia beyond May 1945 was of course that the war against Japan had not yet ended. See Pal, *Campaign in Western Asia*, 460. However, the continued presence of Soviet forces in the region was deemed sufficient reason for the postponement of full British and Indian withdrawal until early 1946, six months after the Japanese surrender.
9. *Supplement to the London Gazette*, 5 August 1943, 3523.
10. Wood was officially granted the honorary rank of colonel on 29 January 1948. Hans Houterman, email message to author, 15 March 2015.
11. *Lost Hospitals of London*, http://ezitis.myzen.co.uk/rnohstanmore.html; Paul Wood, email message to author, 14 March 2015.
12. Legion of Merit (Officer) recommendation, WO 373/148, TNA.
13. Ibid.
14. Organization and functions of B Division, September 1946, KV 4/161, TNA.
15. 'Alan Stuart Roger (Obituary)', *The Herald*, 9 August 1997.
16. See 'Brigadier Bill Magan (Obituary)', *The Telegraph*, 22 January 2010; Andrew, *Defence of the Realm*, 320, 350–1 passim. See also (in connection with the postwar careers of both Kellar and Magan) Philip Murphy, 'Intelligence and Decolonization: The Life and Death of the Federal Intelligence and Security Bureau, 1954–63', *Journal of Imperial and Commonwealth History* 29 (May 2001): 115n83; Tom Bower, *The Perfect English Spy: Sir Dick White and the Secret War 1935–90* (New York: St Martin's Press, 1995), 144–5. Regarding Thistlethwaite and Kellar, see Hughes, *Spies at Work*, 176.
17. Cf. Andrew, *Defence of the Realm*, 352; also Phillip Knightley, 'So What's New about Gay Spies?', *The Independent* (1 June 1997).
18. See Magan, *Middle Eastern Approaches*, 98; Curry, *Security Service*, 270–1.
19. See Andrew, *Defence of the Realm*, 448, for more about Kellar's personality.
20. 'Scots MI5 Spy Was Hero in Terror Plot', *The Herald*, 21 April 2014.
21. 'Alexander James Kellar (1905–1982) – Find A Grave Memorial #5899991', *Find A Grave*, http://www.findagrave.com/cgi-bin/fg.cgi?page=gr&GRid=58999916.
22. Note on future security problems in Mid-East, Appendix B, November 1943, KV 4/384, TNA.
23. Ibid.
24. Report on visit by Mr A.J. Kellar to SIME and CICI organizations, 25 April 1944, KV 4/384, TNA.
25. 'Professor George Michael Wickens (Obituary)', *Globe and Mail*, 30 January 2006, http://v1.theglobeandmail.com/servlet/story/Deaths.20060130.93023387/BDAStory/BDA/deaths.

Epilogue: The Need to Know

> Without publicity, no good is permanent; under the auspices of publicity, no evil can continue. (Jeremy Bentham).[1]

As a concession to the albeit minor active role played by Persian exiles and emigrés in Nazi attempts to influence regional politics, Chapter 5 dealt briefly with the wartime activities of a handful of Persians. However, the central focus of this book and its prequel[2] has not been on them. It has instead been limited to how German covert initiatives and Allied security measures played out in the PAIFORCE theatre, not how they were directly or indirectly affected by the attitudes and behaviour of Persian official-dom and the Persian public-at-large, often referred to as 'the bazaar' or 'the street'. Such popular indigenous opinon might be of sociopolitical significance perhaps, but it had little bearing on the work of the Allied secret services. Without apology therefore, this book (as well as its pre-quel) has not focussed on the wartime Persian polity, nor even on the interface between it and the Allies. They protected Persia from German invasion, subversion, and sabotage, not for Persia's sake but for that of the Allied cause and the survival of the British Empire. The focus has therefore been primarily on a secret war waged on Persian soil between German spies and saboteurs on the one hand and Allied spycatchers on the other. It has been on Persia as a theatre of operations and on the combatants who occupied that theatre: mostly young European, American, Indian, and Soviet Russian men who found themselves operating in a harsh and unforgiving environment — in summer heat so unbearable that even the flies died[3] — far from their homes and often against daunting odds.[4]

A few of these young officers and ORs have left us with a minor but compelling literature of fragmentary memoirs which vividly depicts the difficulty of occupying Persia. Christopher Sykes, who wrote propaganda for SOE in Tehran, also wrote of the process in which moments of war were journaled by ordinary serving men and women:

> During World War II an addendum to King's Regulations laid down that no one serving in His Majesty's forces was to keep a private diary. The rule was ignored by everyone from the Chief of the General Staff to the humblest soldier or sailor who felt some urge to record his thoughts and adventures at so stirring a time, and I know of no official prosecution against those who were guilty of this act of disobedience and 'insecurity'.[5]

Thus it is that in the Documents Collection of the Imperial War Museum (IWM) are to be found descriptive and narrative souvenirs of the daunting challenges faced and rare pleasures enjoyed by the occupiers of Persia:[6] routine garrison duties in unimaginably oppressive heat; coping with sandstorms, snakes, scorpions, and the ubiquitous flies; the café life and cosmopolitan *demi-monde* of Tehran; the terrible ordeal and stoic courage of the Poles who had been forced to migrate to Persia from as far away as northeastern Siberia; vivid impressions of the 1943 Big Three conference; amazement at the massive scale and complexity of the American supply route to Russia; and dismay at the evident degree of corruption, addiction, disease, hunger, poverty, and prostitution in Persian society. These stories, true gems of social history, are a wonderful read and deserve compilation and scholarly treatment, but not here. As might be expected, there is little in them for the intelligence historian, for most of the men and women who wrote them had no inkling of the secret war being waged nearby. Notable exceptions are the memoirs of two major players in covert warfare: Raymond Maunsell (SIME) and David Mure ('A' Force), whose IWM memoirs are important primary sources underlying the Prologue and Chapters 1 and 6 of this book.[7]

Among Allied diplomats who wrote about their wartime service in Persia, pride of place undoubtedly goes to Sir Reader Bullard, who served with distinction throughout the war as British minister (and later ambassador) to Persia, and who wrote lucidly and vigorously after the war of his many years in the diplomatic service. He must be regarded as an unimpeachable source, and *The Camels Must Go* (1961)[8] is probably his most approachable and entertaining work. Unlike so many British career diplomats who came effortlessly to their ascendancy from privileged families, élite schools, and Oxbridge, Bullard's origins were humble. The son of a London docker and a grammar-school pupil, he struggled to gain a decent schooling that would render him fit for a career in the Royal Navy, the teaching profession, or the civil service. There was little money in the family to support him in his quest, and he later described his efforts as a 'curious steeplechase' in 'a world where you flattened your nose against the window of the shop of learning without having the money to go in and make even a modest purchase'.[9] The qualities that sealed his success in those early years — compulsive reading, hard work, tremendous energy, innate intelligence, linguistic proficiency, indefatigable resourcefulness, and above all a large measure of common sense — were to mark his conduct and progress throughout his years in the foreign service as a consular official, minister plenipotentiary, and ultimately ambassador, at a time when that title really meant something quite extraordinary.[10] What is most striking about Bullard the diplomat from the viewpoint of the intelligence historian is his abiding interest in intelligence and counterintelligence matters, which led him to lend the wholehearted support of the British legation to the endeavours of DSO Persia throughout the war. As he wrote in retirement: 'I take a great interest in espionage; I read all the serious books on the subject that I can get hold of.'[11] Another notable British diplomat who wrote about his wartime service in Persia is Clarmont Skrine (*World War in Iran* [1962]). However, Skrine has nothing of consequence to say about security or covert warfare, although he does provide a lucid and convincing justification for the inevitable Anglo-Soviet invasion, effectively countering Persian objections to the Allies' use of *force majeure*. Skrine has also left us with a unique eye-witness account of Reza Shah's final journey into exile.[12]

Among the military commanders who served in Persia, the most accomplished writer is unquestionably Viscount Slim, who commanded 10th Indian Division during Operation COUNTENANCE. His memoir *Unofficial History* (1959)[13] is by far the most vivid account of the Anglo-Soviet invasion bar none. Bill Slim was a gifted — if self-deprecating — humourist who wrote quite extraordinarily well, and his account of the only military operation to be carried out on Persian soil during the Second World War is both readable and amusing. Unfortunately, the same cannot be said of the memoirs by the generals who later commanded PAIFORCE, for whom Persia appears to have been little more than a way station in their army careers and about which they have written relatively little. Most significant are the memoirs of the first PAIFORCE commander, Lord Wilson of Libya — perhaps the most underrated and neglected of Churchill's generals, but an able and popular commander in his day, known to all fondly as 'Jumbo' — who published *Eight Years Overseas* in 1951, in which he addresses the importance of Persian internal security and outlines his plans to counter a possible German invasion through Transcaucasia. His book was later supplemented by a slim memoir published half a century later by his son Patrick Maitland Wilson (*Where the Nazis Came* [2002]), who served briefly as a security-intelligence officer in Persia.[14] Less informative are the memoirs of Sir Henry Pownall (*Chief of Staff* [1972–74]),[15] who headed PAIFORCE from February to September 1943.

Neither this book nor its precursor have been easy to write, because occupied Persia remains geographically, culturally, politically — and most of all historically — obscure to many Western readers, even into the 21st century, for the narrative of Axis and Allied operations in the Persian theatre during the Second World War has been largely overlooked by postwar intelligence historians. Since 1945, and in increasing number since 1995, a significant aggregation of government records dealing with the internal security of wartime Persia has lain dormant and seldom visited in the national archives of Britain, the United States, and Germany. This book and its precursor can therefore claim originality — and not in any clichéd sense — because they are truly the first comprehensive publications of their kind to tell the specific, untold story of wartime covert operations in Persia. Recently, only two historians seem to have taken any general interest in the Persian theatre, producing two significant monographs based on primary sources in the British and American archives. On Anglo-Soviet intelligence relations, Donal O'Sullivan's *Dealing with the Devil* (2010);[16] on Anglo-American diplomatic relations, Simon Davis's *Contested Space* (2009).[17] However, since the former contribution is but one chapter in a broad, multi-theatre study, and the latter a study of policy and diplomacy, these books of are no substitute for a specialized operational intelligence history of Persia.

According Gerhard Weinberg, 'far too much of the historiography of ... the course of World War II has been distorted as a result of the application of hindsight from the experience of the war'.[18] What Professor Weinberg does not say is that this same hindsight has also led to a peculiar kind of prioritization among historians, preventing certain historical narratives from ever being written, let alone distorted. This is clearly how, apart from a handful of cursory, synoptical mentions in the secondary literature, most of the history of German covert operations and Allied security-intelligence measures in Persia during the Second World War has been bypassed and has remained in the archives for over 60 years, barely touched. Indeed, scholarly interest in the Persian theatre *per se*, where — after the swift Anglo-Soviet invasion of 1941 — no conventional battles were ever fought, has been negligible. Perhaps this is because declassification of the Allied records did not begin until the 1970s, continuing at a snail's pace even today, while the Axis records of course remain scarce and fragmentary.[19] But that is to be charitable. Far more likely, it is because postwar historians have generally decontextualized and diminished the strategic significance of Persia. After all, the German-backed Rashid Ali coup in Iraq failed spectacularly in 1941, and the great strategic pincer movement Hitler envisaged in his War Directive No. 32 of 11 June 1941[20] collapsed in 1942–43, effectively denying him the Asian gateways of the Suez Canal and the Caucasus. Thus military historians have unfortunately seen Persia as a sideshow, and any involvement of Allied forces there to have been unworthy of their attention.

Yet, such neglect belies the contextual significance of covert operations in Persia. Over the years since the war, as more and more files have been declassified and released into the public domain, we have become very aware of the Germans' total failure as clandestine planners and operatives in other theatres, especially on the British home front, thanks largely to publications about the codebreakers at Bletchley Park and about the work of the Twenty (XX) Committee and the W Board.[21] However, the files on Persia, open to intelligence historians and the general public since the 1990s, have been overlooked, despite the strategic importance of the region during the war. Especially between 1941 and 1944, the archival records show that Allied communications were repeatedly impregnated with a compelling sense of crisis and urgency in the face of real Axis threats to the occupying forces and to the Persian polity and infrastructure. Such neglect also belies the fact that the Germans attempted to mount covert operations targeting Persia right up to the final months of the Second World War. Until now, no scholarly historians — military or intelligence — have ever examined this question, nor addressed many other intriguing questions relating to German covert initiatives in the Persian theatre.[22] The main difficulty to be found, however, with assembling a cohesive and scholarly narrative of secret warfare in Persia between 1939 and 1945 is the discontinuous and fragmentary nature of the archival records that have survived into the 21st century and that have been declassified for public consumption.

Secret operations are of course supposed to be secret, but for how long do they have to remain a secret? What purposes could possibly be served by withholding 70-year-old case files from historians investigating the failure of the Nazi secret services in a Persia which has since undergone such profound political, social, and cultural metamorphoses that no significant links with its wartime past can be said to exist? Why on earth are there still blank pages and redacted identities in the KISS playback files, for instance?[23] Surely the secrets of a purely notional double-cross of little significance, which involved neither treachery nor vital information, require no such protection today. Nor can one identify any residual continuity between the Nazi secret services and the modern German Bundesnachrichtendienst (Federal Intelligence Service [BND]) that might justify the continued redaction of such files. It is only the British and American services that have a continuous past to nurture and protect, yet they, as the triumphant victors, surely have little to deny and little to fear by revealing names, places, events, intentions, and outcomes that led ultimately to such spectacular success in 1945.[24]

In some instances, particularly where deniability was a concern, there may even have been no written operational records in the first place. It is sobering that the contemporary OSS Secret Intelligence Field Manual states bluntly, as a cornerstone of doctrine for strategic-services training: 'Generally speaking, no records should be kept.'[25] Meanwhile, some records that do exist have undoubtedly been retained by the executive departments still nominally responsible for them (such as MI5 and MI6), and may never see the light of day. Finally, many files that have — in fits and starts through the seven decades since the Second World War — been released into the public domain have been 'weeded' to a degree that makes it difficult to identify people, places, and events with accuracy and consistency.[26] The question of access to information is a crucial one, because this book and its companion — like all 21st-century investigations into events that occurred in the 1940s — could only be driven by the archival records. It is no longer possible to compile an oral, eye-witness history of the secret war in Persia.

Most obviously this is because 70 years later almost no living witnesses remain. More importantly, with the exception of Bill Magan of the IB, individual security-intelligence officers in Persia like Joe Spencer and Alan Roger were not permitted to retain — let alone publish — personal records of their wartime experiences. After the war, Spencer wrote: 'Unfortunately I have no personal papers or notes from those days and have to rely on my somewhat faulty memory, as all my reports were handed over to the War Office, and I no longer have access to them, having left government service.'[27] Unusually, Magan was given permission by MI5 to publish an approved memoir which included his Tehran experiences, but not until 2001.[28]

Even so, this book has benefited immeasurably from the ready availability at Kew of a number of reliable British sources of Middle East
situation reports, including DSO Persia counterintelligence summaries,
CICI Baghdad IB summaries and security-intelligence summaries, MEIC
security summaries, SIME summaries, and PAIFORCE weekly intelligence reviews and special situation reports, as well as serial reports
by the British minister, later ambassador (Bullard) and his military
attachés (Underwood and Fraser). Confusingly, the acronym CICI stood
for Combined Intelligence Centre Iraq, even after the establishment in
1942 of a separate centre in Tehran, which perhaps should have been
called CICP (Combined Intelligence Centre Persia) but never was. In
general, the standard of reporting is excellent: the clear language, vivid
description, logical exposition, consistent organization, and chronolog-
ical continuity of these documents greatly facilitate the construction of
a coherent linear narrative depicting wartime intelligence, counterintelligence, and security-intelligence operations in the region. At the same
time, these reports also provide a contextual background by describing
prevailing conditions within the Persian polity, such as tribal unrest,
political sedition and subversion, endemic corruption, economic problems, bazaar attitudes, and infrastructural sabotage.

One cannot, in this context, overestimate the power of the written
word in the routine yet extraordinary exchange of operational information that was sustained throughout the occupation between Joe Spencer
and Alan Roger in Tehran and Alex Kellar in London. Even in the wartime British naval and military services, including the secret intelligence
and security services, communication standards — in other words, writing standards — were generally high. It can be safely induced from the
liaison between such well-educated men that good security intelligence
and positive operational outcomes may often depend to a significant
degree on the literacy of the spycatchers ... or in this case 'ratcatchers'. Spencer, Roger, and Kellar all came from privileged backgrounds
and had received an élite education, which probably saw them writing
lengthy essays and précising the prose of Macaulay and Trevelyan[29]
from the tender age of 10. The British civil service, especially the
Foreign Office and the Colonial Office,[30] had an incomparable, lengthy
tradition of superb narrative and descriptive writing in the service of
diplomacy and colonial administration, which may be relished by anyone perusing the FO and CO files at Kew. From the stiff, essay-driven
entrance examinations to the daily routine of writing minutes, drafts,
reports, and published documents, 'clerks' at every level were expected
to write not just well, but extraordinarily well. Though from humble

social origins and not a beneficiary of private education, Sir Reader Bullard's lucid despatches to the FO and his vivid correspondence bear eloquent witness to the rigour of his Whitehall training. One of the most interesting things about the British public records is that so many of them preserve not only the perfected final versions of reports and other communications, but also the drafts. It is, of course, particularly enlightening to read many documents authored by Winston Churchill at various stages in the writing process; as a writer he of course owed much to the tradition of good authorship cultivated by the British civil service and British government.

Recently it has been suggested that such records are excessively 'anglocentric' and have too often been used to present the achievements of British counterespionage rather than the work of the German secret services.[31] A reading of this book and its prequel, however, should quickly reveal its lack of biased presentation. No effort has been spared to present the work of the Abwehr and the SD with reference to German sources whenever possible and with respect for German professionalism whenever appropriate. It is through no fault of the author that the German records are sparse, or that many of the German human sources were in captivity and under interrogation when they furnished their information. In fact, Allied interrogation reports go a long way towards compensating for the lack of German records, for most covert operatives 'sang like canaries', once they had acknowledged the irreversibility of their capture and began to respond positively to the humane treatment accorded them by SIME interrogation officers at Maadi and elsewhere. It is largely from these records that one may learn about the Abwehr and — especially — the SD, for very few German records exist.[32]

Allied counterintelligence operations in Persia also yielded several significant Nazi corpora such as the captured Mayr documents and the Franz Mayr diary,[33] together with commentaries on these archival monoliths by security-intelligence analysts and the captured Abwehr staybehind agent Berthold Schulze-Holthus.[34] The Mayr, Gamotha, and Schulze-Holthus files were not finally declassified by MI5 and released to the public until 2004. Without their release, this book and its companion would not have been possible; with their release, a significant lacuna in the history of the Second World War east of Suez may at last be filled. Other single documents of note are the captured diary of SD parachutist Werner Rockstroh and the deceptive Radio Berlin broadcasts of the former SD staybehind agent Roman Gamotha, both of which afford us a rare glimpse beyond the automaton-like stereotype of the Nazi stormtrooper.[35]

Single documents of great interest are to be found in all the archives. In the main Bundesarchiv collections at Berlin-Lichterfelde (BArch) are such curiosities as letters from Himmler to Hitler concerning the deployment of agents Franz Mayr and Roman Gamotha in Persia,[36] as well as the service records of almost all the SS officers and other ranks sent there, formerly stored at the Berlin Document Centre (BDC).[37] At the Bundesarchiv-Militärarchiv in Freiburg (BArch-MArch) are such important papers as the (fragmentary) memoirs and war diary of Erwin Lahousen[38] (including entries concerning the likely invasion of Persia through Transcaucasia in 1942); the file on Operation MAMMUT,[39] which targeted Persian Kurdistan; and various files on the Abwehr special-forces units (Brandenburgers), including some of Admiral Canaris's own memoranda.[40] But the overall scope of the surviving Abwehr and SD records is extremely limited, and their potential for Middle East intelligence historians equally so. Consequently, it is difficult to share the unbridled enthusiasm of the American historian Ladislas Farago for what he overestimated as the scale of the — largely duplicated — German intelligence records held by the US National Archives at College Park, Maryland (NARA). Farago claimed that the German 'machinations' in Persia in 1940–44 were fully covered, and that he had been given full access, not only to the papers of the German Foreign Office, but also of the Abwehr and the SD. 'From them, the whole magnitude of the German manipulations became evident, probably even beyond their scope known to the British authorities,' Farago wrote, greatly overstating his case.[41]

In fact, thanks to their successful codebreaking and the efficiency of SIME and CICI, the British had full measure of the Germans. According to Harry Hinsley, the British were reading both the Abwehr and the SD codes from 1941 onwards. After the breaking of the Abwehr's Enigma in December 1941, SIGINT became an even more valuable source of intelligence. The decrypts of the SD hand cipher, which had been broken early in 1941, but which were read less regularly than the Abwehr decrypts, threw light on the activities of Amt VI, which was interested in the scope for political subversion and propaganda in the Middle East.[42] So, Farago's archival investigations were in reality rewarded solely with his discovery at College Park of the Ettel papers — also to be found at Kew and at the Political Archive of the Auswärtiges Amt (German Foreign Office) in Berlin (AA) — which relate to the evacuation and internment of the German diaspora in 1941, but not to any events after that and definitely not providing the 'full coverage' to which Farago alludes. But the American archives do possess significant collections of records pertaining to the activities of OSS and CIC in Persia, the latter as part of PGSC/PGC, which was responsible for the Lend-Lease supply route across Persia to the Soviet Union (see Appendix A.4).[43] Also, at Whitman College, Walla Walla, Washington (WCNA), are the private papers of Stephen B.L. Penrose Jr, who headed the OSS secret-intelligence section in Cairo from May 1943 onwards, and whose correspondence reveals a great deal about OSS networks in Persia.[44]

However, this book and its companion are based primarily on a wealth of material on wartime Persia discovered in the British archives — at the National Archives in Kew (TNA); in the India Office Records at the British Library (St Pancras) (BL); in the Newspaper Collection at the British Library (Colindale); in the Documents Collection of the Imperial War Museum (IWM); in the Churchill Archives Centre at Churchill College, Cambridge; and in the Middle East Centre Archive (MECA) at St Antony's College, Oxford. All these archives offered up treasures beyond compare which, pieced together, tell the entire story of covert operations in Persia during the Second World War: documents of every imaginable genre — letters, diaries, memoirs, photographic collections, agendas, minutes, reports, articles, speeches, scholarly papers, newspaper and magazine articles, radio broadcasts, propaganda pamphlets, cartoons, cables, telegrams, ciphers, personality traces (or 'lookups'), and personnel records. Yet, for all their abundance now, many of these documents on Persia of inestimable historical value, especially those held by the secret services, could not be accessed for 60-odd years. This was originally because of the 'Fifty-Year Rule' in Britain and the 'Thirty-Year Rule' in the United States and Germany.[45] True, the access problem was alleviated slightly by such interim measures as the Waldegrave Initiative[46] of 1993 and President Clinton's Emergency Order No. 12958[47] of 1995. However, many key documents have until recently been denied to scholars who were left for so long to forage among isolated declassified fragments without historical sequence or context.[48] According to the official historian of MI6, the Waldegrave Initiative 'challenged the traditional British supposition that all official matters were secret until the government specifically decided otherwise'.[49] Yet the records of MI5 and MI6 were granted exemption from disclosure under subsequent legislation.[50] And so even today challenges may still be encountered, and denials of access continue.

One truly appreciates the plight of Sir Reader Bullard when he was preparing to write his memoirs in the early 1960s.[51] Bullard was unable to locate or examine the Mayr papers and other CICI records, which were not ultimately declassified by MI5 until 2004. He was told that the documents he sought were not under Foreign Office control and appears to have been unaware that they in fact resided at MI5 (and — a few — at the War Office). However, according to the principles governing the 'Fifty-Year Rule', the former head of a diplomatic post like Bullard who wished to publish memoirs was permitted by his former employer to see only the diplomatic telegrams and despatches he had sent from Foreign Office posts he had occupied, not classified security files. Though disappointed, Bullard appears to have accepted the necessity for such stringent measures: in his own words, 'there can never be any question of allowing a person sole access to any papers that are still classified. Other writers would naturally be furious if this rule were infringed.' On the other hand, there was slender hope that the Mayr papers, for instance, would be released for general inspection, though why they should not be Bullard did not know. In his opinion, so long as they were kept secret, the Americans would say that the British had forged them or 'that they were forged and we stupidly took them for genuine'.[52]

Problems of access associated with the British 'Fifty-Year Rule' and the American 'Thirty-Year Rule' as they affected writers like Bullard during the 1960s were not eased by the contemptuous attitude of conservative statesmen like Harold Macmillan, who appears to have been in a state of denial about the existence of any public demand for access to materials within the Fifty-Year Rule period.[53] With regard to the forging of documents, it is not possible to find anything in the British archival records that might lead one to doubt the authenticity of the Mayr papers. On the contrary, the fact that they were retained by the authorities for 62 years and then released in their entirety surely militates against any such notion.

If there is a black hole in the archival universe, then it is undoubtedly the Russian archives. Their inscrutability in the 21st century is nothing short of scandalous, belying the very purpose of conservation. The concern here is not so much for the current muddled state of the former so-called Osobyi (special archive), an eclectic trophy archive of looted Nazi records of whose existence we only learned in 1990. Sizeable fragments of it have been repatriated over the years to Germany, Austria, and various other countries, whilst most of the records still gather Russian dust for no good cause. Not all these collections were actually looted; some fell unsolicited into Russian hands, which may perhaps explain the lack of due diligence in curating them. It seems likely, for instance, that Heinrich Müller, head of Amt IV, who defected to the Russians shortly before the end of the war, took with him a large assortment of RSHA files, which he handed over to Soviet counterintelligence (SMERSH). Certainly the Gestapo central registry records were never recovered in 1945 by the Western Allies.[54] To access the captured RSHA collections, now kept at the Russian State Military Archive (RGVA) in Moscow, specifically those in Fond 500, one merely requires archival and linguistic competency (or skilled but costly local researchers), a great deal of time and patience, and an ample budget. However, the real problem for anyone seeking information about the Red Army and the NKVD in occupied Persia is the absolute inaccessibility of relevant Soviet military records at the RGVA. When a Russian-speaking Canadian historian recently visited the Moscow archives and attempted to access records of Soviet military activities in Persia during the Great Patriotic War, he quickly discovered that all the related files were, for some unfathomable reason, still sealed.[55] Perhaps we should not be altogether surprised, for Gabriel Gorodetsky, who has arguably had greater success since 1991 than any other Western historian in penetrating the Russian archives, has written that 'research in the Russian archives is ... governed by a mixture of whim and bureaucratic hazard which undermines the process of research'.[56] This then explains the one glaring deficiency of this book and its predecessor: the total absence of Russian primary sources. If the story of the Anglo-Soviet occupation of Persia is to be told fully, then future scholars will need to face the 'Russian problem' squarely and advocate vociferously for improved access.[57]

Notwithstanding the extensive bibliographies provided at the back of each of these two books on occupied Persia, anyone familiar with the literature on German intelligence and covert operations east of Suez and Istanbul during the Second World War will doubtless notice how seldom there is any reference in the texts themselves to unofficial or academic secondary sources on the subject. This is because both books are pioneering histories; they are the first archival investigations of declassified evidence concerning the secrets of wartime Persia. What their author initially faced was a lacuna, a vacuum, a historiographical black hole, virtually devoid of any valid secondary sources. Therefore his primary role had to be that of detective/storyteller rather than academic scholar. The immediate tasks were firstly the creation of historical context, then a narrative — together with a concomitant identification of persons, places, and activities — and finally an analysis couched in terms of Axis intelligence failure and Allied counterintelligence success. From the very start of the writing process, it was clear therefore that only one methodology could be correct: a concrete, technical approach to the subject matter, not an abstract, theoretical one. Being almost exclusively reliant upon recently declassified primary sources, the author (and the reader) needed to know what happened historically (or did not) and who made it happen (or did not) before anything could be interpreted, and the whys and wherefores could be answered. So, the gauntlet has been thrown: the events and personalities have been duly narrated, described, and (briefly) analysed. It is now for others — who need to know — to take up the challenge and begin the next, more interpretive, problematized stage of historiography on occupied Persia.

Notes

1. Jeremy Bentham, 'Essay on Political Tactics', *The Works of Jeremy Bentham*, VIII (Edinburgh: William Tait, 1839), 314.
2. Adrian O'Sullivan, *Nazi Secret Warfare in Occupied Persia (Iran): The Failure of the German Intelligence Services, 1939–45* (Basingstoke: Palgrave Macmillan, 2014). In this review of the literature, full bibliographical data are repeated for titles cited and abbreviated in previous chapters.
3. Private papers of W.R. Garrett, 2405, IWM.
4. For a well-written, richly illustrated basic introduction to the social experience of wartime Persia, I would strongly recommend Simon Rigge, *War in the Outposts* (Alexandria, VA: Time-Life, 1980), 48–63, 76–99.
5. Christopher Sykes, *Evelyn Waugh: A Biography* (London: Collins, 1975), 203. Extract reprinted by permission of Peters Fraser & Dunlop (www.petersfraser-dunlop.com) on behalf of the Estate of Christopher Sykes.
6. See the following IWM memoirs: 509 Sheppard, 2164 Drax, 2405 Garrett, 3709 Aris, 5810 Webber, 5869 Andrews, 7474 Dunlop, 7939 Gamble, 8006 Dundas, 8093 Bowen, 8125 Christy, 8605 Grimes, 10786 Bell Macdonald, 11631 Williams, 11941 Spiller, 13164 Schonberg, 13165 Thwaites, 13556 Shelton, 15519 Maufe, 15520 Flanakin, 17217 Ball, 17354 Hewitt, 19934 Johnston, and 20366 Speight.
7. 2194 Mure and 4829 Maunsell, IWM.
8. Reader Bullard, *The Camels Must Go: An Autobiography* (London: Faber & Faber, 1961).
9. Bullard, *Camels*, 44, 46.
10. Until relatively modern times Britain had only seven embassies, in only the largest countries; elsewhere there were legations. Beginning in the 1940s, this differentiation was gradually removed, and many ministers-plenipotentiary, like Bullard, became ambassadors.
11. Bullard to Seth, 10 September 1963, GB165-0042-3/11, MECA.
12. Clarmont Skrine, *World War in Iran* (London: Constable, 1962). See also 'Sir Clarmont Skrine OBE (Obituary)', *Asian Affairs* 6, no. 1 (1975): 119.
13. William Slim, *Unofficial History* (London: Cassell, 1960).
14. Henry Maitland Wilson, *Eight Years Overseas, 1939–1947* (London: Hutchinson, 1951); Patrick Maitland Wilson, *Where the Nazis Came*

(Lancaster: Carnegie, 2002). A useful operational overview may be found in Henry Maitland Wilson, 'Despatch on the Persia and Iraq Command Covering the Period 21st August, 1942 to 17th February, 1943', *Supplement to The London Gazette*, no. 37703 (27 August 1946), 4333–40.

15. Henry Pownall, *Chief of Staff: The Diaries of Lieutenant General Sir Henry Pownall*, ed. Brian Bond (London: Cooper, 1972–74).
16. Donal O'Sullivan, *Dealing with the Devil: Anglo-Soviet Intelligence Cooperation during the Second World War* (New York: Lang, 2010).
17. Simon Davis, *Contested Space: Anglo-American Relations in the Persian Gulf, 1939–1947* (Leiden: Nijhoff, 2009).
18. Gerhard L. Weinberg, *Hitler's Foreign Policy: The Road to World War II 1933–1939* (New York: Enigma, 2005), 14.
19. 'No doubt, compared to other subject areas of 20th-century German history the surviving files from intelligence organisations amount to no more than a sad trickle.' Wolfgang Krieger, 'German Intelligence History: A Field in Search of Scholars', *Intelligence and National Security* 19, no. 2 (2004): 186.
20. Hugh R. Trevor-Roper, ed., *Hitler's War Directives 1939–1945* (Edinburgh: Birlinn, 2004), 129–34.
21. See J.C. Masterman, *The Double-cross System in the War of 1939 to 1945* (New Haven, CT: Yale University Press, 1972). For a dissenting view from one who felt that the work of the XX Committee was vastly overrated, see David Mure's correspondence with various former wartime MI5 officers, none of whom agreed with him (2194: 67/321/1-3, IWM). See also David Mure, *Master of Deception: Tangled Webs in London and the Middle East* (London: William Kimber, 1980); *Practise to Deceive* (London: William Kimber, 1977).
22. See Krieger, 'German Intelligence History': 188–90, for a lucid explanation of why German historians have generally failed to engage with their own intelligence history, in the absence of any clear German 'intelligence tradition', and (ibid., 195–6) why so few German spies have published memoirs.
23. See KV 2/1281-1285, TNA.
24. For an informed discussion of the issues associated with the accessibility of British intelligence records, see Len Scott, 'Sources and Methods in the Study of Intelligence: A British View', *Intelligence and National Security* 22, no. 2 (April 2007): 185–205.
25. Secret Intelligence Field Manual — Strategic Services (Provisional), Strategic Services Field Manual No. 5, Office of Strategic Services, 22 March 1944, RG 226, NARA. Available as a download from http://www.soc.mil/OSS/assets/secret-intelligence-fm.pdf.
26. In his capacity as MI5's official historian, Christopher Andrew's occasional talks at Kew, available as a series of podcasts, are helpful to anyone seeking an introductory overview of recent Security Service document releases. According to Andrew, as of 7 February 2012, over 4,900 files had been released by MI5 in the KV series. See http://media.nationalarchives.gov.uk/.
27. Spencer to Bullard, 5 October 1959, GB165-0042-3/7, MECA. Seven years later, Spencer was sure that the Mayr papers were still held in the MI5 archives and could think of no possible objection to any serious author or student having access to them, but 'the official attitude always tends to be very stubborn and obtuse concerning these things'. Spencer to Bullard, 21 November 1966, GB165-0042-3/11, MECA.

28. See William Magan, *Middle Eastern Approaches: Experiences and Travels of an Intelligence Officer, 1939–1948* (Wilby, Norfolk: Michael Russell, 2001).
29. The elaborate prose of the historians Thomas Babington Macaulay (1800–59) and George Macaulay Trevelyan (1876–1962) made them popular with English examiners well into the 20th century.
30. Cf. Thomas G. Otte, *The Foreign Office Mind: The Making of British Foreign Policy, 1865–1914* (Cambridge: Cambridge University Press, 2011), 1–22, 240–4, 393–408. While Otte never specifically mentions the significance of diplomats' and senior clerks' writing skills either before or after Landsdowne's reforms of 1905–6, his analysis of how the mindset of the bureaucratic élite was constituted clearly assumes that such skills underlay the formulation of policy and the smooth functioning of diplomacy and colonial administration.
31. Notably by Emily Wilson, 'The War in the Dark: The Security Service and the Abwehr 1940–1944' (PhD diss., Cambridge, 2003), 3.
32. For a history of the British POW interrogation system, including the Combined Services Detailed Interrogation Centre (CSDIC) at Maadi, Egypt, see Kent Fedorowich, 'Axis Prisoners of War as Sources for British Military Intelligence, 1939–42', *Intelligence and National Security* 14, no. 2 (Summer 1999): 156–78. For a brief but interesting discussion of rendition and the generally benevolent treatment of prisoners of war at Maadi, see Adam Shelley, 'Empire of Shadows: British Intelligence in the Middle East 1939–1946' (PhD diss., Cambridge, 2007), 159–63. Regarding the American system, see Arnold M. Silver, 'Questions, Questions, Questions: Memories of Oberursel', *Intelligence and National Security* 8, no. 2 (1993): 199–213. For a more thorough treatment, see Falko Bell, 'Wissen ist menschlich: Der Stellenwert der Human Intelligence in der britischen Kriegsführung 1939–1945' (PhD diss., Glasgow, 2014).
33. See KV 2/1482, TNA; *NSW*, 111.
34. See KV 2/1480, TNA.
35. The Rockstroh diary and the Gamotha broadcasts are reproduced in full in my doctoral dissertation: Adrian O'Sullivan, 'German Covert Initiatives and British Intelligence in Persia (Iran), 1939–1945' (DLitt et Phil diss., UNISA, 2012), 305–18. Not easy to acquire otherwise, a copy is available in the University College London (UCL) Library.
36. Himmler to Hitler, Einsatz von SS-Führern im Iran, 22 May 1943, NS19/2235, BArch.
37. See 'Personenbezogene Akten' (series PK [Partei-Kanzlei], RS [Rasse- und Siedlungshauptamt], SM [SS-Unterführer und Mannschaften], and SSO [SS-Offiziere]), BArch.
38. Erinnerungsfragmente von Generalmajor a.D. Erwin Lahousen, MSG 1/2812, BArch-MArch; Auszüge Lahousen aus dem Kriegstagebuch der Abwehr-Abt. II des Amtes Ausland/Abwehr, RW 5/497-498, BArch-MArch.
39. Unternehmen MAMMUT, RW 5/271, BArch-MArch.
40. MSG 158/8, MSG 158/38, MSG 158/50, RH 21-2/709, BArch-MArch.
41. Farago to Bullard, 16 November 1966, GB165-0042-3/11, MECA.
42. F.H. Hinsley and C.A.G. Simkins, *British Intelligence in the Second World War*, Vol. 4, *Security and Counter-Intelligence* (New York: Cambridge University Press, 1984), 163.

43. Notably Record Groups RG 165 (Records of the War Department General and Special Staffs [WDGS/WDSS]), RG 218 (Records of the US Joint Chiefs of Staff [JCS]), RG 226 (Records of the Office of Strategic Services [OSS]), RG 319 (Records of the Army Staff), and RG 497 (Records of the Africa-Middle East Theatre of Operations), NARA.

44. Series 8 (OSS), together with additional declassified OSS records, WCNA.

45. For a recent treatment of the issues surrounding the question of restricted access to historical sources, see 'A Note on Sources', in André Gerolymatos, *Castles Made of Sand: A Century of Anglo-American Espionage and Intervention in the Middle East* (New York: St Martin's Press/Thomas Dunne, 2010), xv–xvi.

46. See Richard J. Aldrich, 'The Waldegrave Initiative and Secret Service Archives: New Materials and New Policies', *Intelligence and National Security* 10, no. 1 (January 1995): 192–7; 'Did Waldegrave Work? The Impact of Open Government upon British History', *Twentieth Century British History* 9, no. 1 (1998): 111–26.

47. The full text of EO12958 is available online at Wikisource (http://en.wikisource.org/ wiki/Executive_Order_ 12958).

48. To contextualize recent improvements in accessibility, it is worth reading an informed discussion that predates Waldegrave: Wesley K. Wark, 'In Never-Never Land? The British Archives on Intelligence', *The Historical Journal* 35, no. 1 (March 1992): 195–203.

49. Keith Jeffery, 'A Secret History: Unravelling MI6's Past', *The Telegraph* (22 September 2010).

50. Ibid.

51. In addition to Bullard's *Camels*, a wonderful read is Reader Bullard, *Letters from Tehran: A British Ambassador in World War II Persia*, ed. E.C. Hodgkin (London: I. B. Tauris, 1991). Fitzroy Maclean, who wrote the foreword, found the letters 'immensely readable' and wrote of them 'Bullard's letters give us his personal and unofficial view of events ... with all its attendant domestic and social as well as purely diplomatic problems'.

52. Bullard to Spencer, 20 November 1966, GB165-0042-3/11, MECA.

53. See D.C. Watt, 'Restrictions on Research: The Fifty-Year Rule and British Foreign Policy', *International Affairs* 41, no. 1 (January 1965): 89–95.

54. See the CIA memorandum of 9 December 1971 discussed by Timothy Naftali et al. in 'Record Group 263: Records of the Central Intelligence Agency — Records of the Directorate of Operations: Analysis of the Name File of Heinrich Mueller', RG 263 — CIA Records, Declassified Records, International Working Group (IWG), http://www.archives.gov/iwg/declassified-records/rg-263-cia-records/rg-263-mueller.html.

55. Alex Statiev, email message to author, 14 August 2014.

56. Gabriel Gorodetsky, *Grand Delusion: Stalin and the German Invasion of Russia* (New Haven, CT: Yale University Press, 1999), xiv. See also Gerhard L. Weinberg, 'Unresolved Issues of World War II: The Records Still Closed and the Open Records Not Used', in *Secret Intelligence in the Twentieth Century*, ed. Jan G. Heitmann, Heike Bungert, and Michael Wala (London: Frank Cass, 2003), 23.

57. For further information about Nazi documents in the Russian archives (especially Fond 500), see inter alia Rossiiskii gosudarstvennyi voennyi arkhiv (RGVA), ArcheoBiblioBase: Archives in Russia: B-8, *International Institute of*

Social History, http://www.iisg.nl/abb/rep/B-8.tab5.php?b=; 'Sonderarchiv' Moskau Fondsverzeichnis, *Sonderarchiv Moskau: Informationsseite von Sebastian Panwitz*, http://www.sonderarchiv.de/fondverzeichnis.htm (a useful basic finding aid); George C. Browder, 'Captured German and Other Nations' Documents in the Osoby (Special) Archive, Moscow', *Central European History* 24, no. 4 (1991): 424–45; Kai von Jena and Wilhelm Lenz, 'Die deutschen Bestände im Sonderarchiv in Moskau', *Der Archivar* 45, no. 3 (1992): 457–67; Bernd Wegner, 'Deutsche Aktenbestände im Moskauer Zentralen Staatsarchiv: Ein Erfahrungsbericht', *Vierteljahrshefte für Zeitgeschichte* 40, no. 2 (April 1992): 311–19; Patricia Kennedy Grimsted, 'Twice Plundered or "Twice Saved"? Identifying Russia's "Trophy" Archives and the Loot of the Reichssicherheitshauptamt', *Holocaust and Genocide Studies* 15, no. 2 (2001): 191–244; Patricia Kennedy Grimsted, *Russia's 'Trophy' Archives — Still Prisoners of World War II?* (Budapest: Open Society Archive, Central European University, 2002); Patricia Kennedy Grimsted, 'Why Do Captured Archives Go Home? Restitution Achievements under the Russian Law', *International Journal of Cultural Property* 17 (2010): 291–333. For advice on how to work productively in the Russian archives, see Jeffrey Burds, 'Researcher's Introduction to the Russian State Archive', in *The Russian Archive Series*, ed. S.V. Mironenko and Jeffrey Burds (Pittsburgh, PA: University of Pittsburgh, 1996), 1–9; M.J. Berry and M.J. Ilic, 'Using the Russian Archives: An Informal Practical Guide for Beginners Based on Users' Experiences' (Birmingham: CREES, The University of Birmingham, 2002), 1–35; Michael A. Beier, 'Observations and Experiences from My May 2002 Trip to Saratov, Russia, and Research at the State Archives of Saratov Oblast', *Virginia Libraries* 49, no. 1 (2003), http://scholar.lib.vt.edu/ejournals/VALib/v49_n1/beier.html.

Appendix

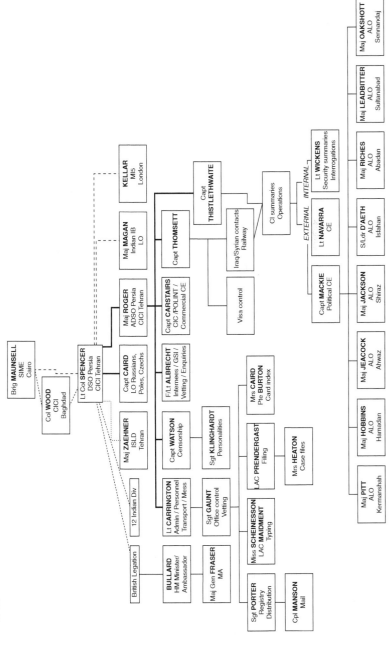

Figure A.1 Organization of DSO Persia

256

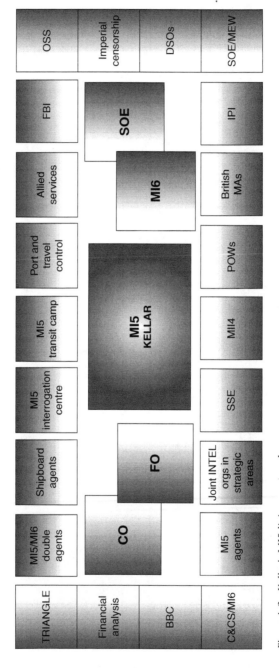

Figure A.2 Kellar's MI5 liaison network

257

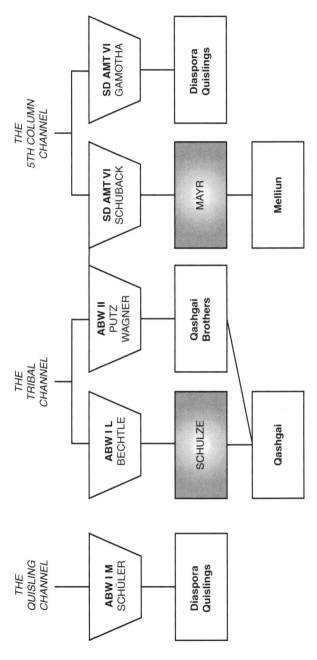

Figure A.3 German operational channels

258

Figure A.4 PGC Lend-Lease supply routes
Source: Wikipedia Commons/PD.

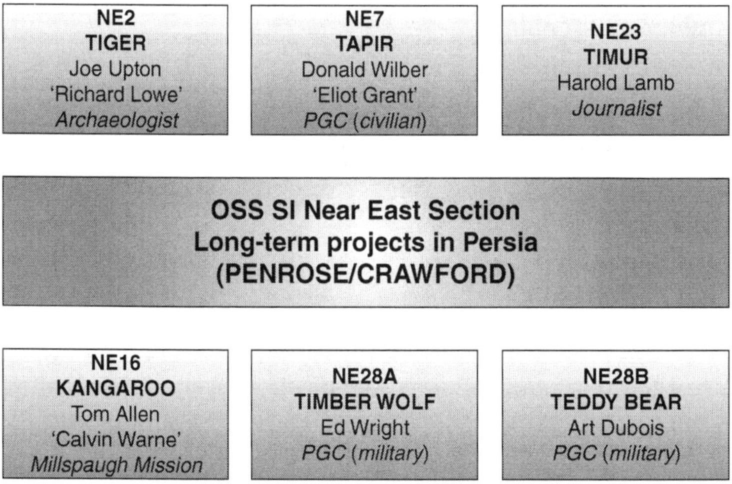

Figure A.5 Long-term OSS SI projects

Select Bibliography

Unpublished documents

Auswärtiges Amt (Berlin) [AA]

Politisches Archiv
R 27330

British Library (St Pancras, London) [BL]

India Office Records
IOR/L/PS/12/656   IOR/L/PS/12/3472A   IOR/L/PS/12/3517

Bundesarchiv (Berlin-Lichterfelde) [BArch]

Persönlicher Stab Reichsführer-SS
NS 19/2235

Personenbezogene Akten
RS/B5043

Bundesarchiv-Militärarchiv (Freiburg im Breisgau) [BArch-MArch]

Militärbiographische Sammlung
MSG 1/2812

Verbandsdrucksachen
MSG 3/667

Kameradschaft 1. Regiment Brandenburg
MSG 158/8   MSG 158/38   MSG 158/50

2. Panzerarmee (PzAOK 2)
RH 21-2/709

Amt Ausland/Abwehr
RW 5/271   RW 5/317A   RW 5/497   RW 5/498

Brown University Library (Providence, RI)

Hay Manuscripts
Ms.47.92

Churchill College (Cambridge)
Churchill Archives Centre [CAC]

CHAR 20/36/8   CHUR 2/168A/135–6

Imperial War Museum (London) [IWM]

Documents Collection

509	7474	11941	19934
2164	7939	13164	20366
2194	8006	13165	
2405	8093	13356	
3709	8125	15519	
4829	8605	15520	
5810	10786	17217	
5869	11631	17354	

National Archives and Records Administration (College Park, MD) [NARA]

Records of the War Department General and Special Staffs (WDGS/WDSS)
RG 165/E281/B251   RG 165/E421/B109   RG 165/E421/B222
RG 165/E421/B581   RG 165/E281/B259   RG 165/E421/B197
RG 165/E421/B357

Records of the US Joint Chiefs of Staff (JCS)
RG 218/GeogFile1942–45/B176

Records of the Office of Strategic Services (OSS)
RG 226/E120A/B22   RG 226/E210/B58   RG 226/E215/B3
RG 226/E210/B261   RG 226/E210/B344   RG 226/E217/B1

Records of the Central Intelligence Agency (CIA)
RG 263/EZZ17/B3   RG 263/EZZ18/B35

Records of the Army Staff
RG 319/E134B/B147

Records of Interservice Agencies
RG 334/E310/B50

The National Archives (Kew, Surrey) [TNA]

Records of the Air Ministry, Royal Air Force
AIR 19/109   AIR 23/5860   AIR 23/5951

Records of the Cabinet
CAB 79/60/26   CAB 146/442   CAB 154/2   CAB 154/112

Records of the Foreign Office
FO 799/8   FO 371/31386   FO 371/40172   FO 371/62077
FO 799/11   FO 371/31387   FO 371/40180   FO 371/68742

FO 847/177	FO 371/31418	FO 371/45502	FO 371/82392
FO 921/3248/1411	FO 371/31419	FO 371/52764	
FO 371/27161	FO 371/35068	FO 371/62059	

Records of the German Foreign Ministry
GFM 33/463   GFM 33/464

Records of the Special Operations Executive

HS 7/31	HS 7/86	HS 7/268	HS 9/1433/9
HS 7/85	HS 7/267	HS 8/971	HS 9/1491/4

Records of the Government Code and Cypher School
HW 20/546

Records of the Security Service

KV 2/173	KV 2/1285	KV 2/1941	KV 4/225
KV 2/230	KV 2/1317	KV 2/2640	KV 4/234
KV 2/267	KV 2/1318	KV 2/2659	KV 4/240
KV 2/272	KV 2/1477	KV 3/88	KV 4/306
KV 2/1133	KV 2/1480	KV 3/89	KV 4/384
KV 2/1281	KV 2/1482	KV 4/161	KV 4/420
KV 2/1282	KV 2/1484	KV 4/192	
KV 2/1283	KV 2/1485	KV 4/223	
KV 2/1284	KV 2/1492	KV 4/224	

Records of the Prime Minister's Office
PREM 3/401/13

Records of the War Office

WO 32/10540	WO 201/1402B	WO 208/1569	WO 208/3094
WO 33/2122	WO 201/2853	WO 208/1588A	WO 208/3163
WO 106/5921	WO 208/1561	WO 208/3085	WO 373/62
WO 201/1314	WO 208/1562	WO 208/3087	WO 373/148
WO 201/1400A	WO 208/1567	WO 208/3088	
WO 201/1401	WO 208/1568	WO 208/3089	

St Antony's College (Oxford)
Middle East Centre Archive [MECA]

GB165-0042	GB165-0199	GB165-0298

Whitman College and Northwest Archives (Walla Walla, WA) [WCNA]

Penrose Papers [PP]
Series 8 (OSS)/B5/F4   Series 8 (OSS)/B5/F8

Published works

Memoirs, autobiographies, biographies, diaries, and correspondence

Anders, Wladyslaw. *An Army in Exile: The Story of the Second Polish Corps*. London: Macmillan, 1949.

Benzing, Klaus. *Der Admiral: Leben und Wirken*. Nördlingen: Klaus Benzing, 1973.

Bower, Tom. *The Perfect English Spy: Sir Dick White and the Secret War 1935–90*. New York: St Martin's Press, 1995.

Brown, Anthony Cave. *'C': The Secret Life of Sir Stewart Graham Menzies, Spymaster to Winston Churchill*. New York: Macmillan, 1987.

Buhite, Russell D. *Patrick J. Hurley and American Foreign Policy*. Ithaca, NY: Cornell University Press, 1973.

Bullard, Reader. *Letters from Tehran: A British Ambassador in World War II Persia*. Edited by E.C. Hodgkin. London: I.B. Tauris, 1991.

———. *The Camels Must Go: An Autobiography*. London: Faber and Faber, 1961.

Colvin, Ian. *Chief of Intelligence*. London: Gollancz, 1951.

Cookridge, E.H. *Gehlen: Spy of the Century*. New York: Random House, 1972.

Eden, Anthony. *The Eden Memoirs*. 3 vols. London: Cassell, 1960–1965.

Ferguson, Bernard, rev. Robert O'Neill and Judith M. Brown. 'Wavell, Archibald Percival, First Earl Wavell (1883–1950)'. In *Oxford Dictionary of National Biography*. Oxford: Oxford University Press, 2004.

Grenfell, Joyce. *The Time of My Life: Entertaining the Troops, 1944–1945*. London: Hodder & Stoughton, 1989.

Hackett, J.W. 'Wilson, Henry Maitland, First Baron Wilson (1881–1964)'. In *Oxford Dictionary of National Biography*. Oxford: Oxford University Press, 2004.

Hamburger, Rudolf and Maik Hamburger. *Zehn Jahre Lager: Als deutscher Kommunist im sowjetischen Gulag*. Munich: Siedler, 2013.

Hickman, Tom. *Churchill's Bodyguard*. London: Headline, 2005.

Höhne, Heinz. *Canaris*. New York: Doubleday, 1979.

Leverkuehn, Paul. *German Military Intelligence*. London: Weidenfeld & Nicolson, 1954.

Mackenzie, Compton. *Eastern Epic*. London: Chatto & Windus, 1951.

Maclean, Fitzroy. *Eastern Approaches*. London: Jonathan Cape, 1949.

———. *Escape to Adventure*. Boston: Little Brown, 1950.

Magan, William. *Middle Eastern Approaches: Experiences and Travels of an Intelligence Officer, 1939–1948*. Wilby, Norfolk: Michael Russell, 2001.

McLynn, Frank. *Fitzroy Maclean*. London: John Murray, 1992.

Mure, David. *Master of Deception: Tangled Webs in London and the Middle East*. London: William Kimber, 1980.

———. *Practise to Deceive*. London: William Kimber, 1977.

Papen, Franz von. *Memoirs*. New York: Dutton, 1952.

Pownall, Henry. *Chief of Staff: The Diaries of Lieutenant General Sir Henry Pownall*. Edited by Brian Bond. London: Cooper, 1972–1974.

Raugh, Harold E. *Wavell in the Middle East, 1939–1941: A Study in Generalship*. London: Brassey's, 1993.

Roosevelt, Kermit. *Countercoup: The Struggle for the Control of Iran*. New York: McGraw-Hill, 1979.

Sayre, Joel. *Persian Gulf Command: Some Marvels on the Road to Kazvin*. New York: Random House, 1945.

Schofield, Victoria. *Wavell: Soldier and Statesman*. London: John Murray, 2006.

Schulze-Holthus, Julius Berthold. *Daybreak in Iran: A Story of the German Intelligence Service.* London: Mervyn Savill, 1954.

Shelton, Francis. *Különleges küldetésem: Ügynök cselloval a II. Vilaghaborüban.* Budapest: Scolar, 2010.

Sillitoe, Percy. *Cloak without Dagger.* London: Cassell, 1955.

Skrine, Clarmont. *World War in Iran.* London: Constable, 1962.

Slim, William. *Unofficial History.* 4th ed. London: Cassell, 1960.

Strong, Kenneth. *Intelligence at the Top: The Recollections of an Intelligence Officer.* New York: Doubleday, 1969.

Sykes, Christopher. *Evelyn Waugh: A Biography.* London: Collins, 1975.

——— . *Four Studies in Loyalty.* London: Collins, 1946.

——— . *Wassmuss: The German Lawrence.* London: Longmans Green, 1936.

Thompson, Geoffrey. *Front-line Diplomat.* London: Hutchinson, 1959.

Thompson, Walter H. *Assignment: Churchill.* Toronto: McLeod, 1955.

——— . *Beside the Bulldog: The Intimate Memoirs of Churchill's Bodyguard.* London: Apollo, 2003.

Trevor-Roper, Hugh R. *The Wartime Journals.* Edited by Richard Davenport-Hines. London: I.B. Tauris, 2012.

Wilber, Donald N. *Adventures in the Middle East: Excursions and Incursions.* Princeton, NJ: Darwin, 1986.

Wilson, Henry Maitland. *Eight Years Overseas, 1939–1947.* London: Hutchinson, 1951.

Wilson, Patrick Maitland. *Where the Nazis Came.* Lancaster: Carnegie, 2002.

Wright, Peter. *Spycatcher: The Candid Autobiography of a Senior Intelligence Officer.* New York: Viking, 1987.

Wynn, Antony. *Persia in the Great Game: Sir Percy Sykes, Explorer, Consul, Soldier, Spy.* London: John Murray, 2003.

Historical and other monographs and edited works

Aboul-Enein, Youssef and Basil. *The Secret War for the Middle East: The Influence of Axis and Allied Intelligence Operations during World War II.* Annapolis, MD: Naval Institute Press, 2013.

Amanat, Abbas and Thorkell Bernhardsson, eds. *US–Middle East Historical Encounters: A Critical Survey.* Gainesville, FL: University Press of Florida, 2007.

Andrew, Christopher and Vasili Mitrokhin. *The World Was Going Our Way: The KGB and the Battle for the Third World.* New York: Basic Books, 2005.

Badiozamani, Badi. *Iran and America: Re-Kindling a Love Lost.* San Diego, CA: East-West Understanding Press, 2005.

Baker, Robert L. *Oil, Blood, and Sand.* New York: Appleton-Century, 1942.

Bamberg, J.H. *The History of the British Petroleum Company. Volume 2: The Anglo-Iranian Years, 1928–1954.* Edited by Ronald W. Ferrier. Cambridge: Cambridge University Press, 2000.

Beck, Lois. *The Qashqa'i of Iran.* New Haven, CT: Yale University Press, 1986.

Bennett, Ralph. *Behind the Battle: Intelligence in the War with Germany.* London: Sinclair-Stevenson, 1994.

———. *Intelligence Investigations: How Ultra Changed History: Collected Papers of Ralph Bennett.* Cass Series: Studies in Intelligence. London: Frank Cass, 1996.

Bentham, Jeremy. *The Works of Jeremy Bentham.* 11 vols. Edinburgh: William Tait, 1838–43.

Boveri, Margaret. *Minaret and Pipe-line: Yesterday and Today in the Near East*. London: Oxford University Press, 1939.

Bullard, Reader. *Britain and the Middle East from Earliest Times to 1963*. London: Hutchinson, 1964.

Caroe, Olaf. *Wells of Power, the Oilfields of South-western Asia: A Regional and Global Study*. London: Macmillan, 1951.

Churchill, Winston S. *The Gathering Storm*. Vol. 1 of *The Second World War*. London: The Reprint Society, 1950.

Clausewitz, Carl. *On War*. Edited and translated by Michael Howard and Peter Paret. Princeton, NJ: Princeton University Press, 1976.

Cleveland, William L. *A History of the Modern Middle East*. Boulder, CO: Westview Press, 2000.

Coakley, Robert W. 'The Persian Corridor as a Route for Aid to the U.S.S.R. (1942)'. In *Command Decisions*. Edited by Kent Roberts Greenfield. London: Methuen, 1960.

Cronin, Stephanie. *Soldiers, Shahs and Subalterns in Iran: Opposition, Protest and Revolt, 1921–1941*. Basingstoke: Palgrave Macmillan, 2010.

———. *Tribal Politics in Iran: Rural Conflict and the New State, 1921–1941*. London: Routledge, 2006.

Curie, Eve. *Journey among Warriors*. London: Heinemann, 1943.

Davies, Philip H.J. *MI6 and the Machinery of Spying*. London: Frank Cass, 2004.

Davis, Simon. *Contested Space: Anglo-American Relations in the Persian Gulf*. Leiden: Nijhoff, 2009.

Deacon, Richard. 'Ilya Svetloff Foils the Nazis'. In *A History of the Russian Secret Service*. London: Muller, 1972.

Dorril, Stephen. *MI6: Inside the Covert World of Her Majesty's Secret Intelligence Service*. New York: Touchstone, 2002.

Erickson, John. *Stalin's War with Germany*. 2 vols. London: Weidenfeld & Nicolson, 1975–1983.

Eubank, Keith. *Summit at Teheran*. New York: William Morrow, 1985.

Farago, Ladislas. *The Game of the Foxes: The Untold Story of German Espionage in the United States and Great Britain during World War II*. Toronto: Bantam, 1973.

Gasiorowski, Mark J. and Malcolm Byrne, eds. *Mohammad Mosaddeq and the 1953 Coup in Iran*. Syracuse, NY: Syracuse University Press, 2004.

Gerolymatos, André. *Castles Made of Sand: A Century of Anglo-American Espionage and Intervention in the Middle East*. New York: Thomas Dunne, 2010.

Goold-Adams, Richard. *Middle East Journey*. London: J. Murray, 1947.

Gorodetsky, Gabriel. *Grand Delusion: Stalin and the German Invasion of Russia*. New Haven, CT: Yale University Press, 1999.

Guedalla, Philip. *Middle East 1940–1942: A Study in Air Power*. London: Hodder & Stoughton, 1944.

Handel, Michael I. *War, Strategy, and Intelligence*. London: Frank Cass, 1989.

Heathcote, T.A. *The Military in British India: The Development of British Land Forces in South Asia, 1600–1947*. Manchester: Manchester University Press, 1995.

Hughes, Mike. *Spies at Work: The Rise and Fall of the Economic League*. Bradford: 1 in 12 Publications, 1994.

Kahn, David. *Hitler's Spies: German Military Intelligence in World War II*. Cambridge, MA: Da Capo Press, 2000.

Keeling, Cecil. *Pictures from Persia*. London: Hale, 1947.

Kirk, George E. *The Middle East in the War.* Vol. 2 of *Survey of International Affairs 1939–46.* London: Oxford University Press, 1952.

Kurowski, Franz. *The Brandenburgers: Global Mission.* Translated by David Johnston. Winnipeg: J.J. Fedorowicz, 1997.

Lenczowski, George. *Russia and the West in Iran 1918–1948.* Ithaca, NY: Cornell University Press, 1949.

Liddell Hart, B.H. *History of the Second World War.* London: Pan, 1973.

Littlejohn, David. *Foreign Legions of the Third Reich.* San Jose, CA: Bender, 1987.

Lovell, Stanley P. *Of Spies & Stratagems.* New York: Pocket Books, 1964.

Macintyre, Ben. *Operation Mincemeat: How a Dead Man and a Bizarre Plan Fooled the Nazis and Assured an Allied Victory.* London: Bloomsbury, 2010.

Mackenzie, W.J.M. *The Secret History of SOE: The Special Operations Executive, 1940–1945.* London: St Ermin's Press, 2000.

Mallett, Derek R. *Hitler's Generals in America: Nazi POWs and Allied Military Intelligence.* Lexington, KY: University Press of Kentucky, 2013.

Masterman, J.C. *The Double-cross System in the War of 1939 to 1945.* New Haven, CT: Yale University Press, 1972.

Meyer, Karl E. and Shareen Blair Brysac. *Tournament of Shadows: The Great Game and the Race for Empire in Central Asia.* Washington, DC: Counterpoint, 1999.

Millspaugh, Arthur C. *Americans in Persia.* Washington, DC: The Brookings Institution, 1946.

Montagu, Ewen. *The Man Who Never Was.* Philadelphia: Lippincott, 1954.

Murphy, Christopher J. *Security and Special Operations: SOE and MI5 during the Second World War.* Basingstoke: Palgrave Macmillan, 2006.

Oberling, Pierre. *The Qashqa'i Nomads of Fars.* The Hague: Mouton, 1974.

Omissi, David E. *Air Power and Colonial Control: The Royal Air Force, 1919–1939.* New York: Manchester University Press, 1990.

O'Sullivan, Adrian. *Nazi Secret Warfare in Occupied Persia (Iran): The Failure of the German Intelligence Services, 1939–45.* Basingstoke: Palgrave Macmillan, 2014.

O'Sullivan, Donal. *Dealing with the Devil: Anglo-Soviet Intelligence Cooperation during the Second World War.* New York: Lang, 2010.

Otte, Thomas G. *The Foreign Office Mind: The Making of British Foreign Policy, 1865–1914.* Cambridge: Cambridge University Press, 2011.

'Press Conference with Veterans of the Russian Foreign Intelligence Service: Official Kremlin International News Broadcast'. *Federation of American Scientists (FAS) Intelligence Resource Program, World Intelligence Agencies, Soviet/Russian Intelligence Agencies* (18 November 2003). http://www.fas.org/irp/world/russia/teheran43.html.

Rafalko, Frank J., ed. *A Counterintelligence Reader.* 4 vols. Washington, DC: National Counterintelligence Center, 2004.

Rahnema, Ali. *Behind the 1953 Coup in Iran: Thugs, Turncoats, Soldiers, and Spooks.* New York: Cambridge University Press, 2014.

Reynolds, Quentin J. *The Curtain Rises.* London: Right Book Club, 1945.

Rezun, Miron. *The Iranian Crisis of 1941: The Actors, Britain, Germany, and the Soviet Union.* Cologne: Böhlau, 1982.

——— . *The Soviet Union and Iran: Soviet Policy in Iran from the Beginnings of the Pahlavi Dynasty until the Soviet Invasion in 1941.* Institut Universitaire de Hautes Etudes Internationales Collection de Relations Internationales 8. Alphen aan de Rijn: Sijthoff & Noordhoff International, 1981.

Rigge, Simon. *War in the Outposts.* Alexandria, VA: Time-Life, 1980.

Rubin, Barry. *Istanbul Intrigues*. New York: Pharos, 1992.

Sayer, Ian and Douglas Botting. *America's Secret Army: The Untold Story of the Counter Intelligence Corps*. New York: Franklin Watts, 1989.

Schubert, Frank N. 'The Persian Gulf Command: Lifeline to the Soviet Union'. In *Builders and Fighters: U.S. Army Engineers in World War II*. Edited by Barry W. Fowle. Fort Belvoir, VA: Office of History, U.S. Army Corps of Engineers, 1992.

Shores, Christopher F. *Dust Clouds in the Middle East: The Air War for East Africa, Iraq, Syria, Iran and Madagascar, 1940–42*. London: Grub Street, 1996.

Smith, Bradley F. *Sharing Secrets with Stalin: How the Allies Traded Intelligence, 1941–1945*. Lawrence, KS: University Press of Kansas, 1996.

Smith, R. Harris. *OSS: The Secret History of America's First Central Intelligence Agency*. Berkeley, CA: University of California Press, 1972.

Smyth, Denis. *Deathly Deception: The Real Story of Operation Mincemeat*. Oxford: Oxford University Press, 2010.

Snow, Edgar. *People on Our Side*. New York: Random House, 1944.

Stephan, Robert W. *Stalin's Secret War: Soviet Counterintelligence against the Nazis, 1941–1945*. Lawrence, KS: University Press of Kansas, 2004.

Stewart, Richard A. *Sunrise at Abadan: The British and Soviet Invasion of Iran, 1941*. New York: Praeger, 1988.

Sudoplatov, Pavel and Anatoli Sudoplatov. *Special Tasks: The Memoirs of an Unwanted Witness, a Soviet Spymaster*. With Jerrold L. and Leona P. Schecter. Boston: Little, Brown, 1994.

Sultanov, Chapay A. *Would the Allies Have Won without Baku Oil?* Baku: Nurlar, 2008.

'Teheran-43: Wrecking the Plan to Kill Stalin, Roosevelt and Churchill: Interview with Russian Intelligence Veteran Gevork Vartanyan'. *RIA Novosti: Russian News and Information Agency* (16 October 2007). http://en.rian.ru/analysis/20071016/84122320-print.html.

United Kingdom. Naval Intelligence Division. *Persia*. Middle East Intelligence Handbooks 1943–1946, 5. Gerrards Cross: Archive Editions, 1987.

Walton, Calder. *Empire of Secrets: British Intelligence, the Cold War and the Twilight of Empire*. New York: The Overlook Press, 2013.

Weale, Adrian. *Renegades: Hitler's Englishmen*. London: Pimlico, 2002.

Weinberg, Gerhard L. *Hitler's Foreign Policy: The Road to World War II 1933–1939*. New York: Enigma, 2005.

West, Nigel. *MI5: British Security Operations 1909–1945*. London: Triad/Granada, 1983.

———. *Secret War: The Story of SOE, Britain's Wartime Sabotage Organisation*. London: Hodder & Stoughton, 1992.

Wilford, Hugh. *America's Great Game: The CIA's Secret Arabists and the Shaping of the Modern Middle East*. New York: Basic Books, 2013.

Wylie, Neville, ed. *The Politics and Strategy of Clandestine War: Special Operations Executive, 1940–1946*. Abingdon: Routledge, 2007.

Yegorov, Victor. *Zagovor protiv 'Evriki': broshenny portfel* [The Plot against 'Eureka': The Lost Portfolio]. Moscow: Sovetskaya Rossiya, 1968.

Official and authorized histories

Andrew, Christopher. *The Defence of the Realm: The Authorized History of MI5*. Toronto: Penguin Canada, 2010.

Cruickshank, Charles. *The German Occupation of the Channel Islands: The Official History of the Occupation Years*. Guernsey, CI: Guernsey Press, 1975.

Curry, John. *The Security Service, 1908–1945: The Official History*. Kew: PRO, 1999.

Hinsley, F.H. and C.A.G. Simkins. *British Intelligence in the Second World War*. Vol. 4, *Security and Counter-Intelligence*. New York: Cambridge University Press, 1984.

Hinsley, F.H. et al. *British Intelligence in the Second World War: Its Influence on Strategy and Operations*. Vol. 1. London: HMSO, 1979.

———. *British Intelligence in the Second World War: Its Influence on Strategy and Operations*. Vol. 2. London: HMSO, 1981.

———. *British Intelligence in the Second World War: Its Influence on Strategy and Operations*. Vol. 3.1. London: HMSO, 1984.

———. *British Intelligence in the Second World War: Its Influence on Strategy and Operations*. Vol. 3.2. London: HMSO, 1988.

Howard, Michael. *Strategic Deception in the Second World War*. New York: Norton, 1995.

Jeffery, Keith. *The Secret History of MI6*. New York: Penguin, 2010.

Motter, T.H. Vail. *The Persian Corridor and Aid to Russia*. United States Army in World War II: The Middle East Theater. Washington, DC: Office of the Chief of Military History, Department of the Army, 1952.

Pal, Dharm. *Campaign in Western Asia*. Official History of the Indian Armed Forces in the Second World War, 1939–45: Campaigns in the Western Theatre. Edited by Bisheshwar Prasad. Calcutta: Combined Inter-Services Historical Section, India and Pakistan, 1957.

Playfair, Ian S.O. *The Mediterranean and the Middle East*. 6 vols, History of the Second World War. London: HMSO, 1954–88.

Stephens, R.W.G. and Oliver Hoare. *Camp 020: MI5 and the Nazi Spies: The Official History of MI5's Wartime Interrogation Centre*. Richmond: PRO, 2000.

United Kingdom. Central Office of Information. *Paiforce: The Official Story of the Persia and Iraq Command 1941–1946*. London: HMSO, 1948.

United States. War Department. Office of the Assistant Secretary of War. Strategic Services Unit. History Project. *War Report of OSS (Office of Strategic Services)*. 2 vols. New York: Walker, 1976.

Woodward, Llewellyn. *British Foreign Policy in the Second World War*. Abridged version. London: HMSO, 1962.

Serial publications

Aldrich, Richard J. 'Britain's Secret Intelligence Service in Asia during the Second World War'. *Modern Asian Studies* 32, no. 1 (1998): 179–217.

'Allied Supply Routes to S.E. Russia'. *Bulletin of International News* 19, no. 6 (21 March 1942): 223–7.

'British Interests in the Persian Gulf'. *Bulletin of International News* 18, no. 19 (20 September 1941): 1193–8.

Bullard, Reader. 'Persia in the Two World Wars'. *Journal of the Royal Central Asian Society* 50, no. 1 (1963): 6–20.

——— . 'Review of *Daybreak in Iran: A Story of the German Intelligence Service*, by Bernhardt Schulze-Holthus'. *International Affairs* 31, no. 3 (July 1955): 392–3.

Cox, Jafna L. 'A Splendid Training Ground: The Importance to the Royal Air Force of Its Role in Iraq, 1919–32'. *Journal of Imperial and Commonwealth History* 13, no. 2 (January 1985): 157–84.

Dovey, H.O. 'Cheese'. *Intelligence and National Security* 5, no. 3 (1990): 176–83.

———. 'Maunsell and Mure'. *Intelligence and National Security* 8, no. 1 (January 1993): 60–77.

———. 'The Eighth Assignment, 1941–1942'. *Intelligence and National Security* 11, no. 4 (1996): 672–95.

———. 'The Intelligence War in Turkey'. *Intelligence and National Security* 9, no. 1 (January 1994): 59–87.

———. 'The Middle East Intelligence Centre'. *Intelligence and National Security* 4, no. 4 (1989): 800–12.

Fedorowich, Kent. 'Axis Prisoners of War as Sources for British Military Intelligence, 1939–42'. *Intelligence and National Security* 14, no. 2 (Summer 1999): 156–78.

Garrod, Oliver. 'The Nomadic Tribes of Persia Today'. *Journal of the Royal Central Asian Society* 33, no. 1 (January 1946): 32–46.

——— . 'The Qashgai Tribe of Fars'. *Journal of the Royal Central Asian Society* 33, no. 3 (July 1946): 293–306.

Garthwaite, Gene R. 'The Bakhtiyari Ilkhani: An Illusion of Unity'. *International Journal of Middle East Studies* 8, no. 2 (April 1977): 145–60.

Grajdanzev, Andrew. 'Supply Routes to the Soviet Union'. *Far Eastern Survey* 11, no. 5 (9 March 1942): 62–6.

Greely, John N. 'Iran in Wartime: Through Fabulous Persia, Hub of the Middle East, Americans, Britons, and Iranians Keep Sinews of War Moving to the Embattled Soviet Union'. *National Geographic Magazine* 84 (August 1943): 129–56.

Guensberg, Gerold. 'Abwehr Myth: How Efficient Was German Intelligence in World War II?' *Studies in Intelligence* 21, no. 3 (Fall 1977): 39–45.

——— . 'Intelligence in Recent Public Literature'. *Studies in Intelligence* 21, no. 3 [Fall 1977]: 47–9.

Harrison, J.V. 'Some Routes in Southern Iran'. *The Geographical Journal* 99, no. 3 (March 1942): 113–29.

Höhne, Heinz. 'Selten Skrupel'. *Der Spiegel* 41, 8 October 1979: 252–7.

John, Michael. 'Anglo-amerikanische Österreichpolitik 1938–1955'. *Historicum* (Winter 1999–2000). http://www.wsg-hist.jku.at/Historicum/HABIL/Beer.html.

Kelly, Saul. 'A Succession of Crises: SOE in the Middle East, 1940–45'. *Intelligence and National Security* 20, no. 1 (March 2005): 121–46.

Kern, Gary. 'How "Uncle Joe" Bugged FDR: The Lessons of History'. *Studies in Intelligence* 47, no. 1 (2003). https://www.cia.gov/library/center-for-the-study-of-intelligence/csi-publications/csi-studies/studies/vol47no1/article02.html.

Kimball, Warren F. 'A Different Take on FDR at Teheran and Yalta'. *Studies in Intelligence* 49, no. 3 (2005): 101–4.

Kirk, Grayson. 'Strategic Communications in the Middle East'. *Foreign Affairs* 20, no. 4 (July 1942): 762–6.

Kramer, Martin. 'Miss Lambton's Advice'. *Middle East Strategy at Harvard (MESH)*, 20 August 2008. http://blogs.law.harvard.edu/mesh/2008/08/miss_ann_lambton_advice.

Krieger, Wolfgang. 'German Intelligence History: A Field in Search of Scholars'. *Intelligence and National Security* 19, no. 2 (2004): 185–98.

Lambton, Ann K.S. 'Persia'. *Journal of the Royal Central Asian Society* 31, no. 1 (January 1944): 8–22.

Lenczowski, George. 'Literature on the Clandestine Activities of the Great Powers in the Middle East'. *Middle East Journal* 8, no. 2 (Spring 1954): 205–11.

'*Life* goes on a Migration with Persian Tribesmen'. *Life* 21, no. 6 (29 July 1946): 99–105.

Lukin, Alexander. 'Operatsiya "Dal'nayi prizhok" '. *Ogonek*, no. 33 (1990) 15 August 1965: 25; no. 34 (1991), 22 August 1965: 25–7.

McFarland, Stephen L. 'Anatomy of an Iranian Political Crowd: The Tehran Bread Riot of December 1942'. *International Journal of Middle East Studies* 17, no. 1 (February 1985): 51–65.

'Memoranda for the President: OSS-NKVD Liaison'. *Studies in Intelligence* 7, no. 3 (Summer 1963): 63–74.

Miller, Marshall L. 'How the Soviets Invaded Iran'. *Armed Forces Journal* 124, no. 7 (February 1987): 30–4.

Motter, T.H. Vail. 'American Port Operations in the Persian Corridor'. *Military Review* 29, no. 6 (September 1949): 12.

Murphy, Philip. 'Intelligence and Decolonization: The Life and Death of the Federal Intelligence and Security Bureau, 1954–63'. *Journal of Imperial and Commonwealth History* 29 (May 2001): 101–30.

Oberling, Pierre. 'Qashgai Tribal Confederacy'. *ELXAN* (7 January 2004). http://elxan.blogspot.com/2004_12_26_archive.html#110435660687558028.

O'Sullivan, Adrian. 'British Security Intelligence in Occupied Persia, 1942–1944'. *Global War Studies* 12, no. 1 (March 2015): 38–56.

Rezun, Miron. 'The Great Game Revisited'. *International Journal* 41, no. 2 (Spring 1986): 324–41.

'Routes to SE Russia'. *Bulletin of International News* 19, no. 6 (21 March 1942): 223–7.

Satia, Priya. 'The Defense of Inhumanity: Air Control and the British Idea of Arabia'. *American Historical Review* 111, no. 1 (February 2006): 16–51.

Schaub, Harry Carl. 'General Lahousen and the Abwehr Resistance'. *International Journal of Intelligence and CounterIntelligence* 19, no. 3 (June 2006): 538–58.

Schulze-Holthus, Julius Berthold. 'Eine groteske Fälschung'. *Die Nachhut: Informationsorgan für Angehörige der ehemaligen militärischen Abwehr* 7 (9 April 1969): 18–26.

Scott, Len. 'Sources and Methods in the Study of Intelligence: A British View'. *Intelligence and National Security* 22, no. 2 (April 2007): 185–205.

Seubert, Franz. 'Die italienische Presse zu den angeblichen Attentatsplänen gegen Churchill, Roosevelt und Stalin'. *Die Nachhut: Informationsorgan für Angehörige der ehemaligen militärischen Abwehr* 8 (15 September 1969): 14.

———. 'Frührot in Iran: Aussergewöhnlicher Einsatz eines Abwehroffiziers im II. Weltkrieg'. *Die Nachhut: Informationsorgan für Angehörige der ehemaligen militärischen Abwehr* 5 (15 June 1968): 2–7.

———. 'Vernichtende Urteile über das Machwerk "Assassinat au Sommet"'. *Die Nachhut: Informationsorgan für Angehörige der ehemaligen militärischen Abwehr* 8 (15 September 1969): 12–14.

Seydi, Süleyman. 'Intelligence and Counter-Intelligence Activities in Iran during the Second World War'. *Middle Eastern Studies* 46, no. 5 (September 2010): 733–52.

Silver, Arnold M. 'Questions, Questions, Questions: Memories of Oberursel'. *Intelligence and National Security* 8, no. 2 (1993): 199–213.

Skrine, Clarmont. 'The Iranian Napoleon: Journey to Internment'. *The Iranian* (24 April 2001). http://www.iranian.com/History/2001/April/Exile/index.html.
Wright, Edwin M. 'Iran as a Gateway to Russia'. *Foreign Affairs* 20, no. 2 (January 1942): 367–71.

Newspapers

Chicago Tribune	*New York Times*	*The Independent*
Daily Mail	*Sunday Times*	*The Telegraph*
Das Schwarze Korps	*The Courier-Mail*	*The Times*
Die Zeit	*The Guardian*	*The West Australian*
Globe and Mail	*The Herald*	*Townsville Daily Bulletin*

Obituaries

'Alan Stuart Roger (Obituary)'. *The Herald*, 9 August 1997.
'Brigadier Bill Magan (Obituary)'. *The Telegraph*, 22 January 2010.
'Field-Marshal Lord Wilson: The War in the Middle East and Mediterranean (Obituary)'. *The Times*, 1 January 1965.
'Gen. Sir Edward Quinan: Commands in India and Iran (Obituary)'. *The Times*, 15 November 1960.
'Professor George Michael Wickens (Obituary)'. *Globe and Mail*, 30 January 2006.
'Prof Terence Mitford: Classical archaeologist and explorer (Obituary)'. *The Times*, 25 November 1978.
'Sir Clarmont Skrine OBE (Obituary)'. *Asian Affairs* 6, no. 1 (1975): 119.

Published documentation and documents

Burdett, Anita L.P., ed. *Iran Political Developments 1941–1946: British Documentary Sources — Iran under Allied Occupation.* 13 vols. London: Archive Editions, 2008.
Farrington, A.J., ed. *British Intelligence and Policy on Persia (Iran), 1900–1949: India Office Political and Secret Files and Confidential Print.* Leiden: IDC, 2004.
Roosevelt, Franklin D. *The Public Papers and Addresses of Franklin D. Roosevelt. 1943 Volume, The Tide Turns.* New York: Harper, 1950.
Trevor-Roper, Hugh R., ed. *Hitler's War Directives 1939–1945.* Edinburgh: Birlinn, 2004.
United States. Department of State. *Foreign Relations of the United States: Diplomatic Papers: The Conferences at Cairo and Tehran 1943.* Washington: USGPO, 1961.
Wavell, Archibald P. 'Despatch on Operations in Iraq, East Syria and Iran from 10th April, 1941 to 12th January, 1942.' *Supplement to The London Gazette*, no. 37685 (13 August 1946).
Wilson, Henry Maitland. 'Despatch on the Persia and Iraq Command Covering the Period 21st August, 1942 to 17th February, 1943'. *Supplement to The London Gazette*, no. 37703 (27 August 1946).

Bibliographical and reference works

Aldrich, Richard J. 'Did Waldegrave Work? The Impact of Open Government upon British History'. *Twentieth Century British History* 9, no. 1 (1998): 111–26.

────── . 'The Waldegrave Initiative and Secret Service Archives: New Materials and New Policies'. *Intelligence and National Security* 10, no. 1 (January 1995): 192–7.

Beier, Michael A. 'Observations and Experiences from My May 2002 Trip to Saratov, Russia, and Research at the State Archives of Saratov Oblast'. *Virginia Libraries* 49, no. 1 (2003). http://scholar.lib.vt.edu/ejournals/VALib/v49_n1/beier.html.

Birstein, Vadim J. *The Perversion of Knowledge: The True Story of Soviet Science.* Boulder, CO: Westview Press, 2001.

British Colonial Policy and Intelligence Files on Asia and the Middle East, c. 1880–1950. IDC, 2006. http://www.idcpublishers.com/ead/455.xml.

Browder, George C. 'Captured German and Other Nations' Documents in the Osoby (Special) Archive, Moscow'. *Central European History* 24, no. 4 (1991): 424–45.

Calder, James D. *Intelligence, Espionage and Related Topics: An Annotated Bibliography of Serial Journal and Magazine Scholarship, 1844–1998.* Bibliographies and Indexes in Military Studies 11. Westport, CT: Greenwood, 1999.

Cantwell, John D. *The Second World War: A Guide to Documents in the Public Record Office.* 2nd ed. Public Record Office Handbooks 15. London: HMSO, 1993.

'Chronology'. *Bulletin of International News* 18, no. 18 (4 September 1941): 1164–90.

'Chronology'. *Bulletin of International News* 18, no. 19 (20 September 1941): 1235–60.

'Chronology'. *Bulletin of International News* 18, no. 20 (4 October 1941): 1301–27.

Clark, J. Ransom. *The Literature of Intelligence: A Bibliography of Materials, with Essays, Reviews, and Comments* (2007). http://intellit.muskingum.edu.

Constantinides, George C. *Intelligence and Espionage: An Analytical Bibliography.* Boulder, CO: Westview, 1983.

Dear, I.C.B., ed. *The Oxford Companion to World War II.* Oxford: Oxford University Press, 1995.

Elwell-Sutton, L. P. *A Guide to Iranian Area Study.* Ann Arbor, MI: J. S. Edwards for the American Council of Learned Societies, 1952.

────── , ed. *Bibliographical Guide to Iran: The Middle East Library Committee Guide.* Brighton: Harvester Press, 1983.

Ghani, Cyrus. *Iran and the West: A Critical Bibliography.* London: Kegan Paul International, 1987.

Grimsted, Patricia Kennedy. *Russia's 'Trophy' Archives — Still Prisoners of World War II?* Budapest: Open Society Archive, Central European University, 2002.

────── . 'Twice Plundered or "Twice Saved"? Identifying Russia's "Trophy" Archives and the Loot of the Reichssicherheitshauptamt'. *Holocaust Genocide Studies* 15, no. 2 (2001): 191–244.

────── . 'Why Do Captured Archives Go Home? Restitution Achievements under the Russian Law'. *International Journal of Cultural Property* 17 (2010): 291–333.

Grimwood-Jones, Diana. 'The Private Papers Collection in the Middle East Centre at St. Antony's College, Oxford'. *Bulletin (British Society for Middle Eastern Studies)* 5, no. 2 (1978): 113–33.

Guide to Collections Relating to Iran/Persia. MECA Guides. Oxford: Middle East Centre, St. Antony's College, 28 May 2008.

Jena, Kai von and Wilhelm Lenz. 'Die deutschen Bestände im Sonderarchiv in Moskau'. *Der Archivar* 45, no. 3 (1992): 457–67.

Kent, George O. *A Catalog of Files and Microfilms of the German Foreign Ministry Archives 1920–1945*. 4 vols. Stanford, CA: The Hoover Institution, 1962–.

Klee, Ernst. *Das Kulturlexikon zum Dritten Reich: Wer war was vor und nach 1945*. Frankfurt: Fischer, 2007.

Lashmar, Paul. 'Mr Waldegrave's Need to Know'. *History Today* 44, no. 8 (August 1994): 5–9.

Milani, Abbas. *Eminent Persians: The Men and Women Who Made Modern Iran, 1941–1979*. 2 vols. Syracuse, NY: Syracuse University Press, 2008.

Mironenko, S.V. and Jeffrey Burds. *The Russian State Archive: A Researcher's Guide*. Vol. IV of *The Russian Archive Series*. Pittsburgh, PA: University of Pittsburgh, 1996.

Moran, Christopher R. 'The Pursuit of Intelligence History: Methods, Sources, and Trajectories in the United Kingdom'. *Studies in Intelligence* 55, no. 2 (June 2011): 33–55.

Murphy, Christopher J. 'Postscript on Sources: SOE at The National Archives'. In *Security and Special Operations: SOE and MI5 during the Second World War*. Basingstoke: Palgrave Macmillan, 2006.

'Outline of Military Operations'. *Bulletin of International News* 18, no. 18 (4 September 1941): 1141–63.

'Outline of Military Operations'. *Bulletin of International News* 18, no. 19 (20 September 1941): 1214–34.

'Outline of Military Operations'. *Bulletin of International News* 18, no. 20 (4 October 1941): 1281–1300.

Polmar, Norman and Thomas B. Allen. *Spy Book: The Encyclopedia of Espionage*. New York: Random House, 1997.

Roper, Michael. *The Records of the Foreign Office, 1782–1968*. 2nd ed. PRO Handbook 33. Kew: PRO, 2002.

Rossiiskii gosudarstvennyi voennyi arkhiv (RGVA), ArcheoBiblioBase, Archives in Russia, B-8. *International Institute of Social History.* http://www.iisg.nl/abb/rep/B-8.tab5.php?b=.

'Sonderarchiv' Moskau Fondsverzeichnis. *Sonderarchiv Moskau: Informationsseite von Sebastian Panwitz.* http://www.sonderarchiv.de/fondverzeichnis.htm.

Tucker, Spencer C., ed. *Encyclopedia of World War II*. 5 vols. Santa Barbara, CA: ABC-Clio, 2005.

'United Kingdom Official Histories of the Second World War: A Progress Report and a Bibliography'. *Military Affairs* 13, no. 3 (Autumn 1949): 170–6.

Wark, Wesley K. 'In Never-Never Land? The British Archives on Intelligence'. *The Historical Journal* 35, no. 1 (March 1992): 195–203.

Watt, D.C. 'Restrictions on Research: The Fifty-Year Rule and British Foreign Policy'. *International Affairs* 41, no. 1 (January 1965): 89–95.

Wegner, Bernd. 'Deutsche Aktenbestände im Moskauer Zentralen Staatsarchiv: Ein Erfahrungsbericht'. *Vierteljahrshefte für Zeitgeschichte* 40, no. 2 (April 1992): 311–19.

Weinberg, Gerhard L. 'Unresolved Issues of World War II: The Records Still Closed and the Open Records Not Used'. In *Secret Intelligence in the Twentieth Century'*. Edited by Jan G. Heitmann, Heike Bungert, and Michael Wala. London: Frank Cass, 2003.

West, Nigel. *Historical Dictionary of World War II Intelligence.* Lanham, MD: Scarecrow Press, 2008.

Wistrich, Robert S. *Who's Who in Nazi Germany.* London: Routledge, 2002.

Young, Peter, ed. *The World Almanac of World War II.* London: Bison, 1987.

Theses and dissertations

Bell, Falko. 'Wissen ist menschlich: Der Stellenwert der Human Intelligence in der britischen Kriegsführung 1939–1945'. PhD diss., Glasgow, 2014.

Kosiba, Harold J. 'Stalin's Great Game: Anglo-Soviet Relations in the Near East, 1939–1943'. PhD diss., Indiana, 1991.

O'Sullivan, Adrian. 'German Covert Initiatives and British Intelligence in Persia (Iran), 1939–1945'. DLitt et Phil diss., UNISA, 2012.

Shelley, Adam. 'Empire of Shadows: British Intelligence in the Middle East 1939–1946'. PhD diss., Cambridge, 2007.

Wilson, Emily. 'The War in the Dark: The Security Service and the Abwehr 1940–1944'. PhD diss., Cambridge, 2003.

Fictional works

Clark, Patrick Nolan. *A Strange Murder in the Persian Corridor.* North Charleston, SC: CreateSpace, 2014.

Havas, Laslo. *Assassinat au sommet.* Paris: Arthaud, 1968.

———. *The Long Jump.* Translated by Kathleen Szasz. London: Neville Spearman, 1967.

Kerr, Philip. *Hitler's Peace: A Novel of the Second World War.* New York: Penguin, 2005.

Le Carré, John. *Call for the Dead.* London: Victor Gollancz, 1961.

Sykes, Christopher. *A Song of a Shirt.* London: Verschoyle, 1953.

———. *High Minded Murder.* London: Home & Van Thal, 1944.

Index

Printed and bound in the United States of America